Heart Beats

HEART BEATS

Everyday Life and the Memorized Poem

Catherine Robson

PRINCETON UNIVERSITY PRESS

Princeton and Oxford

Copyright © 2012 by Princeton University Press
Published by Princeton University Press, 41 William Street, Princeton,
New Jersey 08540
In the United Kingdom: Princeton University Press, 6 Oxford Street,
Woodstock, Oxfordshire OX20 1TW
press.princeton.edu

Jacket Photograph: David Wilkie reciting Robert Burns. Photo by William
Sumits, Time & Life Pictures, courtesy of Getty images.

Library of Congress-in-Publication Data

Robson, Catherine, 1962–
Heart beats : everyday life and the memorized poem / Catherine Robson.
p. cm.
Includes index.
ISBN 978-0-691-11936-6 (cloth : alk. paper)   1. Poetry—Social
aspects.   2. Recitation (Education)   3. Poetry—Study and teaching.
4. Hemans, Mrs., 1793–1835. Casabianca.   5. Gray, Thomas, 1716–1771.
Elegy written in a country churchyard.   6. Wolfe, Charles, 1791–1823.
Burial of Sir John Moore.   I. Title.
PN1031.R626 2012
808.1'07—dc22   2012005139

British Library Cataloging-in-Publication Data is available

This book has been composed in Sabon LT Std
Printed on acid-free paper. ∞

Printed in the United States of America
1 3 5 7 9 10 8 6 4 2

For my sons,

Alexander James and Thomas William Jensen

CONTENTS

FIGURES

ACKNOWLEDGMENTS

Heart Beats has turned out to be a substantially different study from the book I first thought I was writing. Some of the gifts that I have received over the years relate to one of its earlier forms; others were instrumental in helping me to find its ultimate shape. The National Endowment for the Humanities gave me a fellowship to further the writing of a book on unburied bodies, but was extremely supportive (and did not ask me to return its money) when I explained that I had altered my angle of approach. One moment that helped define that new angle occurred in a meeting of UC Berkeley's Nineteenth-Century Studies and Beyond working group when Celeste Langan asked how we might think about meter in a properly historical manner. Other scholars of nineteenth-century British and American poetry were also beginning to pursue this question; I am hugely grateful for the welcome they have extended to me, general garden-variety Victorianist that I am. Most important was my meeting, at a MLA conference panel organized by the estimable Yopie Prins, with Tricia Lootens. Tricia became this book's true interlocutor; she gets to the heart of the matter like no one else I know, and I can never thank her enough for the unstinting generosity of her tough questions and compassionate responses.

At the point that this book transformed itself into a study of Victorian recitation, I received a Guggenheim Memorial Foundation Fellowship and an University of California President's Fellowship in the Humanities. In the period of uninterrupted research and thought that these awards supported, the project changed in two significant ways. The first, an alteration to its historical parameters, was dictated by my new topic; I discovered that I needed to address this story's twentieth-century developments. The second was elective: I redrew its geographical parameters to include a study of the memorized poem in the United States. Because I had to start from scratch to educate myself about the history of the American elementary school, this move significantly extended the time it has taken me to finish the book; how much longer it would have taken had I not had the sterling research assistance and tutelage of Americanist extraordinaire Samaine Lockwood, I dread to think. I am greatly in her debt. I am also very grateful to my other research assistants: Jessica Staheli; Jessica Howell; Elaine Musgrave, who gave meticulous and thoughtful attention to my prose and my notes; and Ryan Fong, for providing wonderfully cheery and resourceful support of many kinds.

The composition of the constituent parts of the book has been materially assisted by numerous other individuals, institutions, and foundations; in addition, I have drawn great benefit from my audiences' comments and questions after my public talks. The "Casabianca" case study came first; I am very grateful to Linda Morris, my former chair, for asking me to give a version of this piece as a fall inaugural lecture for the English Department at UC Davis, my former campus, and to David Simpson for his careful reading of this and other sections. I also thank Kerry Hanlon for her willingness to stand on a chair and recite "Invictus" at numerous Davis events. I wrote most of the chapter on "The Burial of Sir John Moore after Corunna" in the idyllic setting of Villa Serbelloni in Bellagio; I thank the Rockefeller Foundation for this residency and those in my cohort there, especially David Schalkwyk, for comments on my work in progress. I thank Cheri Larsen Hoeckley for inviting me to Westmont College to present a later draft, and her colleague John Sider for suggesting that I include Carolyn Wells's "Overworked Elocutionist" in the book and sending me his researches on this poem. Members of the UC Berkeley working group mentioned above were gracious enough not to complain when I subjected them to a lengthy extract from my lengthy Gray's Elegy study; I am grateful to them for this, and for their insightful responses.

The writing of what eventually became the introduction and Part I was an extended process. I am particularly indebted to Leah Price, who invited me to present any early version of the British history of school recitation to Harvard's Victorianist Colloquium. At that gathering, Stephen Greenblatt and James Simpson posed some challenging questions ("Why do you keep saying 'children were *compelled* to memorize poems?'" asked James. "Would you say 'children were *compelled* to learn to read?'") Such moments were instrumental in helping me to examine a number of my deep-seated prejudices; I hope this has resulted in a more even-handed approach to the topic. It was only, however, in the extraordinarily rich and supportive working environment of the Wissenschaftskolleg zu Berlin that I really got to grips with the task in hand. I would not have guessed that daily exposure to a forty-strong band of evolutionary biologists, cognitive scientists, art historians, legal theorists, and others was what I really needed to understand the stakes of a book on memorized poetry, but the experience was invaluable to me both intellectually and personally; all kinds of conversations, in and out of formal settings, helped me to devise new ways of describing the relationships I came to see within the tangled banks of my researches. I thank all of the Fellows in the Jahrgang of 2008–2009 and most especially Luca Giuliani and the members of his wonderful staff on Wallotstrasse for an exceptional year. I also thank Bill Cohen, Kevin McAleer, Ella Dzelzainis, and Garrett Stewart for their timely and incisive readings of drafts of the introduction.

I first began to develop the ideas which are now in the book's afterword in a piece for the *Times Literary Supplement*; I thank the Nineteenth Century Transatlantic Historical Poetics Group for inviting me to reflect further on "Invictus" at "Crossing the Bar," an immensely illuminating conference at the University of Pennsylvania. I extended my focus to "If –" in a plenary talk for the annual conference of the British Association of Victorian Studies at the University of Glasgow; I thank Kirstie Blair for this invitation and for her earlier spirited emails on the "Casabianca" chapter that began our working friendship. The two reports written for Princeton University Press on my first draft of the complete manuscript gave me much food for thought; I am indebted to each of the anonymous writers for their comments. My last year of revisions coincided with a move from California to New York; I am very grateful for the welcome I have received from my new colleagues in the English Department at NYU and from the many academics, old friends and new, who constitute the Victorianist Collective of the Greater New York area. Turning the manuscript into a book has been a comparatively painless process; I would like to thank my copyeditor Richard Isomaki and all those at Princeton University Press who have worked with me over the years, notably commissioning editors Mary Murrell, Hanne Winarsky, and Brigitta van Rheinberg, editorial assistant Kelly Malloy, and production editor Ellen Foos.

So far I have mentioned the debts accrued at distinct stages of this project; those who have been with me throughout deserve huge thanks too. I am deeply grateful to my friend Ramie Targoff, who read and commented upon pretty much every part of the book as it was written. I also send much love and gratitude to Tom Laqueur and Cathy Gallagher, who continue to play as great a role in my intellectual sustenance and general well-being as they did back in my graduate school days. My involvement with the Dickens Project bestows upon me the exceptional gift of regular interaction with a large community of knowledgeable and convivial Victorianists. I am grateful to everyone who comes to Santa Cruz each summer; my friends John Jordan, Helena Michie, Jim Adams, Carolyn Dever, Jim Kincaid, and Rebecca Stern have been particularly generous in their support of this project, and I give special thanks to my irrepressible suitemates, Carolyn Williams and Teresa Mangum. Lily Hamrick has joined me for many a regenerative walk in the Berkeley hills; my frequent research trips back to England are always enriched by my reconnection with Julian Brown, Jane Leek, Ian Little, Alison Shaw, and Andy Burnett. Ian's nephew Pascal Little deserves a special mention. In 2003, when he was around ten years of age, I filmed his recitation of "Casabianca"; I have shown the video so often that I consider it to have more than recouped the pound-a-line bribe (forty pounds!) I paid him at the time.

Last but not least, I wish to thank my family. Researching and writing the history of working-class scholarship children made me especially aware of how much I owe to my parents, Colin and Patricia Robson. Many of the stories I tell in my second case study are theirs, in the sense that they bear strong relations to their educational experiences at grammar schools in Huddersfield and London between 1946 and 1954, and in a more literal fashion too; most of the volumes I consulted for this chapter were taken from their bookcases or had been put upon my own shelves by them when I was a child. Working in our shared house in Cornwall, where these books now live, I at first thought it was odd that so much of what I needed was immediately to hand, from my mother's hardback *Mrs. Beer's House*, my father's old Pelican copies of *The Uses of Literacy* and his friend Brian Jackson's *Education and the Working Class* to my Puffin editions of *The Country Child, The King of the Barbareens*, and others. It took me a while to realize that I was looking at this the wrong way round; I was writing the chapter because the ideas in these books have always been part of my world. For this, and a great deal more besides, I thank them.

This book has been a part of my sons' lives for as long as they can remember, but they are kind enough not to groan when the topic of recitation comes up. Indeed, thanks to an enthusiasm for Robert Burns on the part of his excellent first-grade teacher Kathleen Doty at Willett Elementary School in Davis, Tom can still perform (under duress) "My heart is in the highlands" and "My love is like a red, red rose." As if to illustrate the random provision of elocutionary instruction in contemporary American education, his twin brother Alex, at the same school but in another class, was never required to recite, but he has memorized "Jabberwocky" off his own bat. I thank them both for being such excellent company and for leaving me alone when necessary. My husband Jamie may not recite, but he has done everything else a partner could do to support me and this project, keeping the show on the road with remarkable cheerfulness throughout. I give him my love and thanks.

◆ ◆ ◆

The photograph of James Wells Champney's painting *The Schoolroom at the Mill and Bars: Recitation Day* is reprinted courtesy of the Pocumtuck Valley Memorial Association, Memorial Hall Museum, Deerfield, Massachusetts. Portions of the first case study appeared as "Standing on the Burning Deck: Poetry, Performance, History," *PMLA* 120 (2005): 148–62, and is reprinted by permission of the copyright owner, The Modern Language Association of America. "Casabianca" is taken from *The Com-*

plete Poems 1927–1979 by Elizabeth Bishop, copyright ©1979, 1983 by Alice Helen Methfessel, and is reprinted by permission of Farrar, Straus and Giroux, LLC. Portions of the third case study appeared as "Memorization and Memorialization: 'The Burial of Sir John Moore after Corunna,'" *Romanticism and Victorianism on the Net* 53 (2009): n.p. Web, September 2, 2011; I thank Kate Flint, who edited this special issue on "Materiality and Memory," and RaVoN for the permission to reprint. An earlier version of the afterword appeared as "The Legacy of Victorian Recitation: The Nation's Favo(u)rite Poems," in "Whither Victorian Studies?" the inaugural edition of *Victoriographies* 1:14–35, 2011; I thank Julian Wolfreys, the editor, and Edinburgh University Press for the permission to reprint. I thank Ron Canfield at SureFire, LLC, for permission to reprint its "Invictus" promotional poster.

Introduction

The core of this book addresses the intersection between everyday life and a mere two hundred lines of poetry: Felicia Hemans's "Casabianca" (1826), Thomas Gray's "Elegy Written in a Country Churchyard" (1751), and Charles Wolfe's "Burial of Sir John Moore after Corunna" (1817). All three works, widely read in schools and continuously reprinted in anthologies, were memorized and recited, whether willingly or unwillingly, in whole or in part, by significant proportions of the population in English-speaking countries for substantial stretches of the nineteenth and twentieth centuries. In consequence, these verses carried the potential to touch and alter the worlds of the huge numbers of people who took them to heart. This book examines the vital connections that were formed between my chosen poems and individuals, communities, discourses, beliefs, and behaviors—primarily in Great Britain, but also, at specific junctures, in the United States of America.[1] In all three case studies, the themes of the given poem and the peculiarities of its movement through time and space determine the stories told and the histories explored. At the same time, these chapters contribute to the book's general examination of the phenomenon of widespread poetry memorization in two national cultures, and consider what might be thought of as the successive phases in the life cycle of the memorized poem. The first study concentrates upon recitation as a physical experience for relatively young children; the second addresses some of the later psychological dimensions inherent within adolescents' and adults' internalization of a poem; and the third focuses upon adults only, asking under what circumstances a work long held within the self might suddenly deliver new and vital meaning.

◆ ◆ ◆

When the topic of verse memorization is raised today, the invocation is often couched within a lament, a mournful regret for the loss of a world in which every individual could readily recite fine-sounding lines from a supply of poems recognizable to all. In Britain the lament is frequently tempered by an acknowledgment that the methods used to achieve such a laudable outcome were perhaps less than ideal and possibly counterproductive. Simple elegiac celebrations are not unknown: Gordon Brown, just days before he assumed the post of prime minister in 2007, could be heard on BBC radio, wistfully casting his mind back to the days he had memorized Gray's Elegy, summoning up some blank verse from Shakespeare, and wishing that schools still required the practice. It is commoner, however, to find a more conflicted response. Commentators generally would like to re-create that lost world—a society, or at least a significant number of individuals, that holds entire poems at its heart—but they want to find a different way of achieving this end. Thus, in the introduction to his anthology *By Heart: 101 Poems to Remember* (1997), the then-poet laureate, Ted Hughes, denigrated the rote-learning method generally used in schools for memorization, and vividly expounded "an array of other less laborious, more productive, more amusing techniques" to secure what he depicts as a life-enriching result (ix). A 1996 *Times Educational Supplement* article entitled "Learning By Rote Kills Verse for Life" had plowed identical furrows (McGavin). Five years before this, a pair of articles in the same publication also argued for the deep value of the memorized poem and suggested nontraditional routes to the goal. In her first essay, the novelist Sarah Neilan told a tale of redemption: after a bout of meningitis had apparently fragmented her brain, she underwent the "life-saving" experience of regaining her mind by recalling the poetry she had learned as a child ("Survival Tactics," 25). In the second article, following what she characterizes as the "amazing response" to the earlier piece, she set forth "the secrets of enshrining words in memory": these were the imaginative and enterprising tricks and turns that her "old teacher and mentor Sister Helena" had taught her in a boarding convent school many years before ("Hook, Line," 27). In all of these writings, the mind's secure possession of a literary work is self-evidently a highly desirable and multivalent good, yet a dislike and distrust of the best-known method of memorization hovers close by and demands the presentation of alternative modes of installation.

Discussions of the topic of the memorized poem are altogether more numerous, more emotional, and less equivocal in the United States. Most are simply distressed by what is imaged as the loss of a common wealth.[2] With the passage of the recitation into oblivion, runs the burden of the stereotypical piece, division has come among the generations and communities of America: where once grandparents, parents, and children, townsfolk and country-dwellers, rich and poor, were united by a joint stock of rich poetic knowledge, now they are fractured and alien to one another. The time when the memorized poem held sway can still be glimpsed, but only just—it is slipping away as the last of those stalwart reciters, those doughty grandmothers and those entertaining great-uncles, reach the ends of their lives. Articles on poetry recitation typically generate large mailbags of letters either from those who still keep the flame alive themselves, or who remember those that did. In 1995, when historian Joan Shelley Rubin appealed in the *New York Times Book Review* for readers' descriptions of the poems they had recited in school between 1917 and 1950, and their feelings about "what the task meant to them at the time and later in life," she clearly tapped a wellspring of passionate remembrance: as one of her 479 correspondents commented, "I have been waiting all my adult life for someone to ask the question you pose" ("They Flash," 264, 271). "A Lost Eloquence," Carol Muske Dukes's op-ed piece in the *New York Times* at the end of 2002, was followed by a comparable flood of reminiscence. During his tenure as the nation's poet laureate, Robert Pinsky initiated what he called the "Favorite Poem Project" in 1997 to record ordinary people reading beloved verse aloud: although this enterprise, designed to reach as broad a constituency as possible, had multiple goals and outcomes, it inevitably spoke with particular resonance to those school-trained reciters of earlier eras and performed a highly valuable service in capturing their voices for posterity.[3] Time after time, individuals expressed gratitude for the fact that their classroom experiences had resulted in a lifelong relationship with a literary work.

Such instances illustrate the heady blend of sentiment, reverence, and downright pleasure that suffuses the idea of the memorized poem in American culture; rarely are its laments for the passing of pedagogical recitation checked by the reservations about rote learning that characterize British considerations of the topic.[4] Nevertheless, individuals on two sides of the Atlantic are united in their belief that there used to be a time when children regularly recited verse at school in their respective countries, but that this time came to an end. One aim of the pages ahead is to bring substance, clarity, and detail to this general and often rather hazily expressed idea, and to account for the significant differences between the ways in which the memorization of verse is remembered and discussed in Great Britain and the United States today. This book is first and foremost a historical examination, but, given the ties that bind us to the topic, it is also in part a study of contemporary attitudes towards a particular poetic practice, and, indeed, to poetry more generally.

At the outset, a few words are in order to suggest some of the arenas in which this specific form of verse memorization should be situated. The process of committing to heart sequences of words in set shapes has a long and significant presence in probably every culture one might care to mention, and thus constitutes an enormous field for analysis.[5] Perhaps the practice that springs most readily to mind is the memorization of religious texts—from the Qu'ran to Bible verses, catechisms to prayers—but even the most casual survey throws up a huge array of other materials for consideration. Nursery rhymes, proverbs, saws, aphorisms, lore and laws, patriotic speeches, oaths, pledges, jokes, mnemonic aids, ballads, song lyrics—the average mind is the repository of innumerable patches of patterned language, memorized consciously or unconsciously; study of the history and influence of any or all of these forms holds the potential to pay handsome dividends. Yet even though the focus is narrowed here to the memorization and recitation of poems in English only—actually, even tighter, chiefly to poems disseminated by the school and knowingly received in Great Britain and the United States as samples of "literature" written in English—then a broad area for investigation still remains. This is a practice that has a relatively long and complex past and a story that, in all probability, will never be over.

Indeed, although this project chooses primarily to look back in time, verse recitation undoubtedly has a forward-looking narrative too. One of the most significant, and certainly most widely reported, signs of revival in the United States is "Poetry Out Loud," a recitation contest instituted in 2005 by the National Endowment for the Arts with generous funding from the Poetry Foundation; this is matched in Great Britain by staged recitations on National Poetry Day and the resuscitation of numerous verse-speaking competitions, such as the BBC-sponsored "Off By Heart" project, for children across the country.[6] The memorization of poetry, then, has not disappeared in either Britain or the United States, and it seems improbable that it will ever vanish completely; for a variety of different reasons, there will always be those in any given community who find this activity appealing and worthwhile, and who will therefore practice it themselves and induce others to do likewise. Further support to recitation is afforded by the range of venues and occasions that exist, and have existed, for its encouragement and performance. For the most part this book will focus on the school as the prime site of propagation, but memorized poetry clearly has strong connections to a range of other institutions, formal and informal. Recitations can occur at the meetings of clubs and societies, in kitchens and parlors, theaters or village halls, pubs and coffeehouses, around campfires and on political platforms, in civic and religious ceremonies, and so forth—any and all of these instances constitute worthwhile areas for examination, and carry histories that inevitably overlap and intersect with the story of poetry in juvenile education.

Nevertheless, important though it is to state that verse recitation has neither died nor has ever been wholly dependent upon the school for its well-being, certain facts do carry a central significance. For defined periods in Great Britain and the United States, the memorization of poetry was not an elective pursuit but a mandatory element of mass educational systems. It is the crucial interplay of two words in that sentence—"mandatory" and "mass"—that created the phenomenon that is of most concern here. Communities containing large numbers of adults who could recite poems that others would recognize only came into existence because even larger numbers of children had performed a particular pedagogical exercise with a limited range of literary works. Although poetry recitation has an influential and interesting history before widespread public schooling was fully established in Britain and the United States, the beginning of the memorized poem's true heyday was in both countries coincident with the consolidation of systems of free, and relatively prolonged, elementary instruction that came about only in the last three decades of the nineteenth century.

In Britain the grasp of this poetic practice, at its very strongest between 1875 and 1900, continued to be felt in the nation's basic educational system, if with progressively diminishing force, for a further forty years. Recitation certainly played a role in other kinds of institution, private and state-supported, inside and outside that historical stretch; in the case studies ahead we will frequently encounter individuals whose relationship with the poem in question did not begin in an elementary school. Nevertheless, it was the presence of this particular exercise in Britain's most extensive but least prestigious system of education that produced both the country's largest populations of reciters and its ambivalent opinions about the practice. In the United States pedagogical recitation had a longer and a broader reach: an important element in the lives of many elementary-school students until around the end of the 1950s, the memorized poem also held a place up to the same date in the high school education received by increasingly significant numbers of young people after 1930 or so. The fact that recitation persisted as a classroom exercise into the teenaged years of many individuals who are still alive today explains to a large degree why current American discussions of memorized poetry differ markedly from their British counterparts. Yet numerous other factors exerted pressure upon poetry's pedagogical progress in Great Britain and the United States, creating divergent histories and contrasting sets of attitudes.

◆ ◆ ◆

This project employs a range of strategies to investigate these various histories and attitudes. Up to a point it is useful to argue that the memorized poem in my chosen contexts has both an institutional and an emotional history; these might also be designated the external and the internal histories of poetry recitation. The institutional or external history can be pursued via relatively familiar forms of historiography; the process by which the recitation of individual works of poetry in English came to assume such an important place within the education of vast numbers of British and American people is at times convoluted and complex, but it is there to be found within a variety of printed sources and other materials.

The next few pages of this introduction provide a summary of my general argument about the development of this phenomenon; Part I of the book devotes itself to a more detailed examination of the rise and fall of verse recitation in British and American popular education.[7] Rightly speaking, however, this latter account should be labeled "Towards a Comparative Cultural History" or some such to indicate that it plots only the major features of a rich territory that offers great scope for further exploration.

My institutional history presents the story of the memorized poem's achieved ubiquity as a materialist formation, not a romantic tale of the superior love of fine literature in days of yore. One strain in the nostalgic lament for the lost world of recitation insists that earlier ages had a truer reverence for poetry, a greater respect for its ability to instill beautiful words, beautifully expressed, into the young. I maintain, however, that the recitation of poetry became an integral part of life for as long as it did for the following reason: at a key moment in the establishment of popular schooling, the practice both shared the same general shape and carried the highest prestige of the limited educational opportunities that those systems could provide. Such a view by no means precludes the possibility that at different times and places, individual educators and students entertained and experienced exactly the kinds of noble feelings about verse that some of those who mourn the disappearance of widespread recitation might wish to believe were directional and mainstream. I nevertheless argue that the history of poetry in the schools, and thus the hearts, of the past is not primarily a story about the wisdom of our elders, and much less of young people's joyful embrace of the literary. Instead I figure it as the haphazard evolution of an exercise that, as a daily practice, often had little to do with either the wonderfulness of poetry or its sustaining presence in the mind of the child or adult.

To be sure, numerous theories about the importance of the practice and the value of its content were certainly expounded at various historical moments and in different cultural climates. The multifaceted nature of poetry recitation meant that it could draw upon a wide range of rationalizations for its place in the curriculum. As Part I illustrates in its survey of the period before the advent of mass education, the presence of poetry— or at least, of verse—in the initial stages of a child's acquisition of literacy was such a pervasive and unremarkable aspect of everyday life that it excited few justifications. The vernacular recitation exercises that began to be demanded of certain more advanced young readers in the later eighteenth and early nineteenth centuries, however, were understood primarily as necessary drill for their elocutionary and oratorical skills. Discussions of these latter practices celebrated the fact that both their external and internal characteristics contributed towards the production of the public speaker. The performance of lines committed to heart strengthened a youth's memory and developed his confidence, self-presentation, and vocal delivery; the lines themselves supplied him with a rich hoard of quotations and an enhanced ability to reproduce effective literary style.

As the nineteenth century wore on and recitation found its secure home in the burgeoning systems of education for the poor, elements of these older justifications migrated into newer pedagogical writings and were placed, with varying degrees of importance, in relation to other arguments. Elocution and oratorical practice dropped down the chart of recitation's extrinsic merits; memory training gained a massive prominence, especially in the United States, and then a falling-off; the exercise of self-discipline and hard work needed to learn long works by heart generally won high marks throughout the period; the improvement of physical health, posture, and accent were significant factors for some.[8] The intrinsic benefits—which is to say, the benefits deriving from intimate knowledge of given works—received progressively greater attention, but also underwent marked shifts of emphasis in different periods and quarters. Memorized poetry was important because of its religious and moral aspect: the individual, both in childhood and in later life, would be guided, improved, and comforted by the principles and sentiments stored within. Memorized poetry played an unrivaled role in the development of taste, in the refinement of the uncultured, in their elevation to a higher plane. Memorized poetry was both a benefit and an agent of democracy, a beacon of civilization, a promoter of patriotism and national pride; memorized poetry brought every boy and girl in touch with the best that has been thought and said, with the greatest literary achievements of their common language. Memorized poetry united individuals with their heritage and with each other. Memorizing and reciting poetry was an essential element of the study of English and American literature; memorizing and reciting poetry *was* the study of English and American literature. For the factions invested in recapitulation theory at the beginning of the twentieth century, children should chant memorized poetry (especially *Hiawatha* and the more stirring ballads) as an adjunct to their progression through the different stages of human development; for those enraptured by a rather fey brand of romanticism, children should recite poetry because children *were* poetry.[9]

Some of these tenets still make sense to us today; others require the excavation and reconstruction of contemporary circumstances for a full appreciation of their relative force. Nevertheless, although certain theories indubitably played a role in getting, and keeping, a particular exercise on mass education's books, they acted for the most part as supportive rather than motivating factors. Overall, they were less important than, in the first instance, specific exigencies, and in the second, the reproductive tendencies of customary practice. The massive and long-running success of recitation in schools was initiated and sustained by its congruence with, and then its deep presence within, the grammar of the institution—the rules that, officially and unofficially, govern an organization's quotidian operations.

Full substantiation of these comments requires detailed examination of the appropriate portions of the educational histories of Great Britain and the United States, but I will say a few more words here to round off the basic outline of my institutional argument. Compulsory poetry recitation figured prominently in what approximated to the founding documents, official or unofficial, of the public elementary systems in these two nations; consequently the practice, at that time formally continuous with their schools' general practices, became encoded, so to speak, in the DNA of mass education. Once established within their regimens, regimens famously slow to change and especially prone to the repetition of the tried and tested, the memorized poem proved to be remarkably tenacious. If verse recitation began its career in popular education as a resonant encapsulation of the highest good that the elementary school could bestow upon its charges, then such a meaning and value only grew larger over the years. For the first half a dozen decades and more of mass schooling, during which successive generations of pupils and students who had undergone this specific form of training went on to become parents and teachers themselves, the recitation of a poem by a child carried an accrued power to signify to listening adults that what they understood as "education" was occurring. Despite the changing tides of pedagogical theory that washed over the elementary school, the ballast of custom served the memorized poem well; the recitation exercise may have had to shift from one corner of the curriculum to another, or to gather around itself at various times substantially different sets of justifications, but the basic practice continued with little alteration.

That poetry memorization as a mass phenomenon was intrinsically bound to the history of a particular institution is illustrated especially well by the British case: when the 1944 Education Act effectively wiped the elementary school off the map and created a new formation, the "primary school," widespread pedagogical recitation disappeared with it. The situation in the United States would seem at first glance less amenable to hard-and-fast historical description. Certainly the absence of any centralized governmental directives meant that mandatory poetry memorization was neither created as a national practice with a stroke of the pen on a given date, as it was in Britain, nor brought to an end when the institution that hosted it was written off in a similarly definitive fashion. Instead, recitation stood at the mercy of the discrete decisions of thousands and thousands of teachers, school board members, county superintendents, and state supervisors; perhaps unsurprisingly, far greater energy was expended in the United States than in Britain on the development and promotion of arguments to bolster the continuation, and in time, to urge the banishment, of the practice. But despite the myriad opportunities for divergence in the States, consensus of opinion generally ruled the day, giving rise to incredibly uniform patterns of behavior across the country and over the decades. The force of customary practice in the continued replication of a time-honored classroom exercise appears, if anything, more marked in the American than the British context. For over a hundred years, the recitation of poetry constituted an act that bore a central relation to American public education's understanding of itself.

And yet the time eventually came when that center could no longer hold. In Britain, mandatory recitation, in general decline after the 1920s, disappeared altogether with the abolition of the elementary school; the practice held on a little longer in the United States, but became an exceptional behavior by the 1960s. Within the culture of these countries three key areas of thought had eventually developed such profound differences, both from each other and from their own nineteenth-century counterparts, that they no longer shared enough common ground to support the continued presence of compulsory memorization in schools. In the first place, understandings of the role of mass juvenile education had undergone significant modulation; second, beliefs about the needs and abilities of the individual child had changed beyond recognition; and third, perceptions of the function of poetry, and its relationship to society, had been utterly transformed. As a result, a phenomenon that for so many years had formed a regular component of mass experience was demoted to the status of an optional pursuit.

This, then, represents one way of understanding the general course taken by verse recitation in Great Britain and the United States during the nineteenth and twentieth centuries. The emotional or internal history of this phenomenon is to my mind as important as, and arguably of greater interest than, the institutional history just outlined. The key questions for this inquiry can be expressed as follows. How did people feel about memorizing and reciting poetry—both at school, and thereafter? How did the necessity of public performance affect children's experience with, and attitude towards, poetry in general and the specific works they learned? What was distinctive about this form of relationship with a poem, and what advantages and disadvantages accrued from it? Did the poems change the children, and did the children change the poems? How likely were they to form opinions about their assigned verses? If they did, what kind of opinions might these have been? What happened to these attitudes and opinions as they grew older? How did adults regard the experiences they had had with poetry in the classroom? Might a poem that still

kept its place within their hearts or heads in later life alter its meaning over time? To whom does a memorized poem belong?

The three case studies and the afterword of this book address different elements of these questions; in each instance, I have attempted to give depth and specificity to my inquiries by embedding them within the discussion of a poem whose thematics offer suggestive connections to the topic in hand. In comparison to Part I's single-minded attention to verse recitation's institutional progress, however, the discussion of the memorized poem's emotional history will inevitably appear somewhat diffuse. Nevertheless, I hope that my explorations of the felt, internal aspects of memorized poetry in British and American society combine to tell a story that both augments and to an extent challenges the arguments put forward elsewhere in these pages.

This complementary history pursues an elusive subject. Some of its difficulties are specific to aspects of the topic in hand. It is, for instance, famously hard to gain access to the feelings of children of the past—whether we consult works of fiction or poetry; memoir or autobiography; oral history or sociology (and at different points in this project I study all of these forms), we are almost always examining reconstructions after the fact. Other difficulties are endemic to all histories—whether we are examining representations of either the child's or the adult's attitudes and sensations, we must carefully consider both the writer's position and the text's specific location in time, place, and genre. But the relative paucity of documentation on what was in actuality a widespread experience presents perhaps the greatest challenge to interpretation. Out of the millions of individuals who memorized verses, only a tiny number represented or recorded their thoughts and feelings about the topic; no large-scale surveys of the views and opinions of those who learned poems at school exist.[10] The records that we do have can be roughly divided into two categories. One category is comprised of works of fiction that present highly critical or otherwise derisive depictions of juvenile recitation; in my first case study I speculate at some length about the possible causes of this negative portrayal. The other category of representations appears primarily within autobiographical texts or anecdotal reports. These, as we shall see in the second case study's extended examination of a subsection of the latter category, are almost always highly positive about the practice.

Although my external argument about poetry recitation tends to stress the unromantically pragmatic and disciplinary function of this compulsory exercise within the institution, other notes are sounded in first-person accounts. Memoirists, autobiographers, essayists, newspaper letter- or article-writers, and those who reply to surveys about the topic are generally adamant, indeed often eloquent, about both the inspirational and the liberating effect of the memorized poem in the classroom and beyond. This is not to say that they all tell exactly the same story about their experiences. Many, but by no means all, of these people explain that they found it relatively easy to commit a poem to heart; although most of them write with relish about their performance on a stage or in front of the class, others recall their mounting anxiety and clammy hands as the appointed time for recitation approached. Despite these divergences, however, writers or respondents generally coincide in their opinions about the ultimate worth of the exercise; their texts explicitly or implicitly make the important points that that which is mandatory is not necessarily unpleasant, and that to be required to do something difficult is not necessarily to be oppressed. On the contrary: for these advocates, school set the bar high when it came to verse recitation, and the expectation that they would make the jump spurred them to feats they might not otherwise have assayed. A successful performance not only brought an exhilarating rush of triumph at the time; it also left them with the secure possession of a beloved work forever after.

At this point it may seem as if my two histories of poetry recitation will be fundamentally at odds, or at least give substantially dissimilar accounts of the practice's meaning and value. To a certain degree, I think this is both inevitable and right. It is a truism that the characteristics of an experience assume different dimensions and significances whenever you alter your point of view, and, to shift my metaphor, a jarring discordance often rings out when analytical histories of a phenomenon are set alongside the memories of those who lived through it. Yet this apparent opposition between the two accounts is only one part of a larger story, primarily because those first-person testimonies come from only one part of a larger population. For this reason, the emotional history must perform a delicate balancing act. On the one hand, it wishes to explore the vivid specificities of personal memories. This project is intensely interested in how any one individual may have experienced the feelings, thoughts, and connections that could be created, inside and outside of the self, by the act of memorizing and reciting a poem. Yet on the other hand, it also wishes to place such experiences in relation to those of the vast numbers of other people who also memorized poems in class. How then do I maneuver between those who left representations, and those who did not—between the loquacious one and the unvoiced many—to create a larger community for our consideration?

To begin with, I find it useful to divide that huge gathering of onetime juvenile reciters into different groups. Positive reminiscences of poetry recitation emanate, we might reasonably assume, from a select constituency: those who valued the poetry exercise and enjoyed meeting, or exceeding, the expectations of their teachers were usually those who did well in education more generally, and such individuals were and are more likely to compose their own texts, or indeed reply to surveys, in later life than those who had not similarly excelled.[11] What, then, are the salient characteristics of others within the larger population? Even though they never experienced the urge to put pen to paper to describe this part of their lives, did a good proportion of people like rising to the challenge of memorizing a poem in school and feel glad to have that work with them for the remainder of their days? Did another proportion of them loathe everything about a classroom ordeal that contained ample potential for humiliation and punishment, and then did they avoid anything that had the least smack of poetry about it forever after? And did a further proportion of individuals, perhaps a large swathe of people in the middle of this immense population of around three or four generations of Britons and Americans, feel, well, frankly indifferent about the whole affair? How many of them just did what they had to do at the time—got through the poem more or less, sometimes badly and sometimes well—and then thought little more about it, whether lines from the schoolroom standard popped up in their mind from time to time, or whether they did not?

In my attempts to imagine the thoughts and feelings of the unrecorded majority, the pages ahead occasionally have recourse to modes of reconstruction that are more akin to the work of the historical novelist than to that of the historian, strictly considered. And it is in these ventures that I will sometimes appear to be closing the gap that just a moment ago began to open up between my institutional and emotional accounts. To my mind at least, it seems likely that the memorized poem exercise was indeed a trial for certain, and perhaps many, students and pupils: it is hard therefore for me to be simply celebratory about juvenile recitation within my study of the practice as a felt experience for huge numbers of people. Sections of the first case study, which include considerations of the anxious body of the reciting child, are especially concerned with this side of the question. Further, in its analysis of a specific constituency of British schoolchildren in the first half of the twentieth century, the second case study will wonder whether even individuals who were very good at memorizing verse might, in certain circumstances, have had complicated and conflicted emotions about both the practice of reciting and the specific poems they held within themselves. On the other side of things, however, I also engage in similarly speculative or hypothetical thinking to create a more expansive discussion of some of the unquestionably estimable benefits of memorized poetry than straightforward documentation would seem to allow. In addition to its examination of mixed feelings about verse recitation, that second case study also explores the role a memorized poem might play in enriching and expanding the mind, and in advancing creative and analytic thought, inside and outside of the classroom, for individuals and communities alike. The final case study configures a more explicitly emotional form of this inquiry, arguing that in times of extreme duress, a poem committed to heart in childhood could bring much-needed solace to an adult in psychological pain.

As a whole, then, this project makes frequent changes to its angles of approach, and hopes thereby to navigate between the Scylla and Charybdis of these particular waters. Aiming to avoid an unqualified lament for the lost world of widespread poetry memorization, the pages ahead strive to keep historical specificity and demographic breadth in view, and to be clear-sighted about the practice's shortcomings. Just as importantly, they wish to steer clear of any blunt indictments of juvenile recitation as some kind of instrument of mass social control. Instead, this book honors the richly satisfying and sustaining inner experiences that could develop out of a simple pedagogical exercise, and argues that works of literature held within individual minds had the power to effect material changes in the world at large.

◆ ◆ ◆

The preceding pages have already made reference to a number of the general topics that the book will explore. Before moving to a discussion of its other concerns and questions, I provide for the purposes of orientation a short overview and explanation of the sections that follow this introduction. As noted, Part I investigates recitation's progress within the mass educational systems that developed in Great Britain and the United States over the course of the nineteenth and twentieth centuries; it concludes with a brief consideration of the factors that affected the constitution of juvenile recitation canons over the years. The histories traced therein are intended to provide a general background for the remainder of the book—a necessary undertaking, given that the chapters within Part II follow idiosyncratic routes rather than a broad path with equal and balanced sections of national coverage.

"Casabianca," the poem at the center of the first of my three case studies, presents the spectacle of a child sailor who is blown to pieces because his sense of duty keeps him standing on deck during the bombardment of his ship; its author, Felicia Hemans, took her inspiration from accounts of the death of a valiant French boy who perished during the Battle of the Nile in 1798. I use this work as a lens to examine the processes whereby the performance of poetry in Britain's elementary schools forged short-term and long-term bodily relationships between individuals and measured language. Looking, among other things, at the history of corporal punishment within mass education, the chapter considers not only what happened to children, but also to poems with regular rhythms, during the process of enforced recitation. The fragmented survival of "Casabianca" in popular consciousness today, I argue, is the last remaining trace of its pedagogical past, of a time when poetry was experienced in and through the body, and when the iamb connected to the heartbeat in a manner that we no longer appreciate, and certainly cannot feel.

The next chapter sets Thomas Gray's "Elegy Written in a Country Churchyard" within a very specific institutional and emotional history, aiming thereby to direct attention to the mingled pain and pleasure that can exist within the possession of a cultural object. The first half of the twentieth century saw progressively larger numbers of academically gifted working-class children in Great Britain receive government-backed scholarships; these awards allowed them to proceed from their public elementary schools to a free secondary education in what were otherwise fee-paying grammar schools. The Elegy, a staple poem for memorization by the highest-achieving elementary-school pupils, is famous for first raising and then dismissing the issue of undeveloped talent within society's lowest echelons. This case study considers how children from such ranks might have felt when they read and recited a work that dubs the poor both unlettered and mute. Further, it speculates about the ability of the memorized poem to stay within those individuals for the remainder of their days, and to act as a constant reminder of the educational and social processes that moved them out of one class and into another—an elevation the eighteenth-century poem deems impossible.

Popular history has it that General Wolfe recited Gray's Elegy to his officers on September 12, 1759, the eve of the Battle of the Plains of Abraham; he concluded his performance, it is said, with the words "Now, gentlemen, I would rather be the author of that poem than take Quebec" (Reed, 204). In the second half of the following century certain soldiers facing combat were more likely to have been thinking of another Wolfe and hearing the relentless beat of a different poetic work within their thudding hearts. My third case study resurrects "The Burial of Sir John Moore after Corunna," a piece all but lost to us today but which was once memorized by countless individuals in the nineteenth century. Charles Wolfe's poem, a reimagining of the hasty interment of a fallen general after one of the land battles in the Napoleonic Wars, was repeatedly quoted by soldiers and other individuals during the American Civil War when they found themselves having to organize, or witness, the burials of dead comrades. In recent years, cultural historians of Great Britain have tried to account for the massive shift in burial and memorial practices for the common soldier that occurred between 1815 and 1915. I argue that the presence of Wolfe's poem in the hearts and minds of ordinary people played its part in creating the social expectations that led to the establishment of the National Cemeteries in the United States, and thus, in due course, the mass memorialization of World War I.

Let me say a few words here about why the case studies are centered on these particular poems. Composed between the midpoint of the eighteenth century and the first quarter of the nineteenth, all three of my chosen works were in general circulation long before they became schoolroom standards in Britain and the United States; all three are by authors from the British Isles; all three are written in abab quatrains; all three focus, one way or another, on death. I find such convergences interesting and will return to each of them in due course, yet none of these points of uniformity played a determining role when I originally drew up my plans for this project. Rather, I chose these three works because they appeared to me to offer opportunities to explore a series of markedly distinct issues within a general consideration of the effects and affects of memorizing verse. In retrospect, I can see that certain other highly popular, much memorized, works could have licensed investigations similar to the ones I ended up conducting. It is also equally apparent to me that I could have explored substantially different questions about widespread poetry recitation, and thus have written a substantially different book, had I selected, say, Wordsworth's "Daffodils," Jane Taylor's "Twinkle, Twinkle, Little Star," and Longfellow's "Psalm of Life" (all of which would have been completely justifiable choices, as would have been Portia's "Quality of Mercy" speech, Holmes's "Chambered Nautilus," Kipling's "Recessional"—or indeed many others).

Although I pay attention to the American history of juvenile recitation in Part I and often to the American reception of British poems elsewhere in these pages, I do not provide a case study centered upon an American-authored poem; given that substantial numbers of American poems were standard fare for memorization in schools in United States and Great Britain over the years, this is perhaps the book's most reprehensible omission. My conscience on this score is somewhat salved by the fact that the most extensive work on poetry memorization has to date been written by Americanist scholars; I think here especially of Angela Sorby's close-grained attention to such poems as Whittier's "Snow-Bound" and Longfellow's *Hiawatha* in her fine book *Schoolroom Poets: Childhood, Performance, and the Place of American Poetry*, and of Joan Shelley Rubin's magisterial tome *Songs of Ourselves: The Uses of Poetry in America*, which considers the recitation of American (and other) poems in the course of its broad survey of the important roles poetry has played for individuals in the United States. That said, I concede that my institutional training in British literature is responsible for a certain bias in this project, which in consequence may appear lopsided to some readers.

To make partial amends, the project's afterword adopts a different stance from the case studies by resuming Part I's comparative mode. It also rings the changes by focusing upon two works that were written during recitation's heyday and that currently hold preeminent status both as, and among, memorized poems in popular culture on two sides of the Atlantic. Positioning W. E. Henley's "Invictus" (1888) as an American national favorite and Rudyard Kipling's "If –" (1910) as a British poem of poems, the afterword conducts a consciously allegorical reading to orchestrate a return to the topic raised in the introduction's opening pages. The memory of mass juvenile recitation, I noted there, arouses very different feelings in the United States and Great Britain. To close the book, I consider in what ways this might be connected to how individuals in these two countries regard not only their nation's educational past, but also their relationships with poetry, with society, and with themselves.

◆ ◆ ◆

In the course of their peregrinations my case studies investigate a wide range of esoteric subjects and histories. Taken as a whole, however, the book positions itself within just a few associated zones of academic inquiry. Both its debts and its desired contributions to the history of education and curricular studies should be manifest. It is also an obvious beneficiary of the lively activity that has over the last twenty to thirty years galvanized three key fields within historical literary studies, namely the history of the book, the cultural history of reading, and reception history.[12] To date, most of the important works in the first two of these areas have been relatively wide surveys of the social functions of authors, or readers, or academic study, or the book trade, in a particular period. Part I of this book follows such leads, aiming to add to these bodies of knowledge by tracking the genealogies of primers, anthologies, and schoolroom reading books and by insisting upon the importance of the often-overlooked chapter of juvenile recitation within mass literacy's history. But within the three case studies this project eschews the general overview and engineers instead a singularly narrow point of entry to its topic. It is my hope that such a reduction of the literary text to no more than fifty quatrains makes workable a capacious form of reception study.

I draw my encouragement to create wide cultural penumbras around short literary works from numerous sources. Analyses of the interplay between an aesthetic object and a broad range of social issues and concerns are today not unusual within research in the humanities. For Anglo-American literary scholars, this general development can be traced back to the 1980s, when historicist criticisms, dividing roughly into a British practice of cultural materialism inspired by Raymond Williams, and the Foucauldian path of American new historicism, made it their mission to break down barriers between seemingly distinct discourses and representations. Yet the landmark explorations in these critical schools, especially the latter, usually addressed themselves primarily to the synchronous forces of a single moment: however invested in, or unconcerned with, the idea of an author such studies might be, and however imaginatively or diligently they reconstruct the informing prehistory of significant topics, they frequently and most famously worked to capture the energies at play at the time of textual inscription. For a considerable number of years, the most promising models for wide-ranging study of a text's subsequent progress through time and its complex relation to social forms were to be found not in mainstream literary criticism, but in the works of literary sociology that came out of the historicist schools.[13] Here, however, most investigations ultimately elected to fold their findings back into a greater understanding of the constitution of the explicitly bookish worlds of, for instance, publishing practices or the politics of literary criticism.

In more recent times the general development of cultural studies, especially the subsection thereof that we might call afterlife studies, has resulted in increasing interest in a given text's ability over time to have meaning and influence in spheres beyond the specifically literary.[14] This project bears a strong family resemblance to works in this line, but there are certain characteristics peculiar to its object of analysis that complicate the relationship. Reception studies, however narrowly or widely they configure the historical, geographical, or demographical area reached by their chosen literary object, usually consider how a specific work has signified or signifies different things to different people in different contexts. This can be examined in minutely detailed or general and abstract ways, but there is a tacit understanding that the dynamic between the semantic content or cultural meaning of a text and its readers is key. In this study, however, no such relationship can be assumed; to put it quite plainly, it is perfectly possible to memorize and recite a poem without much or indeed any conscious thought about either its micro- or macro-particularities.[15] Because this project is always cognizant of the bodily mode by which its literary works were sent out into the world—of the corporeal dimensions of the processes of both memorization and recitation—its discussions can never restrict themselves to the question of how a text's meaning was received. A species of performance history is perforce an element of these reception histories; these are temporal studies of the progress of either a meaning allied with a practice, or simply of a practice alone.

Mentioning the necessity of attention to the body foregrounds a particular irony. Although there is no integral reason why a memorized poem must ever be spoken aloud, the outward expression of lines committed to heart was a mandatory element of the specific historical phenomenon here under investigation.[16] And yet this is a book about the production of sound through the act of verbal recitation that examines only its textual traces, the references in a range of printed materials to what was in one of its chief aspects an essentially oral and aural event. Another version of this project could strive to address this disjunction by including, for example, a CD of reciting voices, or by taking a different form itself, such as that of a radio program. Even so, a major problem would remain. Although it would certainly be possible to incorporate and discuss exceptional, especially professional, performances, the vast majority of the voices in which I am most interested were never recorded; indeed, many of them predate the period in which sound recordings were either easily or commonly made. Instead we must summon up in our head multitudes of everyday recitations, competent and otherwise, spoken in chorus or alone, in and out of the classroom. The inherent difficulties of accessing the sounds of the past explain to a degree why consideration of this key component of many kinds of cultural experiences has only recently become an element of literary analysis. My own attempt to restore a sense of hearing to our apprehensions of worlds that fell silent long ago is particularly indebted to the growing field of Victorian sound studies.[17] It is also intended to counter discussions of literature in its nineteenth- and twentieth-century contexts that argue that this period is characterized by the dissociation of the audible voice and the literary work.[18] From the readerly, if not the writerly, point of view, poetry in Great Britain and the United States had never made a louder noise.

Although these physical aspects of memorization and recitation make this a somewhat specialized variant, my book nevertheless participates in some of the usual projects of reception histories. Accordingly it makes a by-now familiar challenge to the hegemony within academic literary studies of author-centered periodization, the taxonomic principle that, despite some significant exceptions, continues to rule the internal organizations of such entities as university departments, pedagogical anthologies, and professional associations. As mentioned earlier, although I incorporate a number of poems written and published during the period of mass juvenile recitation, my case studies focus upon three works that appeared in earlier eras; I cross other institutional boundaries by looking on occasion at the effects of a British selection of works upon American memorizers and reciters. By making this latter move, I join company with both a growing number of colleagues who interest themselves in Anglo-American literary relations in the nineteenth and twentieth centuries (the essays in Meredith McGill's edited collection, *The Traffic in Poems: Nineteenth-Century Poetry and Transatlantic Exchange* have been especially inspiring to me), and the still larger cohort of critics exploring literature's transnational journeys more generally. Admittedly, I do pay some heed to the individuals who wrote my chosen poems and to the circumstances of each work's composition, but for the most part I choose to spend time in the worlds of the consumers, rather than the producers, of literature.

Loosening the tie that connects a text exclusively to its author and its original national milieu is a liberating experience; once this is done, we gain the opportunity first to glimpse the myriad of other ways in which a literary work might relate to people, eras, and places, and then to see how our ideas about the shape and character of those specific cultures might thereby undergo transformation. The case studies take on the task of exploring some of the myriad relationships, but the remainder of this introduction speaks briefly to the broader ramifications of these reconfigurations and their connection to the book's concern with mass juvenile recitation *in toto*. My guiding question is this: what can we see—either for the first time, or with greater clarity—once this huge involvement with poetry is put back into the picture?[19] To the extent that the responses to this query over the next few pages dwell on academic themes, they are most closely related to my concerns as a practicing Victorianist, but I hope there are issues of interest here for scholars of other areas and for general readers.

My first point can be made relatively quickly. The idea that the ethos of the Victorian era came to a sudden and decisive end has long-standing currency, both in various forms of cultural histories and in general opinion. This notion has played a structural role in the academic arrangement of literature in English; if the texts of the high modernists are taught as the paradigmatic works of the first half of the twentieth century, as they often have been, then it is easy to see why things would look this way. By switching attention from the production to the consumption of texts this project offers a complementary perspective. In Great Britain and the United States, both the practice and a good proportion of the poetic contents of juvenile recitation continued unchanged throughout the period when a revolution in attitudes towards familiar literary forms and conventions is meant to occur; from around the 1870s to the 1930s or so, the formative and arguably dominant relationship that most people ever had with the entities known as "English literature" or "American literature" remained more or less the same. For majority populations in these two countries, then, no break occurred and thus the customary mode of periodization does not apply. In making this argument, I hope to contribute not just to literary discussions but to the growing numbers of studies in other areas of cultural inquiry that argue that many widespread patterns of thought and behavior that came into being in the nineteenth century did not undergo abrupt and radical alteration after the devastation of World War I.

This general emphasis on nineteenth-century origins remains in play as I open up a broader topic. What might we notice about some of the blind spots and assumptions of academic literary studies over the years if the story of the memorized poem were fully restored to view? My answers to this question ground themselves in the following observations:

(1) the nineteenth century witnessed the appearance of two new sorts of engagement with vernacular literature, one of which would be associated with the university and the other with the elementary school; (2) these themselves were epiphenomena of two signal events of the 1800s, the twin explosions in the demographics of literacy and the availability of material to read. It is my contention that the subsequent histories of the university's and the school's differentiated modes of literary study are intimately and somewhat fractiously related; to use evolutionary terms, one might say that the simultaneous but particular developments of these two forms were profoundly influenced by their ecological proximity. Explorations of the different phases of this relationship, I suggest, would yield a more nuanced understanding of how the creation of two specific kinds of reading communities effected a series of schisms of which we are today the inevitable heirs.

Of these schisms, I direct particular notice to the chasm that yawns between ideas about poetry within the university and those that pertain elsewhere. This is an exciting moment to discuss the exact characteristics of this gap. For many years, although there was a bountiful amount of analysis of poetry in its academic contexts, little serious consideration was given to the many roles that poems have played and can play in everyday life. In the first place, studies in the cultural history of reading tended to focus upon the relationship between general readers and texts in prose. In the second, literary studies displayed only partial interest in how poetry's various positionings might work to create site-specific reading behaviors; with a few important exceptions, attention was paid primarily to the history of interpretative practices within the profession itself, or to the question of how and where poetry was read before the advent of mass literacy. Now, however, the many different types of public and personal experiences with the genre that came into existence in the nineteenth century and that are part of life today are beginning to attract the academy's attention. In addition to the books by Sorby, Rubin, and McGill already cited, the work of such critics as Tricia Lootens, Virginia Jackson, and Mary Loeffelholz is increasing our understanding of both the constitution of such relationships and their long-lasting effects.

If poetry's extracurricular activities used to be outside the purview of English departments, then so were some of the groups of poems that correspond to those various sites and forms of poetic engagement. I am most interested in the fate of the canon that constituted itself during the heyday of recitation in British and American mass education. Many of these classroom texts are short poems that possess an apparent regularity of form and whose content makes an apparently unironic appeal, often to love for family, country, and God. Even more succinctly: these seem to be straightforward and simple poems that rhyme. Once the possession of huge numbers of people, such pieces today have a limited circulation, persisting only in the minds of the last generation of individuals who got them by heart; in the memories of their descendants, who heard their parents or grandparents recite them; and, in the company of other sorts of poetry, within volumes like *The Best-Loved Poems of the American People* or *The Nation's Favourite Poems*.[20] I want to ask why many of these verses do not make it into the academy's reading lists. There may seem to be a quick and obvious answer to this question, but I suggest that this is actually a more complicated issue than it at first appears. Only by attending to the intertwined histories of literary studies in the school and the university can we begin to understand certain prejudices and absences within the latter location's analysis of literature in English.

The features and tendencies to be explored are, I believe, both deep-rooted and largely unacknowledged; they have persisted, with only minor alterations, throughout academic literary criticism in the twentieth century and up to the present day, despite the fact there have been numerous and much-discussed changes in the field over this period. Of these shifts, the most significant were prompted by the extensive theory wars that took place within the humanities from the mid-1970s onwards. As a result of the ensuing critiques of the ideological investments and biases of literary studies, both the range of texts examined in academic settings and the stances of those examinations underwent major revision. Just as importantly, these developments prompted a devastating attack upon the concept of transhistorical value. From this point on, the mainstream of literary criticism has generally been loath to declare in print that a text is good or bad; if evaluations of this kind are made, they are invariably situated within defined contexts, historical and otherwise.

No doubt scholars of all fields feel that there are texts from the zones under their watch that do not get a fair crack of the university whip; in the case of texts with a longer history, some of these may have at one time had a happier (or at least, a more noticed) time of things, only to suffer a subsequent neglect, while others may never have received attention in academic contexts at all. There is of course no inherent reason why any given work "deserves" attention; moreover, a commonsensical reader might well point out at this juncture that professors of literature only have so many hours in the day just like everyone else and that choices will have to be made. Nevertheless, the omission of the prototypical "best-loved poems" from today's academic canons seems noteworthy to me because these verses supply a currently important desideratum. Thanks to the rapid growth of various forms of cultural history and analysis, a strong trend in literary studies has been the discussion of works that are deemed to have at one time or another garnered a demographically significant readership—significant, that is, with respect to size or social constitution. Because the poems in the recitation canon were memorized by those huge numbers of ordinary people, we can certainly award them a tick in the first box and debatably in the second one too. And yet many of the pieces continue to occupy the curious status of objects that used to be everywhere and are now nowhere (or very nearly nowhere).

Although it may well be foolhardy to attempt to analyze the meanings of an academic silence, I want to suggest two possible reasons for its existence. First, I suspect that despite all those radical changes to the field of play, most of the "short and simple" poems of the recitation canon retain the power to elicit the kind of dismissive responses that the discipline might like to think it left behind somewhere in the 1950s. Alternatively, or additionally, I believe that many of these verses evoke an even more startling response from a normally voluble community, a response that is no response whatsoever. In other words, these are either bad, embarrassing, or embarrassingly bad poems, about which we do not wish to speak, or they are stupid poems about which we can think of nothing to say at all. This conundrum could be investigated in numerous ways, but I will make a couple of approaches, both of which require that we keep in mind the structural implications of the phenomenon identified earlier—that splitting of literary study into distinct institutional formations under the pressure of a rapidly expanding literate population. It is possible to think more concretely about responses or nonresponses to many of the schoolroom standards if we consider the set of assumptions that functioned as first the grounding, and then the long-reigning, theories of the academic study of English literature. Thereafter, that analysis can be extended and nuanced if we turn to a particular phase of the discipline's development, a phase that witnessed the triumphant success of a single methodological practice.

To begin: the 1860s saw the appearance of new concepts about the associated ideas of the place and function of culture, and the relationship between literature and life. Matthew Arnold, a figure who will loom large in the British history of school recitation, played a key role in disseminating and adapting for English-speaking audiences Continental aesthetic discourse, most particularly Immanuel Kant's theory of the "uselessness" of the work of art, and the artist's—and the literary critic's—necessary detachment from the immediate concerns of the public sphere.[21] A paraphrase of Arnold's derived formulation about the aesthetic realm might run as follows: the required "disinterestedness" of the true work of art meant that, ideally, the poem existed away from the political factionalism and social inequities of the quotidian, creating a place in which individuals could access their best selves, free from the warping particularities of class identities and the petty cares of the moment. Not only art but also its production and its consumption should be placed at a remove from everyday life—the better, on the one hand, to console and inspirit the individual, and on the other, to comment upon the world at large, and thus, by indirect influence, bring it closer to a state of perfection.

Although these ideas were challenged and modified over time, versions thereof became centrally embedded within some of the principal tendencies of academic literary criticism for the next hundred years or so. Of their modulations, the most important was the relocation of the ideal world of art from *above* the level of the broad workaday world (as in Arnoldian theory) or *away* from all involvement with social concerns (as in aesthetic theory's *l'art pour l'art* doctrine) to a place in *opposition* to the mainstream of existence, a mode of life that was increasingly depicted as a debased condition of being. Given especial impetus from the creative and critical writings of key modernist authors (especially T. S. Eliot), this point of view gained a powerful and long-lasting orthodoxy in the academy, not incidentally because it was congenial to thinkers on both the right and left of the political spectrum.

Insisting in their various ways upon distanced relationships between literature and modern life, such understandings held damaging implications for forms of literary engagement that were predicated on no such notions of removal or critique from the margin. Of these, the memorization and recitation of poetry at school—a practice that sought to locate culture at the very heart of general culture—represented perhaps the most widespread example. But ideas about the necessity of critical distance also carried dire consequences for the type of works that were most appropriate for, and thus intimately associated with, such centrist modes. Critics who subscribed to the last, and eventually dominant, concept of literature's required oppositional stance were the most obviously contemptuous of the texts that had been widely enjoyed in the second half of the nineteenth century, and proved especially likely to heap disdain upon the form and content of the verse embraced in that age. To the modernists, and then much of the academic literary criticism that followed in its wake, most of the poetry valued in the Victorian era was self-evidently bad, embarrassing, or stupid, and therefore not worthy of any kind of serious attention. The works of a restricted number of famous poets from this period were, it is true, subjected to analysis, but they too suffered to some degree from versions of these slurs.[22]

Implicitly or explicitly, such rejections or disparagements often carried some kind of link to the cataclysm of 1914–18. It was axiomatic for many years that the poetry best known and most cherished in the second half of the nineteenth century was irrelevant to, and perhaps partly culpable for, a world fragmented by the horrors of the Great War; such ideas both located themselves within, and contributed towards, that general consensus that the Victorian ethos came to a sudden and definitive end.[23]

Certainly it is not hard to see that aspects of nineteenth-century literary culture must have looked unbearably naïve or at the very least misguided after the carnage of trench warfare; Wilfred Owen's excoriating "Dulce et Decorum Est" provides perhaps the casebook example of this bitter theme.[24] Nevertheless, the critical rejection of the poetry held dear in a broad swathe of Victorian contexts was also motivated by other factors, not least the academy's fundamental adherence to the concept of art's necessary distance from the quotidian and the mass. For literary scholars in the first half of the twentieth century, the immediately preceding era was saddled with the clear disadvantage of looking, in its attributes, remarkably similar to, and yet in its disposition demonstrably different from, their own times. The idea that "a literary work was supposed to embody a kind of heterodox or critical relation to modernity" proved especially damaging (Guillory, 140), I would suggest, to works that had been produced or celebrated in the only other society that had experienced the conditions of modern life most denigrated in twentieth-century criticism, but which had neither expected nor wanted all of its literature to position itself as their adversary.

With the seismic shifting of critical paradigms over the last thirty years, a sizable number of Victorian texts once considered beyond the pale of academic interest have now gained secure footholds within the canon. Yet to an almost overwhelming degree it has been works in prose, not poetry, that have received this new attention, with novels enjoying the most notable triumph. To be sure, a few volumes by certain key novelists already carried a long and respectable critical history thanks to their perceived aesthetic qualities, but armfuls of other examples of the genre are nowadays regularly discussed in the university. The onetime best-seller or massive popular success has become an especially favored object of analysis.[25] While at earlier moments in the twentieth century many of these works would have been thought unworthy of study for a whole raft of deficiencies (formal awkwardness or predictability; formulaic themes or plots; triteness; conservatism; sentimentality; and so forth), these very features are now grist to the mill. Today discussions of the ideological forces affecting both the fictions themselves and later judgments thereof are likely to constitute part of the academic inquiry; contemporary interest in the cultural positioning of texts has had the effect of nullifying, or at least contextualizing, judgments about quality.

Numerous arguments could be adduced to explain why scholars otherwise keen to excavate the connections between literature and life have so far been relatively uninterested in many of the poems of the recitation canon. One important contributory factor, I think, has been the hobbling effect of the profession's methodologies, most specifically the technique it considers appropriate for the study of poetry. When confronted with a poem, especially a short poem, critics subject it to a close reading. Yet this reflex action carries its own history, a history that is deeply rooted in that larger story of literary study in the academy. Most famously associated with British Practical Criticism as pioneered in the 1920s and the American New Criticism of the 1940s and 1950s, the technique of close reading typically explores the relationship between a work's ideas and its formal properties and devices. Although any scrap of text can be investigated in this manner, close reading has for several generations enjoyed a special relationship with densely patterned works of literature, which in practice has generally meant poetry. Furthermore, in its purest form—which is to say, when it is performed as an end in itself, not, as is frequently the case today, as an ancillary to other methods of inquiry—the close reading tends to prefer a short work of poetry because it aims to come to a conclusion about the totality of its object of study.

The hallmark of this purest form, as most perfectly practiced by the New Critics, is the discovery of contradictions—tensions, ironies, paradoxes, and so forth—in the relation between content and form.[26] By the end of the investigation, however, such productive oppositions are usually brought to some type of a resolution, thereby demonstrating that the work in question is unified by a more deeply interfused coherence of meaning that could have been foreseen at the beginning of the journey. Certain sorts of poems richly rewarded this type of address; it was a good job, indeed, that dense and knotty works by, for instance, Donne, Blake, and Yeats were short because celebrated close readings thereof found a great deal to say about the many different ways in which they confounded expectations and easy apprehension. But—and here I put it mildly—the poems in the memorization canon do not respond well to the set moves of the close reading, however modified and adapted these procedures may have been in the years since the reign of New Criticism. The very qualities of formal regularity, thematic transparency, and cultural centrality that made the recitational standard suitable for the school's mode of engagement with the literary render it generally unfit for this purpose.

In other words, I am arguing that the tools that literary critics hold in their hands today have been shaped over the years by the objects they have been used to explore. In order to approach many of the "best-loved" poems, we need both to scrutinize the historical lineage and thus the structuring assumptions of our preferred techniques, and to consider how we might develop or resuscitate alternative forms of address. Under these provisoes, aspects of the close reader's art will, I think, continue to prove invaluable; it may be hard to move slowly and carefully through apparently simple verses, but it is a necessary task, given that any and every stretch of language, especially a consciously structured stretch like a poem, might well deliver more than can be seen at first or second glance.

But to expect a schoolroom standard to furnish experiences akin to those offered by the classics of the New Critical canon would clearly constitute a form of short-sightedness in itself; works from one historical tradition cannot be adequately read according to criteria developed within a different, and indeed an opposed, historical tradition. Yet refocusing our vision so that we can look apparent simplicity in the face is no simple matter. For one thing, there are numerous types of simplicity to be found within the recitation canon. For another, the connections between a text and its contexts may prove to be anything but simple: these relationships always carry the potential to develop into a complex affair.

Throughout this project I am therefore asking variants of the following question: how have the different cultural positionings of poetry over the years affected the ways we look at a poem? My book concerns itself with the historical phenomenon of a broadly prevalent mode of relationship between literature and life, but in fact the school provided only one of the many venues and occasions that brought—and still bring—large numbers of people into regular contact with all sorts of poetic forms. More extensive scrutiny of the roles that verse can play in the world off campus would not only develop our understanding of what poetry can mean to people, but it could promote new ways of writing about such bonds. Moreover, such a scrutiny might also have the salutary effect of further questioning the status of the various divisions between academic and popular conceptions of what a poem should be, and what it should be for. To this end, I have attempted in the course of this project to suspend my usual ideas, overt or covert, about what is good in, or about, a poem, and to learn how to appreciate works that were initially impervious to my habitual practices. Recognizing that this is a book written from within the academy and its traditions about a nonacademic relationship with poetry and some nonacademic poems, I have tried to confront my conflicted allegiances whenever they arise.

These, then, are my larger ideas about the scope and potential of this project. I now wish to list, in no particular order, a few of its subsidiary findings. Some of these have been quite surprising to me; certainly many of my first ideas about the topic turned out to be wrong. For example, when it became clear early on in my research that a disproportionate number of the poems in the recitation canon were about death and honor, I assumed that I would ultimately argue that the school had in some way appropriated the practice of commemoration from the church, and that this had something to do with the spread of both secularism and nationalism. I did not expect that I would only begin to understand the relationship between poems of noble martyrdom, education, and organized religion in the British context if I followed the course of first government funding, and then a series of highly influential classroom reading books, as they criss-crossed the Irish Sea. This turned out, then, to be a much more interesting and complicated process than I could have guessed. Other journeys I have taken in these pages also confounded my expectations at various junctures. Sometimes, it is true, they involved a lengthy excursus in a historical field that may at times seem far removed from the topic of the memorized poem, but I hope that the trip is worth it in the end.

I have often thought of this project as the recovery of a lost chunk of the quotidian. Along the way, I have enjoyed picking up some of its chippings, the endlessly repeated *minutiae* of common experience that fall to the side when the practice that holds them together drops out of fashion. The fact that juvenile recitation involved set bodily postures as much as verbal delivery was one such retrieval; the recognition that I should already have known this from my readings of nineteenth-century texts like *Alice's Adventures in Wonderland* was another order of discovery altogether.[27] I experienced versions of that latter realization many times over: the information that I needed was there all along, but I just hadn't been looking for it. The small departmental library at my former University of California campus turned out to contain a whole shelf of recitation anthologies, from a battered old edition of Lindley Murray's *English Speaker* to a varied collection of classroom readers used in the state's public schools in the first half of the twentieth century. The books had arrived there after our Department of Rhetoric was disbanded, I learned, and had been undisturbed, or at least unborrowed, for years.

I found, too, that my sense of the tradition of English literature began to shift; as I compared today's academic canon with the canons of schoolrooms past, not only did the relative magnitudes of various authors start to alter, but different parts of individual oeuvres either came into the light or disappeared from view. It is hard, for example, to overstate the importance that certain works by William Collins, Thomas Campbell, and Robert Southey once held; now they are rarely read. Up to a point I was aware that some of the nineteenth-century Shakespeares were Shakespeares different from the ones we currently possess; the reading scene in *Mansfield Park* (311–12) told me long ago that Cardinal Wolsey's speech from *Henry VIII* used to be considered a superlative set-piece for domestic performance, but who knew that parts of *King John* were regularly visited upon schoolchildren in the nineteenth century? And what I formerly thought of as a personal obsession of Thomas Hardy's turned out to have had a far broader reach; texts invoking the battles of the Napoleonic Wars hung over the classrooms of Victorian and Edwardian Britain just as the poems of World War I loom over the English lessons of British secondary schools today. In addition I have encountered en route not only a large number of poems that I had never read before, but also many

rewardingly quirky but now neglected historical studies. One of my fa-
vorite research finds bears the title *An Unwritten Chapter in the History
of Education.* These investigations of the story of the memorized poem in
general and the tales of my three memorized poems in particular together
constitute my attempt to insert a new chapter into my own education,
and thereby to correct many of the misapprehensions and incomplete
understandings that lurked therein.

◆ ◆ ◆

I may hitherto have given the impression that there are no existing theo-
retical discussions of memorization and literature. This is not quite true.
"Critic"/"Reader," an essay from 1979 by George Steiner, addresses the
topic as an important part of its project of defining the difference between
its two titular figures. To be a critic, the article argues, is to distance oneself
from the art object in order to find one's angle on it; for Steiner, this is es-
sentially a secular act. To know a work by heart so that one might recite
it, however, is to be the highest or consummate form of reader; the inter-
nalization and reproduction of a work of literature is an act that celebrates
its mysterious being and is thus akin to an act of theological worship. In
the course of his essay Steiner makes numerous interesting points about
recitation's place in different times and cultures and tells some especially
effective stories about the deep value of the memorized literary work to
individuals *in extremis.* It is, however, his central dichotomy that most ar-
rests my attention, because it has prompted me to wonder whether one
can combine the perspective of a critic with the devotion of the reader
who has memorized a text. Is knowing a work so that you can judge it an
essentially different act from making a work a part of your being? Is a
critic's study of the memorized poem in some way either an impossible
project, or a project that risks dangerous consequences by clashing the
epistemological and the ontological together?

   To the extent that my book is a historical study, and to the extent that
I do not believe, as Steiner does, that the critic's act of judgment must fi-
nally become part of an evaluation of quality, I do not feel that it is neces-
sarily perilous to bring criticism and memorization into the same frame.
Nevertheless, at numerous junctures in the pages ahead, I have been con-
scious of a sort of spectral barrier, a force separating those two modes of
relation to a literary work that Steiner helpfully defines. Most particu-
larly, I find myself running up against this imaginary divide in my second
case study, when I pose a version of the following question. What role
might memorization of a poem play within literary study in the class-
room, or indeed in any learning environment, when that literary study is
also striving to encourage the critical analysis of the poem? Deliberately

or not, poetry was for years presented to British and American children in a manner that was likely to preclude conscious thought about the words that were memorized or recited. And yet I have ultimately come to think that this was not, and is not, an inevitable result of learning words by heart. On the contrary: I believe it is possible to imagine a kind of teaching that would promote a dialectical relation between an individual's embodiment of a poem and his or her questioning of a poem. In the final estimation, I suggest that such a dynamic oscillation has the potential to create the very best of relationships between an individual and a literary work.

In his illustration of the various differences between critics and readers, Steiner observes that the former abstract small sections of a text to make their points, while the latter, in their ideal form, deliver the work in its entirety.[28] In this respect, at least, I often take on the character of the reader in this book, affording myself the luxury of incorporating whole poems into my text and avoiding, for the most part, close reading's characteristic feature, the truncated quotation. Let me preface my final remarks in this introduction, then, with every single line of "Lord Ullin's Daughter," a ballad that Thomas Campbell composed on a trip to the Isle of Mull in Scotland in 1795:

A Chieftain to the Highlands bound,
    Cries, "Boatman, do not tarry;
And I'll give thee a silver pound
    To row us o'er the ferry."

"Now who be ye would cross Lochgyle,
    This dark and stormy water?"
"O! I'm the chief of Ulva's isle,
    And this Lord Ullin's daughter.

"And fast before her father's men
    Three days we've fled together,
For should he find us in the glen,
    My blood would stain the heather.

"His horsemen hard behind us ride;
    Should they our steps discover,
Then who will cheer my bonny bride
    When they have slain her lover?"

Out spoke the hardy Highland wight:
    "I'll go, my chief—I'm ready:
It is not for your silver bright,
    But for your winsome lady.

"And by my word, the bonny bird
    In danger shall not tarry:
So, though the waves are raging white,
    I'll row you o'er the ferry."

By this the storm grew loud apace,
    The water-wraith was shrieking;
And in the scowl of heaven each face
    Grew dark as they were speaking.

But still, as wilder blew the wind,
    And as the night grew drearer,
Adown the glen rode armed men—
    Their trampling sounded nearer.

"O! Haste thee, haste!" the lady cries,
    "Though tempests round us gather;
I'll meet the raging of the skies,
    But not an angry father."

The boat has left a stormy land,
    A stormy sea before her—
When o! Too strong for human hand,
    The tempest gather'd o'er her.

And still they row'd amidst the roar
    Of waters fast prevailing;
Lord Ullin reach'd that fatal shore—
    His wrath was chang'd to wailing.

For sore dismay'd, through storm and shade,
    His child he did discover;
One lovely hand she stretch'd for aid,
    And one was round her lover.

"Come back! Come back!" he cried in grief,
    "Across this stormy water;
And I'll forgive your Highland chief,
    My daughter!—o, my daughter!"

'Twas vain: the loud waves lash'd the shore,
    Return or aid preventing;
The waters wild went o'er his child,
    And he was left lamenting.[29]

Had I been born in Great Britain some time between 1870 and 1920 and educated in a public elementary school, it is highly probable that I would have encountered this poem when I was nine; "Lord Ullin's Daughter" frequently appeared in the classroom readers for this age group throughout that period and was a very popular choice for memorization and recitation. Had I been the kind of nine-year-old then that I was in 1971, it is likely that I would found it relatively easy and extremely enjoyable to recite this piece alone or in concert. It is also likely, I think (although now I am getting into more uncertain waters), that if I had memorized the poem at this age, then it would have stayed in my head for good; in the years that followed I would have been able to say its lines, out loud or to myself, whenever I had wanted to do so. As it was, the primary education I actually experienced had no time either for recitation or poems like Campbell's; this being so, I had been on this earth for around four decades before I read the ballad in full. I do not intend to start arguing here that this is an important and unjustly neglected poem; I will not begin to make the case that it is a work that everyone should know. Instead, I will just say this: I would have liked to have had "Lord Ullin's Daughter" with me for all those years.

THE MEMORIZED POEM IN BRITISH AND AMERICAN PUBLIC EDUCATION

It is a Friday afternoon, some time in 1910. Elsie Hernsbusher, the blacksmith's daughter, puts down her book and walks to the recitation bench. Both of Elsie's grandfathers were born in Germany, but she and her parents are all natives of the United States, and the family speaks English at home. Now, in front of her schoolmates in the small town of Darien, Wisconsin (pop. 1,249), the twelve-year-old girl prepares to break the silence. On another afternoon in the same year, nearly four thousand miles away in Yorkshire, a boy named Charles William Bond is also on the brink of saying his piece. Charles's father drives a delivery wagon for a local manufacturer of commercial lubricants; just like Elsie, Charles was born in 1898, but unlike her, he is not an only child. On the contrary: he lives (in a village in Mirfield—pop. around 11,000 at this date, but long since part of the West Riding's sprawling conurbation of industrial towns) with one older brother, three half-brothers, and two half-sisters, his five younger siblings the children of his stepmother, Ada. In a year's time, Charles will start work in the local coal-mine as a hurrier; six years after that, he will die on October 9, one of that day's 10,000 Allied casualties at Passchendaele, and his body will never be found. Today, though, he is standing at his desk in Battyeford National School, the long low building on Nab Lane that lies just a short walk away from his family's home.

The information about the two individuals in the paragraph above, plucked from U.S. and British census data and the Imperial War Graves Commission's archive, represents the sum total of all I know for certain about Elsie and Charles. What follows in the next few pages is a series of conjectures about the preparations for the performances that are about to begin in these two widely separated classrooms; thereafter, the bulk of the chapter will conduct a detailed examination of how it was that such behaviors came to form an unexceptional part of huge numbers of lives. Accounting for this process will require the investigation of numerous histories and topics that may at first glance seem to bear tenuous connections to "poetry" or "recitation" *per se*; only by reconstructing a diverse matrix of preconditions will it be possible to understand how poetry recitation eventually found its apparently natural home in public education. My best guesses about the nature and content of two fabricated scenes in Wisconsin and Yorkshire aim to provide glimpses of everyday practice at the zenith of the memorized poem's heyday, visions of experience from the period of classroom recitation's most fully achieved state. We begin, in other words, with our journey's ultimate destination.

And what is Elsie going to recite at the bench in Darien? Here is the section of the 1910 *Manual of the Elementary Course of Study for the Common Schools of Wisconsin* that sets out the list of poems deemed appropriate for the middle and upper forms, which is to say, for children in their fifth to seventh years of study.

147. *Poems Suitable for the Middle Form*

O Farewell. Night. The Skylark. Boy's Song. Morning. To a Butterfly. The Huskers. The Bugle Song. Song of the Fairy. Four Leaf Clover. Autumn. Charge of the Light Brigade. The Night Before Waterloo. Written in March. Under the Greenwood Tree. To the Fringed Gentian.

> —*The Listening Child*, Lucy W. Thacher.

The Sandpiper. The Old Oaken Bucket. Abou Ben Adhem. The Voice of Spring. Herve Riel. To America. The "Three Bells" of Glasgow.

> —*Poems Every Child Should Know*, Mary E. Burt.

The Flight of the Birds. The Beautiful Snow. The Wind in a Frolic. April, Ever Frail and Fair. November. The Bees. Break, Break, Break. The New Year. When Icicles Hang by the Wall.

> —*Poetry of the Seasons*, Mary I. Lovejoy.

148. *Poems Suitable for the Upper Form*: (Many of the following poems should be committed to memory.)

Selections from Hiawatha .... Longfellow.
The Blue and the Gray .... Finch.
My Country 'Tis of Thee..Smith.
Death of the Flowers.. Bryant.
Breathes There a Man With Soul so Dead ....Scott.
The Builders... Longfellow.
The Quality of Mercy is Not Strained........................Shakespeare.
The Planting of the Apple-Tree .... Bryant.

To a Skylark.. Shelley.
October .... Bryant.
What Constitutes a State.. Jones.
Concord Fight.. Emerson.
The Chambered Nautilus..Holmes.
Honest Poverty ....Burns.
Address at Gettysburg..Lincoln.
Pippa's Song.. Browning.
Crossing the Bar ....Tennyson.
Recessional .... Kipling.
March.. Wordsworth.
Selections from Snow-Bound .... Whittier.
Selections from Sir Launfal .... Lowell.
Selections from Evangeline... Longfellow.

(Cary, 105)

Let us assume that Elsie's teacher is a diligent and responsible instructor, who is both fond of poetry and keen to follow the directions in the manual for its most effective presentation in the classroom—as far as is practicable, that is. She intends to get through a good number of the poems in the list with her upper-form students, but will only set them one work to memorize (Cary, 19). This came as no surprise to Elsie; each of her previous five years at school has had its designated poem, and she can easily recite any and all of these works when required to do so, as indeed she has been at the end of each academic year to demonstrate the successful completion of her course of study. (Her favorite is the ditty she learned when she was seven, "Good-Night and Good-Morning"—although she tends to think of it not by its title, but its first line: "A fair little girl sat under a tree . . .").[1] The teacher—Miss Holland, who is twenty-four years old—began working on this year's poem for Elsie and her fellow sixth-years a couple of months ago. Miss Holland has chosen Longfellow's "The Builders." It is not an old friend, not one of the poems she herself learned at school (although quite a few on the list are), but she is rather taken with its seriousness, and thinks it will serve as a fine extension to the morally improving "Memory Gems" that she regularly requires her charges to get by heart (she has a stock of these stored in her head, and the manual provides over forty more snippets in its appendix). Up to now the full-length works her students have memorized have mostly been fairly gentle poems about nature; "The Builders," she feels, will give them a bit more backbone.

As the manual suggested, Miss Holland spent considerable time preparing so that she was "thoroughly at home with the selection" and could "be perfectly at ease before her class" when she read the poem "expressively" to them (103). She had followed that performance with "thought analysis," hoping "to get the pupils to see clearly the pictures suggested by the poem" (103). If you talked to her students, you would probably decide that Miss Holland has done a satisfactory job in this respect. Elsie, for instance, may not like this poem all that much, but she does have two images in her mind's eye when she thinks about it—one of a tumbledown house, with "yawning gaps" and "broken stairways," and the other more like an illustration she remembers from her fourth-year reading book, of a castle solidly constructed of massive and regular stone blocks. Truth be told, though, this is about as far as it goes for either Elsie or her classmates. Miss Holland was unsure how much further she should press with her questions; the manual had said she should "encourage her pupils to abandon themselves to the selection and respond to its beautiful thoughts and music" once she had ensured that they were reading each line with "sufficient expression," so she did not to quiz them directly about the poem's meaning nor exert much energy on explanations of its use of analogy (104). Now she readies herself to listen carefully to Elsie's recitation, to make sure that she is word-perfect throughout each of the poem's thirty-six lines, and that her inflections and emphases fall in the right places. In a few weeks time, after all the children in Elsie's year have demonstrated on multiple occasions that the poem is firmly committed to memory, Miss Holland will have them perform it together. She agrees with the manual's assertion that "there is nothing more inspiring than the recitation of a soul-stirring poem by a class reciting in concert"; she is confident that the piece will provide an excellent and uplifting finale to the school concert at the end of the year (103).

"'The Builders,' by Henry Wadsworth Longfellow. 'All are architects of faith . . .'" As Elsie Hernsbusher begins to speak, let us now travel to Charles William Bond's British classroom. Three years ago, his headmaster (a Mr. G. Greenwood) was sent an inspection copy of W. and R. Chambers's *Poetic Gems: A Selection of Good Poetry for Young Readers*, the preface of which explained that Part I "will be found suitable for children of ten or eleven," Part II for "those of eleven and twelve," and so forth.[2] The table of contents runs as follows:[3]

PART I.

The Brook	Alfred, Lord Tennyson
In a Garden	A. C. Swinburne
Vitai Lampada	Henry Newbolt
The Coming of Spring	Mary Howitt
Little Golden-Hair	Will Carleton
Lady Clare	Alfred, Lord Tennyson

The Baby's Kiss	G. R. Emerson
Robert of Lincoln	William C. Bryant
The Forest Fire	Charles G. D. Roberts
The Voice of Spring	Mrs Hemans
The Slave's Dream	Henry W. Longfellow
The Angel of Patience	John G. Whittier
John Gilpin	William Cowper

PART II.

The Charge of the Light Brigade	Alfred, Lord Tennyson
To a Skylark	William Wordsworth
The Burial March of Dundee	William E. Aytoun
To a Cuckoo	M. Bruce or J. Logan
The Soldier's Dream	Thomas Campbell
The Landing of the Pilgrim Fathers	Mrs Hemans
The Frost Spirit	John G. Whittier
Young Lochinvar	Sir Walter Scott
To the Cuckoo	William Wordsworth
Edinburgh after Flodden	William E. Aytoun
The Skylark	James Hogg
Lament of the Irish Emigrant	Lady Dufferin
The Daffodils	William Wordsworth
Douglas and Marmion	Sir Walter Scott
One by One	Adelaide Ann Procter
Fidelity	William Wordsworth
I am Monarch of all I Survey	William Cowper
The Green Linnet	William Wordsworth
Horatius at the Bridge	Lord Macaulay

PART III.

The Coming of the Snow	James Thomson
A Man's a Man for a' That	Robert Burns
Battle of the Baltic	Thomas Campbell
The Cloud	Percy Bysshe Shelley
The Pied Piper of Hamelin	Robert Browning
The Home of Evangeline	Henry W. Longfellow
A Day in June	James Russell Lowell
The Stag Hunt	Sir Walter Scott
To a Waterfowl	William C. Bryant
Hiawatha's Canoe	Henry W. Longfellow
My Native Land	Sir Walter Scott
To a Daisy	Robert Burns

The Heavens and their Creator	Joseph Addison
The Eve of Quatre Bras	Lord Byron
Morte d'Arthur	Alfred, Lord Tennyson

PART IV.

Recessional	Rudyard Kipling
Sir Galahad	Alfred, Lord Tennyson
The Combat	Sir Walter Scott
On the Receipt of my Mother's Picture	William Cowper
To Autumn	John Keats
The Village Preacher	Oliver Goldsmith
The Armada	Lord Macaulay
Gradatim	Josiah Gilbert Holland
The Chambered Nautilus	Oliver Wendell Holmes
England, with all thy Faults	William Cowper
Elegy Written in a Country Churchyard	Thomas Gray
Introduction to "Endymion"	John Keats
To a Skylark	Percy Bysshe Shelley
King Robert of Sicily	Henry W. Longfellow
The Fall of Wolsey	William Shakespeare
A Father's Advice to his Son	William Shakespeare
The Quality of Mercy	William Shakespeare
Life as a Drama	William Shakespeare
A Lesson from the Bees	William Shakespeare
Lancaster's Dying Speech	William Shakespeare

I choose here to hypothesize that Mr. Greenwood liked the volume so much that he ordered separate paper-bound sets of its constituent parts for the school's top four classes. Charles is one of the older students in Standard V, and thus has temporary ownership of a copy of Part II. Somewhat against the inclinations of Miss Robertshaw, his teacher, the pupils in Charles's class have each been allowed to choose which poem they will memorize and recite. Miss Robertshaw is forty years old; when she herself was in Standard V back in 1882, she had been required to recite 100 lines of verse in front of an inspector to pass the year's examination, and to her mind, this is still the right number of lines for a twelve-year-old child—indeed, as she well remembers, that stipulation was part of the Elementary Code until just ten years ago. But she is thoroughly familiar with the document that has taken the code's place—the *Handbook of Suggestions for the Considerations of Teachers*—and she knows that there are new ways of thinking about recitation. For one thing, it is now believed that "[t]here is no necessity for every child to learn the same passages (for a passage never makes the same appeal to all children) or the same number of lines" (33). In Miss Robertshaw's opinion this creates a great deal of extra and unnecessary work. But she has done what she can to direct her pupils' choices, and is pleased that although the girls are by and large favoring the poems by Hemans, Procter, and Wordsworth, most of the boys—Charles included—have opted for Macaulay's "Horatius at the Bridge." Their book provides two hundred lines from the *Lays of Ancient Rome*, but she has told them they need memorize no further than "But will ye dare to follow / If Astur clears the way?" Which is a shame, in some ways, as this breaks the story off at an exciting point, but she has read the complete extract to the whole class several times and is confident that they have an understanding of what the handbook calls "the general scope of the poem" (34). She is aware that it then goes on to suggest that "with the older children some of the distinctions in diction and form between prose and poetry might be considered," but there really isn't enough time to explore these matters, and in any case, it also states that it "is better to do nothing in this direction than to attempt too much, for the unskilled or irreverent dissection of a poem is destructive to the sense of beauty" (34). She has, however, written the definitions of Macaulay's more difficult words on the blackboard and given the boys plenty of help with their pronunciations ("Herminius" is a particular problem).

Given that such large numbers of the children are preparing this poem, Miss Robertshaw thinks it a pity that the handbook is so set against recitation in unison ("Such a device is the merest mechanical drill, and destroys any value recitation may have" [33]). But she knows that the many occasions on which the boys hear their classmates recite "Horatius" play a helpful part in drumming the lines into their heads—and, if some of them are still shaky on the sequence of the stanzas in the run-up to the end of term when Mr. Greenwood will mark each child's performance out of ten for their reports, she may well revert to a few sessions of group recitation as a remedial measure. Today, however, she has just called on Charles with confidence; if his past performances are anything to go by, he will require only a few promptings to make it all the way through ("Come on, lad: 'Meanwhile, the Tuscan army . . .'"). And Charles is quite looking forward to his moment in the sun. He has always been good at repetition, and is pleased to have a decent poem this year (the worst time was in Standard I, when the teacher made them all do "A fair little girl sat under a tree"—although he does remember how useful it was, when he practiced at home, that his stepmother already knew the soppy thing off by heart).[4] This time around, though, he has worked on his lines alone; he really likes the way the beats of the poem fit the stride of his steps as he marches along the village lanes. But there won't be any moving around in the next few minutes; Charles takes a deep breath, puts his arms straight by his sides, and dives in.

The simplest explanation for the huge success of the memorized poem runs as follows: rote memorization long constituted the dominant method for teaching both reading and other subjects in Britain and the United States, and poetic material worked especially well, for a variety of reasons, in such a form of instruction. For a fuller understanding of exactly how the memorization and recitation of poetry came to be so broadly embraced in these two countries, it is however necessary to examine the practices and assumptions that obtained before the spread of mass education. This chapter therefore starts its historical survey by scrutinizing the experiences of partial populations of individuals at relatively elite levels of society. First it considers the utility of verse and memorization for very early learners, examining the service role played by poetry and poetic devices in the extended period during which rudimentary education in English was understood primarily as a necessary tool to unlock the Bible and Christian scriptures. It then proceeds to the era in which certain kinds of schools began to assign the memorization and recitation of vernacular literary and oratorical extracts, including the most respected poetry of the day, as a task for their advanced readers. Although this innovation of the later eighteenth century reached only a limited number of individuals, and although the justifications for the exercise shared few similarities with the reasons for the continuing presence of verse and memorization in early instruction, such a development was crucial for the subsequent history of poetry in public elementary schools. In the course of time, burgeoning popular education in both Britain and the United States effectively, if unreflectingly, soldered together these two very different species of verse repetition. Poetry's double ability—to foster, on the one hand, prereading and first-reading skills, and to furnish, on the other, prestigious material for recitation—eventually resulted in a progressively ordered system that placed the oral performance of poetry at every step of the way. As the years went by, recited poetry was occasionally, and then increasingly, a contested presence on either side of the join. Nevertheless, an expedient weld between two distinct historical formations and processes managed to hold good in both countries for a substantial number of decades, creating the phenomenon that affected the lives of Elsie Hernsbusher, Charles William Bond, and millions of others.

Precursors to Mass Poetry Recitation

Although we may no longer live in times and places that expect all their young to memorize and recite poetry proper, we generally regard it as both natural and appropriate that verse be part of children's formative experiences and, indeed, feature in their earliest books ("nursery" and "rhyme" still go together like a horse and carriage). If asked to account for this, we would likely begin by talking of the enjoyment that both children and their first educators derive from sharing simple and often amusing verses: as the child hears and then speaks the rhymes, she is clearly developing a range of important skills, but fun is very much to the fore. If pressed to think about how poetry might facilitate not just general learning but the specific art of literacy, we might argue that exposure to the aural and visual homology of rhymed words plays a key role: "the cat sat on the mat" does not appear in today's reading books, but the principle underpinning the construction of such a sentence continues to seem sound. If pushed even further, we might adduce not just the utility of individual matched syllables but also the holistic value of a poetic text in a sequenced set of learning behaviors. Say we imagine the following process. A child listens to a spoken text and repeats it back time after time; once she has committed it to memory, she is introduced to the text on the page, and her preexisting knowledge of its words thus assists her eventual decoding of the printed marks. We take it for granted that the child finds such a process easier and more pleasurable (or less difficult and less unpleasant) if the text in question manifests perceptible rhyming and rhythmical patterns.[5]

These, then, are some of our general ideas about connections between the young and poetry—we think of children's pleasure and facility with verse, and of verse's usefulness in promoting a range of desired skills, especially literacy. Versions of these basic assumptions structured the elementary regimens that preceded and ultimately influenced nineteenth-century practices. Whatever the method of early reading instruction—and there were important, and much discussed, differences between the syllabic, the spelling, and the phonetic methods—both verse and the oral repetition of verse had an habitual presence within basic tuition for hundreds of years before the advent of mass schooling.[6] Yet asserting such a primacy for the poetic is not to claim that the poetry employed was considered important in and of itself. On the contrary: for many centuries verse played only a facilitating role in the learner's progress towards literacy's official goal and its sole true justification, the reading of the Bible.

For all but a tiny minority of the literate population, learning one's ABCs was for a long period a route to divine works only. The route itself was constituted, so far as possible, by religious texts. As Ian Michael comments, "Until at least the end of the seventeenth century the first connected reading for almost all children would seem to have been what it is convenient to call doctrinal: the ABC with the catechism, the primer, the psalter, the Prayer Book, biblical passages and varied prayers and graces"

(138). Although the books used in the first stages of reading ceased to rely exclusively on the Church's literature after this date, primary texts largely continued to understand their fundamental mission in explicitly or implicitly Christian terms for at least the next two hundred years. The importance of this factor cannot be overstated: various secularizing forces came into play in the later eighteenth and the nineteenth centuries in Britain and the United States, but religious, or at the very least, moral, imperatives were for a very long period a tremendous driving force behind and within mass education. The effect this had upon poetry's place and role in the curriculum was profound and complex; in the British case, the eventual centrality of the poem in school reading-book series bore a direct historical relation to its ability to act as an unobjectionable substitute for Scripture in the classroom, but in both countries the recitation of religious or moral verse was frequently considered to be a key component of a child's Christian education. Within this earlier period, however, there are two salient points to be grasped. First, verse's abilities to support reading's first steps were employed to speed learners towards Scripture itself; second, verse's adhesiveness was exploited to fix religious content within children's minds in advance of the church's official texts.

Two of the most influential and widely disseminated texts for elementary learners in the eighteenth century provide good illustrations of the varied ways in which rhyme and rhythm could serve religion. Consider, in this first example, the form of the following biblically themed sentences from the *New England Primer*, which was first published in the late 1680s (Parkerson and Parkerson, 97–99). Although lines such as "In Adam's fall, We sinned all" or "Peter denied his Lord, and cryed" are not exactly poetry, they nevertheless reveal that something akin to verse was an integral constituent of foundational literacy for the huge numbers of Americans who learned to read from this text. Under the prevailing pedagogical climate of the day, these simple couplets would have been repeated again and again and again by child and adult learners alike; the jingling phrases no doubt then stayed within the head of many of those individuals for years after their primer days. Yet such a process is clearly not the same thing as the recitation or the memorization of poetry for poetry's sake. While it was important that the semantic content of the couplets reinforced biblical knowledge, the sentences owed their poetic form to a pragmatic, not an aesthetic, agenda; short-term memorization was enjoined to aid literacy, but such long-term memorization as occurred was a side effect and not a primary objective. But my second example of a prominent early-reading text shows quite different ideas in play. Pedagogue Isaac Watts was explicitly interested in using verse to establish a permanent presence for Christian and moral sentiments within the minds of young children, and thus wished there to be a direct relation between the poems he composed for his collection *Divine and Moral Songs* and memory. If memorization of the text subsequently enabled a smoother transition to literacy, then this was surely a benefit, but one that was secondary to the main goal.

The *Divine and Moral Songs* hold such an important place within both the canon of juvenile verse and the history of recitation that it is worth taking a few moments to examine Watts's expressed aims in detail. Published in 1715 and repeatedly reprinted up to the middle of the nineteenth century, Watts's volume stood unrivaled for the first century or so of its existence as a beginning or early lesson book for hundreds of thousands of British children from comfortable homes. Best remembered today as the originals of Lewis Carroll's witty recitation parodies in *Alice's Adventures in Wonderland*, the poems in this little book were intended to develop a juvenile "relish for virtue and religion" via both ditties of praise and warnings against sinful behaviors (vii). Watts's "Preface to all that are concerned in the education of children" emphasizes the paramount importance of the early introduction of his religious verses into the receptive minds of very small children. He appears to have considered it equally appropriate for the poems to be spoken or sung—to facilitate the latter, he writes, he has "confined the verse to the most usual psalm tunes," and he imagines children both "sing[ing] over" one of his songs "to themselves" and performing them "in the family," in "their daily or weekly worship" (ix).

Watts makes two arguments about the benefits that accrue from his use of poetic form. In the first place, the form makes the child's work fun: "There is something so amusing and entertaining in rhymes and metre, that will incline children to make this part of their business a diversion" (viii). In the second place, and more importantly, "What is learnt in verse is longer retained in memory, and sooner recollected. The like sounds, and the like number of syllables exceedingly assist the remembrance" (viii). The goal, then, is secure installation, rather than the development of literacy—far from picturing the child picking up the book and turning from her reading of one poem to another, Watts suggests that parents and educators strictly control their charges' access to the text: "[Y]ou may turn their very duty into a reward, by giving them the privilege of learning one of these songs every week, if they fulfil the business of the week well, and promising them the book itself when they have learnt ten or twenty songs out of it" (viii). Only once you have got the verses in your head, do you get to keep hold of the book; oral repetition, memorization, and accurate recitation should lead the way.[7]

These brief forays into the *New England Primer* and the *Divine and Moral Songs* illustrate the simple points that verse had a presence in the most elementary of reading books, and that oral repetition of verse had a presence in the early training of children. Within foundational educational experiences, both the shortest of primer couplets and the multiline poem might be spoken out loud on endlessly repeated occasions; such verbal pronouncements of versified material could happen before, during, and after visual perception of its typeset form. Indeed, if we construe "early training" broadly, and consider the many folkloric rhymes and ballads that constituted a child's first exposure to secular literature, then it is fair to assume that repetition of these would often have taken place in the absence of physical texts altogether. Whether required or not, memorization of a wide range of verses would for many individuals have been an inescapable result of the repeated encounters they had with heard or read lines of poetry in their very early lives.

Let us now move forward to the late 1700s to see how the poetic contents and recitatory practices of early juvenile tutelage began to appear, albeit for different reasons and in different forms, in the education of more advanced learners in certain social strata. The period witnessed both a mounting interest in education inside the swelling ranks of bourgeois society and the increasing availability and acceptability of secular (if still moral and uplifting) literature for the proficient young reader. As part of the response to the growing desire and ability of the middling classes to educate their sons, new forms of schooling came into being for those relatively affluent parents who did not want to, or who could not, for religious or other reasons, send their children to the existing possibilities. By and large, the extant forms (tutors, academies, grammar schools, or the subset thereof that later came to be known as "public schools") offered a classical education. Throughout this century, and indeed thereafter, a small but significant tranche of boys in Britain and the United States progressed to the exclusive study of Latin and Greek after they had learned to read in the vernacular. For these pupils and students the recitation of poetry was a required element of their advanced studies; memorizing hundreds and hundreds of lines of Homer, Virgil, and others constituted a long-respected and standard feature of the curriculum.[8] In contrast, the new or newly reconfigured establishments either complemented the ancient languages with living tongues or substituted them entirely. Within their modern curricula the memorization and performance of poetry and prose in English became a recognizable feature of the program of studies (Michael, 287).

It is hard to ascertain the exact degree to which emulation of the classical model influenced this development, but it seems clear that those who ran and patronized the new establishments wished the schools' alumni to be able to make their way in the world as cultured and confident public speakers. To such an end, the recitation exercise, in all its many facets and with its immediate and long-range benefits, supplied numerous important desiderata. The relative popularity of this new educational activity in Britain and the United States can be gauged by the number of textbooks it stimulated; over fifty collections of literary and oratorical extracts in English intended for school use were published between 1770 and 1800 (Michael, 185). While some works presented themselves just as anthologies or miscellanies—themselves a flourishing section of the general market in this period—the presence of the words "Speaker" or "Elocution" in many of their titles indicated that their contents were intended for oral delivery. The best known of these volumes was a 1774 publication called simply *The Speaker*, or, colloquially, "Enfield's Speaker"; this was a collection of readings assembled by William Enfield, a teacher of *belles lettres* at Warrington Academy, a leading school for the sons of Dissenters. The subtitles of a couple of other texts push the point home: William Scott's *Lessons in Elocution* (1779) offers "miscellaneous pieces in prose and verse, selected from the best authors, for the perusal of persons of taste, and the improvement of youth in reading and speaking," while John Walker's *Academic Speaker* (1789) promises "a selection of parliamentary debates, orations, odes, scenes and speeches, from the best writers, proper to be read and recited by youth at school." The *English Reader* of 1799 announced on its title page that it was "designed to assist young persons to read with propriety and effect"; compiled during his retirement in England by Lindley Murray, an American Quaker, this hugely successful book had already reached its thirty-first edition by 1826. Murray's work and Enfield's *Speaker* (still regularly reprinted into the 1850s) were the two schoolbooks used most frequently by middle-class children in both Britain and the United States during the first half of the nineteenth century (Michael, 186; Venezky, 250). From these volumes, large numbers of individuals came to know such works as Whitehead's "The Youth and the Philosopher," Pope's "On the Order of Nature," and Barbauld's "Ode to Content" off by heart.[9]

It is my contention that the series of lesson books that were eventually designed for mass education effected a kind of marriage of convenience between the elementary primers and these "speaker" or "reader" anthologies. Progressively graded classroom readers, as they proceeded from the simplest of "learning to read" rhymes towards, ultimately, bona fide poetry, were not only relatively verse-heavy, but constructed in the expectation that the poetic texts they provided would be learned by heart and recited out loud. To understand how this came about, we turn now to the early stages of popular schooling in Britain and the United States. To what degree did the new schools borrow teaching methods from existing models, elite or otherwise, and to what degree did they generate their own? What distinctive problems did they face, and how did they attempt to solve them? And what kind of presence did poetry have in these classrooms?

One point is indisputable: vocalization, in conjunction with either required or incidental memorization of set phrases and texts, was the defining feature of the emergent systems of the first half of the nineteenth century. The new institutional structures thus adopted time-honored pedagogical methods, but their special circumstances conspired to create an unprecedented reliance upon the oral expression of rote-learned material. The exact nature of these circumstances varied according to time and place—the difficulties facing a teacher with 360 pupils in a single cavernous room on London's Borough Road in 1800 were very different from those experienced by one with four students in a tiny schoolhouse in rural Maine in 1850—but a number of connected factors remained relatively constant. The funds forthcoming for the education of the poor were extremely straitened; proper teaching equipment for classrooms, whether books, writing instruments. or other materials, was in short supply; trained teachers, too, were a scarce commodity. The classroom systems that came into being in these two countries attempted to meet their specific challenges in a variety of fashions, but the strategies employed produced some very similar results—at least in the area of children's relationships to printed text.

Recitation and the Early Stages of British Public Education

The well-known story of British popular education properly begins with the Sunday School movement of the 1780s and then the establishment of day schools in the early decades of the nineteenth century. By 1850, the largest number of children in school attended voluntary institutions set up by the National Society, the educational charity formed by the Church of England in 1811; additional schools were run by the British and Foreign School Society (BFSS, an ostensibly nonsectarian, but functionally nonconformist, entity) and other religious groups, most notably the Wesleyans and Roman Catholics. Thanks to these endeavors, the proportion of the nation's children who received some education in day schools jumped from around 30 percent in 1818 to 60 percent in 1851; even at this later date, however, the average length of such tuition was only of around two years duration.[10] Nevertheless, the fact that over two million children were at school at midcentury represented a remarkable expansion in educational access, one that the charitable bodies were able to effect largely because of the methods developed by two individuals, Andrew Bell and Joseph Lancaster. Both men, associated with the National Society and the BFSS respectively, pioneered the use of monitors; in addition, Bell promoted the teaching manual and Lancaster the reading card. By delegating work to unpaid recruits from the cohort of older pupils, only one teacher, in theory, was required to control an entire school, however large. The difficulties created by employing barely educated juveniles as assistants (or, for that matter, by employing scantily trained teachers) were addressed as far as possible by the imposition of rigid teaching systems, variously codified in easy-to-follow manuals or dictated by the use of severely restricted instructional texts.

Even the briefest consideration of the teaching materials first developed for the new schools reveals the signal importance of verbal repetition in the classroom. Consider, for instance, this extract from Frederic Iremonger's 1817 text, *Dr. Bell's system of instruction, broken into short questions and answers for the use of masters and teachers in the national schools*:

> Q. After leaving the alphabet, how are pages 3 and 4, of the monosyllabic cards, or National Society School Book, No, 1, begun?
> A. By what is termed a *loud* or *repeating* lesson.
> . . .
> Q. What is the manner of saying the "repeating lesson?"
> A. The teacher gives out the words or letters himself, and then the whole class are to follow him by a loud, slow, and distinct pronunciation. (17)

Similarly, in BFSS schools, each monitor would concentrate his group of twelve or twenty pupils' attention on a poster-sized page pasted on a card. After cards showing the alphabet, and words of one syllable, had been mastered, the monitor would proceed to others with phrases such as "Thy way O God" or short passages from the Bible. At all times, he would adopt an unvarying method—the monitor would read aloud, the pupils would parrot back his words.

Vocal repetition, then, was the default mode of instruction throughout the first four or so decades of the nineteenth century. But poetic material—be it in the form of rhyming phrases to aid early learners, versified doctrine, or what we might consider poetry proper—held a fairly minimal place in these years. Several of the *Divine and Moral Songs* made it into the National Schools, via the reading books produced for them by the Society for Promoting Christian Knowledge, but Watts's verses were sung, not recited; as in the Sunday schools, children were exposed to rhymed and rhythmic language primarily through the medium of hymns. The texts used in the schools run by the BFSS made no use of versification whatsoever.[11] Books containing poetry did not appear in British elementary classrooms in any significant quantities until the 1840s. To understand the circumstances of their arrival, we now travel across the Irish Sea.

Loath to involve itself with public education at home because of the vociferous infighting of the different Christian denominations, the British Parliament had no such scruples about imposing school systems upon Ireland as part of its strategies to control the country's Catholic populace. Accordingly it had subsidized the activities of various proselytizing missions from early in the eighteenth century, eventually awarding an annual grant in 1815 to Dublin's ecumenical Kildare Place Society to support, among other endeavors, the publication of "moral and instructive" books (Kingsmill Moore; Goldstrom). Sixteen years later, when the British government cut off the Society's funding and established its own board to superintend Irish elementary education, the new commissioners created their own series of progressively graded readers. Available at very low cost thanks to the government subsidy and the size of the print runs, these titles quickly attracted the attention of schools in Great Britain. From 1840 to 1860 the "Irish Reading books" accounted for around half of the texts used in British institutions and constituted "almost an era in popular education" in themselves, as a government document observed in 1861 (this comment appears in the report prepared by the Newcastle Commission, which had been convened in 1858 to investigate the provision of "sound and cheap elementary instruction" across the country [1:351]). Just as important as the books' physical presence in those classrooms, however, was their influence upon the form of competing volumes: when the British voluntary societies eventually got around to producing their own series of readers, they borrowed their organizing principles from the Irish prototype. A particular model of textbook design, then, established a dominant presence in British elementary schools over the middle period of the century. One of its hallmarks was the plentiful inclusion of poetry.

The Kildare Place Society can be held responsible for this feature. Its members had developed their own library of titles because no existing reading materials were deemed suitable for the children of the poor; further, while wishing to provide pupils with a strictly Christian education in their nondenominational schools, they were extremely anxious about the use of either the Bible or biblical extracts in the classroom, given that whatever choices were made or glosses given would inevitably lean closer to one sect's position and thus further from another's. Verse, however, could function as an uncontroversial conduit for religious and moral sentiments or exemplar; accordingly, the Kildare Place volumes were sprinkled with liberal quantities of poems that fulfilled this function. Other sorts of verses, often about nature or animals, were also included; within all three categories, some of the poems were relatively well-known anthology selections and others nonce compositions. By the point that its operations came to a close, the Society's Cheap Book Committee had produced eighty-five titles, grouped under the headings of "Instructive art or economy," "Natural history," "Voyages, travels, etc.," "Religious, moral and illustrative of scriptures," and "Miscellaneous." It was to this in-house archive that the Irish commissioners turned when they devised their lesson-book series, adapting the five catalogue headings to serve as the divisions within all but the most elementary reading texts themselves, and generally including a selection of verses in each section. For example, around 36 of the 180 pages of the *Second Book of Lessons* are devoted to poetry, including numerous verses by anonymous authors and Watts, Southey's "Father William," Taylor's "My Mother," and Cibber's "The Contented Blind Boy"; the *Fourth Book* has over fifty attributed poems or poetic extracts (Cowper and Milton being the most frequently featured authors, with six and four texts respectively).

The arrival of poetry into school readers for British commoners thus figures as an unlooked-for side effect of an offshore imperial policy. Yet to trace the adventitious textbook history of Great Britain's popular education is to explore only one side of the story. Once children had these books, or ones very like them, in their hands, what were they required to do with the poems therein? The preface to the 1836 *Third Book of Lessons* "recommended that the Pupils be made to commit the best pieces of poetry to memory; and that they be taught to read and repeat them with due attention to pronunciation, accent and emphasis" (iii). But how exactly did a merely recommended practice become a feature of daily classroom life? The next phase in this history—the period directly before government legislation transformed poetry recitation into a compulsory practice—requires that we focus upon the nation's growing cadre of elementary-school teachers. Important changes in their professional education in these years rendered it more and more likely that poems would start to receive a treatment different from other species of reading material in the elementary classroom. Simply stated: instructors began to train their charges to recite memorized poetry because they themselves had been trained to recite memorized poetry *en route* to their certification as teachers.

Growing concerns about both the short supply and the limited competence of classroom instructors for the country's expanding school population had been addressed by the government in 1846 when the Committee of Privy Council on Education, under the direction of James Kay-Shuttleworth, set up a national teacher-training scheme to improve educational standards.[12] Kay-Shuttleworth's measures inaugurated five-year pupil-teacher apprenticeships whereby bright children could stay on at school and receive extra tuition from their head teachers and a stipend in exchange for teaching the younger children. In addition, he devised both a scholarship system to enable the graduates of these apprenticeships to attend newly created training colleges and a teacher-certification

process. Over the next six decades these arrangements supplied the ele-
mentary schools with the majority of their instructors. The development
that concerns us here first appeared in a two-year program of required
studies codified in 1854 for the nation's thirty-four teacher-training col-
leges; this same curriculum was still in force seven years later when the
Newcastle Commission pronounced upon its effectiveness. The men's
course in "English Literature" is summarized in its report as follows:

> [This] includes the history of English literature from Chaucer to Mil-
> ton, with the addition of certain specified books, passages from which
> have to be paraphrased and analysed, whilst questions are set upon the
> style and subject-matter. It is recommended that the books specified
> should be read through with the students in short portion, as exercises
> in language, in illustration of the grammar used in the training school,
> just as Greek and Latin classics are read in superior public schools.
> (1:119–20)

The specified works changed from year to year (in 1860 they were "the
first book of *Paradise Lost*, and . . . *Julius Caesar*"), but students were not
called upon to recite Milton's or Shakespeare's blank verse (119–20). Yet
it was a different story in the women's colleges: the commission com-
mented that their course "resembles the syllabus for the male colleges,
but its subjects are fewer and easier" (123). Like their male counterparts,
the female students were expected to paraphrase and analyze the sen-
tence structures of their assigned texts, but they were excused from the
study of the "history of English literature." What was required of them
instead? The "[r]epetition of passages" from their named works (which
also changed each year—in 1860 they could be taken "in the first year [of
study] from the 5th book of Cowper's *Task*, or from Goldsmith's *Travel-
ler* and *Deserted Village*; and in the second year from the 1st book of
Paradise Lost, or the 1st book of the *Excursion*" [123]).

The inclusion of "English literature" in the training college's program
was a significant innovation, constituting one of a number of midcentury
developments that bolstered the eventual elevation of vernacular literary
studies to the status of a bona fide academic subject throughout the coun-
try's universities.[13] When we pick up the British narrative once more, we
will discover that the memorized poem came into its heyday because of a
set of stringent, and much-maligned, governmental regulations that ex-
plicitly linked the success of a child's recitation to the size of a school's
operational budget. Amid the clamor of thousands upon thousands of
mandatory juvenile performances and in the tense presence of genera-
tions of anxious educators, it will be worth remembering that poetry reci-
tation first entered the education of Britain's nonelite classes because im-

portant changes to the structure of society opened up new worlds of possibility and potential wonder for the poor, and that one of these worlds happened to be a domain called "English literature."

Recitation and the Early Stages of American Public Education

Any attempt to trace a trend within American mass education in the nineteenth century must begin with a caveat: if such a thing could be had as a series of snapshot pictures of the density of provision and types of schooling in every part of the country at set moments in this period, they would each reveal huge variation from region to region, state to state, and in urban, suburban, and rural locations. For the most part, new pedagogical forms originated in the urban centers of the Northeast, and, in due course, of the Midwest, and then spread gradually to other parts of the country; lagged development was a marked feature of sparsely populated and predominantly agricultural areas, especially in the South.[14] An approach to a nationally standardized education came only in the following century, and even here, various factors, especially race, long continued to have a decisive effect upon any given child's potential experiences at school (Kallgren). Yet despite these differences, and at least until the 1860s or so, there was one consistent element that promoted vocalization and memorization throughout the country's developing systems of public education. This was the phenomenon of America's long-term and widespread reliance upon the textbook-as-curriculum.

Having defined the subjects of school study since at least the colonial period,[15] the textbook continued to maintain its hold during the period in which more and more schools were established to serve increasingly larger proportions of the population for longer periods. The most significant force pushing expansion was the Common School movement, an effort to provide free elementary education for all white citizens that spread rapidly from state to state after its origins in the industrialized Northeast in the late 1820s (Button and Provenzo, 84). By 1850, and with marked regional variations, around 45 percent of Americans between five and twenty years of age were receiving some schooling, and the average length of that educational experience—often pieced together over a number of years—was about twenty-two months; as in Britain, this represented a significant increase on attendance figures three decades earlier (Elson, 6). At this midpoint of the century, with only an eighth of the population living in towns of 8,000 or more residents, most individuals in education attended a small ungraded rural school (National Education Association, 97).[16] In an environment that typically had no curriculum and no consistency of teacher from term to term, the textbook was the one entity that brought order and continuity to the educational experience. For the current investigation, the pedagogical methods that were part and parcel of this dependence are hugely significant.

A highly popular subject for cultural representations both in its own time and right up to today, the country schoolhouse of nineteenth-century America occupies a treasured place within romantic versions of the nation's history; it is therefore sometimes hard to separate fact from sentimental fiction in the accounts of everyday life within its roughly constructed walls. The primary importance of memorization and recitation, however, seems indisputable. In many parts of the country specific textbooks were neither supplied nor mandated until late in the century, so children simply brought to class whatever schoolbooks their families owned or could borrow; for many years the teachers that greeted them there were likely to have received little, if any, pedagogical training. These circumstances contributed towards the production of a largely unvarying learning environment. After a child had learned to read from a primer or speller, she habitually spent her time conning a given passage from her own book until she was called to the "recitation bench" at the front of the room; she would then hand her book to the teacher, who would monitor the student for the accuracy with which she repeated the words of the passage (Parkerson and Parkerson, 98–99).[17] In relatively populous schools that had some commonality of textbooks, attempts might be made to group students together according to their degree of advancement; then recitation in unison, or of alternating lines or passages, could occur, but the mode of instruction would have remained constant.[18] In consequence, neither the term "recitation" nor the behavior it denoted had in this period and in this context any special connection to poetry: "the recitation" was required of any and every passage from the book or books available. Whatever its contents—history or geography; civics or nature study; science or legend; story or poem—the text was to be memorized, and then delivered orally. Lessons that required focus not on a book but on the teacher, the blackboard, a map, or a chart also relied heavily on repeated vocalization.

In stressing the continuity of instructional method across all subjects, I do not mean to imply that poetry, in its various forms, held a negligible place within these classrooms. On the contrary, this mode of schooling made great pragmatic use of poetic language's mnemonic properties and capitalized upon the special significance of the recited literary piece. At the early levels of instruction, rhymed and rhythmic phrases could support both the acquisition of literacy and the installation of basic arithmetics into a student's head, as this memoir of school life in the first half of the nineteenth century recalls:

Besides the letters, the teacher taught the smallest ones various little poems, such as "Mary Had a Little Lamb," "Twinkle, Twinkle, Little Star," and

"How doth the little busy bee
Improve each shining hour."

Then there were certain jingles, which were not only poetry, but exercises in arithmetic as well. Fancy a little tot solemnly repeating the following:—

"See me; I am a little child
Who goes each day to school;
And though I am but four years old,
I'll prove I am no fool.

"For I can count one, two, three, four,
Say one and two make three;
Take one away, and two remain,
As you may plainly see . . ." (Clifton Johnson, 52–53)

The instructional advantages of meter and repeated linguistic patterns could also be employed for older children in ostensibly unpoetic lessons: consider, for instance, the incantatory diction and rhythmic pull of the following oral exercise in geography, impressed into the mind of many a young American in the middle years of the nineteenth century:

Maine, Augusta, is on the Kennebec River
New Hampshire, Concord, is on the Merrimac River,
Vermont, Montpelier, is on the Onion River,
Massachusetts, Boston, is on the Boston Harbor,
Rhode Island has two capitals—Providence and Newport,
Connecticut, Hartford, is on the Connecticut River. (Quoted in
    Finkelstein, 82)

Thanks to such habitual practices, the climate of learning in the American classroom was as heavy with rhyme and rhythm as it was with the recitation of memorized material. Within such an environment, how then should we understand the place of the bona fide poem? What differences would there have been between a young child's recitation of an arithmetic jingle and "Against Idleness and Mischief" or of an older child's repetition of a prose passage on the virtues of thrift and an ode such as "How Sleep the Brave"? As would become the case in the British classroom, there were a couple of good reasons why the delivery of Watts's or Collins's poem carried the potential to generate a special aura. First, in all but the worst of instances, it was simply more pleasurable both to perform, and to listen to, a text consciously crafted for aesthetic effect than four lines of instructional doggerel or a run-of-the-mill passage of pedagogical prose. Second, the literary recitation was unlike other lessons because it held a degree of prestigious congruence with other performances that might take place at home or in the community, however plentiful or limited the opportunities for such entertainment may have been.

Within the American context there was one further reason why the poem stood out: the type of books used in the classroom dictated a particular attitude towards the recitation of a literary work. In Great Britain, as we have noted, the vernacular educational texts that were in existence for children of the elite by the end of the eighteenth century did not make their way into the next century's early phases of mass education; instead new materials were developed for what was explicitly understood to be a substantially different population of learners. In the United States, however, specific eighteenth-century works played two important roles in a diverse range of schoolhouses across the growing nation. In the first place, they were both widely used as textbooks themselves for many years, and in the second, they affected both the compilation and apparatus of the next generations of massively influential classroom reading series.

The result of the unbroken line was this: the tradition of oratorical and elocutionary training, as promoted and supported by those late eighteenth-century volumes, continued to exert a perceptible and enduring influence upon the recitation of literary selections in American classrooms. For much of the first half of the nineteenth century, a limited number of textbooks dominated what were effectively only two stages of reading within the classroom. For the rudiments of literacy, the most prevalent manuals were the *New England Primer*, still holding firm into the first three decades of the nineteenth century, and Noah Webster's *Spelling Book*.[19] The learners that advanced beyond the first level would then progress, as Venezky explains, to "readers, speakers, and elocutionary guides . . . consisting of short speeches; historical, moral, and religious selections; and instructions on pronunciation and oral expression" (250). Caleb Bingham's *American Preceptor* (1795) and *The Columbian Orator* (1797), in which the majority of selections were in prose, were highly popular, but the most used text, as already mentioned, was Lindley Murray's *English Reader*, a third of which was devoted to poetry.

Although both the basic texts and these elocutionary speakers continued to crop up in some American classrooms into the middle decades of the nineteenth century, different kinds of books, specifically designed for the burgeoning population of the Common School movement, became increasingly prevalent in these years. The rate of issue of new textbooks jumped from 93 in 1804 to 407 in 1832 (Bartlett, 390); from around this later date onwards, the most important form of publication became the multivolume series, which itself in time evolved into a more explicitly graded sequence of readers. Books 1 through 6 of Oliver Angell's *Union Series of Common School Classics*, for example, first appeared in the early 1830s; between 1840 and 1860, further series of readers were published by Worcester, McGuffey, Swan, Russell, Tower, Sanders, Town and Holbrook, Hillard, Parker and Watson, and others (Venezky, 251; Banton Smith, 390). Thanks, it seems, more to skilled marketing practices than intrinsic merit (neither its contents nor its pedagogical design were markedly different from those of its competitors), the *McGuffey Eclectic Readers* swiftly rose to a preeminent position.[20] Series of stepped textbooks tended to feature poems in all but the very first reader, gradually increasing the number, the length, and the complexity of the poetic extracts with each subsequent volume.[21] A child at the middle of the century who had worked her way through five or six readers could plausibly have left school with her memory stocked with such poems as Gilman's "Mother, What is Death?," Byron's "Destruction of Sennacherib," Hemans's "Better Land," and Bryant's "Thanatopsis"; another might have committed to heart Gould's "Lost Nestlings" and her "Freaks of the Frost," plus Pollok's "Miser" and the "Fall of Cardinal Wolsey" from Shakespeare's *Henry VIII*.

After the Civil War, Venezky notes, "titles like *Elocutionary Reader* or *Rhetorical Guide* were rarely seen" in the schoolbook sequences (252). Instead, the new textbooks provided for growing numbers of children a learning experience in which the first steps of literacy in book 1 were eventually bound, through a series of intermediate stages in intervening volumes, to avowedly "literary" selections in prose and verse (generally a 50/50 split) in books 5 and 6.[22] In this manner the external form of the graded readers introduced a novel structure into the American schoolhouse. At the same time, the arrangement of their internal materials also began to alter habits of learning on a more minute level: unlike the eighteenth-century anthologies, they tended to supplement their readings, short or long, prose or poetry, with questions to guide and test the students' understanding of the given passage or selection.[23] Memorization and vocal recitation of the text was still assumed, but the movement towards memorization *with* comprehension, however haltingly realized in actual practice, was significant; this was a development that would ultimately, as we shall see, play its part in the demise of the recited poem. Yet the emphasis upon elocutionary excellence that these volumes inherited from their "Speaker" forebears did not diminish. Many series included lengthy introductory essays on the correct reading of verse or literary prose, while marks to indicate, for instance, rising and falling inflections, or caesuras, were copiously applied to the poetic or oratorical selections themselves. The new generation of schoolbooks thus perpetuated the long-standing assumption that literary selections demanded a heightened style of recitation and had a more prestigious cultural aura than the workaday informational passages that were, in the lower volumes at least, their textual neighbors.

The best place to witness the special meaning of the performed "piece" was at a regular phenomenon in the American school year that was variously known as "Examination-," "Recitation-," or "Exhibition Day." Generally held at the end of a given term of instruction and treated as an important and enjoyable social event, this gathering also served as a kind of trade show for local investors in education, demonstrating to community members the products of lessons funded by their school-tax dollars. More to the point, in times and places where there was very little external monitoring of educational practice and achievement, Examination Day told parents and local dignitaries whether the teacher they had hired was fulfilling his or, increasingly from the 1870s onwards, her duty (Parkerson and Parkerson, 105). Performances often featured various types of scholarly prowess—the evening might include demonstrations of spelling, grammar, lightning arithmetic, geographical and historical knowledge, and displays of penmanship—but the jewel in the crown was the individual recitation of poetic and oratorical selections. James Wells Champney's painting *Schoolroom at the Mill and Bars: Recitation Day* (1877–87; figure 1) provides a good visual sense of the occasion: here, in a school in rural Deerfield, Massachusetts, in the last quarter of the nineteenth century, a boy stands on the raised dais at the front of the room, and adopts a stylized posture and gesture to perform his piece for an audience of fellow students and townspeople.

A short memoir by Lucia Downing, whose teaching career in Keeler, Vermont, began in 1882 when she was only fourteen years of age, also gives an indication of the place of literary recitation within the event:

> I drilled the scholars on the pieces they were to speak—can remember one of them now "little Dan"—and I told the children how important it was that they should behave well the last day, if never before or after. And school ended in a blaze of glory, a vast and terrifying audience having assembled—entirely out of proportion to the number of pupils. There were fond parents, and grandparents, and aunts and uncles and cousins thrice removed. I think there were twenty-five visitors and only four scholars, but the children did very well. They went through some specially prepared lessons in the various subjects they had been studying; they spoke their pieces without prompting, and they went glibly through the "Instructive Questions and Answers," though if I had made a slip and asked the questions out of order, the results might

1. James Wells Champney, *Schoolroom at the Mill and Bars: Recitation Day* (1877–87)

have been disastrous. . . . Everything went off well, . . . and I went proudly home with twenty dollars, the remuneration for ten weeks of toil.[24] (181–82)

The "Casabianca" case study that follows examines how prose fiction from this period, most famously Mark Twain's *Adventures of Tom Sawyer*, lavishes both pathos and humor upon the topic of the child's anguished preparation of "declamatory gems" for these public performances. For our purposes here it is useful to consider a less emotive issue. How did the regulatory function of this community event affect habitual modes of instruction? The accurate recitation of well-loved and affecting literary pieces on Examination Day often bore a relation not just to the teacher's prestige, but to whether he or she would be rehired for a subsequent term. Consequently instructors had a clear incentive to make elocutionary performance a regular feature of classroom life; Downing's words confirm the obvious fact that frequent drill was a necessity. The next section of the American story will examine how these customary habits became to all intents and purposes formalized into an official requirement. When control of the curriculum moved from the textbook to educational administrators, the recitation of memorized poetry was given a specific slot in the weekly time-table.

The Heyday of the Memorized Poem in Great Britain, 1875–1930s

After the publication of the Newcastle Commission's report in 1861, Britain's system of elementary education was definitively altered by a new set of regulations, the Revised Code of 1861–62. Under these measures, or, to be more accurate, under the measures of the Code as it underwent its own incremental revisions over the next couple of decades, the reach of the memorized poem across Great Britain was to experience its greatest expansion. The first instantiation of the Revised Code established a series of six graded standards with a certain level of competence expected after each year's instruction in reading, writing, and arithmetic; it also ushered in the infamous "payment by results" system, a recommendation of the commission that was implemented with meticulous force by Robert Lowe (Sylvester). Thanks to the financial pressure it exerted on overextended educators, the Revised Code plays a highly important role in the history of memorization in Britain. Because schools and teachers were subject to monetary penalties if their pupils did not individually satisfy visiting examiners that they could meet the prescribed standards, rote learning further strengthened its grip on the classroom. But teaching to the test, as we would say today, did not actually ensure that pupils learned to read; Inspector John Morley lamented in 1868 that while he had heard every child in a certain school's Standard I read with apparent fluency from his or her reading book, not one of them could read the simplest words in a similar, but hitherto unseen, volume (Ellis, *Educating Our Masters*, 94). Such forms of memorization and recitation were one of the inadvertent and undesirable effects of the system; the inevitability of their occurrence helps us to see that the procedures instituted within public education at this juncture were exceptionally good at promoting some kinds of learning practices and skills even as they were exceptionally bad at fostering others. Classrooms governed by the repetitive pedagogical drills that the new regimens encouraged would eventually provide the memorized poem with ideal forcing grounds for its mass propagation.

Yet the recitation of verse did not feature in the original specifics of the Revised Code's six standards for the rank and file of elementary-school pupils. Poetry does get a mention, but only a very brief one—the one-line syllabus for "Reading" for Standard V required that pupils be able to read "A few lines of poetry from a reading book used in the first [i.e. top] class of the school" (a sideways confirmation here that the presence of poetry in classroom readers could now be assumed).[25] Instead, mandatory poetry memorization makes its appearance within the schedule of regulations laid down for that crack corps of the elementary school, the cadre of pupil-teachers. At the end of their second year of apprenticeship, pupil teachers had "[t]o be able to repeat 50 consecutive lines of a secular character from some standard English poet (selected by the managers) with just expression and knowledge of meaning"; at the "end of 3rd year: 40 lines of prose"; at the "end of 4th year: To be able to repeat 100 lines (including the former 50) of the same poet as at the end of the 2nd year with just expression and knowledge of meaning"; at the end of their fifth year, "80 lines of prose." While almost every other feature of the Revised Code came to be "infinitely revised" over the next forty years (to quote the sardonic words of Matthew Arnold, to date the most celebrated member of Her Majesty's Schools Inspectorate), these particular measures stood firm, ensuring that the vast majority of the nation's classroom teachers throughout the elementary school's subsequent existence had experienced an exactly identical training at these stages in their education. When these students graduated to teacher-training colleges, further feats of literary memorization were required of them each year.[26]

It is tempting to view the introduction of compulsory recitation for pupil-teachers in a cynical manner. In common with the rest of Lowe's Revised Code, these regulations seem designed to institute an automated regime, a system that sent the message that it was concerned only with that which could be easily and efficiently tested. But it is worth noticing that when the Newcastle Commission made the suggestion that recitation be added to the pupil-teachers' course, it did so because it considered that this measure would work to relieve what it called "the mechanical character" of their training:

> The constant repetition of the same routine must always tend to cramp and formalize the mind, and this effect is particularly likely to follow where young boys and girls are brought into constant relations with mere children. Something might probably be done to counteract this by exchanging some one of the subjects contained in the present course for others of a more interesting nature. It is an omission in the course that it contains no literary subject whatever, and we think that one of the books of Euclid might be advantageously omitted, and that the pupil-teachers should be required to learn by heart passages of standard English prose and poetry, and to be prepared to repeat portions of them at the annual examination. . . . Learning by heart is a most valuable exercise, and is far too much neglected in elementary schools.[27]

As we noted earlier, verse recitation was substituted for "the history of English literature" to give female students in teacher-training colleges in the 1850s a less demanding course. These two instances show that committing poetry to memory was at this time deemed an interesting and easy activity because it was perceived in contradistinction on the one hand to the "constant repetition" of tiresome instructional tasks, and on the other, to the memorizing of material that was *not* poetry (or "literary" prose). Any notions that we might have about alternative ways to appreciate or learn about poetry are clearly not in the comparative frame.

Further understanding of the ideas behind this new requirement for the pupil-teachers can be gained by turning to a document contemporaneous with the commission's report, Matthew Arnold's annual inspector's report for the previous year. Given that Arnold had served as an assistant commissioner on the Newcastle Commission, it is not surprising that he gives voice to similar themes, but it is instructive to see how he broaches, and then discusses, the topic of literary recitation. Arnold's report is marked by the restrained wit and elegance that lifts all of his writings above the vast swathes of bureaucratic prose produced in Victorian officialdom, but even so, it seems that he may be expressing real rather than assumed weariness when he describes the way in which the educational apprentices have been performing one of the tasks that had previously been required of them in their annual examinations:

> We all complain of the want of taste and general culture which the pupil-teachers, after so much care spent upon them, continue to exhibit; and in their almost universal failure to paraphrase ten lines of prose or poetry, without doing some grievous violence to good sense or good taste, they exhibit this want most conspicuously. (*Reports*, 87–88)

He then suggests that a solution to this problem may however exist:

> [P]erhaps ... the remedy will be found to lie, not in attempting to teach the rules of taste directly—a lesson which we shall never get learnt—but in introducing a lesson which we can get learnt, which has a value in itself whether it leads to something more or not and which in happy natures, will probably lead to something more. The learning by heart extracts from good authors is such a lesson. (87)

Arnold "rejoice[s]" that the new Code will establish this regimen for teacher-trainees:

> This regulation ... I think, no one will be found to attack. Nay, it is strange that a lesson of such old standing and such high credit in our schools for the rich should not sooner have been introduced in our schools for the poor. In this lesson you have, first of all, the excellent discipline of a lesson which must be learnt right, or it has no value; a lesson of which the subject matter is not *talked about*, as in too many of the lessons of our elementary schools, but *learnt*. Here, as in the case of the grammar lesson, this positive character of the result is a first great advantage. Then, in all but the rudest natures, out of the mass of treasures thus gained (and the mere process of gaining which will have afforded a useful discipline for all natures) a second and more precious fruit will in time grow; they will be insensibly nourished by that which is stored within them, and their taste will be formed by it. (88)

Here Arnold eloquently expounds numerous arguments about the value of learning literature by heart; to greater or lesser degrees, these are ideas that will help to guide my investigation of the topic in the case studies that follow. Particularly interesting are his delineations of the range and type of potential benefits of the lesson—he considers, for instance, both its varying meanings across the life span of one person, and how it might be received differently by individuals of minimal and maximal sensitivity to its enriching, nourishing, or cultivating qualities. This is a careful and thoughtful analysis of the ways in which not just the taste, but also the lives, of pupil-teachers might be improved by a simple curricular innovation. And yet—and always allowing for the fact that Arnold's sly pose of languid disdain deliberately and habitually attempts to distance the reader from the essential seriousness and dedication of his educational labors—and yet, might we not at the same time come away from these sentences with a couple of other ideas too? Is there not an intimation here that the daily life of the sensitive inspector could also stand to be improved? And what about the "grievous violence" indirectly inflicted upon poetry and prose by the painful mangling of paraphrase? Would it not be vastly preferable for all concerned—pupil-teachers, inspectors, *and* literature—if the unfortunates at the coal-face of elementary instruction simply attempted to *repeat* the words of the poets?

Mandatory recitation was quickly deemed a success not only in Arnold's subsequent annual reports but in those of his fellow examiners as well. Thanks to the general approbation, the exercise became instituted in the regulations for progressively larger constituencies over the next two decades. Her Majesty's Inspectors were first issued with explicit rules for their examination of "English grammar and literature" in 1870. Under the testing measures of what functioned as an optional "Specific Subject," pupils in Standard IV were required to have "200 lines of poetry, got by heart, and the meanings and allusions mastered," and in Standards V and VI, 250 and 300 lines respectively. In 1875, however, recitations of specified line-lengths were placed in the requirements for the basic standards; at this point all children in public education now had to recite 75 lines of poetry to pass Standard V, and a 100 lines for Standard VI. Although this state of affairs only lasted for three further years, it prepared the ground for recitation's eventual move, in 1882, into every level of the elementary school's curricular program. Categorized at this date as a "Class subject" that could earn the school a shilling a pupil if the standard was "fair" and two shillings if "good," "English" consisted entirely of the following prescribed syllabus:

Standard I   To repeat 20 lines of simple verse
Standard II   To repeat 40 lines of poetry, and to know their meanings

Standard III	To recite with intelligence and expression 60 lines of poetry, and to know their meanings
Standard IV	To recite 80 lines of poetry and to explain the words and allusions
Standard V	To recite 100 lines of poetry and to explain the words and allusions
Standard VI	To recite 150 lines from Shakespeare or Milton, or some other standard author, and to explain the words and allusions
Standard VII	As Standard VI

Nominally optional, the "class subjects" were enthusiastically embraced, quickly becoming, in the words of one inspector's report, "universally taught in the schools" (*Minutes and Reports of the Committee of Council on Education 1882–83*, 255). This pattern—recitation as an all-school practice, with a specific allotment of lines per standard—thus became the norm, persisting as a financially advantageous activity for the school for a further eighteen years, and an encouraged customary practice well into the 1930s.[28] Figure 2 reproduces a report card issued by a London elementary school in 1921; Irene Hines's recitation mark constitutes 7 percent of her total score.

Educational publishing firms were quick to embrace the various commercial opportunities afforded by stringent curriculum control. Texts such as Douglas's *Selections for Recitation Compiled for the Use of Elementary Schools* and Bilton's *Repetition and Reading Book for Pupil Teachers and the Upper Classes of Schools* appeared in the 1860s, and were soon followed by numerous graded series from Longman, Chambers, Collins, Blackie, Bell, Nelson, Jarrold, and Cassell (Ellis, *Educating Our Masters*, 103–27). Frequently compiled or endorsed by "one of H. M Inspectors of Schools" (current or former), such books calibrated their selections to suit the needs of each target constituency as defined within the successive instantiations of the Code. Under the dictates established in its first two decades, the featured works were for the most part drawn from generally respected literary canons of the era; Bilton's volume, for instance, provided suitably-lengthed extracts for the pupil-teachers from Shakespeare, Ford, Milton, Pope, Gray, Merrick, Goldsmith, Cowper, Wordsworth, Scott, Southey, Campbell, [Horace] Smith, Byron, Shelley, Macaulay, Longfellow, Tennyson, and Poe.[29] A more specifically juvenile recitation canon came into shape after the establishment of the all-school metric in 1882; from then on, while tables of contents varied to a degree from series to series and over the decades, certain texts and authors were highly likely to feature therein. Each school year had its classics. For instance, for a good three decades Hemans's "First Grief" was a Standard I

County Borough of East Ham
Education Committee.

KENSINGTON AVENUE SCHOOL.
GIRLS' DEPARTMENT.

Report for term ending July, 1921.
Scholar's Name... J. Hines
Class ...8...

SUBJECT.	MARK OBTAINED.	MAXIMUM MARK.
Reading	9	10
Writing	6	10
Composition	15	20
Spelling	20	20
Arithmetic	17	20
Practical Arithmetic	9	10
Mental Arithmetic	10	10
Needlework	10	20
Drawing	3	10
Handwork	9	10
Recitation	10	10
Oral Subjects	Good	

Number in Class... 7 ...out of ...59
Teacher's Remarks Idene is a very intelligent scholar.
  L. M. Webb
  ....Class Teacher.
  F. F. KETCHER, Head Teacher.
Date...6...July, 1921.

2. A report card from Kensington Avenue School, County
Borough of East Ham, London, 1921

poem, while Wordsworth's "We Are Seven" belonged to Standard II.
Southey's "After Blenheim" and Scott's "Death of Marmion" served Stan-
dards III and IV; Longfellow's "King Robert of Sicily" and Portia's "qual-
ity of mercy" speech from *The Merchant of Venice* provided staple liter-
ary fare for the top two classes in the school.[30]

Between 1900 and 1905, recitation was still referred to as a "compul-
sory" exercise in successive editions of the Elementary Code, but num-
bers of lines were no longer specified. In 1905, the Code and its central-
ized control of the curriculum came to an end; in its stead, and up until
the 1944 Education Act's replacement of the elementary school by the
primary school, the Board of Education periodically issued a *Handbook*

of Suggestions for the Consideration of Teachers. This somewhat haphaz-
ardly revised work consistently supported the practice, but, in accordance
with its name, adopted increasingly permissive tones over the years; for
instance, as noted in the opening focus upon Charles William Bond's hy-
pothetical experiences in 1910, the handbook encouraged teachers to let
children make their own selection of poems to memorize. After we have
examined the processes whereby literary recitation became explicitly
mandated on a different side of the Atlantic, we will begin to consider
how the hold of the memorized poem was gradually weakened in both
Great Britain and the United States by, among other things, this very ges-
ture towards individual selection.

The Heyday of the Memorized Poem in the United States, 1870–1950s

A significant move in the history of poetry recitation in American life oc-
curred in 1862, just as the Revised Code was first being rolled out across
Great Britain. In this year the superintendent of schools in Chicago pub-
lished *The Graded School: A Graded Course of Instruction for Public
Schools*, setting out therein the model curriculum that he had devised for
the institutions under his control (W. H. Wells). Within the increasingly
bureaucratic structures of American public education in the second half
of the nineteenth century, the production of such a "Course of Study"
directive became a key task for senior administrators in urban centers
and school boards in rural areas (Spring, 139). Closely analyzed in the
longer-settled states' growing number of "normal" schools, or teacher-
training colleges, these programs played a structural role in the training
programs of new instructors; thereafter, the implementation of the curri-
cula at the classroom level was both assumed and monitored by close
supervision.[31] Similar blueprints were also important in less developed
areas of the country, in which ungraded schools predominated and over-
sight was more haphazard. Here short-term annual summer institutes,
generally convened in the county seat, allowed instructors to renew their
teaching certificates without having to take a further examination; at the
close of these gatherings, it was the habitual practice for teachers to
pledge themselves to introduce into their own schools the course of study
they had learned about in their few weeks or days of intensive continuing
education (Theobald, 147–48).

   At varying speeds across the length and breadth of the states, then, the
conditions that had in earlier times created highly specific bonds between
a student and his or her own textbook underwent significant alteration.
Now teachers who had some degree of professional training were in-
creasingly likely to possess instructions about how to apportion time to

different subjects for children at each age and attainment level across both the school week and the school term. Just as importantly, the ad hoc use of random and multiple texts in the classroom became a thing of the past as legislatures started to require school districts to order or supply the books mandated by the course of study (Theobald, 107). Within this new culture of learning, poetry took up its securest place in American elementary education to date. Beginning in the 1870s and for a further eighty or so years, it was the general expectation that the memorization and recitation of literary selections would form a regular part of a child's experience each year. Further, from the turn of the century onwards, American educational administrators began to name specific literary works within their curricula, thus involving themselves much more directly than their British counterparts in the business of poem selection.

Before we examine the details of some courses of studies, it is well to remind ourselves of other operative differences between the British and American cases. One effect of the centralization of curriculum control under first the Committee of Council on, and then the Board of, Education in Great Britain is that the basic story of mandatory recitation's progress can be traced by looking at just a few relatively concise documents. While numerous supplementary materials (inspectors' reports, periodical articles, textbook prefaces, and the like) held forth on such topics as the significance of learning poems by heart or the drawbacks of rote memorization, these discussions appeared at some distance from governmental fiat; poetry recitation's place in British education and thus life had both the quality and the appearance of an externally imposed fact. In the United States, however, a country that resisted the creation of a national Department of Education until 1976, the situation was quite otherwise. Here the huge numbers of individual curricular programs produced over the years by school boards and districts were part and parcel of a broad discursive milieu that vigorously and regularly debated the value and the meaning of classroom exercises. This brief account of recitation's heyday in the United States proceeds via attention to a small selection of representative documents; a discussion of the important wider context in which courses of study evolved appears in the next section.

W. H. Wells, the author of Chicago's model school curriculum of 1862, asserts in his preface to *The Graded School* that his program is not groundbreaking or polemical, but rather a combination of "the best elements of the different systems adopted in Boston, New York, Philadelphia, Cincinnati, St. Louis, and other cities" (3). As a synthesis of existing practice, then, the Chicago model looked backwards, but because it was widely copied over the next four decades, it also ended up pointing forwards. *The Graded School* disseminated, or at least endorsed, a certain educational shape across many other parts of the country and thereby affected the lives of millions of individuals. Wells's references to verse recitation appear in his opening remarks and the descriptions of the "Regular Course" for each grade. In the first instance, the "General Directions" for students aged from around eight to fourteen run as follows:

> The [top] five grades should devote about one hour every Friday afternoon, to exercises in composition, declamation and recitation, and reading select pieces. . . . In the [highest two] grades, every pupil should be required to take a part in both the elocutionary and the composition exercise, as often as once a month. When pupils have important written abstracts or other similar exercises to prepare, these may in certain cases be accepted as equivalents for the regular compositions. There may also be instances in which it will be best to accept the reading of a piece of poetry or other selection, as an equivalent for a declamation or recitation; but in all ordinary cases it is better even for the girls to commit to memory the pieces which they recite.[32] (36–37)

In the second, he stipulates that for children in the first three grades, "[r]epeating verses and maxims, singly and in concert" should be a regular event, given that "[a] few simple, easy verses, embodying moral sentiments or useful information, will help furnish an agreeable variety in the exercises" (23–24).

These are the only times that the Chicago course mentions poetry or verse, but its recommendation that the declamation of memorized rhymed and rhythmic language occupy a place throughout the school helped to stabilize recitation's position in an increasingly organized and expansive mode of elementary education. In allocating performance practice a specific slot in the older children's weekly timetable, Wells was both drawing on and solidifying customary behavior; a wealth of other texts reveals that there was broad support for the idea that "two hours of the closing afternoon of each week may be most usefully devoted to declamation, dialogue and select readings," as an 1868 anthology, *Common School Readings,* put it (Swett, 12). That literary recitation was habitually scheduled for Friday afternoons is revealing. Notwithstanding the many stories that dwell with either real or mock fear and trembling on performance anxiety, the activity was clearly considered to be the closest to entertainment and the recreational activities of the weekend that schoolwork ever got. Highly positive descriptions of recitation in numerous memoirs demonstrate that for some children, at least, this was indeed the case.[33]

There is one further feature of the Chicago curriculum that merits brief attention. In common with the new generations of classroom readers produced from the middle decades of the century onwards, Wells placed considerable emphasis on the necessity of comprehension in reading. Such a focus functioned as a frontal attack on the worst aspect of former pedagogical modes, that is, the monotonous and unthinking rote-recitations of any and every textbook passage that had dominated the day in the little country schoolhouse. The preservation of the ultraexpressive literary declamation, however, worked to keep the best element of that older tradition alive. For a good few generations of adult listeners, one of the treasured aspects of the performance of the poetic or oratorical selection may well have been its ability to give physical form to a selective memory of earlier American experience.

In the 1890s courses of study began to grow more detailed; they were also increasingly likely to be separated into discrete sections for different subjects. Within the expanded discussions of "Reading" and "Language," discussions of how children read in the classroom were often joined to a concern about the texts themselves. A glance at an exemplary "Course of Instruction" printed in the 1897 report of the National Education Association's Committee of Twelve on Rural Schools reveals such a tendency. Under "Reading," the first specified reading texts are generally the appropriately numbered textbook, but for all save the youngest children, there are also comments about the necessary enrichment of the standard diet (172). Thus for the nine- to eleven-year-olds, "the reading should be largely of literature, as supplementary reading," while "[t]he reading of good literature, as much as can be carefully read" is enjoined for the eleven-to-thirteens (173). Such attention to the quality of classroom reading materials inevitably had implications for the selection and status of memorized poems within the curriculum. Guidelines frequently emphasized that the pieces should be "appropriate" to the age of the children, but they also made manifest a growing assumption that the recited work should function as the bearer and repository of literary value within the classroom and life more generally. In the rural schools course, the recitation directive is accompanied by instructions that children should memorize "choice selections," and preferably "selections long enough to have unity in themselves" (174, 175).

Subsequent generations of curricular programs made the aims and intentions of such relatively taciturn documents still more explicit; certainly the degree of specificity about which poems were the most "choice" increased exponentially. To be sure, most American classrooms by this point had for many years been using series of readers that regularly allocated certain literary works to certain grade levels, but now educators across the land were more and more likely to be told by their local superintendent's curriculum what kind of words should be ringing out of which children's mouths on those Friday afternoons. The extract from the 1910 Wisconsin course of study reproduced earlier illustrates the "list of suitable poems" approach; other programs opted for narrative descriptions. A 1913 Michigan curriculum, for instance, stated that by the end of the first grade, "each child ought to know by heart ten or twelve Mother Goose rhymes, two or three of Robert Louis Stevenson's poems, and one or two other favorites" and "at least two or three short lyrics and one or two ballads, entirely or in part" at the end of the fifth. Titles of suggested works appear only in the prescriptions for what was in this era most children's last year of education, eighth grade:

> each pupil ought to know by heart one or two of the selections from Shakespeare, beautiful passages from *Snow-Bound* and the *Vision of Sir Launfal*, as well as a few of the lyrics and ballads which are practically memorized in the intensive class-study. The boys, especially, will find pleasure in reciting orations such as "Spartacus," "King Philip" or the "Speech of Patrick Henry."[34]

Courses of study for the next thirty to forty years continued to designate the appropriate contents of the recitation exercise in one or both of these ways. Numbers of lines or poems were sometimes specified ("fifty lines a year memorized in Kansas [1927] and at least one hundred lines a year in Rochester, New York [1929]; . . . one poem for each tenth grade unit in Chicago [1933]," [Rubin, "*Listen, My Children*," 269]), but the standard grid of line requirements per year for each level that governed the practice in Great Britain never had universal purchase across the States. Instead, increasingly interventionist education departments relied heavily upon lists of poems or assigned poetry anthologies, even producing their own volumes on occasion. The canon of works remained remarkably consistent in this period: comparing the 1905–8 *Approved Selections for Supplementary Reading and Memorizing in the Schools of New York, Philadelphia, Chicago, New Orleans, and Other Cities* with a 1925 publication, *Required Poetry for Memorization in New York City Public Schools*, Rubin notes that "approximately two-thirds of the works on the later list appeared on the earlier one":

> Both collections relied for the primary grades on poems expressly for children, with even more Robert Louis Stevenson and Christina Rossetti selections in the 1925 curriculum. Both contained, for grades five through eight, the following: Longfellow's "The Arrow and the Song" and "The Builders"; Bryant's "To the Fringed Gentian" and "To a Waterfowl"; "Abou Ben Adhem"; Robert Browning's "The Year's at the Spring"; Ben Jonson's "It Is Not Growing Like a Tree"; Emerson's "The Rhodora"; Wordsworth's "I Wandered Lonely as a Cloud"; Tennyson's "The Charge of the Light Brigade"; and Shelley's "To a Skylark." (*Songs of Ourselves*, 120)

One further feature of this time span was the performance of poetry within an important institution in the lives of a rising number of individuals, the American high school.[35] Development was once again uneven across the country's vastly different educational landscapes, but in those locations where a sizable proportion of students could reasonably expect to stay in education after elementary school, courses of study that ran continuously from kindergarten to grade 12 created an unbroken chain of experiences with memorized poems. In a manner that had no clear counterpart in British public education until very late in the twentieth century, work in the high school was explicitly understood as building upon studies completed at earlier levels; with regards to recitation, this meant that progressively more complex, and usually longer, poems were to be memorized the higher up the system one moved. At the very top of the high school, recitation's loftiest canon of all was constituted by the poems within another relatively stable set of literary works, those speci-fied in college entrance examination requirements (from 1890 onwards, Rubin notes, "Bryant's 'Thanatopsis,' Gray's 'Elegy,' Lowell's 'The Vision of Sir Launfal,' Longfellow's *Evangeline*, Coleridge's *The Rime of the Ancient Mariner* and the poems of Milton" held secure places here ["Lis-ten, My Children," 264]). It would be wrong to give the impression that the relationships forged between poetry and individuals at the high school level were part of mass experience to the same degree as those produced in elementary schools between the 1870s and the 1950s; numerous fac-tors in different times and places dictated that by no means all students within secondary education ascended to such advanced studies of litera-ture (Urban and Wagoner). Nevertheless, the elevated status of the recited poem in American popular memory was undoubtedly given support by its respected presence at every stage of juvenile education.

Recitation's Heyday, Continued: Shifting Theories, Justifications, Critiques

The differences between the development of British and American popu-lar education in the two countries and the role of pedagogical discourse therein means that the concepts I discuss in this section sometimes have more relevance to one context than the other; nevertheless, there is enough continuity to licence a joint exploration. Parsing the various ideas that inspired and supported recitation's place in curricular programs over mandatory recitation's extended reign is, however, no simple matter; in all its phases justifications come not single spies, but in battalions. But it was exactly this multiplicity, I argue, that allowed the practice to survive the many profound social and ideological shifts that occurred in the de-cades between the 1870s and the mid-twentieth century. While the simple force of customary practice in schools cannot be overestimated, the mem-orized poem could not have maintained its vital presence within British and American education for such a relatively long period had it not been able to muster a wide variety of arguments about its worth. Yet although the exercise's ability to signify many things was one of its virtues, this multivalency also had a damaging effect in the end. Without a single fixed meaning or function, the memorization of poetry at school was vulnerable to attack on a range of fronts.

The following two quotations, drawn relatively randomly from two pedagogical texts, demonstrate just some of the ways that commentators found to love the memorized poem in the first couple of decades of the twentieth century. The former appeared in Percival Chubb's *The Teaching of English in the Elementary and the Secondary School* (initially published 1902, with regular revisions and reissues until 1929); the latter in Paul Klapper's *Teaching Children to Read* (1914):

> [T]he work in memorizing, and the declamation that goes with it, has much value also as a means of confirming the child in correct ways of speaking. But its greatest service is in storing the mind with the priceless treasure of the noblest thoughts and feelings that have been uttered by the race. Especially important is it to make the first impression and memories, which are to impart a tone to one's spiritual system for life, rich and pure enough to outsing all baser and cruder songs, and to set the pitch of character . . . to fashion the norm of his taste . . . To endear by repetition, to accumulate a common stock of old familiar songs that graft themselves deep in the affections and reveal gradually as the child grows, their music and meaning.[36] (48)

> [A] good means of reviewing and applying the masterpiece is to require the children to memorize vital and striking parts. The teacher knows that memorizing literary selections has its educational results: 1. It enriches the vocabulary 2. It develops a storehouse of beautiful expression 3. It give the child a number of lofty sentiments artistically expressed 4. It leaves the child a permanent store of literary gems which grow in beauty and richness as the mind gains insight and appreciation. (45)

Making use of the metaphors of treasure hoarding and organic grafting that Rubin has identified as characteristic of encomiums on memorized poetry ("Listen, My Children," 265–66), these passages address some of the most prevalent topics within the discourse during the first forty years or so of the period in question. Chubb's opening reference to elocution is perhaps a little dated; this justification, prominent in certain forms of middle-class British education from the end of the eighteenth century, and in the American context more broadly in the first half of the nineteenth century, had by this point diminished to a minor theme. An emphasis on the instrumental benefits of memorized poetry, however, was still generally at large, and finds expression in these texts' joint conviction that memorizing and reciting verse would make you a better person, both immediately and in the longer term. When Chubb argues that the internalized poem "impart[s] a tone to the spiritual system," his thoughts are clearly connected to the older, yet still strong, conviction that education's fundamental purpose was to promote the moral development of the individual; his references to other structures of personal virtue ("character" and "taste") are differently angled, but still speak to the general idea that memorization of the "common stock of old familiar songs" improves the child. Klapper, on the other hand, is more consistently interested in aesthetic issues, concentrating on the gifts the individual will gain from the elevated texture and content of poetic language. Once again, such statements are linked to long-standing motifs in these writings: the notion that the memorized poem granted the child access to, and thus the enjoyment of, finely wrought beauty coursed through the majority of discussions.

It is pushing it too far to say that the two passages' points of divergence provide evidence of a significant shift, but Chubb's and Klapper's texts can nevertheless be placed on either side of a rough division that runs between the supportive claims for recitation that were generally put forward between 1870 and 1910, and those more regularly advanced between 1910 and 1940. Broadly speaking, the first period focused on the ways in which the exercise strengthened the ethical condition of the individual, while the second tended to present the memorization of poetry as an important adjunct to the study of literature, English or American as the case might be. To be sure, elements of the older argument lingered on into the later era, while comments about the value of recitation either *as* literary study or *within* literary study can certainly be found in the earlier period. The general trajectory, however, is fairly clear. In keeping with other changes in emphasis in educational thinking over this stretch of time, insistence upon the moral function of a classroom activity gave way to stress upon its place within the academic curriculum.[37]

Within this general schema, however, there were numerous other justifications for recitation in play, some of which enjoyed only brief, or endstopped, periods of popularity in one country or the other. One influential concept was the belief that an individual's ability to remember could be permanently expanded and improved by continued practice in memorizing. Promoting mental discipline as an educational ideal, this was an idea that grew out of faculty psychology, a theory of mind that had particular importance in nineteenth-century American academic contexts. As Kliebard explains, proponents believed not only "that the mind was composed of a discrete set of identifiable faculties waiting there to be exercised," but that there was for "each of the identified faculties a subject perfectly suited to its development" (*Forging*, 8). By the closing decade of the nineteenth century, however, researchers in the field of experimental psychology such as William James and Edward L. Thorndike were reporting that "the faculty of memory was not improved by continued practice in memorizing" and that "abilities developed in one context were not easily transferred to new situations" (cited in Kliebard, *Forging*, 15). It would take some time before such arguments had a demonstrable effect upon classroom practices, but the damage had been done. En route to his own agenda about the necessary relationship between poetry and joy (a theme we will pick up later), British educationalist Arnold Smith summed up the impact of such research on justifications for poetry memorization in his 1915 text *Aims and Methods in the Teaching of English*:

> It used to be held that by this process of learning the faculty of memory was exercised, so that the boy who memorised poetry was cultivating a power of the mind which, having been trained in one direction, was equally available in other directions. Since it has been established beyond all reasonable doubt that this is not so,—that the memorising of poetry will only lead to an increased ability to memorise more poetry, and does not by any means imply the cultivation of a faculty that exists independently of the material on which it has been exercised, it will be seen how utterly useless the learning of poetry must be, unless what is learnt is a source of pleasure to the learner. (101–2)

For most of the nineteenth century in the United States, however, the concept of memory training provided strong support for poetry recitation; its imprint is to be found in a wide range of pedagogical contexts, and is especially evident in the years that experienced the "memory gem" vogue. Compensating for the deficiencies in school libraries and drawing on that idea that the memorization of poetry stocked the mind with a rich supply of jewels, volumes with this title or versions thereof enjoyed a publishing boom between 1880 and 1910; in addition, as noted in this chapter's opening pages, school board manuals sometimes included their own selections. These collections were usually composed of "excerpts from poetry, together with some prose selections, ranging from two to fifteen lines in length and usually classified by grade or subject"; "[m]any teachers in both elementary and high schools," Rubin explains, "devoted ten minutes a day to individual or group recitation of an assigned quotation" ("Listen, My Children," 265). Closely allied to the recitation of poetry that took place at other times within the school week or calendar, this truncated form of the exercise demonstrates quite neatly that in this period the idea of poetry as a beautiful and valuable commodity and the concept of memorization as a form of brain calisthenics came together to form a pedagogical construct of singular power. Although the "memory gem" term had largely dropped out of use by the third decade of the twentieth century, the message about mental training that it helped to disseminate arguably continued to linger on in popular culture far beyond this date.[38]

Another strain in the discourse over roughly the same period derived from the writings of American educational psychologist G. Stanley Hall. A former English teacher, Hall had demonstrated his interest in the literary contents of elementary education early in his publishing career with an 1886 book entitled *How to Teach Reading and What to Read.* When his subsequent works approached this theme, however, they did so in the context of Hall's most famous idea, a theory of childhood development created from a blend of Darwinian evolutionary constructs and, most prominently, Ernst Haeckel's concept of recapitulation (the idea that ontogeny, the individual organism, passes through the same stages as phylogeny, the species). In his seminal 1904 work *Adolescence*, Hall insisted that myth and legend were "the best expression of the adolescent stage of our race"; consequently the best reading matter for children in their teens was to be found in "the literature of the Arthuriad and the Sangrail, the stories of Parsifal, Tristram, Isolde, Galahad, Geraint, Siegfried, Brunnhilde, Roland, the Cid, Orlando, Tannhäuser, Beowulf, Lohengrin, Robin Hood and Rolando" (56). Passages like the following (in a 1908 work by Edmund Burke Huey) produce their own recapitulation of this line of thought:

> Reading, as the study of literature, should be of what our race has voted best, or classic, in its successive stages of culture, the child and youth roughly recapitulating these stages in reading interests and needs. The literature of Teutonic feudalism and chivalry and of medieval romanticism seems especially suited to the nature and interests of adolescents. (198)

Such ideas had an influence upon both lists of works in courses of studies and writings on juvenile recitation more generally; in the 1910s, for instance, it is not unusual to find comments about the innate suitability of ballads for the nine-year-old who is "repeating in little the history of the race, and harking back, at each step, to bygone generations at various periods of racial history" (Arnold Smith, 21).[39]

In common with faculty psychology, hard-line "cultural epoch" theory did not survive much beyond the first couple of decades of the twentieth century. The ideas about poem selection that it had helped to support, however, took longer to die. Admittedly, statements on the importance of matching works to this or that age group had long been a component of discussions of the memorized poem, and were to remain part of the discourse as long as recitation continued.[40] But even though arguments about age-appropriateness could be put forward in many different ways, ghostly traces of Hall's influence persisted well after his concept had fallen out of fashion. David Shayer notes that "as late as 1931" a parliamentary investigation of British elementary schools was "convinced that a great many teachers still hold the Recapitulation theory" (43). This was hardly surprising, perhaps, given that the government's *Handbook of Suggestions for the Consideration of Teachers* of 1927, a mere four years earlier, seems a touch haunted by the idea itself:

> [T]he main story or leading idea of a poem should be within [a child's] grasp, and a well-marked rhythm and swinging metre are most valuable aids to appreciation at this early stage. For these reasons narrative poetry in the form of the ballad generally appeals to young scholars, and English literature affords ample supply of suitable poems of this description, both ancient and modern. Some of the old ballads, and many narrative poems and lays by Scott, Campbell, Cowper, Macaulay, Longfellow, Tennyson, Arnold and many contemporary poets appeal at once to children. (82)

If memory training and recapitulation theory sounded certain notes within the discourse over the years, then the memorized poem's role in promoting and demonstrating pride in one's country or one's empire struck a dominant chord from the beginning of recitation's heyday, and continued to constitute a strong theme as long as the practice continued. The reasons why patriotic enthusiasm increased in the 1870s were different in each of the two countries, but a shared state of heightened nationalist or imperialist sentiment exerted a comparable influence upon American and British education. Respect and reverence both for the symbols of collective identity and for the history of the nation and its sons had demonstrable effects on ideas about how literature should function within the school,[41] making themselves felt not just in discussions about the recitation exercise's importance, but creating new occasions on which verses might be recited and altering the canon of juvenile standards in significant ways.[42]

A passage from *The Companion to the National Union of Teachers Code* of 1906 illustrates how instructors in Great Britain were encouraged to view the memorization of poetry as an adjunct to both institutional activities and national life more generally:

> It is desirable that some of the passages selected for recitation should have a bearing upon the history that any particular class is studying, and a similar use should be made of school songs. National anniversaries may also be made an occasion for reviving many inspiring memories of the past. (Yoxall and Gray, 66)

Drawing on what was in these years a pedagogical vogue for "correlation" of subjects across timetable divisions, classroom focus on, for instance, the nation's heroes or "The Flag" granted the performance of memorized poetry the opportunity to solemnize and diversify the treatment of the topic; in this way, recitation gained an additional justification for its existing presence in the curriculum.[43] Its role in the school's public demonstrations of national and imperial pride was just as important, with one particular twentieth-century insertion into the country's calendar providing the best-remembered annual showcase for juvenile recitation (Rose, 338–41). Invented in 1904 by imperial enthusiast Lord Meath and placed on May 24 (Queen Victoria's birthday), Empire Day eventually became a high point of the elementary-school year, usually functioning as an open-air fete with much-rehearsed pageants, songs and, of course, poetry.[44] Longtime Shakespearean anthological favorites such as *Henry the Fifth*'s "St. Crispin's Day" speech or John of Gaunt's lines on "This royal throne of kings, this scepter'd isle" were obvious choices for performance, as were Cowper's "England, with all thy faults" and Campbell's "Battle of the Baltic" and "Ye Mariners of England"; works by modern poets also had a strong presence. Many of these new poems featured in school recitation throughout the year as well. Patriotic verses like Kipling's "English Flag," Newbolt's "Drake's Drum," and Henley's "England, My England" joined the classroom's repertoire rapidly after their first appearances in print, proving that this was a canon with no inherent resistance to new works *per se*.

Across the Atlantic, a wider range of occasions gave even greater prominence to the recited poem's ability to provide communal events with a rousing focus. Recitation had a central place in days of national jubilation or remembrance, such as the anniversaries of presidential inaugurations, Arbor Day (a "mainstay of the public school calendar by the 1880s"), and Memorial (originally Decoration) Day (Rubin, *Songs of Ourselves*, 171). Over the years, and thanks in part to its presence within the high school as well as the elementary school, the recited poem also became a customary feature of other sorts of commemorative or jubilatory gatherings in or out of class, from local or regional centennials to the veneration of national icons. The country's poets formed an especially important group of worthies in the schoolroom pantheon; as Angela Sorby demonstrates with reference to the cult of Longfellow, the birthdays of the authors of the country's most memorized poems were opportunities simultaneously to celebrate the school's culture of recitation and to use recitation to celebrate the culture of the school, and, by extension, the nation (1–34). The successful performance of a poem such as "Paul Revere's Ride" ticked many boxes at once; general pride in American history, literature, and culture was affirmed as neatly as were the individual achievements of hero, poet, and reciter.

These various nationalistic positionings of poetry within public education show how recitation's subsidiary supporting claims could, with simple changes of tack, adapt themselves to changes within the larger climate of pedagogical discourse. Rubin comments, for instance, that "the enhancement of patriotic fervor was not entirely separable from moral instruction, because patriotism was a subset of 'love for that which is good and ennobling'" ("Listen, My Children," 268). When the instrumental view of recitation began to cede to increasing emphases upon the memorized poem's role within the classroom subject of English or American literature, the nationalistic or imperialistic argument still held. Under this dispensation, memorization of "the noblest thoughts and feelings that have been uttered," as Chubb puts it, was important not just, or not so much, because poems made a child nobler, but because those poems represented his literary heritage, and thus gave him a source of pride in the cultural achievements of his nation. Being able to reproduce your country's most revered poetic works was in this period an important constituent of an essentially nationalistic form of literary study.

In time, however, the relocation of poetry memorization from a moral to an academic register began to weaken the exercise's position within juvenile education. The next section will identify the two principal angles from which the deathblows came, but we can prepare the ground for that postmortem examination by studying the emergence of some damaging themes within recitation discourse. Of particular importance was a growing anxiety about the shortcomings of rote memorization and mandatory performance as educational activities. As long as pedagogues had concentrated on recitation's role in the training of character, then the self-discipline required to memorize and recite a long poem counted towards the exercise's sum of virtues. But when the terrain of value shifted, commentators became more likely to worry about the negative aspects of enforced drill. Such themes come to the fore most prominently when discussions of the practice include reports of watching and hearing children perform; at these junctures, the discrepancy between idealistic theories about the memorized poem and the daily reality of an uninspired classroom makes itself felt with particular force. The exercise always carried within itself the potential to degenerate into the most leaden and meaningless of rote activities; perhaps, as the years went by, it became progressively harder for this unchanging stalwart of the school curriculum to access the energy required to lift itself to a higher level. Certainly written concerns about the possible unpleasantness and mindlessness of the activity began to appear with increasing frequency after the 1910s.

Let us tackle the question of enjoyment first. The desire for recitation to be a happy experience can certainly be found within the older discourse; whether linked to ideas about ethical improvement, patriotic uplift, or sensibility to beauty, there is often an insistence that the child should both like the poem and like reciting it, at times in somewhat uneasy tandem with stern statements about the value of hard work. Within the newer concept of the exercise as an important component of literary study, the necessity of pleasure took up a rather different position. In his 1925 text *On the Teaching of Poetry*, British writer Alexander Haddow explains the relation between the two in the following manner. "Poetry is one of a group of subjects," he states, that promote the "development of the aesthetic sense"; "joy in beauty" is an essential element of both recitation and the classroom analysis of a literary work (3). For Haddow there should be no divisions between being enraptured by a poem, knowing it by heart, and being able to understand it; ideally, appreciation (that more moderate term for loving literature) and academic study are indissolubly bound. In consequence, the idea that displeasure might enter the continuum at any point is painful to him:

> I would have no compulsion. I would have only those who wish to read, try, and I would have you deal gently with all who really try. I have had a little girl of ten say to me, almost in tears at her own failure, "I can feel it in the right way, but I can't get it into my voice," and this after I thought she had done it well. (59)

"During the poetry lesson," he insists, "there must be no blight on the joy" (59):

> Let them choose for themselves the poems they are to learn by heart, each choosing his own favourites. Thus only can we develop a taste for poetry, and train the ear to the variety of beautiful sounds. Thus only can we rouse in them some idea of the wealth of poetry that lies before them. (68)

Other commentators were less emotional than Haddow, but still worried that the prevailing modes of teaching were counterproductive. "Poetry which is learnt by heart under compulsion and the fear of punishment is not only valueless to the learner, but likely to associate the reading of poetry with a feeling of distaste," opines Arnold Smith, the writer whose dismissive comments about memory training we noted earlier (101). Arthur Quiller-Couch, professor of English at Cambridge and editor of the influential anthology *The Oxford Book of English Verse*, is similarly concerned about the effects of the distinctly nonideal conditions of mass recitation. As he informs his undergraduates in the second decade of the twentieth century, he has spent "a great part of the last ten years in watching some 320 Elementary Schools" while fulfilling his duties as a magistrate in Cornwall.[45] In consequence, he finds it difficult to be sanguine about the lives of the vast majority of individuals in the country, badly nourished as they are by the meager diet of poetry force-fed to them in their youth, and hard to concentrate upon his ostensible topic, the study of English literature within the academy:

> My thoughts have too often strayed from my audience in a University theatre away to remote rural class-rooms where the hungry sheep look up and are not fed; to piteous groups of urchins standing at attention and chanting "The Wreck of the Hesperus" in unison. (*On the Art of Reading*, vii).

Quiller-Couch's pronouncements find play and poignancy in a Miltonic reference that his privileged listeners would no doubt have appreciated; the children of some far-flung Cornish parish, in contrast, are locked into an inflexible and joylessly impersonal relationship with Longfellow's schoolroom standard.[46] This is clearly not how things should be. "Can you not give them," he asks the students, the future policymakers of his country, "in their short years at school, something to sustain their souls in the long Valley of Humiliation?" (76).

This Bunyanesque statement may sound distinctly old-fashioned, but Quiller-Couch's worry that mass recitation is mindless as well as joyless connects to a growing consensus in the twentieth century: more and more commentators felt that children should comprehend the poem that they were memorizing. This, however, was a tricky subject to negotiate within the discourse proper. Presenting their programs for ideal teaching behaviors and strategies, pedagogical writings operate as an exhortatory and inspirational genre; in consequence they are rarely entirely frank about the baseline facts of quotidian classroom practice. But the truth of the matter was this: whereas even the least gifted or motivated of individuals could supervise unthinking rote recitation, only certain sorts of teachers were themselves good at understanding poems, and only skilled and enthusiastic members of this subset could get their charges to discuss and comprehend the literary work up for memorization. At this particular juncture, then, there was considerable potential for a gap to open up between what should be, and what was—between the prescriptive and the functional curriculum.

It is interesting to compare the ways in which different writers, in various types of pedagogical documents, approach the question of comprehension. More realistically cognizant of actual conditions, perhaps, texts intended for everyday use by members of the teaching profession appear unwilling to insist upon a goal of full understanding. Certainly a staple guide for British rank-and-file instructors, the 1906 *Companion to the National Union of Teachers' Code* cited earlier, seems to makes a virtue out of a necessity. "So long as the poetry chosen for repetition is good in itself, and has a fascination for the children," it temporizes, "it is of little moment whether or no they wholly comprehend what they learn. Indeed an element of incomprehensibility is perhaps part of the fascination. This should be remembered in selecting poetry for children. The pieces must of course have a meaning for them, but not necessarily their full meaning" (32).[47] Writers at a greater remove from the chalk dust took a firmer line. In 1899 William James asserted that "the best method is of course not to 'hammer in' the sentences by mere reiteration, but to analyse them and think" (cited in Klapper, 47); in *How to Teach the Fundamental Subjects*, authors Kendall and Mirick insisted in 1915, "It is of primary importance that a pupil understand the thought before beginning to commit a selection to memory" (14). "He may not appreciate fully the significance of the passage," they continue, "but it should convey sense to his intelligence or he should not learn" (15).

Such calls for thoughtful apprehension were often situated, as the James quotation reveals, within writings that attacked rote learning not because it was the killer of joy, but because it was perceived to be an outmoded pedagogical technique. In the United States, where "mere reiteration" had formerly held such a dominant and, at times, valorized presence within the classroom, the backlash was especially noticeable, if only, at first, in particular quarters. Here, from the end of the nineteenth century onwards, as Gill and Schlossman argue, "opposition to . . . the tyranny of memorization . . . would soon become a badge of honor among educators who viewed themselves in the vanguard of progressive education"; both the emergent "child study movement" (an offshoot of G. Stanley Hall's theories) and mothers' clubs (later to evolve into parent-teacher associations), voiced dissatisfaction with what were known as "memoriter" tests and the excessive amounts of homework required for children to pass them (33). Eventually these concerns passed to the mainstream. It is hard to gauge exactly how far the discrediting of rote learning in general affected the specialized literary variant, but the increasingly popular belief that drill was not an appropriate activity for the modern classroom inevitably affected attitudes in the longer term.

In the context of British mass education, where memorization *per se* had in contrast experienced an officially validated relationship only with the poetry exercise, sea changes in social attitudes and pedagogical thinking had different effects on the landscape. In 1937, just a few years before the country would let go of juvenile recitation altogether, the *Handbook of Suggestions* issued that year stated that "if the teaching in the Junior School has been successful, it will be found that the children not only like their poetry, and, to some extent, understand it, but also know a good deal of it by heart" (372). Apparently unwilling either to give up quite yet on the memorized poem or to make an explicit endorsement of rote learning, the governmental document retreats to the passive voice to express its hope that a subtle osmosis will have "stored the young child's active memory . . . with fine and gracious fragments of poetry and prose" (372).

The Ending of Mass Poetry Recitation

The introduction has already made some summary statements about the demise of wide-scale poetry memorization in the two countries under scrutiny. To recap: in Great Britain, the elementary school, the institution that had hosted recitation in one way or another since the introduction of the Revised Code in 1862, was abolished by the 1944 Education Act. Its replacement, the primary school, founded itself upon a set of social ideas and teaching philosophies that had little tolerance for what were perceived as either the activities or the modes of instruction of the past; in consequence, the compulsory performance of a memorized poem had no place here.[48] Yet it is probably more accurate to say that British recitation ended not with a bang but a whimper; after the link between its successful performance and the size of a school's budget was severed at the end of the nineteenth century, the practice was still broadly prevalent for a further two decades, but there was something of a falling-off in the 1930s before the nation's memorization culture reached its definitive terminus at the close of World War II. In contrast, the memorized poem in the United States continued to hold its own—generally in the elementary school, and for certain constituencies of students in the high school—throughout the 1950s. Yet by the 1960s (and once again allowing for significant degrees of variation across different zones of educational provision), recitation in the American classroom was well on the way to becoming a fringe pursuit.

The previous section illustrated how cracks in the memorized poem's defenses began to appear long before the edifice finally fell. The real wrecking balls, however, swung from two principal locations, designated here for convenience as the "learning to read" and the "something to read" camps. To explain the process whereby poetry recitation achieved its customary presence at each standard or grade of the elementary school, I have argued that classroom readers and curricular programs of mass education fused together two dissimilar, but superficially congenial, pedagogical traditions. At the base, or lower levels, of literacy acquisition, rhymed and rhythmic text bore a hereditary connection to the development of reading skills; at higher levels, literary selections in English functioned as worthy and improving reading material. But over time, verse memorization's right to exist within either location was at first challenged and then ultimately rendered untenable. From one angle, theories about optimal methods of teaching reading sidelined the idea that memorizing verses was an appropriate activity during the first steps of literacy; from the other, a growing consensus that recitation was inimical to the study of poetry put paid to its presence in the literature class. As we have seen, numerous other justifications for the activity could be, and were, thrown out to provide lifelines, but the memorized poem's connections to these two prime fastnesses had been key. When their constituting principles changed, both strongholds turned against the practice. Without this support, recitation could not survive as a mandatory mass phenomenon.

The two relevant developments within the "learning to read" base are easy to summarize. The first grew out of the concept that the vocabulary encountered by novice readers should be strictly monitored to ensure logical and steady progress; the theory dictated that (1) a lesson should introduce only a fixed number of new words, and (2) each subsequent lesson should repeat words already learned to build familiarity. Venezky notes that some innovative American primers and readers had already begun to distinguish "selection-specific vocabulary" in the 1820s and 1830s; by the middle of the nineteenth century most textbook series were demonstrating some awareness of a need for phased introduction and repetition. These ideas eventually achieved their high-water mark in the 1960s, when "control of reader vocabulary by frequency of occurrence became a fetish for basal reader design" (256). By this point, however, even the simplest of verses for early learners had long lost any claim to pedagogical appropriateness or utility in relation to this fundamental classroom objective. Teaching the youngest pupils to memorize and recite little poems might be worthwhile for other reasons, but no instructor would have considered the activity to form part of the royal road to literacy.

The pervasive effects of a growing emphasis upon silent reading, the other principal shift, are harder to quantify, but they also helped to render time-honored classroom traditions obsolete (Venezky, 261). Although reading aloud remained the primary mode for beginning readers and had a defined place in the education of their more advanced schoolmates, the importance of encouraging the unvoiced form was an increasingly dominant theme in pedagogical writings and teacher-training courses from around 1910 onwards. Eventually the twentieth-century classroom became a much quieter place than its nineteenth-century counterpart. The recitation of poetry had grown out of a learning culture characterized above all by vocalization; the injunction that pupils should read in their heads created another world altogether.

Just as changing ideas about best practices in literacy training separated the memorized poem from reading instruction, its bond to the classroom's need for, and uses of, reading material also gave way in the end. As we have seen, perceptions of the primary purpose of recitation at higher levels of the school shifted according to time and place. Although the vocal reproduction of literary selections had originally been stimulated by that eighteenth-century desire to bring competent readers into relation with their culture's most prized writings, this impetus had on occasion played second, or even third, fiddle to other concerns during the exercise's heyday in mass education; the quality of the verse assigned for memorization had sometimes been of less importance than the exercise's perceived significance in improving the individual and the community through its form, or its content, or both. Nevertheless, recitation had nearly always operated as some kind of adjunct to the reading of literature, a role that became ever more prominent when understandings of the basic purpose of primary education elevated academic development above moral training. Eventually, however, developing ideas about appropriate modes of rudimentary literary study in the elementary school altered classroom attitudes and behaviors to such a degree that the memorized poem lost its common cause with English or American literature. To put this in another way: over the years there was less and less overlap between the accepted meanings and functions of two entities that in earlier times and other places had sometimes appeared practically identical.

A full explanation of this shift would require its own separate study; suffice to say here that major alterations in perceptions about what poetry was, and what it was for, played their part, as did new concepts about childhood development, especially in relation to education in general and literature in particular. In essence, the change drew upon a seemingly paradoxical combination of ideas about freedom and rigor. On the liberatory front, poetry came to bear an increasingly important association with creativity, individuality, and self-expression, and the child's necessary access thereto. The encroachment of this concatenation of beliefs upon the recitation exercise makes itself manifest in those recommendations, evident in the later periods of the memorized poem's heyday in both Great Britain and the United States, that children be only "encouraged" to memorize, and that each child should "choose" the poem that appealed to him or her most. Inevitably, though, the trajectory implicit within such gestures gradually led the classroom poetry session further and further away from what now looked like the fixed and impersonal form of mass mandatory memorization and towards other, apparently looser, more self-realizing, activities. By the end of the 1930s, for example, forward-thinking British elementary-school teachers who enjoyed

teaching poetry were less likely to be insisting that the class commit reci-
tational standards to memory than urging each pupil to compose his or
her own verse—and perhaps even free verse at that (Shayer, 103–34).

On the other, rigorous, side of things, moves towards discussion and
analysis within the literature lesson served to make the conflicted relation
between recitation and comprehension appear ever more awkward.
Teachers had long been encouraged to make their charges think and talk
about the poems to be memorized, yet given the daily pressure of more
immediate or achievable duties, it must have been tempting to let this dif-
ficult and amorphous task slide. But as pedagogical training developed
and was influenced by movements within the study of specific subjects at
the university level, the literature lesson began to take a different shape;
instructors were increasingly likely to believe that it should include dis-
cussions not only of what a given poem meant, but of how it achieved
those meanings. Admittedly, such assumptions more readily affected be-
haviors in secondary, or high school, education, but their modes of think-
ing had some effect upon the lower-echelon institution as well. Whether
content, or form, or content and form together, was the topic for conver-
sation, talking about the poem that constituted the classroom's reading
material came to seem progressively more important than, and indeed
increasingly antithetical to, the recitation of the work in question. In ad-
dition, the third and fourth decades of the twentieth century witnessed
other forms of engagement with literature that similarly challenged the
value of recitation. For instance, and especially in the United States, the
vogue for "life studies" project-work encouraged by the burgeoning field
of educational psychology meant that poems might be explored to see
how they presented solutions to, or perspectives of, the problems of exis-
tence.[49] Memorization and performance had even less contribute to such
an endeavor than they had to literary analysis.

This account of the memorized poem's passing would be incomplete
without a brief word about the eventually problematical nature of the
verses themselves. Recitation discourse had long contained voices that
worried whether this or that piece or category of poetry was a suitable
object for the exercise of juvenile memorization. Beginning in the 1860s,
as we shall see in the next section, important objections were made on the
grounds of literary quality, but from the end of the nineteenth century
onwards, complainants usually addressed the issue of thematic and age
appropriateness, expressing doubts about the wisdom of exposing chil-
dren to gloomy or bloodthirsty works. These latter concerns cropped up
in discussions of the ideal nature of poems within both the "learning to
read" and the "something to read" camps outlined above. In time, how-
ever, discomforts with the morbid or the violent were subsumed into an

attitude that turned out to be far more extensively hostile to the traditional contents of the recitation canon, that is, an impatience with whatever was perceived to be either adult-oriented, or otherwise archaic, esoteric, or exotic.

Pronounced with increasing emphasis from the 1920s onwards and reaching full volume in the 1970s, the new watchword was "relevance." Implicitly, this meant "of relevance to children's lives": if the contents of a stretch of text did not connect in obvious ways to a child's immediate experiences in the world, then it was deemed in many quarters to have no place in popular elementary schooling. This was a criterion that many poems that were once massively assigned just could not satisfy. Whether undergirded or not by recapitulation theory, earlier ideas about the importance of adventure or imagination within childhood development continued to have some play and thus provided support for the survival of certain schoolroom standards, but a large number of their erstwhile comrades looked woefully out of fashion in the new light. In consequence poems about the Assyrian coming down like a wolf on the fold or architects of faith working in these walls of time eventually dropped out of lower-level public education; in their stead came verses on, for instance, playground games, the passing of the seasons, or the importance of friendship. Such favoring of children's poetry of the everyday was coincident with the disfavoring of memorization; when these new poems entered and altered the schoolroom canon, they brought along no default connection to the practice of recitation. On the other side of things, when the old faithfuls were dismissed from class, they each took with them an increment of the declamatory mode that had been an indivisible element of their former presence.

The Major Phases in the Constitution of Recitation Canons

Numerous references to the form and contents of recitation canons have appeared in the preceding pages but there are aspects of their histories and makeup that merit a separate focus here. Because any canon is in essence an abstraction or a convenient fiction, some words of caution are in order first. It is easy enough to provide the names of works assigned or made available for memorization in a specific time and place, but any lists of, or summary statements about, the poems most frequently recited across extended periods and locales should be regarded simply as nets thrown into the wide seas of daily pedagogical practice—catches that only bring in certain samplings from the vasty deep. Part II of this book is expressly designed to tug against generalizations about groups of works; its case study structure asserts that there is a distinct tale to tell about how each and every poem gained or lost its presence in cultural memory. These points acknowledged, this section nevertheless offers a description of some of the principal trends that affected practices of poem selection for juvenile recitation over the years.

As in the broader history, there are three main phases for attention, each subject to tendencies already partially described and each demonstrating certain national variations. The general narrative is one of eventual, but not absolute, conservatism. There are significant areas of overlap between the sets of poems that correspond to each era and each country, but in truth very few poetic selections persisted in the mainstream all the way from the last third of the eighteenth century into the first half of the twentieth in both Britain and the United States (those set-piece Shakespearean speeches that are untroubled by sexual references experienced the best survival rates). Juvenile recitation canons came to assume their most stable forms in the heyday of the memorized poem. In this period, the works inside series of graded readers manifested strong continuity diachronically, with a good proportion of tables of contents staying the same over the years, and synchronically, in that there was considerable duplication from one publisher's sequence to the next (copying was endemic both domestically and across the Atlantic divide). Yet variances and incremental changes happened everywhere and all the time. Both title-by-title alterations and broader categorical developments occurred; innovations were promoted or enacted from time to time by official educational bodies or enterprising compilers and editors; shifts in other contiguous canons wrought their effects. Nevertheless, three generations of individuals in either country between 1880 and 1930 could conceivably have been assigned a near-identical set of poems for memorization over the duration of their school years, albeit under the sway of different pedagogical justifications and from textbooks with varying amounts of annotation and apparatus.

To begin the historical survey, we return once again to the two heterogeneous forms of English-language poetry recitation that existed at the end of the eighteenth century, those that depended upon (1) the rhymes in primers or books for infant readers, and (2) the literary extracts in elocutionary anthologies. The first group of works can be characterized as a selection of verses that tailored religious and moral ideas to suit little minds. Many of its members were nonce compositions that simply "thr[ew] important truths and precepts into a poetical form," as a later volume put it (*Sacred Poetry*, 3), but it also contained some poems that were to become enduring celebrities, such as "How doth the little busy bee," and, in later years, "Twinkle, Twinkle, Little Star" and "My Mother." The latter group was very differently constituted. Its prototypical works were also largely virtuous and uplifting in content, but in order to win their places in the "Speaker" volumes, they had to fulfill two secular requirements as well. Selections needed to possess both a fitness for dramatic declamation and the status of prized specimens of vernacular literature (their appearance in other kinds of anthologies in the period generally figuring as a good proof thereof). Numerous passages of Shakespearean blank verse occupied secure positions in this lofty collection; works by such authors as Pope, Thomson, Cowper, and Addison also had a strong presence (Michael, 198).

Now, had a hypothetical (not to say anachronistic) compiler attempted to bring together these two sets of poetic texts as part of his creation of a graded series of school readers in, say, 1810, he would have found himself in a quandary. The verses for the first book would have seemed worlds away from those destined for the final one in the sequence, and he would have been hard put to know how to traverse the gap in the intermediate volumes. Yet when pedagogues and publishers began to produce progressive series for public education in the second phase for our consideration, the 1830s to the 1850s, this potential problem did not arise; the disparities between the two groups of works were smoothed out to such a degree that there was no obvious wrenching of gears as each volume stepped up the level of difficulty. This worked itself out in nationally distinct fashions, but both the British and the American canons of pedagogical verse that came into being in this period were subject to a cultural climate that put its primary stress upon the moral function of mass education. In consequence, the idea that books for the classroom should contain texts that were considered elsewhere to be models of literary excellence had less sway than the belief that poetry was useful inasmuch as it provided an ideal conduit for Christian teaching.[50]

Although this move meant in effect that the conceptual justifications behind the primer's poems triumphed over those that underpinned the anthology's, it did not follow that all of the latter volume's literary selections were necessarily ejected. Instead, a kind of winnowing process went into operation. Works that could fill the morality desideratum became ever more firmly lodged within subsequent generations of reading books, whereas those that could not were likely to be dropped. Usually this involved a judgment about content; for instance, the British compiler of an 1849 volume entitled *Poetry for Schools* notes in his preface that he excludes Pope and Dryden because they lack "passages for the moral and religious principles of which I would willingly make myself responsible" (Cook, vi). At other times, works might be avoided because suspect behaviors were associated with their authors. As Elson explains in *Guardians of Tradition: American Schoolbooks of the Nineteenth Century*, compilers of textbooks in the United States after the 1820s were sometimes loath to feature poems by such reprobates as Byron, Coleridge, Burns, and, in due course, Poe—this last despite the fact that his "European reputation should have pleased . . . nationalists" who were ever keen to enlarge the proportion of American pages in the country's readers (226). There was always the possibility that such high-minded standards would not be applied—Byron's stirring martial works were never excluded from the popular McGuffey series, for example, and "The Raven" would become a schoolroom classic—but a broadly moralizing tendency prevailed. As a result, literary selections in the higher-numbered books within reading sequences became unified by their unobjectionable ethical concerns to a much greater degree than the works that had been collected together for earlier "Speaker" volumes.[51]

It was thanks to this sifting that the progression of the recitational canons from the simplest of religiously didactic jingles to, for example, works like Gray's Elegy or "Thanatopsis" was rendered less obviously awkward than it might have been. The appearance of continuity was further bolstered by the fact that bona fide literary selections, if sufficiently short and not too complex in their diction, could also be lodged at the beginner and intermediate levels of the reading series. On the whole, though, the low-number volumes tended to be heavily populated by instances of the nonce compositions that had long been a regular feature of the primers, spellers, and early readers. Although some nonattributed verses superseded their humble origins and were silently copied elsewhere, thus becoming in the process repeat, rather than onetime, offenders, a substantial proportion of the poetical sections of British and American reading series over the middle years of the nineteenth century were true one-offs, specific to a single volume.

Subsets of the work of that prolific author Anon., then, these little poems constitute a species of literature that has understandably attracted little critical attention. Probably quite often "the composition of the anonymous compilers" of the reading series themselves, as Matthew Arnold was to observe with distaste in 1860, such pieces were usually written in the textbook poem's default meter of common, or short, measure (*Reports*, 87–88). Yet this was not always the case. Take, for instance, an excerpt from a twenty-line work in *Cobb's Juvenile Reader No. 2*, published in Baltimore in 1831, which otherwise provides a representative example of the typical content of thousands of works that were produced, memorized, and performed in this period:

If I do right, my weary head
Shall find rest upon my bed;
Freely opening every plan
To the eyes of God and man.

Days in joy shall then be past,
Each one happier than the last;
And every year that hurries by
Finds me well prepared to die. (141)

Considered *en masse*, these quite literally undistinguished poems helped to make the era's recitational repertoire an essentially hybrid affair. Parts of it behaved according to our understanding of how canons conventionally function: individual named works reappeared time after time in distinct but associated publications intended for specific reading environments. The remainder of its component parts, however, manifested the more curious ability both to change and stay the same. Which is to say, a relatively large quantity of the classroom's literature relied upon neither the presence, nor the repetition, of specific charismatic texts to create the canonical hallmarks of coherence and reproduction, but constituted itself instead through the thematic, tonal, and formal unity of a constantly shifting set of works.

Before moving on to the third and final phase, I will make one further observation about this essentially moral period of juvenile recitation. It was not only the requirement that poetry fulfill a religious duty that shaped the evolution of the pedagogical canon; its ability to stand in for Scripture also resulted, I believe, in the creation of certain thematic foci therein. To substantiate this assertion, I will concentrate for the moment on a British development, but the story I tell also has purchase in the American context. An earlier portion of this chapter tracked the train of circumstances that placed a single set of textbooks in huge numbers of British classrooms in the middle decades of the nineteenth century. Within the Irish readers, as we noted, poems played an important role in representing the main events and themes of the Christian story that would otherwise have been illustrated by excerpts from the Bible if this had been permissible. Of these events, none was more important than the crucifixion of Christ. While both this series of schoolbooks and their emulators, early and late, included many different sorts of verses, the fact that they contained a distinct cluster of poems that variously incarnated the martyrdom of Jesus had significant long-term effects. Over the years, this nucleus acted as a kind of magnetizing force that drew in other texts that performed a similar function, thus establishing within the canon a key subset of works whose central theme was noble sacrifice.

The general process I describe here is, I believe, a common feature of canon evolution. Works whose themes duplicate, or otherwise resemble, those of works already lodged in a certain anthological form stand a much greater chance of being adopted in subsequent versions thereof, always assuming that their particularities satisfy other local requirements; in this way, competing demands for variety and continuity are both satisfied. I draw special attention to the "Christ by other means" poems because they continued to exert a significant shaping force upon the pedagogical canon in recitation's heyday, an era that coincided, as already noted, with the period in which schoolroom literature was called upon to serve increasingly imperialistic and nationalistic ends. In this climate, those long-serving classroom poems that extolled the selfless laying down of life for a larger cause could bend themselves, with greater or lesser ease, to the prevailing wind; further, the presence of this time-honored group also helped to dictate the preferred characteristics of newly composed patriotic verses that joined the canon in this period. In consequence, children in British mass education were far more likely to find themselves reciting poems about bravery in the face of defeat than verses celebrating victory; furthermore, their larger stock of works was habitually, rather than incidentally, marked with the stamp of death.[52] A full attempt to understand these specific and general morbidities of emphasis would examine a range of contributory factors and comparative contexts; nevertheless, I wish to suggest that the larger history of the schoolroom canon here under scrutiny played a strongly deterministic role.

Heightened nationalist fervor also had another structural effect in the third and final phase of canon development. As the poetry lesson became increasingly linked to ideas about the promotion of patriotic pride in the rich artistic heritage of the nation and the language, then the presence of undistinguished verses within educational readers began to seem more problematic. This concern intersected with the general move towards academics previously outlined. In those places and periods in which the prime duty of mass education was believed to be the inculcation of moral habits and thoughts, then the purpose of the recitation exercise inhered above all in its ability to promote upright behavior via the disciplinary rigor of performance and the ethical content of the words pronounced. But, over time, wherever and whenever a stress on schooling's academic function came to the fore, the perceived quality of the verse assumed a greater importance. In effect, the pendulum now swung back to the "Speaker" volumes—not to the exact set of poems that had found favor therein, but rather to their informing insistence upon the literary excellence of the pieces.[53]

Altered conceptions of the meaning of the recitation exercise once again did not necessarily mean alterations in the poem selection. For the most part, named works that had already survived earlier shifts of opinion simply solidified their position as classics of the classroom. Yet other sorts of compositions—one-offs; those that carried either no author's name, or the name of an author without literary status elsewhere—now fell under explicit attack. Matthew Arnold regularly complained about the inferior sources of the poetry in graded readers in his annual inspection reports. We do not know whether or not it was at his personal instigation that pupil-teachers were expressly required to repeat lines "from some standard English poet" in the rules laid down in the first edition of the Revised Code, but it is tempting to think that his desire to rid the classroom of nondescript literature led to the subsequent emendations for the higher echelons of the general elementary-school population that stipulated that their verse be taken "from Shakespeare, or Milton," or from that convenient catchall, "some other standard author." Concerns about quality were also expressed across the Atlantic. In an 1891 magazine article, Harvard president Charles W. Eliot fulminated that "there are a great many readers that seem to have been composed especially for the use of children. They are not made up of selections from recognized literature, and as a rule this class is simply ineffable trash" (cited in Banton Smith, 120). Such poems should be cast out; instead, "we should substitute in all our schools real literature for readers."

To the extent that attributed works became more prevalent, the route that Eliot advocated was generally followed, as far as possible, by the new generations of textbooks produced in both countries towards the end of the nineteenth century; in addition, as we have seen, the courses of study that laid out the poetic curriculum in the United States became increasingly likely to name individual works for memorization. While the poems assigned to the youngest two or three year-groups in elementary education on both sides of the Atlantic tended to belong more obviously to the category of "juvenile literature" than to Arnold's and Eliot's desired "real literature," here too an author's repute carried weight: certain apparently simple and sufficiently short works by poets with canonical standing elsewhere were repeatedly reprinted ("We are Seven," "The Arrow and the Song," and the most famous eight lines of *Pippa Passes* are prime examples), as were verses by authors perceived to be children's laureates, such as Stevenson and Rossetti, and additionally in the United States, Larcom and Thaxter. In general, though, the achieved canons in both countries were now and at every standard or grade level essentially patchwork affairs, stitching poems held in high or general esteem to works that had currency in the classroom only, and laying verses with long pedagogical service records alongside others that had recently appeared. In all aspects—not excepting their inclusions of the odd local peculiarity—the two lists of poems from the Wisconsin course of study and the Chambers volume provided in the opening pages of this chapter are representative of the state of affairs that pertained in the United States and Britain in recitation's heyday. For comparative purposes, appendix 1 sets out in schematic form further information about the works and the identities of their authors; appendixes 2 and 3 present additional snapshots of some prototypical groupings of poems from this final period.

PART II

CASE STUDIES

Felicia Hemans, "Casabianca"

The boy stood on the burning deck
    Whence all but he had fled;
The flame that lit the battle's wreck
    Shone round him o'er the dead.

Yet beautiful and bright he stood,
    As born to rule the storm;
A creature of heroic blood,
    A proud, though child-like form.

The flames rolled on—he would not go
    Without his Father's word;
That father, faint in death below,
    His voice no longer heard.

He called aloud—"Say, Father, say
    If yet my task is done?"
He knew not that the chieftain lay
    Unconscious of his son.

"Speak, Father!" once again he cried,
    "If I may yet be gone!
And"—but the booming shots replied,
    And fast the flames rolled on.

Upon his brow he felt their breath,
    And in his waving hair,
And looked from that lone post of death
    In still, yet brave despair.

And shouted but once more aloud,
    "My father! must I stay?"
While o'er him fast, through sail and shroud,
    The wreathing fires made way.

They wrapt the ship in splendour wild,
    They caught the flag on high,
And streamed above the gallant child,
    Like banners in the sky.

There came a burst of thunder sound—
    The boy—oh! where was he?
Ask of the winds that far around
    With fragments strewed the sea!—

With mast, and helm, and pennon fair,
    That well had borne their part—
But the noblest thing which perished there
    Was that young faithful heart![1]

Beating Time: Exploding the Rhythm of the Heart

Love's the boy stood on the burning deck
trying to recite "The boy stood on
the burning deck." Love's the son
    stood stammering elocution
    while the poor ship in flames went down.

Love's the obstinate boy, the ship,
even the swimming sailors, who
would like a schoolroom platform, too,
    or an excuse to stay
    on deck. And love's the burning boy.

"Casabianca," Elizabeth Bishop (1946)

Of all the many retellings—usually ribald, scurrilous, or just plain silly—of Felicia Hemans's poem "Casabianca," Elizabeth Bishop's response is perhaps the only one that is consciously attentive to the status the work once held as a preeminent choice for memorization and recitation by English-speaking children.[2] Hemans had based her poem (first published in the *Monthly Magazine* in 1826) on accounts of the death of a young Corsican sailor in 1798, informing her readers in an explanatory note that "Young Casabianca, a boy about thirteen years old, son to the Admiral of the Orient, remained at his post (in the Battle of the Nile) after the ship had taken fire, and all the guns had been abandoned; and perished in the explosion of the vessel, when the flames had reached the powder" (Hemans, ed. Wolfson, 428–29). Bishop, 120 years later, presents us with a double vision of children in solitary torment: we see both the boy-sailor of reimagined Napoleonic history waiting steadfastly for the paternal word of release that will never come, and his unhappy descendant, the reciting child of a later age, doomed to stand on "the schoolroom platform," his own version of the burning deck, until the task is done. For Bishop, both the spectacle of recitation and the action of Hemans's poem itself offer twin opportunities. In the first place, she mines these two tableaux to furnish us with peculiarly novel and striking definitions of the emotion of love (each of the poem's four declamatory, declarative sentences has a contraction of the words "Love is" at, or near, its beginning). In the second, she offers an analysis of the paired scenes, finding love not only at the center of the two acts of filial obedience, but also the essence of every other element of the ultimate desolate vision— the ship, the swimming sailors, and finally, not just the obstinate, but also the burning, boy. In Hemans's heroic ballad, love, subsumed in bravery and fidelity, does not speak its own or its associated name until the very last line of the poem, when we are forced to imagine the fiery destruction of the boy's "young faithful heart." For Bishop, love is strewn all around.

In granting the performance history of "Casabianca" equal billing with its subject matter, indeed, in proposing a profound connection between the two, Bishop's poem preempts and inspires the examination I conduct here. By virtue of the uncanny alliance of its thematic concerns and its function in Britain's systems of pedagogical recitation, Hemans's poem plays an unusually defined role in the country's cultural imagination, first standing over its own century, and then haunting the next, with a doggedness rarely matched by other literary works. It is, for once, no exaggeration to state that this is a poem that takes on a life of its own— or perhaps I should say, with respect to the macabre circumstances of the boy's demise, a death of its own. In consequence, "Casabianca" presents one of literature's most arresting examples of a corpse that cannot be laid to rest: just as the boy's body, blown into smithereens over a wide area of the Mediterranean, can never be gathered up and placed in a single, fixed grave, so has his poem eluded decent burial in the dark and backward abysm of time. This is not to say, though, that the author of the poem has also enjoyed a continuous celebrity; for much of the last century Felicia Hemans was covered in obscurity. (Significantly enough, I, like many others whose undergraduate education was completed before the mid-1980s, first encountered the name of Mrs. Hemans, arguably the most widely published, most widely read poet of the nineteenth century (McGann, 182), interred deep in a footnote to the penultimate stanza of Wordsworth's "Extempore Effusion upon the Death of James Hogg," an elegy for quite a different dead poet.)[3] But if the main body of Hemans's work has only recently been exhumed, her noble boy has always stood apart.

Because of its standing as British culture's favorite performance piece, "Casabianca" lodged itself so firmly inside the national mind that adults today often know the poem without knowing that they know it. Eminent romanticist Jerome McGann gives his account of what is also, on occasion, a North American experience:

> And one of those [poems] that ran in my mind for years began "The boy stood on the burning deck." It wasn't until I was far gone as a scholar that I learned that the author of the poem was Felicia Hemans. Many more years went by before I started to realize how many worlds were not well lost because I hadn't known that poet's name. The fault wasn't my mother's. She had the poem by heart and didn't think I needed the name. (ix)

As the difference between the son's "mind" and the mother's "heart" signals,[4] the poem's hold on later generations is far more tenuous: for us, the poem may persist in our heads, but certainly not in its entirety. It lives on only in shreds and tatters, gobbets even; blown by the four winds to wash up into consciousness at the unlikeliest of moments and in the strangest of places. The first line is probably familiar to many above a certain age; the first quatrain, if it survives at all, endures primarily in parodic versions, which tend to manifest a risible juvenile smuttiness ("knickers" are often in there for the British),[5] and a preadolescent delight in substituting bathos for the expected pathos (sometimes painful "blisters" turn out to rhyme with a self-evidently ridiculous feminine presence, "sister's").[6] The poem has beaten time's effacement, but lost its integrity.

This case study will investigate the processes by which "Casabianca" established itself at the heart of one culture, and attempt to understand how it has managed, in an admittedly fragmented condition, to haunt another (even if today's Britain has forgotten the story of the grisly death that lies beneath). Within this scrutiny, I ask how it happens that a poem that is important to the people of one historical period becomes laughable, distasteful, or simply meaningless to those of another. In general, responses to this familiar question, posed of many a nineteenth-century gem whose value has plummeted, examine both a work's content, its semantic meaning, and its formal arrangement, or generic conventions. "Casabianca" stands indicted of serious crimes in both arenas. In its supposed celebration of juvenile self-sacrifice, unflinching heroism, and unquestioning fidelity to the father's word, it evidently participates not only in an especially lachrymose sentimentalism, but also in the glorification of war and a concomitant upholding of patriarchy. In the formal arena, the poem commits, if possible, even graver sins: not so much in choosing the simplest of closed forms, the ballad stanza—common, or short measure—but more in maintaining with apparent regularity its rhymes and rhythmic patterns, Mrs. Hemans demonstrates an allegiance to practices deemed second-rate, at best, and certainly unsophisticated, by the academic establishment for most of the twentieth century.

In the last thirty years or so, critical paradigms have changed significantly, allowing the work of a popular female writer of the first half of the nineteenth century to regain the respectful attention that it attracted in the period of its initial publication. Feminism in general, and the remapping of the terrain of Romantic literature in particular, has brought Hemans back into literary discourse, stimulating a wealth of intelligent analysis that has culminated in the publication of two new scholarly volumes of her poetry. No longer neglected and despised, Hemans's poetry, it turns out, does indeed possess those sterling attributes of ambiguity, complexity, and irony that are generally discovered once a work is subjected to academic scrutiny of any stripe. But while I applaud and learn from the varieties of ways in which Hemans's work has in recent years undergone skilful dissection and rearticulation,[7] I myself am interested in "Casabianca" more as a discrete cultural entity than as part of a substantial poetic oeuvre. Here I am interested not in canon debates fuelled by identity politics, but in the specific reception history of one particular work[8]—a reception intimately linked to its position within a particular system of dissemination, and, further, with the corporeal dimensions of that system. Furthermore, while I plan to make an argument about how the meaning and value of a poem can change from generation to generation, I do not intend to set my discussion against a historical panorama of the shifting literary, cultural, and academic contexts that inevitably alter our perception of a work over time.

My claim, instead, is that the body of an individual who reads "Casabianca" at the beginning of the twenty-first century is different, in important ways, from the body of an individual who read "Casabianca" at the end of the nineteenth century. In truth, I could make this claim about any poem that has been in circulation for the last hundred years or more, but I choose to focus on the reading history of "Casabianca" for the following reason. This particular poem grants us an especially good opportunity to follow the course of a pedagogy that had as one of its immediate goals the right ordering of the child's body and mind, but that often continued to work its rhythms throughout the remainder of that individual's days. Which is to say, for as long as "Casabianca" was assigned as a school poem, children were subjected, however successfully or unsuccessfully, to an educational praxis that made a profound physical and emotional connection between the literature it assigned and the bodies that read that literature. Freed from, or deprived of, such training, we, the children of later, differently disciplined ages, will never feel the beat with quite the same urgency.

Until relatively recently in the history of literary criticism, such a claim would have sounded fairly ludicrous. After all, it has been a central credo in this, as in other areas of study, that whatever else may change, bodies and bodily experience remain the same.[9] Paul Fussell's pronouncement in his classic study *Poetic Meter and Poetic Form* encapsulates the received, nay commonsensical, opinion on the relation between literature and the human frame. "The modern reader of poetry in English," he writes, "despite his vast differences in extrinsic and learned attitudes from, say, his Elizabethan counterpart, has still the same kind of physique and personal physiological rhythms as his forebears. These will still seem to seek satisfaction and delight in ways which accord with experienced rhythmic traditions of Modern English" (90). Or, to put it another way, systole and diastole produce, for nineteenth- and twentieth- and twenty-first-century persons alike, the same rhythm of mortal existence—in the words of contemporary poet (and undertaker) Thomas Lynch, "a steady iambic tally / of this life's syllables, stressed and unstressed" (49). But here lies the difference: when we do not learn by heart, the heart does not feel the rhythms of poetry as echoes or variations of its own insistent beat. We contemporary readers no longer hold poems with regular iambic rhythms at our core; no longer, if we are children, feel our pulse rates quicken as we approach the work-in-hand, aware that we must calm the racing thudding of our hearts to have any hope of reproducing the poem's own rhythms effectively, or at least acceptably; no longer, if we are adults, feel ourselves glide into the mesmeric state of the reciter of the successfully memorized, fully internalized poem, when body and words beat as one in measured familiarity. "Casabianca," the most memorized, the most recited poem of them all, allows us to historicize meter and the heart together, to think about our relationship to literature in the most corporeal of ways.

◆ ◆ ◆

In the introduction to her edition of Hemans's work, Susan Wolfson lays out a chart of the major phases in the poet's reception history, demonstrating how a steadily rising nineteenth-century popularity came to founder in a long, but eventually interrupted, period of neglect in the twentieth century. At the beginning of her publishing career in 1808, Hemans's poetry was accepted with tentative praise, but already by the 1820s the "icon" of "Mrs. Hemans" had "emerged as England's premier 'poetess,' celebrated as its epitome of 'feminine' excellence" (xiii–xxi). While her poems were read with respect and admiration by reviewers, fellow poets, and intellectuals alike during her lifetime, a significant change occurred in 1835 with Hemans's death, an event that ushered in a period of widespread popularity that was to persist throughout the Victorian period, both in Great Britain and in North America.

A variety of sources—letters, memoirs, and allusions in contemporary novels—reveal that Hemans's work held an important place in the drawing rooms and parlors of a broad swathe of middle- and upper-class life. "Every young lady had a copy of her poems," claims Amy Cruse in her study of *The Victorians and Their Books*, and "older people too, of cultivated tastes, praised Mrs. Hemans" (177). Certainly some readers still engaged with the longer poems (Mary Ann Evans enthusiastically recommended *The Forest Sanctuary* to a friend in 1840, declaring "I can give it my pet adjective—exquisite" [quoted in Cruse, 179]), but in general the short works, many of which Hemans had originally published in magazines and annuals, were the most beloved. Now firm anthology favorites, poems like "The Better Land" (admired so much by Florence Nightingale that she copied it out to send to her cousin [quoted in Cruse, 178]), "The Graves of a Household," "He Never Smiled Again," "Evening Prayer at a Girls' School," "The Child's First Grief," and "England's Dead," experienced broad circulation. The reach of many of these works was extended further by the fact that they were frequently set to music, and thus provided domestic entertainment in any home with a piano. Recitation in the home had also become a well-established pastime by the mid-1840s, while afternoon and evening "penny readings" at respectable venues grew increasingly popular in this period (Mayer). In all of these performance opportunities the work of Mrs. Hemans occupied an unrivaled position, apparently bringing tears and smiles to a wide range of audiences. Although there are clear signs that critical opinions of her poetry were beginning to change by the 1880s, increasing in condescension and moving towards outright antagonism, Mrs. Hemans continued to hold her own in the anthology market in general, and in the recitation anthology in particular, right up to the end of the century.

At the dead center of Felicia Hemans's popular reputation stood "Casabianca." But while this piece became a general anthology standard like many of the others, it was the poem's pedagogical role that ensured its cultural ubiquity. In retrospect, it almost seems as if Mrs. Hemans, with some uncanny sixth sense, had deliberately set out to fashion a poem uniquely suited to child recitation. Thanks to Elizabeth Bishop, we have already noticed that the boy who stands on the burning deck is directly analogous to the boy who stands on the classroom platform: both are meant to keep stock-still and perform their assigned tasks until the patriarch (parent or teacher) tells them that it is time to go. Just like brave Horatio at the bridge (the subject, in truncated form, as noted at the beginning of Part I, of another popular piece for children), the boys must stand alone in the face of doom. It is hard to decide whether the correspondence between the steadfast boy and the performing child occurred to the compilers of Victorian textbooks—certainly I have discovered no prefatory materials or editorial commentary to support such an idea— but whatever they may have felt about the poem, they seem to have seen enough of the right stuff in "Casabianca" to make it far and away the most anthologized work in all classes of nineteenth-century schoolroom readers. Presumably they were drawn to the poem's exciting mix of bravery, suspense, history (albeit history seen from the "wrong" side),[10] naval engagement, and a child hero—perhaps to some of the very elements that today might make us wary of placing this combustible piece anywhere close to delicate young minds. It is hard to take the time to work through "Casabianca" carefully: even with newly awakened expectations of the potential subtleties of Hemans's verse, one is liable to be swept along by the false memory of preexisting familiarity. But if we are able to perform this task, we are likely to conclude that this work is deeply unsuitable for juvenile perusal, let alone juvenile memorization.

Horror and violence saturate the poem. For most of its verses, we are directly encouraged to imagine the child's terror as the prospect of unimaginable pain and the impending sight and smell of his own burning flesh come closer and closer with the advance of the rolling, wreathing, streaming flames. Actually, it is much worse than this—because Hemans, that celebrated icon of devoted maternity and gentle femininity, tells us that the boy feels the "breath" of the flames "Upon his brow" and "in his waving hair," these fiery caresses become the poem's single, and singularly perverse, touches of the loving presence of a mother, a mother who may well be the narrator of the tale, but who is otherwise absent from the scene of action, and can do nothing to alter its outcome.[11] Of course, apparent parental abandonment lies at the heart of the boy's emotional torment, for the child, unaware that his father lies "faint in death below," believes, like Christ, that he has been forsaken.[12] All this is bad enough, but the worst is yet to come. When the flames finally reach the powder kegs, we must contemplate the blowing apart of the boy's entire body ("The boy—oh! where was he?"), its scattering up into the air and then down into the waves with all the other debris of the exploded ship. Then, most horrible of all, we return in the poem's last line to something that no longer exists. All the better to suffer its loss, its fragmentation, we focus at the end on the wholeness, the integrity of the life-center of that boy's being, his "young faithful heart." But just as "mast, and helm, and pennon fair" are now only bits of rope, wood, and cloth littering the disturbed waters of the Mediterranean, so too has that beating heart been blasted into muscle, tissue, valves, "heroic blood" and all, into now unrecognizable particles of humanity that have already dropped sizzling into the sea.

Such an exposition of the literal events of the poem may seem unnecessarily gory. I accept that "Casabianca," for most of its stanzas, wants us to think of courage, not *coeur*—of the stoutness of the heart rather than its vulnerability, its capacity to be destroyed. Perhaps it is anachronistic to imagine that our nineteenth-century forebears pictured the poem's visceral devastation in quite this degree of anatomical detail, but if they did, we should not for a moment assume that this would have made them hesitate to assign "Casabianca" to child readers. As discussed in Part I, there was a specific historical reason why verses able to represent the biblical story of noble martyrdom first appeared in the classroom reading books used in British mass education; Hemans's poem certainly furnishes a prime example of what I have already dubbed "Christ by other means." But for a fuller understanding of the prevailing pedagogical climate in which the apparent physical and psychological sadism of poem like "Casabianca" circulated, it is important to remember that in some respects, the religious culture of the nineteenth century operated according to norms that seem wholly alien to us today. Mrs. Sherwood's *History of the Fairchild Family* of 1818 is often cited for the casebook illustration of the mores of another world: this book, one of the most-read children's works of the nineteenth century, contains a grisly scene in which an earnest Evangelical father takes his young children to observe a corpse on a gibbet for their spiritual good. To be sure, attitudes towards the appropriate relationship between the child and the facts of mortality varied according to time and place. Nevertheless, it is fair to say that in the heyday of recitation, a poem's focus on disturbing themes, while not exactly a prerequisite for its inclusion in a reading series, was *not* a cause for its exclusion. Colin McGeorge's quantitative analysis of three widely used British and American series of school readers from the 1870s and 1880s demonstrates that between one-quarter and one-third of the pages in these texts make reference to death in some way, most frequently as a result of violence or war. Certainly some contemporary writers spoke out against gloomy preoccupations in juvenile literature: "Avoid dismal pieces," counseled the author of an 1891 handbook on recitation for teachers in public elementary schools; "young children should look to the light, not to the darkness" (Burrell, 83). But while gentle ditties like "Twinkle, Twinkle, Little Star," "My Mother," and "Hang Up Baby's Stocking" were well represented in volumes intended for the youngest of readers and reciters, the body count mounts up swiftly thereafter.

Part I has already made some observations about the constitution of the pedagogical recitation canon within Britain's public educational system, noting that the children therein would have been familiar with numerous morbid poems. While the ultrapatriotic utterances of poets like Kipling, Newbolt, and Henley eventually flooded in to swell the nation's increasingly imperialist image from the last decades of the nineteenth century on, the roll call already contained a number of doughty old stalwarts. Campbell's "Mariners of England" (1801) and "Hohenlinden" (1803) and Southey's "Battle of Blenheim" (1798) had been turning up for service for many years, appearing in such textbooks as Leitch's *Juvenile Reader* (1839), Douglas's *Selections for Recitation Compiled for the Use of Elementary Schools* (1869), and, from the 1870s onwards, in the numerous graded series from publishers like Chambers, Collins, Blackie, Bell, Nelson, Jarrold, and Cassell (Ellis, *Educating Our Masters*, 103–27). Away from mass education, upper-class scholars may well have spent three-quarters to four-fifths of their time on Latin and Greek and ancient history and geography, but, by the end of the century at least, when it came to the recitation of English verses, they too encountered the same martial standards, as Cornish's *Public School Speaker* (1900) attests.[13] But if old soldiers never die, then the young sailor was still more resilient: within school reading books for the full range of social classes, "Casabianca" is almost always present.[14]

And at what age did British children first make acquaintance with Mrs. Hemans's thirteen-year-old? As Part I explained, the Revised Code laid down its most comprehensive regulations for mandatory recitation within Britain's public elementary schools in 1882: from this point onwards a child in Standard II had to "repeat 40 lines of poetry, and to know their meanings." This was however the position in the graded readers from Chambers, Collins, Blackie, and others that the forty-line "Casabianca" had already been occupying for some years; the new requirement simply codified the prevailing assumption that the poem was fitting fare for the nation's eight-year-olds. There is no indication that the matching of this particular text to children of these tender years caused any disquiet to educators during Britain's recitational heyday. Indeed, the bond may seem relatively benign to us too if we compare it to other pedagogical choices that could be, and were, made. "Sometimes a teacher's enthusiasm led to rather inappropriate results," remembered a Sussex man of his state education in the first two decades of the twentieth century, "as at Harting Combe, where eight-year-olds in Standard II began to read Shakespeare and had to learn by heart the scene from *King John* where Arthur pleads with Hubert not to put out his eyes" (W. E. Palmer, 17, quoted in Burnett, *Destiny Obscure*, 159). An article from *The Teachers' Aid* in 1887 reveals that this particular instructor was not unusually sadistic. Advising teachers to think carefully about the choice of pieces that pupils will perform in their examinations, it urges its readers not to "select hackneyed ones. . . . it would be well to avoid 'Mark Anthony's oration' from *Julius Caesar*, and 'Heat me these irons hot'" (419–20).

There are undoubtedly elements of late Victorian and early Edwardian experience in British classrooms that still have the power to shock, or at least trouble, us. In the overall scheme of things, the fact that a few children might have had nightmares about imagined medieval eye-burning, or that boys and girls everywhere were regularly thumping out lines about blood and guts and fiery death, may seem neither here nor there. I certainly do not wish to make heavy weather of the potential psychological pain that could be caused by the internalization of disturbing literary material, nor, on the other side of things, to downplay the genuine pleasure that many children gained from the experience of recitation. Nevertheless, it seems only honest to point out that in common with many educational experiences in this period, the learning of a poem at school was generally a compulsory, not an elective, pursuit, and that the threat of physical pain could hang heavily over this compulsion. To put this more plainly (indeed, to call a cane a cane)—although we can probably find evidence of pockets of more enlightened educational policy, in which children were encouraged to learn through gentle and caring methods,[15] corporal punishment was an integral and unignorable part of British pedagogical practices, just as it was more generally of child-rearing practices, at all social levels throughout the nineteenth, and well into the twentieth, century. Both at home and at school, children received physical "correction" for a range of undesired behaviors and demeanors, from physical unruliness to laziness, from cheekiness to dumb insubordination. They also could be beaten—or threatened with beating—for the failure, or inability, to learn, or to complete an assigned task successfully.

It is perhaps a little too glib to assert that the boy who stands stammering because his attempt to recite a poem has just gone down in flames knows to his cost that learning by rote can be practically indistinguishable from learning by the rod. However, the atmosphere in which a poem like "Casabianca" would have been learned at school was invariably one that involved the child's body—not necessarily through overt physical punishment, but perhaps through the threat of it, or more likely, through the inevitable physiological symptoms that accompany the experience of public recitation in a testing environment. In seeking to understand this environment, and the child's reaction to it, I shall have recourse first to the patchy records of actual disciplinary behaviors in classrooms in this period, and second, to the scenes of pedagogical correction that occur with startling regularity in its contemporary fiction.

Corporal punishment was so widespread in British schooling in the nineteenth century that we should be warier than we have been about the precise application of some of Michel Foucault's ideas to Victorian society. Certainly the theory of power in the highly influential *Discipline and Punish* that argues that control of the populace becomes a question of mental, rather than bodily, practices in this period, is more obviously relevant to the situation south of the Channel than to the north, given that corporal punishment was repeatedly outlawed in French schools in the nineteenth century and a comprehensive ban eventually ratified in 1887.[16] In Britain, such a prohibition did not make its way through Parliament until 1986.[17] To speak more specifically about the practices of birching, caning, and so forth in British schools across the class spectrum, however, is surprisingly difficult, for there are few reputable historical studies of this phenomenon, and those accounts that do exist are bedeviled by two, often interlinked, factors. In the first place, they often have an uncomfortable tendency to slide towards pornography, and in the second, they frequently draw their supportive illustrations from sources that might reasonably be assumed to have a rather creative relationship to the real.[18] Nevertheless, there is enough hard evidence from the relatively sober testimonies within governmental, and also judicial, investigations, to convince us that "the English vice" is not mere flagellant fantasy.

It is often maintained that the nation's mania for beating was given prestige by Eton, Harrow, Westminster, and the other bastions of upper-class education, and then duly imitated elsewhere. French commissioners Demogeot and Montucci made the following report after visiting English public schools for Napoleon III in 1866:

> The whip . . . is one of those ancient English traditions which continue because they have continued. . . . A foreigner finds it difficult to conceive of the perseverance with which English teachers cling to this old and degrading custom. We have read in Dr. T. Arnold's works an eloquent dissertation in favour of flogging which has not in the least convinced us. Flogging is not fitting and not decent. One is astonished to see English teachers remove a garment which the prudery of their language hesitates even to name. (Quoted in Gibson, 66)

That the practice made its way down the social scale to the schools of the middle classes is readily apparent from the comments of Arnold *fils*, who, in the same year, makes clear his distaste for what was to him a savage abomination, and one that made his country embarrassingly anomalous in Europe. Writing with more hope than assurance, he argued that flogging "will more and more come to appear half-disgusting, half ridiculous, and a teacher will find it more and more difficult to inflict it without a loss of self-respect. The feeling on the continent is very strong on this point" (*Schools and Universities*, 113). Unfortunately, as British education progressively extended its empire over the working classes, it carried into the new dominions its tried and tested disciplinary techniques, so that the procedure Arnold despised was, if anything, more, rather than less, prevalent by the end of the century. "Every single teacher of every rank had his cane," wrote former teacher and subsequent inspector F. H. Spencer, reflecting back over pedagogical experiences that began in 1886.

"We used these canes, not often brutally, but commonly, without much discrimination and without scruple, indeed without thought" (73).[19]

Given the systemic nature of the phenomenon, and the lack of any truly systematic studies of its practice, it is hard to make a confident assertion that children were regularly beaten for the specific crime of failing to make an adequate recitation of an assigned poem. While "punishment books," daily logs kept by head teachers in state schools of names of offenders, nature of offenses, and meted punishment, were officially mandated from 1870 onwards, few have been saved, and, anyway, in the quotidian rush of school life, classification is necessarily a crude affair, and we can only assume that the headings "disobedience," "insubordination," "unsatisfactory work," or even plain "laziness" cover a multitude of sins. If we alter the angle of approach, however, and turn from the archive to the library of nineteenth-century fiction, we find a wealth of examples of the connection between failed child-performance and retributory corporal punishment. We should certainly think carefully about the status of such evidence in the context of an attempt to discover what "really" happened in any given classroom, but there are nevertheless benefits to be had from such a survey. One of these, as we shall see, is the opportunity to witness a particular literary genre mount a defamatory action upon the hegemonic sway of another, but we may also gain an useful sense of the affective experience of pedagogical beating, as it was represented to a readership who very likely had undergone, or witnessed, similar trials themselves.

Whatever type of punishment, whatever age or whichever sex of child, whatever level of school we are looking for, we can find it somewhere in the nineteenth-century novel. A tap with a ruler on the outstretched palm of the youngest board school infant; a dozen strokes from the bunch of twigs on the back of the girl's neck in the genteel charity institution; fifty stinging, lacerating lashes from a whipping willow switch on the buttocks of England's richest and highest-born sons—the beatings come thick and fast. "Torture in a public school is as much licensed as the knout [or whip] in Russia," claims the narrator of *Vanity Fair* (86), and certainly the names of Thackeray's preceptors—Dr. Swishtail, Dr. Birch, and so on—make the point with cutting brevity. Yet the upper echelons of education have no monopoly on pain and suffering in the period's fiction. In the lowest depths of Arthur Morrison's East End, school punishments may seem relatively puny compared to those meted out by fathers and policemen, but they are part of life, all the same: *Child of the Jago* Dicky Perrot gets "handers" (caning on the palms) at the Honey Lane Board School after copying answers from his neighbor's slate (86). Indeed, a novelistic episode of juvenile education that *doesn't* forge the bond between learning and hurting is the exception: the sentence "I am going to teach you a lesson" is far more likely to preface a sound thrashing than, for instance, a disquisition on the Norman Conquest or the physical geography of Greece. In *Jane Eyre*, the eponymous heroine may watch Helen Burns birched at Lowood for apparently "slatternly habits," for standing wrongly and not cleaning her nails (65), but the archetypal scene of child punishment in the Victorian novel follows the child's inability to complete his given task to his educator's satisfaction. In *David Copperfield*, the protagonist feels the weight of his stepfather's displeasure when he cannot remember his lessons:

> I hand the first book to mother. Perhaps it is a grammar, perhaps a history, or geography. I take a last drowning look at the page as I give it into her hand, and start off aloud at a racing pace while I have got it fresh. I trip over a word. Mr. Murdstone looks up. I trip over another word. Miss Murdstone looks up. I redden, tumble over half-a-dozen words, and stop. (103)

What then? A hurled book, a cuff to the head, then "a lithe and limber cane," and eventually the "fleshy cuts," "the double tooth," the "deep prong" of schoolmaster Creakle's daily floggings at Salem House (104, 106, 141). In the novel that bodies forth the muscular-Christian world of Thomas Arnold's Rugby, Tom Brown's school days are regularly punctuated by cuts and blows, but it is the mistranslation of two words in an oral examination that summons the beloved Doctor's rage:

> "Triste lupus, stabulis," began the luckless youngster, and stammered through some eight or ten lines.
> "There, that will do," said the Doctor; "now construe."
> On common occasions, the boy could have construed the passage well enough probably, but now his head was gone.
> "Triste lupus, the sorrowful wolf," he began.
> A shudder ran through the whole form, and the Doctor's wrath fairly boiled over; he made three steps up to the construer, and gave him a good box on the ear. The blow was not a hard one, but the boy was so taken by surprise that he started back; the form caught the back of his knees, and over he went on to the floor behind. (155)

When we narrow our focus from "failure to perform a given task" to "inadequate recitation" *per se*, then nineteenth-century fiction still has much to offer. Samuel Butler's autobiographical novel *The Way of All Flesh* presents one of the era's most devastating depictions of child punishment: four-year-old Ernest is thrashed by his home-schooling Evangelical father, the Reverend Theobald Pontifex. The intimate alliance between the acquisition of literacy and the infliction of pain is telegraphically signaled at the moment that the subject of the child's education is first introduced: "When Ernest was in his second year, Theobald . . . began to teach him to read. He began to whip him two days after he had begun to teach him" (120). The specific offense for which we see him beaten is mispronunciation—not, in this instance, in the recitation of a poem, but in the singing of a hymn. I quote the scene in full:

Ernest was to choose the first hymn, and he chose one about some people who were to come to the sunset tree. I am no botanist, and do not know what kind of tree a sunset tree is, but the words began, "Come, come, come; come to the sunset tree for the day is past and gone." The tune was rather pretty and had taken Ernest's fancy, for he was unusually fond of music and had a sweet little child's voice which he liked using.

He was, however, very late in being able to sound a hard "c" or "k," and, instead of saying "Come," he said "Tum, tum, tum."

"Ernest," said Theobald, from the arm-chair in front of the fire, where he was sitting with his hands folding before him, "don't you think it would be very nice if you were to say 'come' like other people, instead of 'tum'?"

"I do say tum," replied Ernest, meaning that he had said "come."

Theobald was always in a bad temper on Sunday evening. Whether it is that they are as much bored with the day as their neighbours, or whatever the cause may be, clergymen are seldom at their best on Sunday evening; I had already seen signs that evening that my host was cross, and was a little nervous at hearing Ernest say so promptly "I do say tum," when his papa had said he did not say it as he should.

Theobald noticed the fact that he was being contradicted in a moment. He got up from his arm-chair and went to the piano.

"No, Ernest, you don't," he said, "you say nothing of the kind, you say 'tum,' not 'come.' Now say 'come' after me, as I do."

"Tum," said Ernest, at once; "Is that better?" I have no doubt he thought it was, but it was not.

"Now, Ernest, you are not taking pains: you are not trying as you ought to do. It is high time you learned to say 'come,' why, Joey [his three-year-old brother] can say 'come,' can't you, Joey?"

"Yeth, I can," replied Joey, and he said something which was not far off "come."

"There, Ernest, do you hear that? There's no difficulty about it, nor shadow of difficulty. Now, take your own time, think about it, and say 'come' after me."

The boy remained silent for a few seconds and then said "tum" again.

I laughed, but Theobald turned to me impatiently and said, "Please do not laugh, Overton; it will make the boy think it does not matter, and it matters a great deal;" then turning to Ernest, he said, "Now, Ernest, I will give you one more chance, and if you don't say 'come,' I shall know that you are self-willed and naughty."

He looked very angry, and a shade came over Ernest's face, like that which comes upon the face of a puppy when it is being scolded without understanding why. The child saw well what was coming now, was frightened, and, of course, said "tum" once more.

"Very well, Ernest," said his father, catching him angrily by the shoulder, "I have done my best to save you, but if you will have it so, you will," and he lugged the little wretch, crying by anticipation, out of the room. A few minutes more and we could hear screams coming from the dining-room, across the hall which separated the drawing-room from the dining-room, and knew that poor Ernest was being beaten.

"I have sent him to bed," said Theobald, as he returned to the drawing room, "and now, Christina, I think we will have the servants in to prayers," and he rang the bell for them, red-handed as he was. (123–25)

If Butler's savage denunciation of a particular form of respectable Victorian domesticity concentrates its violence around the failed production of a single consonant, Thomas Mann's similarly autobiographical and contemporaneous exploration of bourgeois German life, *Buddenbrooks*, provides us with a comprehensive taxonomy of the scripts that the children of this comfortable merchant family must perform for their elders.[20] Indeed, the novel begins in the middle of a stalled recitation—"And—and—what comes next?"—for eight-year-old Antonie has stumbled in the midst of her catechism, always the urtext of child memorization, and must receive assistance from her mother: "Tony," prompted the Frau Consul, "'I believe that God'—" (7). Far more fortunate than Ernest, Tony picks up the thread:

Once more she repeated "What comes next?" and went on slowly; "'I believe that God'—" and then, her face brightening, briskly finished the sentence: "'created me, together with all living creatures.'" She was in smooth waters now, and rattled away, beaming with joy, through the whole Article. . . . When you were once fairly started, she thought, it was very like going down "Mount Jerusalem" with your brothers on the little sled: you had no time to think, and you couldn't stop even if you wanted to. (7)

Perched contentedly on her grandfather's knee, young Tony has no way of knowing that this ability to internalize her society's commandments will eventually doom her to a disastrous marriage, but *Buddenbrooks* makes it equally clear that the *inability* to get the text right, while bound to make you miserable at the time, will not deliver happiness or freedom in the long run either. The life of Tony's nephew Johann, or Hanno, is presented through a series of scenes of failed recitation, and although we do not see him suffer the same kind of physical punishment as poor Ernest, the psychological torments he endures are perhaps just as disturbing. As Tony's and Hanno's nurse stand over his bed and discuss the seven-year-old's unhappiness with the rigor of his new school ("Poor darling! Have they whipped him yet?"), the child sits bolt upright and, still sleeping, begins to recite. "He is saying his piece," explains his nurse, and proceeds to tell Tony about the agonies of grief the child experiences for the different figures—the "little man," "the nursery clock," "the waggoner"—which appear in the poems he must memorize from his reader, "The Boys' Magic Horn" (357–60). Later, when Hanno must perform in public on the occasion of the family firm's hundredth anniversary, the terrors that possessed him in the night are now visible in broad day:

> [H]e was to recite to Papa a poem learned painfully by heart, with Ida Jungmann's help, in the little balcony on the second floor. . . . He knew well what would happen. He would begin to cry, would not be able to finish for crying; and his heart would contract. . . .
>
> Hanno took up his position on the threshold of the living room and let his arms hang down. Obediently he raised his head, but his eyes—the lashes drooped so low that they were invisible. They were probably already swimming in tears.
>
> "This is the day of our—" he began, very low. His father's voice sounded loud by contrast when he interrupted: "One begins with a bow, my son. And then, much louder. Begin again, please: 'Shepherd's Sunday Hymn'"—
>
> It was cruel. The Senator was probably aware that he was robbing the child of the last remnant of his self-control. But the boy should not let himself be robbed. He should have more manliness by now. "Shepherd's Sunday Hymn" he repeated encouragingly, remorselessly.
>
> But it was all up with Hanno. His hand sank on his breast, and the small, blue-veined right hand tugged spasmodically at the brocaded portiere.
>
> "I stand alone on the vacant plain" he said, but could get no farther. The mood of the verse possessed him. An overmastering self-pity took away his voice, and the tears could not be kept back: they rolled out from beneath his lashes. . . . He put his head down on the arm with which he clung to the portiere, and sobbed.
>
> . . . "Well," said the Senator harshly, "there is no pleasure in that." He stood up, irritated. "What are you crying about? Though it is cer-

tainly a good enough reason for tears, that you haven't the courage to do anything, even for the sake of giving me a little pleasure. Are you a little girl? What will become of you if you go on like this? Will you always be drowning yourself in tears, every time you have to speak to people?"

"I never will speak to people, never!" thought Hanno in despair.[21] (375–76)

In comparison to these home horrors, Hanno's fears of school, of "catastrophes at the recitation hour," are relatively muted (491), and the next time we witness his enforced performance, the outcome is quite different. Now a fifteen-year-old at high school, Hanno escapes exposure when, thanks to a schoolfellow's judiciously placed open book, he is able to fake his recitation of the lines of Ovid that "were to have been learned by heart" for that day (544).[22] Although Hanno's school exerts discipline through a system of public humiliation and demerits rather than corporal punishment, the disjunction between the assigned passage's content and its deployment in the classroom is readily apparent:

With trembling voice, his face working, he read of the Golden Age, when truth and justice flourished of their own free will, without laws or compulsions. "Punishment and fear did not exist," he said in Latin. "No threats were graven upon the bronze tables, nor did those who came to petition fear the countenance of the judges . . ." (564)

All in all, *Buddenbrooks* counterpoints its dissection of a script-bound society with far more set pieces of destructive recitation than I can examine here (though I might just mention that tongue-tied Hanno, as he predicted, never does "speak to people, never," for he is laid in an early grave in the chapter that directly follows the painstaking anatomization of that overly regulated high-school day).

Mann may conduct the most thoroughgoing attack on the damaging psychological effects of enforced public performance for children, but, as should be more than apparent by now, he chooses a popular target. Two more examples, this time drawn from nineteenth-century American comic fiction, should push the point home, both extending the geographical and cultural boundaries of this particular investigation and bringing us back concretely to the memorized poem. Stephen Crane's ironically titled short story "Making an Orator" from the end of the nineteenth century shares *Buddenbrooks*'s concern for the long-term effects of mandatory recitation:

In the school at Whilomville [the tale begins] it was the habit, when children had progressed to a certain class, to have them devote Friday afternoon to what was called elocution. This was in the piteously ignorant belief that orators were thus made. By process of school law, unfortunate boys and girls were dragged up to address their fellow-scholars in the literature of the mid-century. Probably the children who were most capable of expressing themselves, the children who were most sensitive to the power of speech, suffered the most wrong. Little blockheads who could learn eight lines of conventional poetry and could get up and spin it rapidly at their classmates did not undergo a single pang. The plan operated mainly to agonize many children permanently against arising to speak their thought to fellow-creatures.[23] (625)

In the course of the story we witness Johnnie Tanner's dash through a parliamentary speech on the loyalty of the Irish regiments and Susie Timmens's blue-lipped and whispered reiteration that "she would be Queen of the May," while "the phlegmatic Trass boy . . . calmly spoke undeniably true words concerning destiny" (627). Readerly emotion, however, is focused on the plight of our hero, Jimmie Trescott, who instead of "eight lines of conventional poetry" is saddled with all fifty-five thundering strides of "The Charge of the Light Brigade" (625). Despite feigned illness, despite desires that the schoolhouse might erupt in flames, Jimmie must inevitably make his way to the stage at the front of the room, where "he bowed precariously, choked, made an inarticulate sound, and then . . . suddenly said 'Half a leg . . .'" (628). Four, five, six balked attempts later, the indignant, angry teacher finally acknowledges that Jimmie is never going to make the distance, and sends him back to his seat with the looming punishment of a detention, and a repeat performance the next Friday. In the minds of Jimmie and his sympathetic narrator, the whole experience is "worse than death," "a spectacle of . . . torture," akin to a "lamb brought to butchery," an "exhibition" no more "edifying than a dog-fight," and the children's bodies, accordingly, are "as pale as death," the pictures of "unnecessary suffering," and gripped with "ignoble pain" (625–29). For Jimmie, "on this day there had been laid for him the foundation of a finished incapacity for public speaking which would be his until he died" (629).

All this, and not a cane in sight. Conversely, Mark Twain's depiction of this pedagogical phenomenon some quarter of a century earlier in *The Adventures of Tom Sawyer* shows in no uncertain terms that the performance of reciting scholars on Examination Day is entirely backed up by both the threat and actuality of "rod and ferule" (131–38). By this stage in the text, we are already all too familiar with the "merciless flaying[s]" of schoolmaster Dobbins, and thus take our delight along with the pupils when, through a concatenation of rather improbable machinations, he is comprehensively humiliated in front of the entire audience, scholars, parents, dignitaries of the town and all (a captive cat, lowered down from the attic space above the platform, flails desperately in the air until her claws sink into, and then remove, the teacher's wig, revealing the glorious vision of the teacher's bald pate, which has been surreptitiously gilded, at an earlier moment of the master's drunken befuddlement, by the sign-painter's boy). The "terror and suffering" experienced by Dobbins's pupils ("Only the biggest boys, and young ladies of eighteen and twenty, escaped lashing. Mr Dobbins's lashings were very vigorous ones, too" [132]) is thus displaced from center stage by the altogether more humorous topic of their revenge, but we should not therefore discount the role that beating has played in the preparation of the "declamatory gems" for public performance. Both prose—Tom Sawyer's own choked rendition of "the unquenchable and indestructible 'Give me liberty or give me death' speech"—and, better represented, poetry, comes to us under the sign of the rod. And which poems? "You'd scarce expect one of my age to speak in public on the stage," "Mary Had a Little Lamb," "The Assyrian Came Down," and, of course, "The Boy Stood on the Burning Deck" (133).

From this plethora of examples (and I do not even venture into the obsessive repetition of schoolroom beatings in contemporary juvenile fiction and boys' own weeklies and annuals), I venture to make a couple of points. In his essay "Sparing the Rod: Discipline and Fiction in Antebellum America," Richard Brodhead argues persuasively that the prose fiction he examines "is singularly open to middle class disciplinary imaginings at this time not because the disciplinary is everywhere, but because of the way fiction's position as a cultural category is configured at this moment" (90). Which is to say, the novel of the period deliberately presents odious tableaux of "bodily correction" as part of a strategy to advance its own, differently organized "correctional model," one that makes "warmly embracing parental love the preferred instrument for authority's exercise" (92). While some adjustments must be made for the various national, cultural, and historical contexts of the works I have presented in the last few pages, Brodhead's explanation certainly offers a useful starting point for an examination of this topic. However, when the focus is narrowed from general pedagogical and parental beating to punishment for inadequate recitation, we might reasonably assume that the novel may have an additional, and equally self-interested, axe to grind. If the novel, as Brodhead claims, is keen to propagate the message that it offers a kinder, gentler mode of inculcating discipline within young people, might it not also be attacking the right of the short poem, and its compulsory memorization, to constitute the prime representation of "the literary" in elementary curricular programs of the developed Western world in the nineteenth century? There are many complex reasons why vernacular poetry becomes the preeminent literary genre once juvenile education begins to spread beyond the traditional tiny, classically trained, elite from the eighteenth century onwards (Guillory, 85–133), and there are also obvious practical factors, connected to straitened resources of time and money, why a forty-line poem constitutes a much more teachable entity than a four-hundred-page novel in all but the most utopian of classrooms. Nevertheless, the number of times that prose fiction chooses to lay into what it sees as the derived physical and psychological effects of the practice of poem memorization, and the ferocity of those attacks, suggests that there may well be a specific animus at work here.[24] As a genre that in the nineteenth century frequently opts to follow the full course of an individual's life, the novel might well be expected to reflect back upon what its readers would recognize as familiar childhood experiences, but the frequent bundling of pain and poem in its pages ought really to alert our suspicions.

While we are reflecting on how the pecking order between different genres in different eras and settings might determine the presentation of one sort of literature within another, we might start to think about how current rankings of past cultural forms affect the kinds of general conclusions we reach about those other times. Let us consider, for instance, the orthodoxy of the most significant account to date in Victorian studies of the prime relationship between the literary and the construction of subjectivities in this period. In a landmark essay (and explicitly the one on which Brodhead builds his particular edifice), D. A. Miller advanced the notion that the novel played a key role in drilling its nineteenth-century consumers "in the rhythms of bourgeois industrial culture": "Discipline in Different Voices: Bureaucracy, Police, Family and *Bleak House*" maintains that "the characteristic length" of the era's fiction trained the reader to engage and disengage, to accept and internalize the "close *imbrication* of individual and social, domestic and institutional, private and public, leisure and work" (83).

This elegant and compelling piece extends Foucault's argument about the pervasiveness of technologies of interiorized power in the period to suggest that the archetypal nineteenth-century fiction, in both its form and its content, constructs a self-regulating model of subjectivity for character and reader alike: "Discipline," as Mr. Bagnet of *Bleak House* is fond of stating, "must be maintained." But at least in the latter decades of the nineteenth century, the experience of novel reading came to an individual who had *already* received a comprehensive schooling in quite a different discipline, quite a different relationship between the literary and the self, and one that involved the concept of rhythm in a far more direct manner. Because we have lost sight of this pedagogical history, and because, with some important exceptions, the practitioners of Victorian studies tend to think and write about the novel as the primary, synecdochal genre of the period, the role of the memorized poem as a tool of culture has not been adequately explored. However seriously or lightly we wish to take the novel's charges about the connection between the poem and the infliction of actual bodily punishment, we know enough from other, less interested, sources to assert the following: the learning and performing of poetry was a common part of nineteenth-century childhood, and it was, from the first to the last, a corporeal experience.

I am not interested in suggesting that there is any simple, causal relationship between the beat of the line and the beat of the cane. Neither do I wish to follow the route pioneered by such critics as James R. Kincaid and Eve Sedgwick who, with Swinburne as patron saint, and the Freud of "A Child Is Being Beaten" as resident theorist, intimate that when beating, children and literature are present, then sexual excitement must be there too—whether in the person or persons of the flogger, the floggee, or the gentle reader. Instead I feel constrained to tell the tale of a less titillating, and, I suspect, much more widely felt experience—a soberer story in which the threat or the reality of corporal punishment did not send the mass of juvenile memorizers on a thrilling side-trip to sexual arousal, but were linked to quite a different set of physical sensations. The child's acquisition of the literary at school was a corporeal experience inasmuch as the anticipation, and then the actuality, of performance would likely be attended by the fear, or at least the anxiety, of failure—and thus palpitations, clammy palms, shaking legs, and pounding hearts were part and parcel of the genre in a testing environment. As we shall discover in the next case study, those children who, conversely, found distinct pleasure in their recitations—in the extraordinary richness and intensity of poetic language, and their own competence therewith—would nevertheless also be caught up into a heightened state of physical awareness. Throughout the subsequent course of an individual's life, too, the poem inhabited the body in a manner that is now hard to comprehend, or indeed, substantiate—for many, the memorized poem lurked deep within the self, ready to be called up not so much by a conscious act of rational retrieval, as by simply allowing the body to utter what the body stored, in a state that approached something like a trance.[25] I am thus claiming (and now I draw closer to the topic of meter) that the compulsorily memorized poem inserted itself into an individual and established its beat in sympathy with, or in counterpoint to, his or her own preexisting bodily rhythms. When an era's people learned poetry by heart, then, their relationship to measured language—and especially to regular meter—carried a distinct, corporeal difference from that experienced by readers of other, alternatively disciplined, ages.

Thus, while we may wish to agree with Miller's thesis that the Victorians were undergoing training through their on/off novel reading in the new rhythms of their culture, this notion must be underpinned by a recognition that these individuals had *already* learned a far more fundamental lesson from the bodily discipline of poetry. As readers in the late twentieth and early twenty-first centuries, our continuity with Victorian consumers of novels is not so hard to conceptualize: we too alternate between periods of happy isolated immersion in satisfyingly fat books and necessary stints in the bustle of everyday affairs, for we too, like those first inhabitants of the industrialized age, understand our lives as a series of hours meted out between private and public, leisure and work. When we read poetry, however, there are few lines connecting us to the memorizing population of long ago. Because that particular technology of dissemination fell out of pedagogical favor, we now find it hard to appreciate the special relationship between body and poem that was created by a highly structured set of circumstances.

Any attempt we might make to understand that alliance, however, has been hampered by the issue raised in the introduction: many of the poems that formed one side of the bond became for many years bywords for the very worst kind of poetry. It is now possible to see that this rejection was an aftereffect of the long-prevailing system of mass recitation in education's least prestigious venue, but recognition of this fact was blocked for decades by literary criticism's general refusal to admit that its standards of adjudication were related to the historical conditions of a work's production and reception. As previously outlined, thanks to numerous paradigm shifts, "Casabianca" is no longer a self-evidently "bad" poem and today has a place in the academic canon. I would argue, however, that this work's recuperation has been achieved not through an understanding of its specific institutional travails in a defined period, but by means of two other, by now highly familiar, strategies. Initially the work was restored to us as an item of interest because of the social identity of its author, and then, as a follow-on, through a variety of theoretical approaches that have opened up numerous opportunities for the exploration of its proclaimed or tacit ideological messages.

Thus "Casabianca" is currently fascinating to critics because of Hemans's adroit, indeed antinationalist and feminist, critique; because she writes a poem about one of the British navy's and ultra-British hero Admiral Nelson's greatest victories from the perspective of a lone (and young) Corsican midshipman; because in an age of masculine imperialism she devotes a mother's care to the individual, to the doomed child. Others applaud Hemans's unflinching depiction of the waste of war; her refusal to end the poem with a transcendent vision that would turn the child's corpse through art "into something rich and strange"; the honesty of her final vision of fragmentation.[26] There again, it appears to another critic that Hemans speaks as an advocate of empire, that her "powerful, unstable fusion of domestic and military values" restores "military endeavor to its originary purity and innocence" (Lootens, "Hemans and Home, 241). Whatever the tack, though, and to whatever degree that these interpretations might repeat, or contradict, the opinions of nineteenth-century readers, the redesignation of "Casabianca" as an object of legitimate scholarly interest has been achieved through attention to its semantic content, and an analysis of that meaning in relation to different historical contexts and values—primarily those in play at the time of the poem's composition, and those that inform critical perspectives today.

What these readings have rarely done, however, is attempt to consider the *form* of this poem in relation to changing contexts. Such attempts in nineteenth-century studies are far outweighed by considerations of the forms of prose fiction, which, it seems, is assumed to exist in a more dynamic conjunction to social and cultural shifts.[27] When investigations of this type are, however, conducted on a poetic text, effort is usually expended to position a poet and his or her stanzaic or metrical choices within literary history, rather than history more generally considered. Thus, in the case of "Casabianca," if the topic is touched upon at all, it is probably to note that Hemans employs a traditional folk-song measure, and perhaps to gesture towards the ballad revival movement that gathered strength after the publication of Bishop Percy's *Reliques of Ancient English Poetry* in 1765, and encouraged both antiquarian collection of time-honored standards and the widespread appropriation of its stanzaic patterns by poets in the Romantic era.[28] Yet the minute particulars of Hemans's deployment of this form's meter are generally ignored[29]—presumably because it is assumed that there is little to say, or worse, because we fear that the only thing we could say would plunge us into a quagmire of adjudication. After all, if we know anything about "Casabianca," we know it is a "ti-dum ti-dum ti-dum ti-dum" poem—and at some deep level of our being, we believe that this is self-evidently—and eternally—a bad thing: after all, is it not axiomatic that successful, or strong, poets deviate from the set rhythm of a given line, while weak poets stick to it? It is my contention, however, that it is exactly this "ti-dum ti-dum" factor that we need to examine and to reunderstand in relation to history. And I believe that the historical context we must consider is not the moment that Felicia Hemans sat down to write a poem, but the subsequent experience of her work in the mouths and bodies of thousands of children in the nineteenth and early twentieth centuries. By examining how a pedagogical practice both embraced and then overemphasized consistent rhythm, we shall come closer to understanding not only the fall of "Casabianca," but also one of the special sources of twentieth-century antipathy to formal regularity, an antipathy we have tended to believe is free from historical or ideological conditioning. For purposes of clarity, I shall confine my attention primarily to the topic of meter, despite the fact that the history of our changing attitudes towards rhyme offers equally rich food for thought.[30]

Given that memorization of literary material became a standard element of Victorian curricular design, it is not surprising that the texts that were most frequently assigned tended to be those written in closed forms, those that manifested regular rhythmic patterns and consistent rhyme schemes. Such poems at least gave a fighting chance of successful recitation to the largest number of children, children who would inevitably manifest a wide range of abilities. Although like Elizabeth Bishop we might well see an ominous or ironic connection between the topic of child torture within "Casabianca" and the experience of its recitation, the truth of the matter is that a child in Standard II, say in 1882 in a board school in Manchester, would think itself a deal luckier to be assigned Mrs. Hemans's poem than, say, forty lines of *Macbeth*. It was hard mental and physical labor to memorize and perform "Casabianca," but better that than many other texts—whether you love or hate its "message" (if we can decide what that is), you cannot deny that it is thrilling and exciting, and has a boy hero with whom to identify—a feature perhaps of more significance to our hypothetical Lancastrian child than to us. True, its narrative could have a stronger forward thrust, but once you get past the maddening near-repetitions of the boy's three utterances, it is mostly plain sailing. Furthermore, its diction is relatively uncomplicated. Despite that strange foreign polysyllabic title (which, in any case, none but the superliterate know, or connect with the poem, which suggests that many reciting children did not have to state it, or promptly forgot it if they did), 86 percent of the words in the poem are monosyllables and 13 percent disyllables. This leaves only three "hard" words ("beautiful," "heroic," and "unconscious," significantly enough), while in the semantic sense, the only "difficult" linguistic items are "chieftain," "gallant," and "pennon"— words that might not have been that unfamiliar to eight-year-olds forced to ingest archaisms on a regular basis. But much more to the point, "Casabianca" is relatively easy to memorize because of its form.

As noted, the poem is written in the standard closed ballad stanza, also known as common (or short) measure, which is to say, quatrains consisting of alternating iambic tetrameter and trimeter lines, and rhyming abab. When Wordsworth stated in the preface to his *Lyrical Ballads* that meter works to soothe our pain, he probably was not implying that a regular rhythm might help a reciting child escape the chastisement of the rod (260–61), but the fact remains that the ballad stanza does help us out with some intrinsic *aide-mémoire* features. It is of course hard to make absolute distinctions here between those elements of the genre that are inherently easy to remember, and those that we assimilate more quickly simply because they resemble the form of materials we have already committed to memory, but it is fair to say that the rhymed quatrain constitutes the most familiar organization of patterned language in English, and that it has a long history both as a sung and a spoken form.[31] Usually organized as one divided sentence, or two sentences with a natural pivot or place for breath, the quatrain is long enough to paint a discrete scene; to express a contained thought; to feature dialogue in the form of question and response; or to describe a narrative movement; but not long enough to permit much complicated elaboration. And while rhymed couplets close in upon themselves and offer no convenient bridge to the succeeding lines, an alternate rhyming scheme helps to lead us forward. Above all, the regular pattern of four iambs, three iambs, four iambs, three iambs offers tremendous security. Built from accumulations of the most familiar foot, the heartbeat of English poetry, the tetrameter/trimeter combination also seems to have established its supremacy as the most memorable form through a couple of other features. In the first place, a pattern of alternating line lengths seems easier to keep in order in our heads than a series of potentially interchangeable same-length lines; in the second, the relative shortness of both the tetrameter and the trimeter lines makes it more probable that absolute regularity of meter will be maintained. Or, to put it another way, the author of a poem has less scope for variation in a four- or three-beat line than in, for instance, a line of iambic pentameter. The form that Felicia Hemans chose for "Casabianca," then, was inherently a form that would be unlikely to deviate from its prescribed duty.

But here's the rub. It is not actually true to say that Hemans wrote a poem with an absolutely regular unvarying meter. The rhythm is certainly consistent enough to make the poem that necessary thing, a work that could be memorized by a diverse population, but what happened, I believe, is that "Casabianca" *became* an ultraregular poem, and thus a byword for unthinking jog-trot meter, through that very process of constrained and unthinking recitation that we have been examining. Because meter aids the process of memorization, meter becomes the dominant force whenever a poem has to be committed to memory, and will, if necessary, triumphantly overthrow the meaning of a line. This is readily apparent once we consider the performance history of "Casabianca's" very first words, which are, as we have noted, often the poem's only surviving fragment. Hemans opened her poem with an irregular line, a line that places its second strong stress on the word "stood": "The BOY STOOD on the BURNing DECK." If mimetic meter—meter that enacts or resembles the action or thing described—is a feature of the work of "good" poets, then Hemans earns her stripes, for here we are pulled up short by two adjacent stresses, and movement is arrested in the line just as it is for the boy, who is quite literally going nowhere. And yet who, outside the hypereducated elite, actually says it in this way? Half-knowledge of the words as a derided remnant of another age, or the beginning of something like a smutty limerick, dictates that a singsong rhythm override the sense of the line, and so most British people, at least, would chant "The BOY stood ON the BURNing DECK." How would a child in a state of bodily anxiety have recited it? Not slowly, not with feeling, not thinking about how to fit sense to the syllables, meaning to the meter—instead, when you've got to get through something, you gallop along with your eyes on the finishing post, with no desire to introduce significant pauses or reversed stresses or indeed anything that might hamper the progress of your thumping hooves. When he finally made it to the end, would not the reciting boy also be likely to murder the tender pathos of Hemans's final irregular, meditative stress on "that YOUNG FAITHful HEART" by chucking in for good measure his own unstressed "and" between "young" and "faith" to regularize, and thus speed up, the line?

The point I am making is this: "Casabianca" has come to be remembered as a poem with uniform meter because of the particular circumstances of its assimilation into a culture. Poems that were already fairly regular, and thus suitable for a certain practice, became more and more so through that practice. Once individuals were no longer put through this specific pedagogical mill, and thus "forgot" why unvarying rhythm had been such a necessary and desirable element therein, then the particular poems that had been worn out in its service became pariahs. Now, too, there was additional force behind scholarly disparagement of metrical regularity in the abstract. Generally derided in theoretical discussions of prosody over the years, uniform meter in the twentieth century carried the extra burden of all those barely educated nineteenth-century recitations. A regular poem has typically been perceived as a bad poem, a lying poem, a false poem: "regularity we feel is meaningless and irregularity meaningful," says Cunningham (163); "we must reject effects of appliqued metrical regularity" agrees Fussell (*Poetic Meter*, 91). It is of course far more accurate to say that a regular poem is a low-status poem, but because academic literary studies have forgotten the history of pedagogical recitation, this fact has not been on the table for discussion.

Suffice it to say that the decks were absolutely stacked against Mrs. Hemans's boy: history brought in its revenges against a poem that had for a time represented the essence, the acme of "the literary" to a large and diverse constituency. "Casabianca" was in a sense sent back to where it came from, to the place of popular song, to the ballad's natural home with the folk. Even now when fashions have changed and Felicia (no longer Mrs.) Hemans is warmly invited back into the room, the cut of her measures has been decorously ignored because of our intact belief that her poem doesn't quite make it in that department. After all, great poems achieve "organic meter" and effect "prosperous departures" from external form. But, as we have seen, poets do not have control over the journeys their works make over the years; over how their poems are read, and by whom; over the circumstances of acquisition, performance, and retention. "Casabianca" simply could not be that ubiquitous, recited that many times by so many individuals—willing or unwilling, proficient or incompetent—without undergoing certain processes of exaggeration, overfamiliarization, and ultimate rejection.

◆ ◆ ◆

If "Casabianca" is not as regular as it became, in a metrical sense, then neither is its relationship to historical record quite as straightforward as one might imagine. I have deliberately devoted most of this chapter to the poem's life and times in the heyday of British recitation. I wish now to draw back, if not exactly to the events of August 1, 1798, then to the closest approximations thereof that we can find in the various accounts of what happened on the fateful night when the Battle of the Nile culminated in the deafening explosion of the French flagship *L'Orient*. This, claims Brian Lavery in his definitive study *Nelson and the Nile: The Naval War against Bonaparte 1798* was "the first battle of annihilation in maritime history . . . the finish of the French Navy as a force capable of counterbalancing British power . . . [an event that] carried within itself the germ of Trafalgar" (302).[32] Of the seventeen French ships in the conflict, only four survived, and while only 895 British sailors were killed or wounded, the defeated force lost over 5,000 men. Reports by those present, written in dispatches, letters, logs, and memoirs, published immediately thereafter or at some point in the following century, concur on the general sequence of moves made by the two squadrons in the shoals of Aboukir Bay, although all specify a different moment (some point in the evening between 9:37 and 11:30) when the mighty 120-gun ship finally blew up. Raking shots from the *Alexander*, a British ship, had started a fire in the stern cabin of *L'Orient*, which rapidly spread across its decks. (Had tins of paint been left lying around in "true French carelessness," as Admiral Sir George Elliot would have it in his memoirs, published some sixty-five years after he had stood aghast on the deck of the *Vanguard* as a young midshipman? [quoted in Lavery, 196]. Other British accounts tend to think so.) The heat from the flames was so intense that it began to melt the tar between the planks of the *Swiftsure*, and, aware of the danger of the powder magazines igniting, this ship, like all the others in the vicinity, began to retreat as rapidly as it could. From the *Goliath*, purser Samuel Grant saw "the French three decker in a blaze to the water's edge very near to us. It was the most melancholy but at the same time the most beautiful sight I ever beheld" (quoted in Lavery, 198). When the flames finally reached the magazines, the ship exploded, wrote Chaplain Wyllyams, "with a crashing sound that deafened all around her. The tremendous motion, felt to the very bottom of each ship, was like that of an earthquake. The fragments were driven such a vast height into the air that some moments elapsed before they could descend" (quoted in Lavery, 199). Nearby, the *Franklin* was showered with burning debris, "red-hot pincers, pieces of timber and rope on fire"; nine miles away on land in Alexandria, the staff of General Kleber saw "a bright flame rising rapidly through the air. The flame became thicker and in a moment it turned into a black smoke, across which, for several minutes, sparks of light were visible" (quoted in Lavery, 199).

But the boy—oh! where was he? Or rather, where had he been? The chances are he hadn't been standing on that burning deck. In fact, none of the extant accounts place him in that lone post of death in still yet brave despair, nor was his father, it seems, faint in death below. Wolfson gives the commonly held belief in her notes to "Casabianca" that Hemans's "likely source, but with revisions" for information about the battle was Robert Southey's tremendously popular *Life of Horatio Lord Nelson* (first published in 1813, and frequently reissued).[33] With revisions indeed, for after his wonderfully paced account of the battle, Southey's only two sentences about the topic run as follows: "Among the many hundreds who perished, were the commodore, Casa-Bianca, and his son, a brave boy only ten years old. They were seen floating on the wreck of a mast when the ship blew up" (154). But might Hemans have been privy to different versions of the story? Her brothers and her husband were army, not navy, men who in later years fought against Napoleon's forces on land rather than sea, but perhaps they heard tales from other, and earlier, theaters of war. Certainly a variant account of the fate of young Casabianca appeared in the memoirs of Sir John Theophilus Lee (quoted in Warner, 87–88). These were printed in 1836, just a year after Hemans's death, but his story of that famous night might possibly have been in circulation ten years earlier when she wrote her poem. And yet Lee's narrative tells a tale that, if anything, is even further removed from Hemans's vision than Southey's picture of father and son clinging to the wreckage together. Recalling a time when he himself was barely eleven years old and the *Swiftsure*'s midshipman, Sir John does not grant us an image of a proud, though childlike form standing in noble isolation on the deathstrewn deck as he waits for his father's word. Instead, the scene that Lee paints has a different kind of pathos, for it replaces the boy's gallant beauty with pitiful mutilation; a child who will not move with a child who cannot move; and paternal abandonment with paternal care:

The son of Casabianca had lost a leg, and was below with the surgeon, but the father could not be prevailed upon to quit the ship even to save his own life, preferring to die beside his son rather than leave him wounded, and a prey to the flames, thus placing parental affection in a most trying and awful situation, as if to show the extremities to which it may be carried. (Warner, 88)

Now it is certainly true that Lee here describes a scene below deck that he could not have seen himself (and indeed, his view of the events *upon* the burning decks was not continuous, for he was sent at a crucial moment to "bring a few bottles of ginger beer from the cabin locker" for his commander Captain Hallowell and other senior officers [quoted in Warner, 87]), but we do know that the *Swiftsure* managed to pick up eleven of the *L'Orient*'s seventy survivors (this from a crew of over a thousand men), and thus he had had the opportunity to meet true eyewitnesses. But what of it, after all? In the battle of representations of the Battle of the Nile, Hemans and her boy undoubtedly carry off the spoils. This fact was made transparently clear some twelve years after the publication of Lee's *Memoirs*, when a certain Captain Plunkett issued his translation of the French Captain E. Jurien de la Gravière's text *Sketches of the Last Naval War*. "At ten o'clock an explosion, which shook the surrounding ships and covered them with the flaming wreck, announced to both fleets that the *Orient* was no more," runs de la Gravière's sober record, but at this point Plunkett sees fit to add his own footnote:

The following lines upon the death of young Casa Bianca, who was a midshipman in the Orient, commanded by his father Commodore Casa Bianca, under Admiral Brueys, struck the translator as so beautiful, that he inserts them:— (198)

And there stands "The boy stood on the burning deck" in its entirety.

Of course, whatever version of the story inspired Felicia Hemans to pick up her pen, poetic license then afforded her a time-honored right to reimagine the scene in whatever ways she wished within her verse; appending an explanatory historical sentence or two to a literary text was also a well-established convention, and one particularly dear to her own practice. When we peruse this note, however, it is perhaps not its large-scale deviation that is most surprising. Hemans's apparently inaccurate insistence therein that the boy "remained at his post" is of course the work's controlling conceit; without this revisioning of this scene of naval history there would be no poem, or at least, not this poem. But what about the other, less consequential, alterations? It would seem wrong to read much into the tiny error that makes Casabianca's father the admiral, rather than the commodore, of the ship, but how should we understand the transformation of the child from a ten-year-old boy, as in all the sources, into one "about thirteen years old"? Is this a mere slip of the pen?

In 1826 Hemans was surrounded by boys, for she had five sons, and at this point had effectively been their only parent for eight years. Shortly before the birth of his last child, her husband had decamped to Italy "for his health," never to return again and never to provide any support for his family (Hemans, ed. Wolfson, xxi–xxvi). Living with her mother in rural Wales, and helped to some extent by her sister and brothers, Hemans was nevertheless the main financial provider, always fighting to find enough space and time to write the poems that kept them living at a reasonable standard of gentility. "I have been pursued by the household troops through every room successively," she wrote wearily to a friend when the boys were three, five, six, seven, and ten years of age, "and begin to think of establishing my *metier* in the cellar . . . When you talk of tranquillity and a quiet home, I stare about in wonder, having almost lost the recollection of such things, and the hope that they may probably be regained some time or another" (Hemans, ed. Wolfson, 486). Constantly on call to the needs of her family and their "incessant clatter of obstreperous sound," Hemans at the same time knew that the day would come when her boys would "long for, and be launched into, another world to the green fields in which they are now contented to play around me" (quoted in Chorley, 1:143). When she silently changed Casabianca's age from ten to thirteen, her oldest son Arthur was himself thirteen. Once she had conjured up her vision of the child's desperate plight, was it just too painful to visit this punishment on a boy of any tenderer years, on a mere slip of a lad? Did Arthur stand for all boys, for all *her* boys? Did his bravery in the face of his father's desertion give strength to the boy on the burning deck? It is impossible to know, of course, and although one could certainly speculate about the wider meaning of the abandoned child or the significance of the courageous boy in Hemans's life and work more generally, I choose not to make that move here.[34] Instead, I close this case study with a vision of all the children that take their places in this particular history—not just the young Corsican boy Giacomo Jocante de Casabianca, but also those other ten- and eleven-year-olds, George Elliot and John Lee, who had the luck to be standing on the decks of British ships on August 1, 1798, and thus lived to tell the tale. And not just thirteen-year-old Arthur Hemans, but eleven-year-old George, ten-year-old Claude, nine-year-old Henry, and eight-year-old Charles too. And most of all, perhaps, all those nameless boys and girls who at one time mounted a wooden platform and recited "The boy stood on the burning deck."

"I have always . . . written," confessed Felicia Hemans in a letter to a friend a couple of months before her death, "as if in the breathing times of storms and billows" (quoted in Chorley, 2:212–13). At an earlier moment she had expressed the hope that she would prove that "the *discipline of storms* has, at least, not been without purifying and ennobling influence" (2:285). Hemans had no way of knowing that out of the thousands of lines she composed in her short life, one short poem would cause countless children to catch their breath and experience the discipline of poetry in every vibrating fiber of their little bodies. On the topic of her own physical health, the poet believed her "greatest foe" to be "'the over-beating of the heart'" (Hemans, ed. Kelly, 441). Critic Ian Jack also made a cardiological diagnosis in 1963 when his survey *English Literature 1815–1832* opined that Mrs. Hemans "took the pulse of her time and helped to prevent it from quickening." "The general level of her work is high," he continued, "but unfortunately it almost always stops short of memorable poetry" (168). These words would have made little sense to the boy who had felt "Casabianca" through the rapid beats of his young (though not necessarily faithful) heart.

Thomas Gray, "Elegy Written in a Country Churchyard"

The curfew tolls the knell of parting day,
    The lowing herd wind slowly o'er the lea,
The ploughman homeward plods his weary way,
    And leaves the world to darkness and to me.

Now fades the glimmering landscape on the sight,
    And all the air a solemn stillness holds,
Save where the beetle wheels his droning flight,
    And drowsy tinklings lull the distant folds;

Save that from yonder ivy-mantled tow'r
    The moping owl does to the moon complain
Of such as, wand'ring near her secret bow'r,
    Molest her ancient solitary reign.

Beneath those rugged elms, that yew-tree's shade,
    Where heaves the turf in many a mould'ring heap,
Each in his narrow cell for ever laid,
    The rude Forefathers of the hamlet sleep.

The breezy call of incense-breathing Morn,
    The swallow twitt'ring from the straw-built shed,
The cock's shrill clarion, or the echoing horn,
    No more shall rouse them from their lowly bed.

For them no more the blazing hearth shall burn,
    Or busy housewife ply her evening care:
No children run to lisp their sire's return,
    Or climb his knees the envied kiss to share.

Oft did the harvest to their sickle yield,
    Their furrow oft the stubborn glebe has broke:
How jocund did they drive their team afield!
    How bow'd the woods beneath their sturdy stroke!

Let not Ambition mock their useful toil,
    Their homely joys, and destiny obscure;
Nor Grandeur hear with a disdainful smile
    The short and simple annals of the poor.

The boast of heraldry, the pomp of pow'r,
    And all that beauty, all that wealth e'er gave,
Awaits alike th' inevitable hour:
    The paths of glory lead but to the grave.

Nor you, ye Proud, impute to These the fault,
    If Memory o'er their Tomb no Trophies raise,
Where through the long-drawn aisle and fretted vault
    The pealing anthem swells the note of praise.

Can storied urn or animated bust
    Back to its mansion call the fleeting breath?
Can Honour's voice provoke the silent dust,
    Or Flatt'ry soothe the dull cold ear of death?

Perhaps in this neglected spot is laid
    Some heart once pregnant with celestial fire;
Hands, that the rod of empire might have sway'd,
    Or waked to ecstasy the living lyre.

But Knowledge to their eyes her ample page
    Rich with the spoils of time did ne'er unroll;
Chill Penury repress'd their noble rage,
    And froze the genial current of the soul.

Full many a gem of purest ray serene
    The dark unfathom'd caves of ocean bear:
Full many a flower is born to blush unseen,
    And waste its sweetness on the desert air.

Some village Hampden that with dauntless breast
    The little tyrant of his fields withstood,
Some mute inglorious Milton here may rest,
    Some Cromwell guiltless of his country's blood.

Th' applause of list'ning senates to command,
    The threats of pain and ruin to despise,
To scatter plenty o'er a smiling land,
    And read their history in a nation's eyes,

Their lot forbade: nor circumscribed alone
    Their glowing virtues, but their crimes confined;
Forbade to wade through slaughter to a throne,
    And shut the gates of mercy on mankind,

The struggling pangs of conscious truth to hide,
    To quench the blushes of ingenuous shame,

Or heap the shrine of Luxury and Pride
    With incense kindled at the Muse's flame.

Far from the madding crowd's ignoble strife,
    Their sober wishes never learn'd to stray;
Along the cool sequester'd vale of life
    They kept the noiseless tenor of their way.

Yet ev'n these bones from insult to protect
    Some frail memorial still erected nigh,
With uncouth rhymes and shapeless sculpture deck'd,
    Implores the passing tribute of a sigh.

Their name, their years, spelt by th' unletter'd muse,
    The place of fame and elegy supply:
And many a holy text around she strews,
    That teach the rustic moralist to die.

For who, to dumb Forgetfulness a prey,
    This pleasing anxious being e'er resign'd,
Left the warm precincts of the cheerful day,
    Nor cast one longing ling'ring look behind?

On some fond breast the parting soul relies,
    Some pious drops the closing eye requires;
Ev'n from the tomb the voice of Nature cries,
    Ev'n in our Ashes live their wonted Fires.

For thee, who, mindful of th' unhonour'd dead,
    Dost in these lines their artless tale relate;
If chance, by lonely contemplation led,
    Some kindred spirit shall inquire thy fate,

Haply some hoary-headed Swain may say,
    'Oft have we seen him at the peep of dawn
Brushing with hasty steps the dews away
    To meet the sun upon the upland lawn.

'There at the foot of yonder nodding beech
    That wreathes its old fantastic roots so high,
His listless length at noontide would he stretch,
    And pore upon the brook that babbles by.

'Hard by yon wood, now smiling as in scorn,
    Mutt'ring his wayward fancies he would rove,
Now drooping, woeful wan, like one forlorn,
    Or crazed with care, or cross'd in hopeless love.

'One morn I miss'd him on the custom'd hill,
 Along the heath and near his fav'rite tree;
Another came; nor yet beside the rill,
 Nor up the lawn, nor at the wood was he;

'The next with dirges due in sad array
 Slow through the church-way path we saw him borne.
Approach and read (for thou canst read) the lay
 Graved on the stone beneath yon aged thorn:'

THE EPITAPH.

Here rests his head upon the lap of Earth
 A Youth to Fortune and to Fame unknown.
Fair Science frown'd not on his humble birth,
 And Melancholy mark'd him for her own.

Large was his bounty, and his soul sincere,
 Heav'n did a recompense as largely send:
He gave to Mis'ry all he had, a tear,
 He gain'd from Heav'n ('twas all he wish'd) a friend.

No farther seek his merits to disclose,
 Or draw his frailties from their dread abode,
(There they alike in trembling hope repose,)
 The bosom of his Father and his God.

"Three cheers for mute ingloriousness!": Cultural Capital and the Scholarship Boy

> The best boy in a good school told me a few days ago, on being asked the meaning of the word "mansion," which occurred in his repetition,—"Please, sir, it isn't in the notes."
>
> Report of Her Majesty's Inspector Mr. Boyle, 1876 (439)

> When I think of all those of good intelligence left behind stage by stage I feel like echoing Granville-Barker: "Oh, the waste of [them] . . . oh, the waste, the waste!" Or even more strongly, Empson: "The waste remains, the waste remains and kills." Still today we should say that, far more than we wish to recognise.
>
> Richard Hoggart, *A Local Habitation, 1918–40,* 1988 (181)

At the age of fifty-one, having received the nomination for the presidency of the United States at the 1860 Republican National Convention,

Abraham Lincoln found himself besieged by requests for information about his formative years. According to his onetime law partner William H. Herndon, Lincoln was unwilling to make himself the subject of any extended study and "deprecated the idea of writing even a campaign biography" (2). In response to a plea from a journalist on the *Chicago Tribune*, the presidential candidate is said to have expressed himself in the following manner:

> Why, Scripps, it is a great piece of folly to attempt to make anything out of me or my early life. It can all be condensed into a single sentence, and that sentence you will find in Gray's Elegy,
> "The short and simple annals of the poor."
>   That's my life, and that's all you or anyone else can make out of it. (2)

As things were to turn out, Lincoln hugely underestimated the powers of biographers and historians to make a great deal out of his life, including his first seven years in Knob Creek, Kentucky, and the subsequent fourteen-year stretch in Spenser County, Indiana. Within these early periods, Lincoln's scant formal education often proves of particular interest: every possible detail has been minutely examined in the attempt to find the source of the statesman's formidable literary skills and to explain how an impoverished backwoodsman came to write some of the world's most moving and resonant speeches. Lincoln's own account, in the third-person autobiography he eventually agreed to give to John L. Scripps in that summer of 1860, is terse: he reckoned that "the aggregate of all of his schooling did not amount to one year. He was never in a college academy as a student, and never inside of a college or academy building till since he had a law licence. What he has in the way of education he has picked up. After he was twenty-three and had separated from his father, he studied English grammar—imperfectly, of course, but so as to speak and write as well as he now does." "He regrets his want of education," Lincoln added, "and does what he can to supply the want" (Lincoln, 4:62).

That Lincoln should have quoted a line from the "Elegy Written in a Country Churchyard" in an offhand comment about his uneventful existence in rural poverty is not, on one level, surprising; Thomas Gray's poem is one of the most frequently cited poems in English literature and acts as a kind of cultural shorthand for a range of topics. Yet on another level, and with the benefit of historical hindsight, the disjunction between the sixteenth president of the United States and Gray's poem is arresting. Put in the simplest terms possible, the course of Lincoln's life unites two states of being that the Elegy declares to be unbridgeable. For the speaker of the poem, the poor, whom he pictures in both the plodding daily

rounds of their existence and the quiet sleep of their deaths, are by defini-
tion those whose lives and graves will not be significantly marked in any
way. Gray's examples of what cannot come forth from the common or-
ders are explicitly drawn from the epoch of a bitter civil war: in the tran-
quil churchyard surveyed by the speaker in the fading light of day, there
may well lie the remains of those who had the potential gifts or powers
to equal Hampden, Milton, or Cromwell, yet their uneducated and im-
poverished condition would have rendered such emulation impossible:

> . . . Knowledge to their eyes her ample page
> Rich with the spoils of time did ne'er unroll;
> Chill Penury repress'd their noble rage,
> And froze the genial current of the soul.

"Th' applause of list'ning senates to command" cannot be the lot of a
man whose opening life-story is capable of being contained within "The
short and simple annals of the poor." Such a man will necessarily be
"guiltless of his country's blood." Such a man will never read his "hist'ry
in a nation's eyes" nor yet receive the lasting tribute of a football-field-
sized memorial edifice in the ceremonial center of his capital city. Al-
though Gray's poem voices the opinion that extraordinary talents may
reside within the hearts, minds, and hands of the poor, it does not recog-
nize any mechanism, personal or social, that would result in the exercise
and acknowledgment of these talents in the wider world. Lincoln's jour-
ney "From Log Cabin to White House" is wholly unimaginable within
the Elegy's figuration of cultural and political realities.[1]

I begin with this willfully ahistorical alignment of Abraham Lincoln
and the Elegy neither to celebrate the triumph of the self-made statesman
nor to castigate the apparent conservatism of the poet, but rather to open
up an investigation of the poem's class politics in periods and circum-
stances far removed from the time of Gray's writing. Given the brevity of
Lincoln's formal schooling, it is unlikely that the poem would have been
assigned to him as a text for study in what he called the "ABC" class-
rooms of his youth; in common with many other dedicated working-class
autodidacts in the nineteenth century, he would instead have encountered
the ubiquitous Elegy during the rigorous self-education to which he sub-
jected himself thereafter. Yet the largest groups of individuals who have
known this poem did not discover it for themselves, but learned it under
the auspices of the school and through that institution's pedagogical
practices of memorization and recitation. For these people, Gray's Elegy
had the potential to carry distinct and particular sets of meanings and
significances that we shall explore in this chapter. "The real relation of
Gray's great poem to the present stage of our history," mused G. K. Ches-
terton in 1933, "will probably not be understood until a later stage"

(151). I take these words as an encouragement to consider the Elegy in the ages that first experienced mass elementary education.

To make the "Elegy Written in a Country Churchyard" the focus of one of this project's three main case studies is in many ways to bow to the inevitable: for complex historical and cultural reasons, most compellingly laid out in John Guillory's elegant inquiry in *Cultural Capital*, Gray's poem has come to stand for literature's best object, "the poem" itself (85–133). Although no longer commanding the same sort of reverence that it received for the first two centuries of its existence, the Elegy is nevertheless still with us, showing no signs of losing its eminence within the high literary canon of academic study and scholarly discourse. However, just like "Casabianca" and "The Burial of Sir John Moore after Corunna," Gray's Elegy also once occupied an indisputable position within the juvenile canon. This chapter exploits the Elegy's status as the school's quintessential literary object to investigate a number of key questions about the memorized poem. Gray's poem readily lends itself to the forms of analysis I adopt elsewhere in these pages—for instance, it would be relatively easy to discover instances in which the phenomenon of mass recitation "altered" the Elegy, just as it "altered" "The boy stood on the burning deck," or to speculate, as I will in the final case study, how widespread knowledge of a set poetic sequence of sentiments might contribute to changes within individuals and society more generally—but I choose other approaches here. Most prominently, I ask how the circumstances of a poem's acquisition affect the ways in which the words of Gray's Elegy—or indeed those of any other poem—are understood and enjoyed.

Before we set off, I will lay out a general summary of the poem; crudely reductive though it is, my schemata aims to provide a rough map of the major features in the work's topography to guide us on our journey. Readers of the Elegy usually agree that the poem falls into three main parts. The opening seven stanzas constitute the first section: herein we are both introduced to an unnamed speaker, who stands alone watching a plowman walk home after his day's work, and presented with a series of sensuously evocative scenes of rural life. Initially, in the most extensive of these, the speaker's immediate surroundings are vividly realized: as the light departs, we hear a sequence of sounds from far and near, from the ringing of the curfew, the lowing of cattle, and the "drowsy tinklings" of distant sheep bells to the droning of a beetle in flight and the melancholy hootings of an owl in an "ivy-mantled tow'r." The eye then takes over from the ear: the speaker's vision moves downwards from the tower and "those rugged elms" to "that yew-tree's shade." In that shade, the sight of the greening burial mounds of the village poor confirms that we are within the "country churchyard" of the poem's title. Summoned up by a sense of what these "rude forefathers" will "no more" do, each of the next three stanzas presents imaginary tableaux of moments from lives structured by labor: morning, when the men were roused from their beds to begin work; evening, when they returned from it to the "blazing hearth" and the familial embrace; and finally, the working day itself, spent in the fields at the time of harvest or plowing, or tree-felling in the woods.

At this point, a shift from the concrete to the abstract signals the beginning of the poem's second, and longest, section: lines 29 through 92, sixteen stanzas in all, are taken up with a complex sequence of musings that are richly studded with personifications and hypothetical cases. "Ambition" and "Grandeur," we learn, should not despise the simple lives of the poor because the grave awaits the aristocratic, the powerful, the beautiful, and the rich as surely as it awaits those without such qualities; the proud should not look coldly on the unremarkable graves of the lowly, for neither ornate tombs and memorials nor the influence of such friends as "Honour" and "Flatt'ry" possess a superior force that would keep death at bay. From line 45 onwards, we encounter a nexus of new thoughts that encompass the theme already introduced in my opening focus on Lincoln: perhaps the outward appearance of this undistinguished graveyard, this "neglected spot," belies the value of what it contains—perhaps an individual of truly outstanding ability, a potential visionary, or imperial leader, or great poet, lies here. Ah, our muser continues, but without education and under the repression of poverty, how could such individuals have developed the gifts within themselves? Yes, he decides, just as nature creates miracles of beauty that are never appreciated, so men who could have done great things have been born into circumstances that did not allow the blossoming of their talents—yet such circumstances, he continues, also put a limit to their potential "crimes" and saved them from possible excesses and evils. The poor have instead led quiet and uneventful lives. The final four stanzas (lines 77 through 92) of the poem's central section then take the speaker back to a direct consideration of the burial sites that have stirred up these thoughts: even these, humble and clumsy though their markers may be, ask for our sighs, for none of us wish to die and be forgotten; at the point of death—and beyond—each of us requires the sympathy and pious sorrow of another.

A dramatic change of focus then occurs: attention turns to the particular story of the life and death of a single individual. Both the identity of the individual addressed as "thee" in line 93, and the meaning of this third, and final, section of the Elegy have excited considerable critical controversy;[2] suffice it to say here that most readers feel that the speaker ends the poem by conjuring up a daydream that allows him to imagine his own early, mourned, death. And who is the mourner? "Some kindred spirit" who is led "by lonely contemplation" to investigate the fate of the author of the poem. In the speaker's fantasy, an old peasant encountered in the graveyard supplies the kindred spirit with the sorry tale: the strange and moody young man, often glimpsed in listless or desperate attitudes upon the "upland lawn," "at the foot of yonder nodding beech," or "hard by yon wood," suddenly disappeared; three days later, the villagers saw his coffin carried along the "church-way path" for burial. "Approach and read (for thou canst read) the lay, / Grav'd on the stone beneath yon aged thorn," commands the "hoary-headed swain." The last three stanzas of the poem are comprised of this epitaph:

> Here rests his head upon the lap of Earth
> 	A Youth to Fortune and to Fame unknown.
> Fair Science frown'd not on his humble birth,
> 	And Melancholy mark'd him for her own.
>
> Large was his bounty, and his soul sincere,
> 	Heav'n did a recompense as largely send:
> He gave to Mis'ry all he had, a tear,
> 	He gain'd from Heav'n ('twas all he wish'd) a friend.
>
> No farther seek his merits to disclose,
> 	Or draw his frailties from their dread abode,
> (There they alike in trembling hope repose,)
> 	The bosom of his Father and his God.

"A youth to Fortune and to Fame unknown"? How are we to calibrate the youth's exact social rank, especially in relation to the "rude forefathers" with whom he now shares a resting place? Just how "humble" was his "humble birth"? How did he come to receive the embrace of "Fair Science"? And when "Melancholy mark'd him for her own"—was this in any way because of his relationship with "Fair Science"? Are the kindred spirit and the friend "gain'd from Heav'n" one and the same? Who composed these verses? And who paid for the tombstone? Leaving us with a series of unanswered questions, the Elegy comes to a close.

The majority of this chapter will be concerned with that central section of the Elegy and its famous preoccupation with the question of undeveloped human potential. For good or ill, Gray calmly informs us, the lot of the poor inevitably limited the range of their activities to the narrow sphere of their immediate surroundings, denying them the possibility of any significant participation in world events or culture. By unraveling the poem's imbrication in the politics of the class structures and educational institutions of its immediate world in the mid-eighteenth century, Guillory has argued for the Elegy's essential importance to bourgeois readers: Gray's verses validate this particular social group, he claims, by setting its rise to power against the poor's absolute inability to rise. Yet if we consider the meaning of the Elegy in later periods, eras that experienced the extension of education, and thus the possibility of individual advancement, to mass, rather than partial, populations, then some very different issues come into view. Thanks to the specific curricular design of widespread educational programs in both Britain and the United States, Gray's Elegy gained the potential to become known not just to the upper and middle classes, but by members of every stratum of society. The words of the poem, then, were eventually read and recited by the poor themselves, the very people it dubs both unlettered and mute.

How did that feel to them? How might we begin to understand the emotional and intellectual dimensions of this historical irony? To find a route through the territory, I take my bearings from a couple of points about the Elegy, as it was taught in the closing decades of the Victorian era and the first few decades of the twentieth century. In the first place, mainly because it was a relatively long poem, but in some degree because of its complex diction and concepts, Gray's Elegy was habitually assigned to what were generally the "top" classes, or final stages, grades or standards, of the public systems here under scrutiny: the poem can thus legitimately be considered as a kind of capstone, or summation, of the elementary educational experiences of huge numbers of individuals. In the second place, and once again because of the "difficulty" of the Elegy, the poem was probably taken to heart, in both senses of the phrase, only by those pupils who were particularly academically able—who were (in what was often a literal, as well as a figurative, position in the schoolrooms of these times and places) at the "top" of their classes. This chapter attempts to imagine the thoughts and feelings of those "top achievers," the exceptionally gifted within the ranks of the poor. My other strategy to delimit a path grounds itself upon a profound national difference between the two countries in this study: in Britain, in a manner never mirrored to any significant extent across the Atlantic, numerous systems (at first ad hoc, and then official) sought to abstract the academically able poor child out of his or her elementary school and into what was intended to be both an extended, and a more intensive, education. Gray's poem undoubtedly had a massive importance in American educational, and thus social, contexts, but I choose here to concentrate on the question of its reception by British pupils. What might the Elegy have meant to individuals who underwent the experience of leaving one class and entering another?

It perhaps goes without saying that many of the children who were very good at committing poems to heart and performing them on demand were also those who succeeded in examinations; proficient recitation was often one element of a general competence that was rewarded in various different ways in the elementary classroom, and which, in certain circumstances, led to the highest prize of all, a scholarship to the grammar school. When a literary object is disseminated as a portion of official school culture, and when its internalization and reproduction are part and parcel of that school's testing systems, how does that influence the ways in which the literary object is experienced in childhood and thereafter? While many of the individuals whose autobiographical writings I examine hold forth upon the sheer sensuous joy of literary language, some also reflect upon other, distinctly less positive, experiences with poetry in the classroom. One of the lessons learned is that working-class pronunciation is undesirable; another is that the poems assigned either ignore or denigrate the lower strata of society. Does culture, then, have the power to betray the heart that loves it? Although the successfully memorized poem undoubtedly played a role as acquired cultural capital, a pleasing and often permanently possessed symbol of that expertise that might enable an individual to rise first within the educational, and then the social, system, it also carried the potential to act as a persistent reminder of the school's ability to alienate an individual from his or her earliest associations.

In 1957 a pioneering work entitled *The Uses of Literacy* identified the former "scholarship boy" as a significant presence in the ecology of Britain's adult social structures; its author, Richard Hoggart, isolated a distinctive psychological type that, he claimed, had come into being within the peculiar class dynamics of the scholarship system that Britain had progressively, if haphazardly, extended in the first four decades of the twentieth century.[3] While in certain respects resembling the age-old structures that had enabled some of the country's poorest sons to attend grammar schools free of charge, the arrangements put in place from 1902 onwards were for the first time centrally planned and publically financed; these measures created a sizable, and, increasingly after Hoggart, a recognizable constituency.[4] *The Uses of Literacy* characterizes erstwhile scholarship-winners as the "anxious and uprooted," a group marked out by "their lack of poise, by their uncertainty" (241). While careful to qualify his assertions and categorize the range of variations within the type, Hoggart nevertheless maintains that the representative individual is unable to bring his internal and external affiliations into comfortable equilibrium: "He has left his class, at least in spirit, by being in certain ways unusual; and he is still unusual in another class, too tense and overwound" (250). As the century progressed, more and more former scholarship children came to positions of prominence in all areas of society, reaching Number 10 Downing Street as surely as they won prestigious literary prizes, but the image of the essentially split self of the class-crossing individual was unaffected by the relative worldly successes and failures of actual cases. In Britain's cultural imagination the onetime scholarship boy is forever a lost soul.

Gray's mournful verses, we have already noticed, experience a radical break in their structure: while the first two-thirds of the poem concentrate for the most part on undifferentiated collections of the rural poor in life and in death, its final stanzas focus upon that singular individual, the youth of "humble birth" who managed to gain an education before succumbing to an early grave. *The Uses of Literacy* argues that the child who made the journey from a working-class home to the middle-class grammar school also experienced a feeling of internal division; Hoggart is too restrained, however, to suggest that all of these individuals, in their later lives, were necessarily haunted by a sense of the death of their earlier selves. Nevertheless, the abiding icon of the scholarship boy is always shot through with melancholy. In the light I have chosen to cast upon my investigation, Gray's poem can be seen as this figure's very own elegy.

◆ ◆ ◆

The story of the Elegy's ascent to cultural ubiquity has often been told (Guillory). First published anonymously as a sixpenny quarto pamphlet on February 16, 1751, Gray's poem was rapidly reprinted in the months that followed, appearing in both authorized and pirated editions and a wide variety of magazines and miscellanies. "Everybody read it, in town and country," states Edmund Gosse in his 1882 biography of Gray; "Shenstone [the poet, at home in Shropshire], far away from the world of books, had seen it by 28th March. . . . It achieved a complete popular success from the very first, and the name of its author gradually crept into notoriety" (105). In the final paragraph of his brief chapter on Gray in *The Lives of the English Poets* in 1781, Samuel Johnson refers in a matter-of-fact manner to the high esteem in which "the common reader" holds the poem; no rarefied literary object for a coterie audience, the "Churchyard" has been embraced, he states, because it "abounds with images which find a mirrour in every mind, and with sentiments to which every bosom returns an echo" (4:184).

As Guillory observes in his detailed investigation of the poem's attraction for an emerging bourgeoisie in the second half of the eighteenth century, Johnson here identifies what is usually acknowledged as the "most striking formal feature of Gray's poem": "its phrases sound familiar even in the absence of identified pretexts, as though it were the anonymous distillation of literary *sententiae*" (87). For the aspiring middle classes, then, Gray's Elegy offered in a readily assimilable form the cultural cachet of classical learning, one of the traditional hallmarks of the elite, without the laborious and costly necessity of an extended classical education. Just as the poem constantly reappeared in anthologies and poetry collections destined for their drawing rooms and private studies, so it rapidly became a regular selection in the school textbooks produced in this era by and for this class. Its position in Enfield's *Speaker* both reflected and accelerated the poem's rise to omnipresence in middle-class vernacular education (p. 45). By the end of the Victorian era, however, the "Church-yard" had also come to be a fixed feature of the pedagogical literary landscape at the two extremities of the social scale. Once classical grammars and then the "public schools" began to study English literature as well as Latin and Greek, children might be found mumbling the Elegy in the most elite of institutions,[5] but they were also stuttering out its phrases in the lowliest of surroundings, thanks to the specific requirements of the nation's burgeoning system of mass elementary education and the series of graded textbooks its regulations brought forth. A similar picture obtained across the Atlantic: Gray's Elegy figured in a wide selection of nineteenth-century American schoolbooks, often doing duty not just as a piece for recitation, but also as fit copy for parsing exercises or as an example of a literary form ("An Elegiac stanza consists of four heroic verses rhyming alternately; as, 'The curfew tolls the knell of parting day . . .'" [Butler and Noble, 189][6]).

By 1900, then, the poem's uncanny ability to seem familiar even on first acquaintance was rooted less in its presentation of what sounded like translations of time-honored classical dicta and more in its thorough and longtime saturation of the cultures in which it continued to circulate.[7] "The Elegy has so worked itself into the popular imagination," opined Leslie Stephen in 1909, "that it includes more familiar phrases than any poem of equal length in the language" (97). For Gosse, too, the poem is "more thickly studded with phrases that have become a part and parcel of colloquial speech than any other piece, even of Shakespeare's, consisting of so few consecutive lines" (98). Writing in 1998 about the Elegy's influence upon Thomas Hardy, critic Dennis Taylor notes that a study of the *Oxford English Dictionary* reveals that "more words are quoted from Gray, proportionate to the size of his oeuvre, than from any other poet. . . . Of the 195 words cited from the "Elegy," only nine are clearly labeled as obsolete, rare, poetic, and so on (custom'd, haply, inglorious, jocund, lea, long-drawn, madding, "note of praise," wonted) while the rest are now standard" (464). For Taylor, it is an "amazing paradox . . . that no poet has been more accepted into our language, even though he is supposedly the poet of poetic diction and a language far removed from the language of the age," but focus on the Elegy as a text for widespread memorization makes its thoroughgoing infiltration of everyday linguistic usage seem, on the whole, rather unsurprising. Stephen was exaggerating when he wrote,

"Everyone knows [Gray's] poetry by heart," but certainly thousands and thousands of people were given the opportunity to learn the Elegy at school, and this inevitably had an effect upon how they expressed themselves thereafter (97).

As demonstrated in the case of "Casabianca," mass familiarity can have a disastrous effect upon the reputation of a literary work, particularly when that familiarity has been achieved in the context of a low-status institution, such as the elementary school. The Elegy appears to have been protected from such a fate by numerous connected factors. In the first place, the highest virtue of Gray's poem had always been located in that effect of preexisting familiarity: the very point of the Elegy was to tell what was already known, again and again and again. But just as significant was its accrued value of exemplarity: thanks to the genealogy of its reception, the work had come to stand, at least in the periods here under investigation, as English literature's "poem of poems," to quote Gosse's late nineteenth-century judgment. While not, in his opinion, "the most brilliant or original or profound lyric in our language," the Elegy "may almost be looked upon as the typical piece of English verse." Within the circular course of this logic, Gray's work, for this critic and many more, was thus believed to "combine[ ] in more balanced perfection than any other all the qualities that go into the production of a poetical effect," and consequently it represented the ideal object for literary study (97). What is so remarkable about the Elegy is that it managed to play this role for such a wide range of communities over such an extended stretch of time. The second hundred years of the poem's existence, the period running from the mid-nineteenth to the mid-twentieth century, witnessed a significant growth in the number of contexts in which "literary study" could be performed; the term (or its equivalents) came to describe the classroom's valiant attempts to pronounce the word "jocund" just as much as it covered the composition of paragraphs in *belles lettres* or scholarly tomes. Further, agreement over the question of what constituted "literary study" within these venues, and all the others in between, underwent important changes of emphasis over the years. Nevertheless, the Elegy reigned supreme, singularly successful in its ability to claim preeminence in all the subtly shifting canons of "English literature" that corresponded to these various enterprises in different periods. It is probably impossible to state definitively to what degree the poem's status in one particular world affected its standing, positively or negatively, in another, but the fact that the Elegy enjoyed multiple citizenship in a significant number of domains is indisputable.

The Elegy's importance at the secondary school level in Britain was maintained, to a large degree, by its position within the lists of prescribed texts for model courses of instruction and, still more influentially, for external examinations. Most significant here was the placing of Gray's poem at the symbolic center of the nineteenth century's most successful poetry anthology, a text that held an important presence in secondary school syllabi up to World War II, and even, in some cases, beyond. As the poet Patricia Beer recalls in her 1968 autobiography *Mrs. Beer's House*, her third-form English lessons at a grammar school in Devon in the early 1930s were organized entirely around a single section of this book:

> There was one poetry lesson a week and this consisted of working through Book III of Palgrave's *Golden Treasury*. One by one, in the order laid down by the selector, the poems were put before us by Bullo [the senior English master], read, discussed, and often learnt by heart. (177)

To Beer, enraptured by poems in general ("I enjoyed them all so much that I learnt most of them by heart even when not required to do so, and I can recite them to this day" [177]), the identity of the anthology's best poet was clear:

> [T]he great love of my life—I use the expression seriously—at this time was T. Gray. I knew nothing about him personally; it never occurred to me to read a biographical study of him. I knew him only by his work, but this was most plentifully represented in the *Golden Treasury*: he was the undoubted laureate of Book III. (180)

Preferring "his minor reflections on the state of man and the world" to "his weightiest sayings," the schoolgirl Beer liked Gray's "Ode on the Pleasure arising from Vicissitude" most of all (181). For Palgrave, however, one poem ranked far above the others: the *Treasury*'s introduction states that the Elegy contains "perhaps the noblest stanzas in our language." Generations of British secondary schoolchildren thus studied Gray's Elegy in textbooks and lessons that told them that this poem represented the loftiest heights of English literature.

Although the books used in American high school classrooms were different, the message remained the same. In this institution, in common with its compatriots *The Rime of the Ancient Mariner* and works by Milton, the Elegy typically rubbed shoulders with native productions from the pens of Longfellow, Bryant, and Lowell. As noted in Part I, from the last decade of the nineteenth century onwards, American "high schools preparing students for college entrance requirements . . . routinely subjected to intensive scrutiny" the works in this narrow canon (Rubin, "Listen, My Children," 264). For many of these students, this go-round with Gray's Elegy would build upon previous classroom experience; as in Britain, the poem was often assigned in the earlier grades of the high school as well.

To discuss secondary and high school practices in Britain and the United States is to consider phenomena reserved, until relatively late in the day in this project's historical scope, for a privileged minority of individuals. I wish now to focus our attention upon the Elegy's place in mass educational experiences by exploring its relation to the elementary school's habitual pedagogical exercises; it is in these contexts, I contend, that the discord between the words of the poem and the individuals who recited them sounds most powerfully. In Britain, Gray's poem has a history within this institution for a good sixty years or so, up until the early 1930s.[8] But just how did this 128-line poem fit into the minds and syllabi of mass public education?

Part I's summary of the recitation requirements laid down by central government demonstrates that in the first twenty years of elementary-school recitation, an unabridged Gray's Elegy sometimes fitted the bill, and sometimes did not; if the length of a given work exceeded or fell short of the stipulated line-requirement, however, it was common practice either to truncate it, or to make up the difference with other poems, or parts of poems.[9] Although relatively few schools prepared their pupils for the stringent measures of the "Specific Subjects" options in the 1870s, some ambitious teachers evidently thought the effort worth making. The records of a small village school near Bristol provide an interesting case in point. Writing to Her Majesty's Inspector Mr. Balmer in 1874, teacher Elizabeth Harwood petitioned to add "English Literature" as subject for testing in the following year, and hoped that her chosen texts would "meet with [his] approval." "I have selected Cowper's 'Winter Morning' for the sixth std from line 1 to 300," she writes, "and Gray's 'Elergy' [*sic*] for standard 4." This slip of the pen notwithstanding, Miss Harwood's plan apparently paid off: the inspector's report for 1875 notes, "This little school has again passed a very satisfactory examination . . . The extra subject Literature appears to have been carefully taught."[10] But this school seems somewhat exceptional; widespread knowledge of the Elegy in British public education cannot properly be said to begin until the 1882 Code regularized recitation requirements throughout the curriculum and made them an achievable target for the vast majority of the country's elementary schools.

From this date onwards, Gray's poem settled into the position it was to hold for many years; in nearly all cases it features in school readers' selections for pupils at the very end of their elementary education. As the leaving age gradually crept up over the years, Gray's poem also drifted upwards, as if it became its melancholy task always to represent the final stage of the process—or perhaps, in its embodiment of more than could be reasonably expected of the average elementary-school child, to stand for that which could never quite be reached.[11] There is some evidence that the poem was on occasion assigned to classes lower down the school, but Gray's Elegy generally appeared at the point that a child's formal education came to a close. Its position in *Poetic Gems*, the volume surveyed at the beginning of Part I, is typical: Gray's Elegy is placed in Book IV of its four-volume set and, as the rubric states, is intended "for children of thirteen and upwards." In 1907, when this series was published, the overwhelming majority of individuals in England finished school at thirteen. Exactly how many of them, then, would have made it to page 144 to hear the curfew toll the knell of parting day?

We turn now to a thorny question: how can we judge how difficult it would have been for any given child to commit to heart all thirty-two four-line stanzas of the Elegy? Exceptional juvenile feats in the realm of poetry memorization are not unknown. The thirteen-year-old Winston Churchill, famously indolent at school, was apparently able to recite some twelve hundred lines of Macaulay's *Lays of Ancient Rome*, and records of other champion child performers, such as David Wilkie, the bekilted Burns expert, certainly exist. But how would an eleven-year-old lad from a Lancashire mill town have fared in 1894? Or a fourteen-year-old girl in a Gloucestershire village in 1920? It seems to fair to assume that many children, trained from the first in regular drills of rote learning, would have had a certain competence with extended sequences of measured verse; personal experience with our elders, and, in this respect, definitely betters, confirms that individuals in many English-speaking countries who completed their elementary and secondary schooling before 1940 or so were and are much more likely to be proficient poetry reciters than those educated in later periods. But while it is just about possible for me to believe that nearly all of the children of Standard II in, say, a national school in Birmingham would have been able, with some prodding, to mumble out the forty lines of "Casabianca," expecting everyone in Standard VI to get through a poem over three times as long seems a different proposition altogether. What proportion could do it, then or at any other time?

Worth recalling at this juncture is the fact that an important element of the mystique that had gathered around the Elegy was the story of its recitation in a testing environment. As I mentioned in the introduction, the beloved tale of the behavior of General Wolfe before the Battle of Quebec was regularly trotted out not only in biographies and editions of Gray's works, but also, on occasion, in surveys of English literature and the notes or introductions of anthologies, including those used in schools. Gosse provides a version of the legend in his book on the poet:

> It was while Gray was quietly vegetating in Bloomsbury that an event occurred of which he was quite unconscious, which yet has singularly

endeared him to the memory of Englishmen. On the evening of the 12th of September, 1759,— while Gray, sauntering back from the British Museum to his lodgings, noted that the weather was cloudy, with a S. S. W. wind,—on the other side of the Atlantic the English forces lay along the river Montmorency, and looked anxiously across at Quebec and at the fateful heights of Abraham. When night-fall came, and before the gallant four thousand obeyed the word of command to steal across the river, General Wolfe, the young officer of thirty-three, who was next day to win death and immortality in victory, crept along in a boat from post to post to see that all was ready for the expedition. It was a fine, silent evening, and as they pulled along, with muffled oars, the General recited to one of his officers who sat with him in the stern of the boat nearly the whole of Gray's *Elegy in a Country Churchyard*, adding, as he concluded, "I would prefer being the author of that Poem to the glory of beating the French tomorrow." [12] (144–45)

As Gosse proceeds to tell us, the inevitable hour came the next day; the foe was vanquished and the territory gained, yet for Wolfe the paths of glory led but to the grave. Within the space of twenty-four hours he had, however, secured a place in his nation's history, both military and literary. For Gosse, the soldier's performance bestows upon poetry a tremendous accolade, elevating the Elegy to a position that its own merits would never have warranted: "No finer compliment was ever paid by the man of action to the man of imagination," he continues; "sanctified, as it were, by the dying lips of the great English hero, the poem seems to be raised far above its intrinsic rank in literature, and to demand our respect as one of the acknowledged glories of our race and language" (145).

The bias of Gosse's presentation cries out for some comment—the biographer's relative weighting of the achievements of Gray and Wolfe comes as no surprise after that mischievous opening focus upon our vegetative poet, a man prone to making mild metereological observations while "sauntering" home to dinner after a light day's graft in the British Museum. Consistently sniffy about the inherent qualities of the Elegy (not "the most brilliant or original or profound lyric," we remember), Gosse here makes Wolfe's recitation of the poem a more important, or at the least, a more socially significant, act than Gray's composition thereof. To be sure, other commentators who invoked the Wolfe anecdote were usually less concerned to establish a hierarchy between writing and reciting, but the repeated yoking of the verses on the page to the story of their reverential performance inevitably contributed to the conception of the Elegy as a poem that could and should be learned by heart.

Yet the gallant general, we might note, recited "*nearly the whole* of Gray's *Elegy in a Country Churchyard*" (my emphases), not the poem in its entirety. How far did he get, then? Did Wolfe make a conscious choice to end at line 92, thereby evading that puzzling turn to the problematic "thee" that the poem takes in the next line? Did he lop off the last nine stanzas deliberately—after all, on the night before a battle, who needs the "drooping" youth, all "woeful wan," stretching out his "listless length" under a "nodding beech"?—or did he simply fade away into the solemn stillness of the Canadian dusk, memory losing the fight with conscious will and forcing him to call it a day at whatever point he foundered?

Many others, in far less charged circumstances than Wolfe, have been defeated by either the sheer length of the poem or the stumbling block of its potentially interchangeable stanzas. We might have expected a fellow poet, and one of Gray's keenest readers to boot, to have been able to get it right all the way through to the end, but Thomas Hardy admits in his disguised autobiography that such a feat was beyond him. Recalling an experience that occurred in 1899, he writes as follows:

> At the beginning of June Hardy was staying at a country-house not many miles from London, and among the guests was the young Duchess of M——, a lady of great beauty, who asked him if he would conduct her to the grave of the poet Gray, which was within a walk. Hardy did so, and, standing half-balanced on one foot by the grave (as is well known, it was also that of Gray's mother), his friend recited in a soft voice the "Elegy" from the first word to the last in leisurely and lengthy clearness without an error (which Hardy himself could not have done without some hitch in the order of the verses).[13] (Florence E. Hardy, 326)

The anecdote reveals that the duchess could do what the author could not: the Elegy separates the wheat from the chaff, confounding all but a few reciters.[14]

But to return to the specific consideration of our hypothetical school-child's attempted acquisition of the poem *in toto*: what traces remain of his or her experience with the Elegy? Honesty compels me to admit that the pickings are slim, at least when compared to the bulk of stories, albeit in a range of genres with greater and lesser relationships to verifiable fact, about the other works in this study. When individuals put pen to paper to write about the phenomenon of the memorized poem, they are far more likely to conjure up a burning boy than a plodding plowman. Yet exceptional cases do occur. Describing his mother, an illegitimate child of a Scarborough slum, in his autobiography *Nine Lives*, Sydney Cross Harland recalled that "her memory was remarkable. When she was over ninety she correctly recited much of Gray's *Elegy in a Country Churchyard* in a strong Yorkshire accent."[15] Orphaned while still an infant, Eliza Fitzgerald was taken out of the workhouse to be fostered by a North Riding farming couple and, in their care, managed to stay on at a village school ("walking the four miles a day") until she was fourteen. Did she learn that poem in 1882, her last year in education? Was she one of those who triumphantly met the challenge of the highest standard's most testing requirement?

Another example, this time drawn from around thirty years later in the memorized poem's history, relates to an educational environment that was probably very different from that which Eliza would have experienced. On April 22, 1960, the *London Times* featured a 1,200-word article entitled "Gray on a White Night: Reconstructing the Elegy through the Small Hours." With the following words, "A Correspondent" begins his or her minutely detailed account of the fight to remember all of the stanzas in the right order:

> When I was 12 years old a beloved old teacher suggested that I learn Gray's "Elegy" and I gladly did so. It did not inebriate me as had Shelley's "Skylark," nor Vaughan's "Retreat" (the poems I had just learnt), but I found it immensely satisfying, and as I grew older it gave me a sense of contentment merely to say the lines. (16)

Given that the writer goes on to tell us that she, or (more likely, I think) he, originally memorized the poem "nearly fifty years" ago, we can calculate that this pedagogical guidance occurred in the early 1910s; to hit upon the type of school in which the recommendation was given is a harder matter altogether. Yet the point to this piece is not any primal scene of recitation, but the struggle to reach and reassemble that which continues to lurk within the mind a half century later. As an almost clinical case-study of the process of rearticulating the once-memorized poem, of reaching down into "that pit of forgetfulness which, like a net far below a pond, must hold so many ill-assorted scraps and broken-off threads of experience," the article directs a fascinating light on the connective tissues of the Elegy, on the system of ligaments that stretch over its bones and cartilages to keep it in shape. "The first seven or eight verses came as easily as ever (allowing for a few hesitations over adjectives)," but then false promptings rush in and must be resisted; instead, the painstaking art of the forensic scientist is employed for the true reconstruction of Gray's anatomy. Eventually, having made it to line 60, the "Correspondent" can go no further:

> Furious at my defeat, but by now wakefully curious, I got out of bed and fetched the *Oxford Book of English Verse*. Everything I had recalled was correct so far and here was my gap: "Th' applause of list'ning senates to command." I shut the book quickly before I had read further and started off with this severely small clue. But with that line came the next; again rhymes hinted at their partners and sense—

and small remembered groups of words—contributed enough to re-
store the whole . . . this back-stepping from rhyme and conclusion to
rhyme and opening statement was sheer delight, as satisfying as solv-
ing a crossword clue and, for some reason, far more flattering to one's
self-esteem.

The poem is restored—not, we should note, in its entirety, for our mental
reciter spurns "the last section of the poem where the hoary-headed swain
takes over" on the grounds of its artistic inferiority ("Why is this uncon-
vincing, conventional eighteenth-century bit of nonsense tacked on to the
end of this flawless piece of writing?" he—or she—asks, unconsciously
echoing Walter Savage Landor's famous opinion that the Elegy's coda
was akin to a tin kettle tied to the tail of a noble dog). Deliberate choice,
then, not the failing of memory, creates a truncated form; the writer states
that "At 12, presumably, I learnt it [all]."

Widely different though the cases of the Yorkshire farmgirl and the
Times correspondent may be, they show us that the placement of the
Elegy in all those textbooks for children just before, or at the beginning
of, their teens was definitely not an empty gesture, a perfunctory nod to
the English "poem of poems" from hidebound publishers. Though to a
certain degree Gray's Elegy may have operated in elementary pedagogies
as the literary equivalent of the formal parlor or the best china—neces-
sary to establish the respectability of the household, but used only on rare
and special occasions—the recitation of this long poem was not beyond
some eleven-, twelve-, thirteen-year-olds. But for how many of them
might a successful recitation of Gray's Elegy in elementary school have
represented the final fading glimmerings of their formal education? "Rob-
ert Campbell left the school to-day," wrote a disconsolate Scottish school-
master in the daily record he published under the title *A Dominie's Log*
in 1915 (Neill, 58).[16] Robert, one of his most able pupils, had that day
celebrated his thirteenth birthday: "He had reached the age-limit. He be-
gins work tomorrow morning as a ploughman. . . . Truly it is like a death:
I stand by a new made grave, and I have no hope of a resurrection. Rob-
ert is dead" (58). On the other side of things, though, just how many of
those highly able children would have had the opportunity to develop
their talents further? For how many of them might their prowess with the
Elegy have imaged in little a general proficiency that licensed a rise to a
new school, to a new realm of potential, to a new place in society? Knowl-
edge ceased to unroll her ample page to Robert Campbell after he turned
thirteen (ceased to unroll it, that is, within any official educational sys-
tem); it is a fair guess that chill Penury proceeded to repress his noble rage
and freeze the genial current of his soul as he broke the stubborn glebes
of Dumfriesshire. Eliza Fitzgerald, who had maybe not all but "much of
Gray's Elegy" permanently installed within her memory "scrubbed, baked,

washed, ironed, milked cows, fed pigs, calves and hens, and worked in the field"; as far as we know from what her son tells us, her lot circumscribed not only her virtues, but also any potential crimes, and she never strayed from the cool sequester'd vale of York. But what about the latter-day embryonic Hampdens, Miltons, and Cromwells whose promise was not only acknowledged in the elementary school, but rewarded with sufficient financial assistance to persuade their parents to allow them to continue their educations?

Aligning the Elegy with the historical question of how potential talent within a mass population has, or has not, been recognized is to summon up the most well-known remarks in this poem's extensive critical reception. In the opening pages of *Some Versions of Pastoral*, William Empson makes these observations:

> Gray's Elegy is an odd case of poetry with latent political ideas:
>
>> Full many a gem of purest ray serene,
>>   The dark unfathom'd caves of ocean bear;
>> Full many a flow'r is born to blush unseen,
>> And waste its sweetness on the desert air.
>
> What this means, as the context makes clear, is that eighteenth-century England had no scholarship system or *carrière ouverte aux talents*. (4)

This is not to say that earlier and other readers of the poem had not noticed its focus upon the wastage of higher powers in the lower orders: on the contrary, from the *British Magazine*'s acknowledgment in 1751 of the "just regard shewn by the author to humble stations" to a 1927 advertorial for Selfridge's department store, "The Duty of Discovering Merit," a wide range of commentators have felt that Gray's presentation of the topic constitutes the Elegy's most interesting and innovative feature.[17] But the fame of Empson's analysis resides within the following argument: while the poem depicts this human wastage "as pathetic," "the reader is put into a mood in which one would not try to alter it." He continues:

> By comparing the social arrangement to Nature he makes it seem inevitable, which it was not, and gives it a dignity which was undeserved. Furthermore, a gem does not mind being in a cave and a flower prefers not to be picked; we feel that the man is like the flower, as short-lived, natural, and valuable, and this tricks us into feeling that he is better off without opportunities. (5)

According to Empson, the sleights of hand with which the poem's reactionary views are disguised render those views distasteful not only to those who would dislike them however they were presented, but also to those who might otherwise uphold their content in a different context:

Many people, without being communists, have been irritated by the
complacence in the massive calm of the poem, and this seems partly
because they feel there is a cheat in the implied politics; the "bour-
geois" themselves do not like literature to have too much "bourgeois
ideology." (5)

The Elegy, then, for Empson (and most critics and readers today) is a
conservative document. I reserve a more extensive consideration of this
issue for later stages in my chapter; for now I simply observe that Gray's
poem has over the years been embraced at numerous points around the
political spectrum.[18] Instead, my attention here is claimed primarily
by that opening insistence that the "Full many a gem" stanza points to-
wards the lack of a "scholarship system or *carrière ouverte aux talents*"
in eighteenth-century England. According to Guillory, this is a "perversely
brilliant intuition" on Empson's part, and one that prompts the later
critic to investigate how the "gem" lines signify "a problem of social mo-
bility, which is . . . specific to a certain historical class structure" [95, 93]).
In a brilliant gesture of Guillory's own, his chapter on "Mute Inglorious
Miltons" then restores the school that Gray excises from the poem's land-
scape, bringing into the picture not only the poet's own disquisition on
educational opportunity, the fragment "The Alliance of Education and
Government," but also his "Ode on a Distant Prospect of Eton College"
and the work that followed the Elegy in Enfield's *Speaker*, Anna Laetitia
Barbauld's "Warrington Academy." Guillory makes these moves to dem-
onstrate the crucial role played by educational establishments in the in-
creasing degree of upward mobility achieved by the bourgeoisie in mid-
eighteenth-century England. While there were no structures in place to
lift the brightest and best of the village poor out of the muck and into the
glare of the nation's eyes, at this historical moment the *carrière ouverte
aux talents* happened to be more of a reality for the educated and effec-
tive *middle-class* man than it had ever been before. But a "scholarship
system" *per se* has less relevance to Guillory's argument about eighteenth-
century social conditions; or rather, this part of Empson's intuition does
not play a role in helping him to unlock the puzzle of how the Elegy came
to assume its position of canonical centrality in vernacular education. For
my purposes, however, it goes to the heart of the matter.

When we consider the historical context of Empson's *own* moment of
composition, we will more readily understand why he should have made
this particular remark. *Some Versions of the Pastoral* was written in the
1930s, the end point of what historian G. A. N. Lowndes would call the
"Silent Social Revolution" in his 1937 book of this name. The phrase, as
Lowndes uses it, refers to the general extension of education to Britain's
mass population, but we can also apply it more narrowly (albeit, as we
shall see, somewhat ironically) to a battery of measures instituted in the

first four decades of the twentieth century that sought to allow the ablest children of the working classes to continue their educations beyond elementary school. By the time Empson was writing in 1935, the resultant scholarship system had come to be a well-known feature of the educational landscape. It is pushing it too far to say that every gem of purest ray serene was now given the opportunity to gleam forth among the chalk-dust of the form-room, or that flow'rs no longer blushed unseen and wasted their sweetness in the muddy furrows of the shires or the back alleys of the metropolis, but at this point in the century the most academically accomplished children of the impoverished ends of the social scale stood a fair chance of winning a scholarship to the local grammar. Such children, I readily acknowledge, are not exactly nascent forms of the hypothetical horny-handed geniuses of statecraft and poetic inspiration that haunted Gray's imagination; nevertheless, an examination of the range of educational possibilities for such potential scholars over the years not only takes us to an informative context in which ultimately to set the reception of the Elegy, but also shines a strong light on major social and cultural trends in British history.

◆ ◆ ◆

The roots of England's scholarship culture reach back to the Middle Ages; arrangements that benefited students without means had an important place in the establishment of numerous forms of educational institutions. For instance, in return for praying for the dead, scholars with no worldly connections like Chaucer's "thin clerk" could gain admission to the colleges of Oxford and Cambridge, many of which received their endowments in exchange for the celebration of masses for donors' departed souls; famous schools like Winchester and Eton that eventually became bastions of the elite also had at their inception provisions for free places for various categories of children, such as founder's kin or local residents. The institutions of greatest importance to our inquiry here, though, are the grammar schools. Established over the centuries—some evolving from the schools attached to the great cathedrals or chantries; many others founded in the boom of sixteenth-century Anglicanism and mercantilism; variously strengthened with gifts and endowments, and often granted royal charters—these establishments were by definition schools "in which the learned languages are grammatically taught," as Johnson's *Dictionary* put it, and most of them held in their history some connection, for however long or short a period, with the provision of free education for at least a proportion of their pupils.

Our scrutiny begins in the era that saw the extension of basic education to the general populace. Before the government involved itself in the full-scale provision of compulsory education, relationships between existing grammar schools and the growing numbers of elementary schools run by the Church of England and the nonconformist denominations developed in piecemeal fashion. J. Campkin's 1858 autobiography, *The Struggles of a Village Lad*, an uplifting tale issued by the Temperance Society that plots the progress of a Band of Hope supporter, provides an useful illustration of a single location's range of educational establishments, and the possibility of movement between them, during the first third of the nineteenth century:

> In our village there was no lack of schools. There was the Grammar School, where none were allowed to go but gentleman's sons; then there was the National School, taught by Mr. Pepper, who used to cane the boys and girls so much that they all declared it was a shame. Besides these, there was the dame school, the mistress of which did not cane the children, but pulled their ears, and pinned them to her apron. (4)

Campkin (presented in the story as one "Frank West") is the son of the village handyman, and makes his way first from the dame school to the national school ("a penny a week"), and then, because of a fortuitous meeting on the road with the new master of the grammar school, to that institution.[19] Impressed that a local urchin is reading Simpson's *Euclid* in the lane, the teacher tests West on a few problems, and then gives him the following information:

> In October next there are to be three boys admitted into the school free of cost, and if you like you can try to get one of the scholarships. There will be an examination, and those three boys who acquit themselves the best will be admitted. . . . There will be questions from the Scriptures, Grammar, History, Arithmetic, and the First Book of Euclid. (54)

"Can any boy try?" West asks. "Yes, if they are of good character, and can bring a certificate of baptism and a written recommendation from one of the trustees," comes the reply (54). Assailed by gloomy doubts ("there are thirty-six candidates for the three scholarships; the greater part of which have been to excellent schools, and what can you do against such as these?" [62]), the plucky lad nevertheless girds up his loins for the examination that, contravening the master's description, actually turns out to contain what is to Frank a wholly incomprehensible Latin paper. His prowess in the other sections, however, is more than sufficient unto the day, and he wins not only one of the coveted awards but also in due course and, we are led to believe, in large part thanks to his forswearing of all spirituous liquids, a place at Cambridge. Frank and his similarly estimable brother ultimately attain respected positions within the two fields traditionally associated with humble scholars, the church and education.

While the main trajectory of this providential narrative is broadly predictable, some of the author's incidental pronouncements are more surprising. An interestingly early plea for the prolongation of the education of the poor constitutes one such moment:

> How little do parents [writes Campkin] imagine the harm they are doing their children by taking them from school at such an early age! Who can tell what is buried in the mind of a child, which might, with culture, wake up the genius of a Milton, a Shakespere, a Watt, or a Stephenson? ... alas, this is denied to the agricultural poor, as their employers think that they are only created to be machines for life. (46)

It is not hard to hear Gray's quiet tones behind this lament; we notice, however, that the utterance not only recasts some of the exemplary luminaries but also the terms of the social problem. Leaving to one side Campkin's shift of emphasis upon who is to blame for the current state of affairs—are the parents culpable, or is it the fault of the employers?—we can pay full attention to his revision of the Elegy's position on unrealized talent: the issue now is not the absence of educational opportunities for the poor, but rather the limitation of their education to a few early years. For a significant proportion of the upper, middle, and even working classes at this stage in the nineteenth century, Campkin's complaint would have offended their beliefs about the appropriate accommodation of the "lower orders": in the words of R. H. Tawney in the 1920s, elementary education was perceived for many years as "a self sufficient kind of education designed for a particular section of the community" (35). The idea that children from all backgrounds and of all levels of achievement should receive an extended two-part education, first in a primary, and then in some form of secondary, school, would not receive full governmental implementation until nearly a hundred years after the publication of *The Struggles of a Village Lad*. What happened instead in the intervening years was the progressive, albeit gradual, extension of a scholarship system.

The partial solution to the problem that Campkin raises rhetorically, and then addresses with West's elevation—the selection, by competitive examination, of the brightest children in the elementary school for a free grammar-school place—became a little more of a reality in the years that followed the reception of the 1864–68 Royal Commission, but not without a cost to the less academically able sons of the poor who might previously have received a free place on local residence grounds. While many of the Taunton Inquiry recommendations were ignored, an Endowed Schools Commission was established to promote the more effective use of endowments in line with a new classification system, which divided schools into three socially differentiated grades. As Digby and Searby comment in *Children, School and Society in Nineteenth-Century England*, these moves effectively reduced the total number of free places, which were seen as "suspect because they gave a place . . . to boys of an inferior social class to that predicted for the school," but they worked to promote the merit-based scholarship, providing "a narrow ladder of opportunity for the very gifted" (12). In a haphazard and regionally uneven fashion, awards specifically intended for "high fliers" from local elementary schools gradually began to appear; by 1878, for instance, Leeds Grammar School had "four scholarships every year of £20 for two years for boys under thirteen who had been in Public Elementary Schools and had passed the examination in the sixth standard." After legislation in 1891 allowed local school boards to fund these scholarships, the likelihood that individual grammars would offer competitive places to elementary-school children increased further; in the 1890s Sheffield Grammar School had four awards, Wigan twenty-five, and London as a whole some five hundred by 1893. In 1900 there were around 5,500 scholarships available by competition to high-achieving pupils from what were now the free elementary schools, national, board, or otherwise. Just under a third of a million eleven-year-olds were in education by this point, the vast majority of them attending those free institutions. The chances of winning an award were thus around a hundred to one, but subject to pronounced geographical variations; there were no central governmental structures in place to regulate the system or ensure that a coherent network covered the country.

Moving into the 1900s brings us to the era that saw both the increase of the number of grammars across Britain and the progressive reinforcement of this particular educational formation's hegemonic power at local and national levels. The grammar school was to weather a wide range of reforms throughout the first two-thirds of the twentieth century, but it is fair to say this highly influential social structure came to be associated with two main ideas over this long period. In the first place, the grammar school did not lose what was by 1900 a long-standing reputation as a solidly middle-class preserve and bastion of middle-class values; in the second place, however, and at the same time, the grammar school became increasingly perceived as the natural and appropriate destination for the brightest children of the working classes.[20] This state of affairs was largely unaffected by the changes wrought by the 1944 Education Act, a piece of legislation that is today broadly, although inaccurately, imagined to have brought the possibility for upward mobility via education into Britain's social scene for the very first time.[21] Even though the introduction of the comprehensive system in the 1960s and 1970s did away with the grammar school in many (although by no means all) parts of the country, the strange fact that this particular institution had signified both of these messages at the same time continued to have an incalculably huge effect upon British culture and politics; indeed, because of the time lag between individuals' educational experiences and their executive or cultural power in the social sphere, the complex consequences of this hybrid formation still make themselves felt in profound ways today.

To concentrate upon this phenomenon is to bring into focus one of the factors that contribute to the continuing, and much-discussed, differences between the two countries in this study. In his 1945 autobiography *A Cockney on Main Street*, upholsterer's son and taxi driver Herbert Hodge (b. 1901) reflected upon the question of national divergence in the following manner: "The American boy," he writes, "grows up in a community 'dedicated to the proposition that all men are born free and equal'" (quoted in Rose, 361–62). Hodge was not so naïve as to believe that this resulted in actual freedom and equality in the United States; as Jonathan Rose notes in *The Intellectual Life of the British Working Classes*, "He was outraged when the Chicago police ransacked the home of an elderly black lady, disgusted by the American 'dollar complex' and success-at-any-cost ethic" and found "[l]abor-management hostility in Detroit . . . worse than anything he had seen in Britain" (361). "But," Hodge continued, "because [Americans] are all of them dedicated to the proposition they do tend to behave in their social intercourse as if it were so. And that is at least the beginning of true democracy. We'll never get as near as that to democracy until we've abolished our caste system of education" (361–62). Invidious tendencies have certainly warped the bias of American public education over the years—inequitable racial and economic segregational practices spring most readily to mind[22]—but the systems that prevailed in Britain in the late nineteenth and first half of the twentieth centuries found no footing across the Atlantic. While scholarship programs have at different times and places enabled gifted students to make the transition from high school to college, American states have never established wide-scale, publically funded programs to abstract high-achieving elementary-school children out of the mass free institutions and into prestigious fee-paying alternatives. In Britain, however, the grammar school, simultaneously selective and nonselective, "free" and fee-levying, took up a pivotal position in the complex and evolving structure of British twentieth-century state education. In consequence, it has played a directional role in the operation of the country's class system.

At the beginning of the twentieth century, the apprentice system and the Higher Grade schools allowed certain high-achieving elementary-school pupils to continue their education within what were largely indigenous working-class structures. Many more of these children, of course, would simply leave school as soon as they could and get a job. But as a result of a series of government measures instituted in the next four decades, the educational and, in due course, professional opportunities for exceptionally promising children of the poor were gradually but decisively transformed. In effect, bright children were systematically removed from the lower classes through the medium of the grammar school and for the most part relocated within the middle classes, happily or otherwise, for the rest of their lives. In his account of the developments in these years, A. J. P. Taylor remarks that "[e]ducation, usually a solvent, produced in England a further hardening of class lines" (170). It is hard not to agree: as we shall see, a controlled number of scholarships allowed a proportion of the ablest working-class children to move a little up the social scale while long-standing patterns of economic inequity and class division remained generally unchanged.

Reflecting upon the Elegy in the essay quoted earlier, G. K. Chesterton constructed a historical allegory around the departing figure glimpsed in the poem's first stanza; already at the midpoint of the eighteenth century, he reckons, the humble plowman is "passing out of the sight and reach of that learned and sensitive and secluded gentleman," the speaker, and moving into a new age that Gray "could not understand" (125). But "[w]hen the ploughman comes back out of that twilight," Chesterton continues, "he will come back different. He will be either a scientific works-manager or an entirely new kind of agrarian citizen great as in the first days of Rome; a free peasant or a servant of alien machinery; but never the same again" (126). As things transpired, Gray's plowman-plus-education did not overturn the existing structures of society; of the range of outcomes that Chesterton imagines as possibilities from his vantage point of the mid-1930s, only the first came to pass. The plowman, if he possessed some portion of that potential genius that might have lain in the graves of his forefathers, now ascended from the elementary school to the grammar school, and thence to a respectable job with a decent salary, or, if he could once more buck the odds and win a further scholarship to university, thence to a slightly more respectable job with a slightly more decent salary. He would then plod, or perhaps even drive, homeward from the scientific works; there his busy housewife would ply her evening care; his children would run to lisp their sire's return.

The chief concern of the administrators who reconfigured the structures of English education in the first years of the twentieth century was "with the academically highly able and the grammar schools," rather than with the development of increased opportunities for majority populations (Sanderson, 24).[23] The 1902 Education Act, masterminded by Sir Robert Morant, abolished the small independent school boards and set up 200 Local Education Authorities (LEAs) that could use the rates both to create municipal or county grammar schools and to provide grants to the existing endowed establishments; by 1906, these provisions were helping to fund over 25,000 scholarship places, nearly a fivefold increase upon the 1900 number. The new grammar schools, just like the old, were conceived of as fee-paying institutions; regulations laid down in 1904 also ensured that their curricular design emulated the existing model in important respects (minimum study times were set for arts subjects, largely to ensure that pupils learned the Latin that was necessary for potential entrance to Oxford or Cambridge). In 1907 further measures aimed to increase the flow of bright children into both these schools and the existing grammars: higher grants were now given to those schools that offered 25 percent of the number of entrants of the previous year to scholars from elementary schools. Five years later, nearly 35 percent of all pupils in grammar schools were free placers, some 52,583 children in all. This meant that the majority of their schoolfellows continued to be "middle-class fee payers of very mixed ability," but, as Sanderson comments, "the scholarship Regulations of 1907 were . . . a vital part of the ladder of opportunity between the elementary school and the grammar school" (24). Although huge geographical variations still obtained, by 1914 a child from a public elementary school had roughly a forty-to-one chance of obtaining a free place.

Educational proposals and enactments over the next thirty years were mainly directed towards the inch-by-inch extension of various postelementary opportunities for the huge bulk of what were considered to be less academic children, but a few policies continued to increase the number of scholarships to grammar school: in the 1920s Sir Charles Trevelyan, the president of the Board of Education, encouraged LEAs to bring the proportion of grammar schools' intake from elementary schools up from 25 to 40 percent, and in the 1930s a grammar-school building program increased the number of places overall. All of these measures sought to afford extended educational opportunities for poor-but-bright pupils (and, not incidentally, to realize their talents for the ultimate benefit of the nation). Nevertheless, the number of children from public elementary schools who made it to grammar school, although much larger than pre- and early-twentieth-century totals, still constituted a relatively small proportion of the age cohort. Between 1931 and 1941, a working-class boy stood rather less than a one-in-ten chance of entering a selective secondary school. At all points in the first four decades of the twentieth century, to win—or to be perceived as on the way to winning—a free place at the grammar school was to be separated from the majority, to be marked out as a special figure in both the schoolroom and the community. Still, in the general scheme of things, the aggregate of these children formed a significantly sizable social trend. Now, even if you were a youth to fortune and to fame unknown, your humble birth might not preclude your eventual study of Fair Science in all her many guises. But what would be the consequence of this? Would Melancholy also mark you for her own?

◆ ◆ ◆

Obvious sites for the investigation of this question are the autobiographies of those who began their lives in the British working classes. Thanks in large part to the magisterial annotated critical bibliography of *The Autobiography of the Working Class* produced by John Burnett, David Vincent, and David Mayall, it is today relatively easy to access these documents in large numbers; among them exists a substantial quantity of testimonies written by those whose years of elementary-school attendance occurred in the period stretching between the last decade of the nineteenth century and the beginning of World War II. Unsurprisingly, nearly all the autobiographies of this class and era address the scholarship issue in some way; Jonathan Rose, an important recent interpreter of the genre, notes that such memoirs tend to be written by those who did well at school, while those "whom the system failed were much less likely to record their lives on paper" (148). Consequently success at elementary school frequently looms large, often constituting the first significant experience of self-affirmation that set the memoirist on his or her journey to the eventual act of autobiographical composition. Further, the fact that a large number of the autobiographers made their careers in teaching, that traditional province of the poor scholar, also helps to explain a repeated concentration upon the relationship between individual development and educational structures.

A representative example of this particular story occurs in the reminiscences of Derek Davies (b. 1923); the son of a Midlands metalworker, Derek ultimately became the headmaster of a school in Devon. Although some autobiographers record that their prowess at school won them special attention from the age of eight or nine onwards,[24] Davies' narrative bears witness to the common practice of moving children likely to pass the "Scholarship" out of their large classes into a specially taught set in the year before they turned eleven and took the selective exam (which hence also came to be known in this period as the "11+").[25] Once in this set, Davies notes, "I was one of the pampered and protected elite." Yet the attrition rate was severe: "Each year about a dozen started the course. About seven or eight were finally entered for the examination and usually two or three at most passed" (ed. Goldman, 28). The numbers were still more brutal in Star Road School, the West London elementary attended by Joan Hughes (b. 1928). Of the fifty girls in Class Five, the upper half were allowed to take a preliminary test; the eight who passed this proceeded to intensive training for the full examination. One child out of these eight succeeded: only Hughes scored high enough to win a Junior County Scholarship.[26]

But how far did the funds awarded by a scholarship go towards meeting the true cost of attending grammar school? "My mother knew we could not cope with uniform, books, satchel and hockey-stick," wrote Bim Andrews (b. 1909) of her sacrifice of a Cambridge County Scholarship won in 1920. "She was realistic and right. . . . So I was inserted into the Higher Grade School which, like my father's pub, was at the bottom of the street" (quoted in Burnett, *Destiny Obscure*, 161). As early as 1877, Oxford don and city councillor Thomas Hill Green had been insisting that "scholarships merely equivalent to whole or part of the school fees are not sufficient to enable really poor boys to continue their school education. Scholarships must carry some payment toward maintenance" (quoted in Marsden and Jackson, 204). At different times and places in the first four decades of the twentieth century, certain awards from LEAs included such a maintenance grant as well as tuition costs, but many others did not; conditions changed, too, after an economy campaign introduced in 1932 converted many free places into "special places" with a means-tested scale of fees. Parents were repeatedly placed in difficult positions; even if they were generally in favor of allowing their child to take up his or her place at the grammar school (and many, as numerous memoirs reveal, were not), this move had the potential to invoke all kinds of worries. Household income inevitably affected deliberations—over the period under scrutiny, the children at public elementary schools came from a broadening range of socioeconomic levels, and expenditure that constituted a hardship for one family would be more easily covered by another—but the attitudes and personalities of different mothers and fathers would also have played a contributory role.

For an array of reasons, then, many of those awarded scholarships never went to grammar school. In Bradford in 1926, 60 percent of free-place winners did not take them up; ten years later in Manchester, 20 percent of awardees were still turning their places down. And even if children from financially strapped homes did begin to attend the grammar school on a scholarship, how long would they stay? Once the official school-leaving age was reached, and if jobs were readily available in the immediate area, the temptation to allow—or push—a child to enter employment must have been strong, and all the more so if that child were not enjoying, or succeeding, in the grammar school. Some children, on the other side of things, desperately wished to stay on, but the combination of monetary pressures and parental anxieties, often compounded by insensitive local rules and regulations, made continued attendance impossible. In his chapter on school experience in the invaluable study *Destiny Obscure*,[27] John Burnett relates the story of Edith Williams, who had won a scholarship to Cyfarthfa Castle Secondary School in 1910: "though doing well there, she had to be withdrawn when the cost of textbooks became too great in a family of eight children, and after the LEA had written to inform parents that if they withdrew children for this reason, they would be exempt from the usual fine for early withdrawal." How did Edith feel about this? "I was heartbroken and bitter, and my sense of deprivation was so great that I nursed this grievance for many years afterwards" (161).

For this girl, the experience of leaving grammar school inflicted a deep wound; for other children, the experience of attending grammar school cut them to the quick on a daily basis. Just as most autobiographies written by individuals born into the working classes in this period contain a discussion of "the Scholarship," so do the memoirs of scholarship winners invariably broach the topic of class consciousness, as it might manifest itself in and out of the classroom. Indeed, awareness of this issue had for generations formed part of the discussion of the grammar school, as key paragraphs from the Taunton Inquiry of 1864–68 reveal:

> At several schools the free scholars were made to sit in a different part of the room; at another the two sets of boys were separated by a "partition breast high." The use of the playground was a continual problem. In one it was divided "by an imaginary line between the boarders and free boys and a penalty imposed on transgressors." (*British Parliamentary Papers*, 2:478)

Hard physical divisions may have disappeared by the twentieth century, but the testimony of one former scholarship-child after another certainly suggests that the "imaginary line" around the "free boys" and girls continued to make itself felt. The memoirs, admittedly, record a range of responses; conditions varied from school to school, decade to decade; and even within a single institution, subjective attitudes to, or experiences with, the same circumstances might differ greatly. In the telegraphic account of his early years that he supplied to a French publisher in 1928, D. H. Lawrence (b. 1885) registers the isolation of this cohort as a simple unemotional fact of grammar-school life:

> [W]ent to elementary school—at age of twelve won a scholarship for Nottingham High School, considered best day school in England— purely bourgeois school—quite happy there but scholarship boys were a class apart. (300)

In its essential details, Lawrence's experience was probably shared by many; for others, though, that consciousness of being in "a class apart" was excruciatingly painful. Burnett provides some distressing illustrations of this, prefacing the quoted testimonies with the following remarks:

> Perhaps most sharply felt and expressed was the sense of social inferiority and isolation in the large, post-1902 secondary schools, where the scholarship holders were often more intelligent than the fee-payers, and, not infrequently at the top of the class, but could find themselves socially ostracized by a mixture of envy and contempt.[28]
> (161)

The school experiences of Kathleen Betterton (b. 1913), whose father was a liftman on the London Underground, were not obviously cruel, but they were just as transformative after she had won a prized place, with "all found," to Christ's Hospital, which was (and is) a boarding institution. Here, Betterton writes, "one of the first questions put to new girls by the rest was always—'Are you a scholarship girl?'" (quoted in Burnett, *Destiny Obscure*, 211). In some schools, "free placers" were continually reminded of their status, and therefore could never forget the exact position of that place in relation to their fee-paying counterparts.

It would be daft to claim that working-class scholarship winners had any kind of monopoly on the humiliating sensations of class discrimination; it would be equally wrongheaded to suggest that they formed the only category of individuals to suffer lifelong effects therefrom. Yet British scholarship boys and girls often found themselves in a particularly unenviable place; if their presence in a grammar school was seen as bringing a working-class element into a middle-class preserve, then their experience was especially difficult. The opportunities among schoolchildren to oppress a sensitive scholarship boy or girl must have been legion, but while I do not wish to minimize the potentially severe effects of this kind of treatment, they are not my immediate concern here. Instead, I am more interested in the psychological dimensions of a working-class child's absorption into the culture of the secondary institution. Arguably, the twentieth-century grammar school ended up teaching its free-place pupils more about class than about the classics; it is in the rift opened up by this part of the school's education that I wish to set our further investigation of Gray's Elegy and other memorized poems.

Whether or not a particular grammar school presented itself, overtly or covertly, as a middle-class institution, and whether or not an individual scholarship-winner suffered class-motivated discrimination therein, the fact remains—children from working-class backgrounds who attended grammar school in the period in question, and indeed beyond, acquired a perspective that could not help but distance them from the expectations and assumptions of their home communities. The memoirs of Richard Hoggart and Kathleen Betterton help us to see that the culture of a school and one's experience in it could differ in marked ways, and yet still have the same ultimate effect. Hoggart, an orphan brought up in great poverty by his grandmother with financial assistance from the Board of Guardians, writes of his grammar school, like a huge number of ex-working-class memoirists, with gratitude and respect. Cockburn High School, though imposing and impressive to the young Hoggart, occupied a fairly modest position in the hierarchy of secondary educational establishments in Leeds. During his period there, Hoggart explains, "just over half of [its] pupils were still fee-paying," but "fees must have been so slight that even quite small self-employed grocers or tailors or hardware-shop owners could afford them"; the children of "local doctors," on the other hand, went "to one of the Yorkshire public schools or, probably after some preparatory training, to Leeds Grammar School, an independent foundation near the middle of town which also took in the sons of solicitors, accountants, plain aspirants and the like, as Leeds Girls' High School did for the girls" (*A Local Habitation*, 158).

Within Cockburn, and its consequently relatively narrow range of social grades, Hoggart remembers "no snobbery or bullying":

> This was because for the first time in our lives we were in an environment created not by accident but by selection, an environment whose main purpose was to train clever children to make effective use of their brains. There was competition, inevitably; but since we were all being pushed from outside we tended, with a good sense we were not aware of having, not to compete overtly among ourselves. The school thought of itself as training us in more than the use of our brains; it offered diluted versions of some public-school values: a healthy mind in a healthy body, responsibility towards the community and the like. But these values were not urged with any great conviction. Brains plus tenacity were the main things. (159–60)

Hoggart thus nicely positions his school's range of class affiliations, but sees them as secondary to a praiseworthy emphasis upon its pupils' academic development and earnest application. Nevertheless, he makes it quite clear that his first walk from the back-to-back houses of his poor neighborhood to the grammar school high on the hill was a symbolic journey "out of Hunslet and the life of Hunslet," "towards ways of life, ways of seeing life, which Hunslet did not offer but which as the weeks and months passed I saw could be offered in other places and were in some important ways preferable" (156). He was not quite alone as he walked across the moor:

> Other boys and a smaller number of girls, but in all no more than a trickle, thirty-odd scholarship holders a year, out of the 65,000 people

who lived in South Leeds, were coming out of the crowded streets, togged out in their silly new blazers and even sillier caps, starting the journey away, getting on to the first of the little launching pads. From now on their main friendships would be of the classrooms not the streets; they would dance to different drums. No parents would go with them, that first day or any other. In the early months the boys and girls would not talk to each other en route; that came later if at all. As you pushed off, out of the gravitational pull of your own small ring of streets through others you knew less and less well as the rings widened outwards, the accretions of memory all thinned out: you were enclosed within yourself, looking nervously but doggedly ahead, one person going though what would have seemed to outsiders like featureless, dull streets to a new order of life, new words, new ways of behaving, new kinds of excitement, a novel sense of possible openings-out, "prospects." (156–57)

Putting Hoggart's account of this definitive break next to Betterton's depiction of the effects of her secondary-school days at Christ's Hospital from 1924 onwards yields some interesting results. A boarding school has more opportunities than a day school to exert its influence upon its charges; as Betterton describes it, the intense process of acculturation worked to reorient the child from the world of home to the world of school:

> The school absorbed us completely into itself, tolerating no other loyalties. Dimly we discerned a divergence between home and school standards, but we could hardly help believing that the school was always right. Parents lost their authority; it was never precisely stated, yet it was often plainly implied, that they were foolish or misguided in their outlook. Headmistress, matron and mistresses by degrees loomed more important in our minds. The weekly letter home, written under supervision on Sunday evenings, the three half-holiday visits from parents—these during term-time were our only family links. Home, though nostalgically remembered, became remote and foreign. Of this gradual process we were at the time unconscious, yet it exercised a strong psychological influence. It produced division, doubt, a sense of divided allegiance. (Quoted in Burnett, *Destiny Obscure*, 211)

To a certain degree, the feelings that Hoggart and Betterton describe partake of the general experience of transition from childhood to adulthood, a process that for many people shifts the weight of emotional importance away from the family group and towards the individual, away from the parental home and towards the structures that succeed it. For the scholarship child, however, these common sensations are greatly magnified and played out across a sharply differentiated social landscape. Whether or not the alma mater is regarded with affection or loathing, ex-working-class autobiographers repeatedly represent their grammar-school days as an education away from their origins; whether or not the school is explicitly identified as a middle-class structure, it is inevitably associated with systems of individuation, regulation, competition, and self-advancement that are presented as antithetical to the prevailing ethos of working-class life. For middle-class children, the assumptions and expectations that patterned grammar-school life were generally more of a piece with the structures of belief that existed at home; for them, "getting on" in their education was part of their appointed role on earth. For working-class children, "getting on," even when admired and encouraged as it so often was by proud parents, relations, and neighbors, meant leaving those very families and communities behind.

To present the inner tensions of "the scholarship boy" in this manner is to follow quite deliberately in the path first explored by Richard Hoggart in 1957. The *Uses of Literacy*'s original presentation of the scholarship boy is admirably judicious; with all the delicacy of a natural scientist, Hoggart subdivides the species, remarking thoughtfully upon the various innate characteristics and environmental circumstances that might result in scholarship-winning children taking up a wide range of different jobs or attitudes. The fact that a working-class boy has undergone a spell at grammar school cannot tell us what level of success he will attain in the world, nor—and perhaps this is the more important point—can it tell us how that individual will ultimately regard the social arrangements of that world.[29] Hoggart is careful to say that those who do not fulfill their early promise, at least in society's eyes, are the most likely to be afflicted by a severe sense of inward division, but in his estimation the difference between these individuals and those who have gone on to win the world's glittering prizes is a question of degree, not kind:

> I am sometimes inclined to think that the problem of self-adjustment is, in general, especially difficult for those working-class boys who are only moderately endowed, who have talent sufficient to separate themselves from the majority of their working-class contemporaries, but not to go much farther . . . this kind of anxiety often seems most to afflict those in the working classes who have been pulled one stage away from their original culture . . . yet . . . it is interesting to see how this occasionally obtrudes (particularly today, when ex-working-class boys move in all the managing areas of society) in the touch of insecurity, which often appears as an undue concern to establish "presence" in an otherwise quite professorial professor, in the intermittent rough homeliness of an important executive and committee-man, in the ten-

dency to vertigo which betrays a lurking sense of uncertainty in a suc-
cessful journalist. (243)

Quoting a near-contiguous passage from *The Uses of Literacy* in a com-
monplace book published in 2002, the poet (and former scholarship boy)
D. J. Enright (b. 1920) argues that this unease constitutes a never-to-be
satisfied spur to success for his high-achieving comrades:

> Permanently in irksome debt, morally speaking, to his origins, the
> scholarship boy doesn't have to do well, he has to do brilliantly, mak-
> ing sure to become a top professor at Oxford or Cambridge, one of the
> best writers around, a great inventor, a celebrated surgeon, a senior
> politician (not that he thinks much of politicians). He must be offered
> a peerage (which naturally he will decline) and above all he needs to
> make a lot of money—not because he reveres money, for he certainly
> doesn't, but because it is the objective proof of success, and he can give
> it to his parents (who are long since dead). In short, he can never do
> sufficiently well, never be "usual" enough. (100)

The bright working-class individual, Hoggart argues, cannot "acquire
the unconscious confidence of many a public-school-trained child of the
middle-classes. He has been trained like a circus-horse, for scholarship
winning" (248). The process begins at elementary school, where "he is
likely to be in some degree set apart" (244); once he has made it to the
grammar, there is no going back. For the archetypal scholarship-winner
under Hoggart's microscope, the worlds of home and school exist as two
distinct entities: they are patterned by incommensurate sets of ideas, as-
sociated with two different classes, and productive of a profound internal
division.

◆ ◆ ◆

According to Hoggart and other former scholarship children, then, the
experience of attending a grammar school opened up a lifelong rift
within: the fact and form of their secondary educations revealed to them
a new way of being and a new way of perceiving the structures of society,
not to mention their ambiguous status therein. Yet if the grammar school
sent out these messages in a general and all-pervasive manner, some of its
lessons had the potential to deliver a much more pointed exposition of
the theme of class difference. Where would scholarship winners learn
that a broad chasm yawned between the two worlds in which they now
existed? Most explicitly, it was lessons in the humanities that told work-
ing-class children of the minor or absent importance of the poor to their
great island's story;[30] what were they, after all, but the mulch of centuries

of British life—that which had made no history and had written no great literature? Britain's heroes had not come from penury; it was entirely illogical to imagine that Britain's great poets could have been inspired by an unlettered muse. Why on earth would you subject the short and simple annals of the poor to academic scrutiny in the classroom? This was not even a question that could be framed or raised: scholarship winners, in company with all but the most somnolent of their classmates, had already discovered at earlier stages of their educations that the lower ranks were of negligible interest. In the curricular design of its history and English lessons, the grammar school was merely continuing on a line that the elementary school had tacked with considerable exactitude. Indeed, the elementary school had not only taught its pupils this message, but had insisted that they memorize, and recite it, to the class.

I have, then, finally maneuvered this chapter round to a consideration of one of the questions that constituted the original motivating forces behind the project as a whole. What did children make of a process that asked them to commit to heart a work that either bore absolutely no relation to their own lives or, more disturbingly, told them that they—or, at least, the social stratum with which they were associated—did not count in the overall scheme of things? It is a question that took some time to take shape in my head, but it must have been there, if only in wordless form, on the numerous occasions when I listened to my grandmother recite her one memorized poem, Newbolt's miniepic "He fell among thieves." (Or rather, as the opening of her word-perfect delivery had it, "He-fell-among-thieves-by-Sir-Henry-Newbolt"—evidently my grandmother's elementary-school teacher was one of the few who insisted on the inclusion of titles and names of authors at the beginning of a recitation.) Here is Newbolt's poem in the full glory of all its forty-eight lines:

> "Ye have robb'd," said he, "ye have slaughter'd and made an end,
>   Take your ill-got plunder, and bury the dead:
> What will ye more of your guest and sometime friend?"
>   "Blood for our blood," they said.
>
> He laugh'd: "If one may settle the score for five,
>   I am ready; but let the reckoning stand 'til day:
> I have loved the sunlight as dearly as any alive."
>   "You shall die at dawn," said they.
>
> He flung his empty revolver down the slope,
>   He climb'd alone to the Eastward edge of the trees;
> All night long in a dream untroubled of hope
>   He brooded, clasping his knees.

He did not hear the monotonous roar that fills
    The ravine where the Yassin river sullenly flows;
He did not see the starlight on the Laspur hills,
    Or the far Afghan snows.

He saw the April noon on his books aglow,
    The wistaria trailing in at the window wide;
He heard his father's voice from the terrace below
    Calling him down to ride.

He saw the gray little church across the park,
    The mounds that hid the loved and honour'd dead;
The Norman arch, the chancel softly dark,
    The brasses black and red.

He saw the School Close, sunny and green,
    The runner beside him, the stand by the parapet wall,
The distant tape, and the crowd roaring between,
    His own name over all.

He saw the dark wainscot and timber'd roof,
    The long tables, and the faces merry and keen;
The College Eight and their trainer dining aloof,
    The Dons on the daïs serene.

He watch'd the liner's stem ploughing the foam,
    He felt her trembling speed and the thrash of her screw;
He heard the passengers' voices talking of home,
    He saw the flag she flew.

And now it was dawn. He rose strong on his feet,
    And strode to his ruin'd camp below the wood;
He drank the breath of the morning cool and sweet:
    His murderers round him stood.

Light on the Laspur hills was broadening fast,
    The blood-red snow-peaks chill'd to dazzling white;
He turn'd, and saw the golden circle at last,
    Cut by the Eastern height.

"O glorious Life, Who dwellest in earth and sun,
    I have lived, I praise and adore Thee." A sword swept.
Over the pass the voices one by one
    Faded, and the hill slept.[31]

    I try to imagine the day at Teesdale Street Board School, an elementary
school that served one of London's poorest districts in Bethnal Green,

when Eileen Adams (b. 1912) stood up to recite this poem. What would she and her classmates have made of such sensational imperial violence—the sickening thrill of the sweeping sword and those blood-red peaks; the contrast between the treacherous denizens of the Hindu Kush and our oh-so-noble nameless hero, separated from his country, his countrymen, and, ultimately, his head, but never from his unswerving code of honor? Is it possible that those schoolchildren thought about the differences between their lives and the life reviewed by the quintessential English gentleman on the night before his death? Not for Eileen the comfortable upper-class home in rural England; sporting and popular success at public school and then an Oxbridge college; travel to the furthest limit of empire to explore the untamed reaches of the East—instead Eileen, sharp as a tack and top of her class, would leave school at fourteen and work in an East End sweatshop making silk blouses for couturiers on Bond Street; she would marry at twenty-two, give birth to my mother, and then contract the tuberculosis that would keep her a semi-invalid in a slum-clearance-era council house in Chingford on the outskirts of London until her death in 1990. I have no wish to stake my all on the inevitability of identification in our reading processes: we do not necessarily or even primarily look for representations of ourselves, or of people like us, in the literary work in our hands or on our tongues, and it's a truism that much of our pleasure and interest in the arts comes from the immersion they offer in previously unimaginable and unknown worlds, lives and emotions. Very likely it was in this vein that the schoolchildren of Teesdale Street Board School experienced and enjoyed "He fell among thieves," if indeed they considered its content very much at all. But what if one of those East Enders, at the time or in later life, thought about Newbolt's poem and wondered how he or she might fit into the story it told? If this work were assigned today, a schoolchild whose parents or grandparents had come to Britain from South Asia might, with reason, find its assumptions more than a little galling. But back in the first few decades of the twentieth century, where would you have found someone like yourself, or like one of your ancestors, in the poems that you recited in your elementary-school classroom?

England's poor are in Newbolt's poem, though it is hard to spot them at first. They lie at the very center of the poem, and they lie where they lie in Gray's Elegy, in the very same country churchyard. "The mounds that hid the loved and honour'd dead" stand in lineal descent from the poem of poems, even if Newbolt has thrown in "loved" and detached the prefix from "unhonour'd" to leave untroubled his dream of an English rural idyll. But the turf still heaves "in many a mould'ring heap," and the rude forefathers of the hamlet sleep on, forming an organic community of ancestral English dead that in Newbolt's poem serves as counterpoint to the singular death of the British hero overseas, the man who fell among thieves (which is to say, among foreigners). Did any of the children notice that this was the only way that their forebears contributed towards the constitution of national identity? Time and again, the poems assigned for memorization in Britain's elementary schools carried the implicit message that the poor were, well, pretty much like dirt, the soil, the loamy clay—a necessary medium, to be sure, but an unchanging and undifferentiated substrate that was part of nature, not culture. They were part of Britain's history inasmuch as they had been there all along, but none of her noble words and deeds had come out of this lowly bed, this lap of Earth. And which verses put forward this sad-but-true, regrettable-but-inevitable message in the clearest terms of all? When Eliza Fitzgerald and all those other bright pupils at the top of their classes recited Gray's Elegy in their final year at elementary school, did they ever consider what relation there might be between their own piping voices and the noiseless tenor of the poor? Did scholarship hopefuls wonder if their ambition mocked the useful toil, the homely joys and destiny obscure of their parents, and their parents before them? Did it occur to them to cast one longing, ling'ring look at those who had been left behind?

To frame such questions is to excite some reasonable objections. In the first place, I concede that one can certainly memorize a poem without ever considering its meaning—indeed, as I argued in the last case study, the experience of enforced and stressful recitation would for many militate against any temptation whatsoever to analyze a work's content. But we should not close the door on the possibility that some individuals may have thought about the words they stored so deeply within themselves; we shall explore this issue more fully in our analysis of this book's third case study, but it has a necessary presence in this chapter too. In the second place, to wonder about the existence of such ideologically aware reactions in the era under scrutiny may seem highly anachronistic—may seem to impose upon an earlier age perspectives that became generally available only in the latter half of the twentieth century. Once again, however, we shall find that although responses to the schoolroom canon varied greatly, some of them do demonstrate sensitivity to its class assumptions. We might imagine that a resurrected Sir Henry Newbolt would snort in disbelief if he could read my stereotypical early-twenty-first-century, predictably left-leaning, sentences about "He fell among thieves," but even he, at least at the beginning of the 1920s, knew that accusations of class bias could be, and were, levied against the way poetry was being taught in schools. As the chairman of the 1921 government inquiry into "The Teaching of English in England," Newbolt was duty-bound to record the existence of opinions he did not share:

Literature seems to be classed by a large number of thinking working men with antimacassars, fish-knives and other unintelligible and futile trivialities of "middle class" culture, and, as a subject of instruction, is suspect as an attempt to "sidetrack the working-class movement." . . . We were told . . . working men felt any attempt to teach them litera- ture or art was an attempt to impose on them the culture of another class. (252–53)

We may not find the point of view attributed here to "working men" ex- pressed quite so unambiguously in the memoirs and oral histories of those who memorized poems at school, but it is sometimes there, nevertheless.

So exactly what kind of responses to the recitation exercise can we find in the autobiographies of those who attended elementary schools? First and foremost—and in direct opposition to the fear and trepidation that this book has hitherto clustered around its subject—these writers remember the experience with pleasure. Admittedly, as we have noted before, we are here examining special, not representative, cases—indi- viduals who take the trouble to write their autobiographies are often those for whom the written word has had a lifelong charm. Even when this acknowledgment has been made, however, it is hard not to be caught up in these rapturous evocations: the excitement of poetic meter and dic- tion are remembered in delighted detail—the racing rhythms, the hissing of sibilants, the chiming of rhymes, the novelty of pronouncing out-of- the-ordinary words. Yet the most ardent celebrations of recitations past tend to locate their pleasure not in any cumulative comprehension of a poem's meanings, but rather in the physical sensation of a fine-sounding word or phrase, or in the incantatory or dramatic thrill of prolonged rhythmical declamation, or in the two combined. The analytical powers of the mind are less commonly invoked; it is the body and the senses that are fed by poetic language and its performance.

Dorothy Parker famously insisted that the most beautiful words in the English language are "cellar door"; for these memoirists, too, the seman- tic content of poetic diction often plays a subsidiary, or even an absent, role in the seductive charms of recitation. Anne Treneer (b. 1891), who won a scholarship to St. Austell County School in Cornwall and then went on to become an English teacher, devotes pages and pages of *School House in the Wind*, her autobiographical trilogy, to memories of intoning poetry at school and away. "A child said to me once that she liked poetry because she liked the taste of the nice words in her mouth," she remarks at one point; "Tennyson's poetry gave me that voluptuous pleasure" (220). Kathleen Woodward (b. 1896), author of *Jipping Street*, had the minimum of schooling before she had to start work, but language had her in its sensuous lure nevertheless. The protagonist of this disguised autobiography learns many of the *Sonnets from the Portuguese* by heart: these were "oh, sweet and savoury words, to the sound of which I so often went to sleep." "There was nothing that brought sweeter music to my soul than the sound of beautiful words," she comments at an earlier moment; "[t]he Blessing, for example in the Communion Service: 'The peace of God, which passeth all understanding. . .'" (137).

Woodward here connects the mellifluence of Barrett Browning to that of the Book of Common Prayer; many other autobiographers also conflate the pleasures derived from the language of poetry and the language of religion. The cadences of the King James Bible and the rich diction of Victorian hymns exhilarated rhythm-seeking and word-hungry pupils in similar ways to their assigned literary pieces, often penetrating as deeply into their consciousnesses as the memorized poem. "'O measureless might, ineffable love' and 'Who hath believed our report' sound to me now as no other words ever sound," records Albert Mansbridge (b. 1876), founder of the Workers Educational Association, in his autobiography, *The Trodden Road* (12). In church or chapel, Sunday school, morning assembly, or scripture lesson, children could thrill to what Patricia Beer calls the "rich and splendid" words they sang and spoke even if they had little or no conceptual grasp of their actual import (42); further, the pleasure of pronouncing this language and committing it to memory did not need to connect with any orthodox religious feeling (although equally there was no reason why it should not do so).

When these memoirists record the enjoyment they derived from fine-sounding words, then, it matters little to them whether these words came from the zones of poetry or religion. The line between these two different worlds is blurred in a comparable manner when we examine the representation of the pleasures of sustained verbal performance. Certainly, the hypersensitivity that overcame some children when they recited verse could in some ways resemble a spiritual trance, whether or not the words had anything to do with religion; once again, this did not necessarily have anything to do with any apprehension of semantic content. Generally in *The Country Child*, the 1931 fictionalized autobiography of Alison Uttley (b. 1884), schoolroom recitation of divine and secular texts is just part of the daily round: "she learnt to sing-song like the other children, and to recite the Creed and the collects and Gray's *Elegy*. She spent sunny afternoons learning 'The Motherless Boy,' 'The Blind Girl,' and 'Casabianca'" (48). Yet on one significant occasion, the memorized poem provides if not exactly a religious, then definitely a transfiguring, experience. After she wins a shiny half-crown for reciting Addison's "Spacious Firmament" to the local vicar, she repeats her performance in the empty farmhouse kitchen, telling the furniture and the fire her guilty secret that she intends to buy a copy of *A Thousand and One Nights* with the money. She recites "in a low, quiet, vibrating voice," with "her fingers tightly clasped, and a rapt expression on her face"; "a force electrified the room, and the air trembled with thoughts and waves of feeling from the things unseen" (75–76).

If pleasure in recitation occasionally assumed a spiritual dimension, then the opportunities poetry offered for passionate declamation often excited children of a dramatic bent. As Flora Thompson (b. 1876) tells us in *Lark Rise to Candleford* (1939), although most of the pupils in her North Oxfordshire national school hated the "portry" in their *Nelson's Royal Readers*, she and her brother were entranced by such works as "'The Slave's Dream'; 'Young Lochinvar'; 'The Parting of Douglas and Marmion'; Tennyson's 'Brook' and 'Ring out, Wild Bells.'" "'Lochiel's Warning,'" she tells us, "was a favourite with Edmund, who often, in bed at night, might be heard declaiming 'Lochiel! Lochiel! Beware of the day!'" (181). For Janet Hitchman (b. 1916), an orphan shifted around from foster home to foster home, institution to institution, reciting the verses she had learned at school supplied a parallel pleasure to that of making up her own stories and poems, and provided one of her few escapes from a difficult and largely friendless childhood. "I ruled the world in my head," she recalls in her 1960 autobiography *The King of the Barbareens*; "I frequently bumped into people while I was muttering 'The Charge of the Light Brigade.' Sometimes I stood at the edge of the pavement declaiming 'Ruin seize thee, ruthless king / Confusion on thy banners wait' to passing cars" (121).[32]

The pleasure afforded by any aesthetic experience is nearly always a composite affair. Frequently in these reminiscences what is presented as a bodily thrill in either poetic language or the performative dimension of recitation must also have been fueled by mental enjoyment or interest in the story a poem told, or in the series of images and ideas it presented, not to mention the other sources of gratification, extrinsic to the merits or content of a given poem, that this exercise could access. Yet we should not downplay the importance of the purely aural and oral dimensions of spoken poetry; Patricia Beer recited what was to her the "mumbo-jumbo" of

> Grat his een baith bleer't and blin',
> Spak o' lowpin ower a linn

not quite as reverentially as she spoke the words of her beloved T. Gray, but with considerable delight nevertheless (179). Time and again, these memoirists record that as children they were intoxicated with "the sheer magic of words," with "the wonder of words in their own right," as Hoggart puts it, when he describes his first, uncomprehending, reading of Swinburne's poetry in Hunslet Public Library at the age of eleven (*Speak-*

ing to Each Other, 26). Sound without (at least immediate) sense had its own power to fascinate.

Yet it is important, I think, to notice that this experience did not take place at school. For Hoggart, reading "Atalanta in Calydon" was a private matter, both because he discovered the poem on his own, and because he pronounced its words, first in his head in the library, and then out loud after he had memorized it, for himself alone. The delight that Hoggart records here has much in common with the experience of literary rapture described fairly regularly in the autobiographies of working-class autodidacts in the nineteenth century—finding your own way to a piece of dizzyingly lovely poetry and memorizing it for yourself seems to offer a distinctive, often triumphant, form of joy. The examples of Alison Uttley, Flora Thompson's brother, and Janet Hitchman have already shown us that a poem acquired at school might also yield this sensation, but their remembered recitations actually took place in the kitchen, in the bedroom, and on the street. So are melodies heard away from the classroom sweeter than those heard within? When poetry was experienced at school, could the sounds that might entrance a child elsewhere prove to be her undoing?

For the British, since at least the end of the eighteenth century, the spoken word has been intrinsically linked to the question of class difference; to raise this topic is to gesture towards a complex range of issues, most notably explored by Linda Mugglestone in her book *Speaking Proper: The Rise of Accent as Social Symbol*. A thorough investigation of the relationship between recitation and the sociocultural dimensions of pronunciation would require its own full-length study;[33] suffice it to say here that the children who must have suffered most on account of their accents were exactly those who have stood at the center of this chapter's concerns, the scholarship boys and girls. The act of entering any school has the potential to teach a child patterns of language usage and pronunciation that differ from those he or she has employed at home and elsewhere. Children who attended elementary school in the nineteenth and twentieth centuries frequently learned to switch between registers; Thomas Hardy describes this verbal dexterity nicely, telling us that Tess Durbeyfield "who had passed the Sixth Standard in the National School under a London-trained mistress, spoke two languages; the dialect at home, more or less; ordinary English abroad and to persons of quality" (*Tess of the d'Urbervilles*, 12). An elementary school, then, often taught its charges a new ways of speaking; the pupils would most certainly employ this learned pronunciation, with no doubt varying degrees of success, when they performed their institution's most self-consciously linguistic act, the recitation of a poem.[34] And yet would this elementary-school English pass muster at the grammar school? As we know, the teachers in the national and board schools were frequently products of the working classes themselves; elocution courses at teacher-training college, often supplemented by earnest programs of self-improvement, would have done what they could to graft a new accent onto the existing stock, but did such individuals really speak, and could they really teach, "proper English"? Among the pupils themselves, the types of English spoken, both original and acquired, would show some variation, but the children at elementary school were more or less in the same boat, broadly speaking (or speaking broadly). To step into the grammar school, however, was to enter a different linguistic universe; many working-class pupils discovered that their way of talking was the clearest marker of their social difference from both the teachers and the other pupils. Scholarship children, sociologist Judith Okley remarks, "whose accents deviated from the forms deemed 'proper,'" might be subjected to "strategic mimicry and ridicule" during any part of the school day (68). Such discrimination could be most precisely applied, however, in the performance of poetry in the English lesson.

Picture the scene. A scholarship boy, in the West Riding of Yorkshire, is asked to read, or perhaps recite, Keats's "Ode to a Nightingale" by his English master. He begins:

> 4 words only of *mi' art aches* and . . . "Mine's broken,
> you barbarian, T. W.!" *He* was nicely spoken.
> "Can't have our glorious heritage done to death!"
>
> I played the Drunken Porter in *Macbeth*.
>
> "Poetry's the speech of kings. You're one of those
> Shakespeare gives the comic bits to: prose!"

Who better than Tony Harrison to capture in his bitter wit and wordplay the pernicious dynamics of this particular class encounter? If Hoggart stands firm as the scholarship boy's premier analyst, then Harrison is his foremost poetic chronicler. Like his fellow Leeds-man (or, to use the local expression that he has made more widely known, "Loiner"), Harrison is also a scholarship boy himself, despite the fact that he constitutes something of an historical anomaly, a later and less typical flowering of the earlier, more common, phenomenon. Born in 1937, Harrison came of secondary-school age after the vast majority of scholarships had been done away with by the provisions of the 1944 Education Act, but the "independent foundation" of Leeds Grammar School, which gave him an award in 1948, received no funds from the public purse and was thus free to continue in the old ways.

Many of Harrison's poems, most notably those from *The School of Eloquence* sonnet sequence, draw upon the by-now familiar phenomenon of the scholarship winner's experience of division—within himself, from his parents and his community, from the world into which his learning and his talents take him—and place the grammar school's tutelage in the politics of class at the very center of that rift. For our purposes, the couplets quoted above (from the pair of poems entitled "Them & [uz]" in the sonnet cycle) dissect the cruelty of the "nicely spoken" master's attack on the pupil's working-class Yorkshire accent with devastating nicety. In subsequent lines the speaker will wreak a long-deferred revenge on his teacher's historical ignorance about poetry and pronunciation—was that ode not written by "Cockney Keats?"; shouldn't the master have known that "Wordsworth's *matter/water* are full rhymes"?—but this is knowledge gained at a later stage of life, and is of no help to the humiliated youth. How many other working-class children received similar lashes from the tongues of politely, or not so politely, patronizing educators, men and women wrapped in both the full fig of academic black and a sense of their unassailable class-superiority? Who else was pinioned on the crucifix of the "dropped aitch," the shibboleth of Received Pronunciation that does for Harrison's schoolboy (even if, in time, he will be able to see that his "broken" English can transform his aching heart into "art")?[35]

Albert Mansbridge's previously quoted autobiography offers up a similar story, though he declines, or perhaps is unable, to probe the wound to any great depth. Originally a country boy, the young Mansbridge moved to London with his family and became a champion reciter at school and in any other available venue:

> Once at Band of Hope I got through Macaulay's *Spanish Armada* and was given a penny; but mostly it was "Tell me not in mournful numbers," or "All the architects of faith." Imagine a small boy of five or six years old standing before a meeting of the Women's Co-operative Guild, of which my mother was a pioneer member, pouring out the sentiments of mature poets! (13).

In 1886 Mansbridge passed the scholarship examination to win a place at Sir Walter St. John's School in Battersea, and, for the first time, "was brought into contact with boys whose fathers belonged to the professional rather than to the working class." Now, however, his obvious ability to memorize verse was no longer enough to win him a place in the limelight:

> [M]y great ambition was to act in a Speech Day play, and I worked hard to qualify as Antonio in *The Merchant of Venice*, but my cockney accent (it wasn't, it was Gloucestershire) was said to be too marked. Like Antonio himself, I was "certainly undone." (18)

"One of those / Shakespeare gives the comic bits to: prose!"? Mansbridge didn't even get to be Shylock's attendant Launcelot Gobbo, though he does tell us, apparently without rancor, that "[a] year later I was a charming servant maid in the French play. . . . I have never forgotten the words I burst out with" (18). Presumably his working-class accent proved less of an impediment when he was speaking a foreign language and playing a menial. "[T]he speech of kings," the poetry of his own "glorious heritage," was placed out of his reach.[36]

Other children no doubt mimicked the new tongue more easily, acquiring and perfecting its pronunciations and lexicon just as they worked on the grammar school's other lessons. "By this time," recalls Anne Tibble (b. 1912) of her days as a scholarship girl in Northallerton, "I had two quite opposing sets, inner and outer, of values, and two kinds of speech. With unconscious snobbery I imitated the gentry's way of saying certain words, such as 'girl.'" "Their way was preferable," she continues, "[b]ut I kept ready not a few pithy turns of phrase which belong to dialect. These prevented the family of accusing me of 'putting it on'" (125). Register switching continued a fact of life for many individuals after the changes instituted by the 1944 Education Act: "There were children who became bilingual, speaking BBC English at school but roughening up when they got home," comment the sociologists Brian Jackson and Dennis Marsden in their important 1962 study *Education and the Working Class*. The grammar-school system, they note, was still creating highly skilled linguistic chameleons: sometimes "on the public platform, the orthodox working-class child spoke the idiom better than the native-born. It was worked into the very grain of their ambitions" (98).

Children were very likely conscious that they were "putting on" a new voice at school; were they similarly aware that the words they learned and recited might be speaking against them? Numerous individuals record with some surprise that they never thought to question their classrooms' angle of approach to class matters. "History was a matter of battles and kings, and trying to remember their dates," recalls Amy Gomm (b. 1899), the daughter of an electrician. "We'd hear, in passing, of certain villains who 'rose up in revolt.' It was years before we realized that they might have had a point of view" (39–40). Outside school too, working-class children frequently overlooked the political assumptions of their favorite reading matter, and performed acts of cross-class identification that they later found mortifying, perplexing, or, at the least, amusing. Jonathan Rose provides numerous illustrations of this phenomenon, most particularly in relation to the public-school stories that "were a staple of children's papers." Robert Roberts, one of thousands and thousands of children who adored Frank Richards's tales in the *Gem and Magnet*, only questioned this allegiance in later life, noting, "It came as a curious shock to one who revered the Old School when it dawned upon him that he himself was a typical sample of the 'low cads' so despised by all at Greyfriars" (quoted in Rose, 163, 124). Patricia Beer records a similar experience with *The Scarlet Pimpernel*:

> We all identified absolutely with the persecuted aristocrats of the story. It seemed not to occur to one of us that had we lived then we should by reason of our social status have been *sans-culottes* dancing round the guillotine, rather than *vicomtes* escaping in carts. (101)

Beer, that highly accomplished reciter of "most of the poems in Palgrave's *Golden Treasury*," also took her poetry as read; she explains that memorizing a poem in its entirety diminished any desire to take issue with its contents, and made placid acceptance more likely than analysis and dispute. Not that this lessened her pleasure in the exercise:

> Educationists would think this was a terrible way to teach poetry; for me, it was pure magic, pure enchantment. I loved the poets' tone of calm authority; they suggested nothing, they stated, not aggressively but with conviction. It was like listening to an argument that had already been won, to a debating motion that had already been carried, to a recorded programme where nothing could go wrong. (177)

Perhaps other individuals shared these feelings; this would explain to a degree why autobiographers tend to locate their pleasure in poetry's sensuous effects and its performance, and say little about their engagement with the possible meanings of any given work. Beer's words certainly help us to see that the manner in which poetry was presented to children in the classroom must have been hugely influential. As discussed elsewhere, the disciplinary strictures and pedagogical methods that were dominant for many years in mass education were hardly likely to produce classrooms filled with questions; Herbert Spencer lamented in his 1904 autobiography that it was plain to see that the "established systems" encouraged "submissive receptivity instead of independent activity" (1:338). But the rigors of rote learning and mandatory testing cannot be held wholly responsible for the hermetic seal around the closed poetic object that Beer describes. The reasons why a poem, as distinct from other items on the curriculum, did not invite inquiry were inevitably informed, in however a diluted or confused a manner, by prevalent notions about what "literature" was, and what it was for.

The evolution and modulation of such concepts over the past few centuries is a complex, and much discussed, affair. Both the introduction and Part I of this book gave historical accounts of the changes within the elements of those concepts that affected the school's version of literary study; in addition, they demonstrated how understandings of recitation's place in connection to, or within, that study were subject to alteration in the period under scrutiny. Here I wish to make an alternative approach to these issues, and to concentrate, for the moment, on some of the continuities in the relationship between theoretical understandings of classroom literary study and the practice of recitation. An early statement from the man credited as the main architect of British mass education provides an useful starting point for a discussion of some dominant tenets. In 1841, when J. Kay-Shuttleworth described the curriculum he had devised for his model teacher-training college in Battersea, he set out ideas that would subsequently inform his design of the pupil-teacher scheme, the system in which later government legislation would first make poetry recitation mandatory.[37] For Kay-Shuttleworth, the "course of reading in English literature" carries a tremendous importance:

> It . . . forms one of the most important elements in the conception of the objects to be attained in a training school, that the teacher should be inspired with a discriminating but earnest admiration for those gifts of great minds to English literature which are alike the property of the peasant and the peer; national treasures which are among the legitimate sources of national feeling. (339)

Let us consider the key points of this short but complicated amalgam of seemingly egalitarian and avowedly nationalistic opinions. The teacher, it seems, may exercise a certain amount of "discriminat[ion]" in the investigation of a literary text, but adjudication must be allied to "earnest admiration." And why should literature be admired? Because it contains "those gifts of great minds," gifts that are now the property of rich and poor alike; England's heritage, made glorious by authors past, swiftly becomes a heritage that also contains manifest evidence of its laudable democratizing tendencies. This fact, of course, would already be front and center both to the trainee's sense of self and her current endeavors: she, most likely a child of the poor herself, would at that very moment be readying herself to teach those masses, preparing to lay before them Knowledge's ample page, rich with the spoils of time. Inspired, no doubt, by his thoughts of the country's great literature, Kay-Shuttleworth employs poetic gestures of his own in his invocation of an archaic and alliterating "peasant" to represent one pole of British society against the "peer." Ninety years after the composition of Gray's Elegy, then, the peasant appears not as the subject of literature, not as the figure without access to literature, but as the owner of literature; for this educational thinker, the peasant is the same as the peer, at least (or, we might say, only) in his relation to the great wealth of English letters. Literature, in Kay-Shuttleworth's formulation, does not discriminate between the rustic and the noble; while differences of rank and fortune may continue to make themselves felt elsewhere, the nation's literature offers a realm in which all members of English society can participate equally, regardless of their position. And still further: to possess these gifts from England's great minds is to reach a "legitimate" and emotional understanding of the privilege of being English.

Gears will inevitably clash when we attempt to bring Kay-Shuttleworth's exhortatory sentence into relation with the daily reality of poetry teaching in the country's elementaries between 1875 and the 1930s.[38] Nevertheless, while I would not want to insist that his credo came to underwrite every literature lesson throughout this period, its compact expression of a series of charged ideological constructs offers a neat encapsulation of what turned out to be a remarkably long-lived set of assumptions about how and why poetry should be taught in the school. Indeed, I would argue that the general cloud of feeling inspired by this concatenation of ideas hovered over school poetry for as long as mass education's dominant mode of "teaching literature" included the assignment of verse for memorization. We can see how well the theory would eventually fit the practice: the gifts of "great minds" are to be placed within all those little minds in the classroom; the child of the peasant (or his descendant) will then own the nicely rounded, complete-in-itself "property" of the poem as surely as the child of the peer; the legitimate sources of national feeling will thus be possessed equally by all the nation's subjects.

But neither the theory nor the practice, we might notice, opens up much room for caviling and quarreling with the contents of any given work in the nation's canon. First of all, how might a hypothetical ideal instructor approach the works of English literature that she will teach? A little "discriminating," we remember, could accompany her "earnest admiration," but how far would this really go? Depending on the individual teacher's bent, she might discriminate so far as to rank one poem, or poet, above another, according to her own lights, or the opinions of an authority; she might judge one stanza's exercise of meter or choice of diction superior to that of the next's; she might, perhaps if she were very daring, decide that poem A expresses a given theme more successfully than poem B. But would she share, or encourage, such acts of relative admiration in the classroom? Would these kinds of discussions really help her towards the required goal of installing the poem in her pupils' heads?

As we have already discovered, evidence from many sources must be weighed up if we are to reconstruct the contents of the literature lesson over the years: educational directives and histories (official and otherwise), textbook prompts, and depictions of schoolroom scenes in memoirs and fiction alike all tell significantly different stories, which are bound to bear different relations to actual daily events. But perhaps I can venture to assert the following points as we attempt to think once again about the kinds of interpretative climate that could or could not exist around the poem when it was regarded as an object for memorization. Part I's opening focus suggested that a responsible and thoughtful teacher would try to make sure that her pupils had a secure general sense of the work before they started to chant; she would explain unusual words and supply paraphrases of difficult lines; she would furnish the historical information necessary to understand its arcane references. If she were teaching one of the higher standards, her pupils might conceivably spend some time identifying rhetorical figures, scanning lines, or understanding the constraints or opportunities of a particular verse form—though it must be admitted that there is not a great deal of evidence for these activities at the elementary-school level. In any eventuality, such a collection of pursuits would probably constitute the furthest limits that "discrimination" might reach—and the vast majority of classes would be unlikely to travel anything like this distance. Figuring out what a poem "meant" would be contained within a circumscribed area; questions and discussion, hypothesis and conjecture, would, if they occurred at all, be limited to the investigation of how the poem achieved that meaning.

Yet if "discrimination" only went so far as this, then "admiration" had an infinitely longer rein. How could it be otherwise, when the objects to be dispensed were presented as the great gifts of great minds? We have already noticed that school reading books habitually included a certain amount of adulatory biographical information about the featured poets; introductions and notes to poems were studded with terms of praise and favorable evaluations of merit. Of course, any given teacher or perhaps a particularly reckless pupil might choose to disagree, but the nimbus of approbation around the text must have rendered such acts unlikely. Further, the poems' contents themselves often made it evident that the poetry exercise was about veneration, not contention and debate; for reasons discussed in Part I, a large proportion of the poems in the juvenile canon featured not only valorous and sacrificial acts, but valorous and sacrificial acts that were to be understood as actually having taken place, and more often than not in the service of Great Britain herself.[39] In addition, this was a message that was brought clearly home by the linking of the juvenile performance of memorized verse with days of national or imperial celebration. All the more reason, then, not to subject the juvenile canon to suspicious, disloyal scrutiny.

And yet. Despite all these reasons, and all the other reasons why a schoolchild might not choose, or be able, to compare a poem's sentiments to any kind of an alternative perspective, there must have been times when the content of a given work was just too much to swallow without some form of protest, expressed or not. Interviewed for an oral history project in the late 1960s, a laborer's daughter remembered that as a little girl she had recited a poem for Empire Day, a poem that celebrated the great ships that brought England her bread and butter. "And somehow or other," she told the researchers, "it stirred a bit of rebellion in me. I thought, where's my bread, where's my butter? And I think it sowed the first seeds of socialism in me, it really did" (quoted in Rose, 339). After World War I and its unprecedented casualties, the poems of martial glory that continued to be assigned in schools must have had more than a hollow ring to hundreds of thousands of grieving children. A. J. Mills, the son of a disabled veteran and a charlady, cannot have been the only one to have hated reciting "The Charge of the Light Brigade" (Rose, 339).

While these instances represent extreme cases, they do help us to see that it is not wholly unrealistic to imagine that elementary-school children considered the words they had to store within themselves for the recitation exercise, and, on occasion, disagreed with them. How often such dissenting responses might have been prompted by poems with seemingly blatant ideological biases, we cannot know. Still harder is it to work out whether works with subtler, or more equivocal, messages could have brought forth similar feelings. If the events in a poem occurred in an earlier historical period, or were set in a foreign country or alien society—would that make it less likely that a child might compare the piece's attitudes and assumptions to what he or she knew about the way the world went? For Mills, probably neither the gap of time between hostilities in 1854–56 and 1914–18, nor the difference between the slaughter of a cavalry brigade and either the wounding of his father or the deaths of over a million soldiers, rendered the sentiments of Tennyson's poem any less immediate or troubling; we can readily appreciate why he would not wish to trumpet its lines aloud. But what if your assigned poem talked about peasants in olden times? If you were the daughter of a shop assistant in Preston at the end of the nineteenth century, or the son of a road mender in 1920s Newcastle, how likely would it be that you might take the words of Gray's Elegy personally? And whether you did or not, was there the least possibility, one, that you would feel the stirrings of a proto-Empsonesque critique within your mind? Or two, would you glory in the differences between your existence and that of an eighteenth-century plowman, and inwardly celebrate the fact you now possessed the highest treasures of the nation as surely as any scion of the aristocracy? Or three, would the question of class not enter the equation at all, because to experience the joys of literature was to be taken to a place blissfully free of its contentious claims?

I pose these questions for rhetorical purposes only. I have not found, nor can I imagine finding, traces of such attitudes recorded in childhood. Versions of all these opinions, though not necessarily about the poem in question, do exist in the adult writings of ex-working-class children educated in the period under scrutiny. From their general approaches to life, literature, and class, we can hypothesize that a Richard Hoggart or a Raymond Williams would end up in the first camp;[40] an A. L. Rowse in the second;[41] an Albert Mansbridge—at least from the perspective of his fiercest detractors[42]—in the third. These former scholarship boys' routes to their published views are of course personal and complex, and I cannot make the case that their eventual standpoints originated in thoughts first held in the elementary school. But even in the face of all these admissions about the ultimate mystery of what generations of children actually felt about this particular aspect of an everyday classroom activity, I wish to keep in play the possibility that some pupils—the most thoughtful, at least—formed critical opinions about the contents of the poem that was installed within.

Let us hold that notion in place for one moment while we revive two other key ideas about the memorized poem. In the first instance, I wish to refocus attention on the conceit that has underwritten my study of the scholarship boy's progress: the perfectly recited piece functions as an apt image of success at school, inasmuch as proficient reproduction played an important role in helping a child rise within the educational structures of the times and places under scrutiny. In the second instance, I bring back into view one of this project's fundamental tenets: the poem committed to memory in childhood could remain with you for the rest of your life; of all the lessons learned in school, this one had a strong tendency to stay put. At the crossing-over point of these two "facts"—the shaded area in another great Victorian construct, the Venn diagram—the memorized poem turns out to be not just the sum total of its words, images, and meter but potentially a permanently held symbol of that ability to win prizes, to take in and repeat back the culture of the school.[43] So how might certain individuals—let us say former scholarship boys and girls—feel about this entity that lies within? In memory's golden casket gleams a gem of purest ray serene—or perhaps, for the sake of argument, let us imagine it to be a cultured pearl. These men and women may take delight in its glowing form and enjoy its intrinsic beauty; they may take pleasure in the fact that their talents and their labors helped them to acquire and retain such a valuable object; they may be proud that their ownership of such a jewel has allowed them to move in higher social circles. They may very well feel all of these sensations simultaneously. But what if, at the same time, and despite all those soothing layers of lustrous nacre, they could still sense the grit of pain at the pearl's center—still feel that deep within that poem there existed something that hurt, something that told them that some people are worth more than others? What if your education, your amassing of cultural riches, set an unbridgeable, guilty, rift between the place you began and the place you ended up, between the people the poem said didn't matter and those that did? What if you left one class for another but never felt at home again? Any poem that is disseminated by the school will hold some trace of what that schooling meant to an individual. How will this effect be magnified if the contents of the poem bore some sort of a relation, as they so often did, to the question of who is valued in a society, and who is not?

◆ ◆ ◆

In 1958, long before Pierre Bourdieu's more thoroughgoing codification of a theory of cultural capital, Stuart Hall wrote an essay entitled "A Sense of Classlessness." Responding to the recent publication of *The Uses of Literacy*, Hall had this to add to Hoggart's analysis:

> The "scholarship boy" who retains some sense of allegiance to his family and community has constantly to draw the distinction within himself between the just motive of self-improvement (which took him to university in the first place) and the false motive of self-advancement ("room at the top"). This is because culture, education and learning, like the other "commodities" of our society, have accreted to themselves a social value in a hierarchy of status symbols. To learn or to read is no longer a process through which the individual broadens and deepens his experience for his own sake ... they are, in themselves, modes of propulsion up the status quo. (26)

Up to this point I have walked a more or less gloomy line, seeking to relate the anxieties of the class-crossing scholarship boy in the twentieth century to an eighteenth-century poem's apparently dismal perspective on the ultimate appropriateness of an unjust social structure. For the most part, I have had in my sights those stanzas in the Elegy, primarily lines 29 through 84, that reflect upon the effective brake placed upon genius *in potentia* by the absence of education and the presence of poverty; I have considered how these might sound when education became broadly present in a world in which poverty still existed, in a world in which some of those poor began to receive extended schooling. I have exploited the largely depressing implications of this juxtaposition to deliver a harsh indictment of the meaning of the memorized poem in everyday life: inasmuch as poetry was received under the sign of the intensely class-conscious social structure of the school, then poetry, I have argued, became a charged signifier of that social structure—especially when (back to lines 29–84 again) the content of the assigned poetry appears to reinforce a homologous view of differentiated social grades. But now I wish to take up an oppositional stance and ask what happens if, in closing, we shift our attention to other topics within the poem. What objects and relations might swim into view if we stand in a different spot? Where might we end up if we think about the elementary school's memorized poem not in connection to "self-advancement," as Hall says, but to "self-improvement"?[44] What if the poem learned at school provided a "mode of propulsion" not up (or not just up) the ladder, but to another place entirely? What if it took you, for example, to a country churchyard? And what if it showed you a man who stood still and allowed his mind to rove?

To consider the opportunities Gray's Elegy offers for transport is to begin at last to honor the genuine pleasure and benefit that many elementary-school children derived from poetry in their English lessons. So far, my account of any positive emotions associated with the recitation exercise has been strictly delimited: I have quoted passages from autobiographies, memoirs, and novels that focus on the special thrills and delights of speaking poetic language, but on closer inspection these turned out to be performances, short or long, that were largely unconcerned with content and usually conducted away from the classroom. To explain why this should be so, I have mustered a variety of causes, ranging from the problems attendant upon the pronunciation of a single letter to the prevailing tendencies of widely applied pedagogical theories and practices. But is it now possible to leap over this discouraging barrage to find evidence of poetry's power at school, evidence of occasions when teacher and pupils shared the excitement of exploring a work together? And, more importantly for this particular study, can we discover instances when memorization and recitation formed an integral element of that pleasurable journey?

"English literature was the subject most often singled out for praise," writes Jonathan Rose in his chapter on accounts of elementary-school life (157). It is tempting to speculate that this particular lesson was all the more attractive because of the tedium of the others in the timetable, but perhaps such relative thinking is out of place here. Despite huge practical and conceptual barriers, inspirational educators managed to make their pupils excited about poetry: this is an astounding fact. Certainly the comments that Rose quotes are more than heartening, and rightly commemorate the efforts of those hard-pressed teachers of another age. "Thinking back, I am amazed at the amount of English literature we absorbed in those four years," wrote Ethel Clarke (b. 1909), the daughter of a railway worker in Gloucestershire. "I pay tribute to the man who made it possible . . . Scott, Thackeray, Shakespeare, Longfellow, Dickens, Matthew Arnold, Harriet Beecher Stowe and Rudyard Kipling were but a few authors we had at our finger-tips. How he made those people live again for us!" (quoted in Burnett, *Destiny Obscure*, 159). The extraordinarily prolific popular novelist Edgar Wallace (b.1875) made it clear in his reminiscences that only one lesson shone out of the wasteland of his dreary board-school years. For this adopted son of a Billingsgate fish porter, literature alone could carry him out of the life of London's poor and into another world:

> There were golden days—poetry days. We learnt the "Inchcape Rock," of that Sir Ralph the Rover who sailed away
>
> And scoured the seas for many a day.
> At last grown rich with plunder's store,
> He steered his course for Scotland's shore.
>
> And Casabianca, and Brave Horatius, and so by degrees to the Master. I learnt whole scenes of *Macbeth* and *Julius Caesar* and *Hamlet*, and could—and did—recite them with gusto on every and any excuse. (Quoted in Rose, 158–59)

Good teachers evidently enraptured their pupils with the exciting stories and spellbinding language that the poetry in the textbooks could offer. Yet it also seems that certain children responded to the poetry lesson because this was one of the few times and places in their lives where they were encouraged to think precisely about a defined object, and to figure out how it created its ideas and effects. Such procedures can of course be practiced in relation to the widest range of natural and cultural artifacts, from a snowstorm to a sonata, a bluebell to a Burne-Jones, but in the curricular programs that prevailed throughout the history of the British elementary school, if any class session could clear room for communal intellectual and imaginative investigation, then it was usually the English lesson. Rare educators might foster these processes in a variety of ways: John Allaway (b. 1902), for instance, mentions a vividly iconoclastic teacher, Tommy Cross, who broke down the barriers between "History, Geography and English" at his Higher Elementary School in Sheffield in 1915 and "set us to work a great deal singly and in twos and threes, and as we worked he moved round among us asking questions and giving advice and encouragement" (ed. Goldman, 49). But most frequently, if such a climate was ever created at school, it was created around the focal point of a poem.

Where might a poem take you? It is easy to see how the rich otherness of the worlds that were frequently depicted in the juvenile canon could offer the enchantment of escapism, especially for children who had every reason to wish themselves away from the drab narrowness of their straitened environments; memoirists repeatedly assert that the visions of the poets offered a seductive respite from the bleakness of everyday life.[45] But if poetry offered a voyage outwards, it could also, and perhaps more productively, offer a voyage inwards, especially if a skilled and enthusiastic educator could excite the imagination and intelligence of his or her pupils. I have spent much of this chapter connecting literature in the classroom to the processes that enabled a clever child to rise towards that room at the top, but it is time now to think about the poem's role in the creation of a room of one's own. For all individuals, regardless of social and economic status, investigating a poetic work with the guidance of a good teacher had (and has) the potential to open doors within the mind, but for elementary-school children, particularly those from impoverished homes, the experience could be still more significant. In the best of circumstances, a poem, and perhaps especially a memorized poem, could create an internal space that had few enough correlatives in their external worlds.[46] It could create a place for mental exploration and contemplation.

Let us go now to a board school in Walworth, another of London's poorest districts, in the early 1930s. A teacher, Bert Linn, is introducing the class to a new poem. Nearly fifty years later, in a memoir written in 1977, his pupil Wally Horwood (b. 1922) remembered how he did it:

> Bert would dissect a poem line by line, phrase by phrase, and even word by word. There are those today who say that you shouldn't do that; that the work should be appreciated as a symmetrical whole. Had Bert attempted this, we would have quickly become bored with words and idioms we simply couldn't understand. As it was, we were able to eventually appreciate not only the final structure but all of the fine detail which went to build it. By working in this way he added enormously to our knowledge of our own great language. (Quoted in Rose, 167)

As Rose notes in his response to this passage, Linn "brought close reading to the slums," but that was not all. Memorization also played a key role in Linn's strategies: the teacher gave each boy a line of the poem to learn by heart, and then called on them to recite in order. "His methods might be frowned on today," comments Horwood, "[y]et they were extremely effective, instilling into so many of us boys from the grimy back streets of South London a love of poetry and fine writing that has enriched a lifetime" (167). It would be easy to pick at Horwood's account—to draw a direct line between the language of valuation that he employs and the concept of cultural capital; to suggest that the rich gift of "fine writing" might have played its part in palliating a justified working-class anger with the economic inequities that kept (and keep) those back streets of South London grimy—but to make only these moves would be to miss some important points about what the teacher taught and what the pupils learned. If we emphasize only the negatives, we might not notice that a poem provided not only a focus for the pedagogical encounter, but also, thanks to the process of memorization, a potentially perpetual resource for the exercise of thought.

Is this an impossibly utopian view of the poetry lesson? "It is a favorite theory of yours," warns the Canadian humorist Stephen Leacock in a 1928 essay entitled "Come Back to School," "that the literature class was a real treat, or at least that if you only had listened to your teacher properly, you would have got something for your whole life" (183).[47] Certainly many classroom sessions would have been intellectually uninspiring; certainly many children did not enjoy them or get very much out of them at all. But every so often, teachers like Bert Linn showed their charges how exciting it could be for them to enter the world of a poem, and to enlarge their own worlds by taking that poem inside themselves. Wherever recitation from memory was positioned—it could precede exploration and discussion of the work, or it could follow those activities, or, best of all, it could do both—when the movement away from words on a page towards words in the head and on the tongue was fused with understanding, then it could ignite a tremendous and transformative charge.

The moment when the voice of the poet is made suddenly and urgently present in the tones of a young individual holds obvious dramatic potential; while prose fiction, as we saw in the last case study, tends to attack or satirize juvenile recitation, the play and the film have readily mined the rich possibilities of this essentially performative occasion. *Dead Poets' Society* (1989) provides perhaps the casebook examples, but another work, Alan Bennett's 2004 play *The History Boys* offers a more thoughtful examination of the educational opportunities of the memorized poem in the classroom.[48] When Posner, a sensitive sixth former, recites Hardy's "Drummer Hodge," the act initiates an exemplary pedagogical encounter between the pupil and Hector, his English teacher. In response to Posner's tentative ideas and questions, the teacher gently sets the poem in a range of illuminating contexts, directing the youth's attention to some of the possible meanings and significances—historical, literary, biographical, psychological—of Hardy's choices, from the poet's decision to give this dead soldier a name,[49] to his construction of the compound adjective "uncoffined." Posner recites; pupil and teacher explore; and then Posner recites again. In the course of this sequence, Posner and Hector are united with their spectral equivalents, the adolescent Hodge and the sixty-something Hardy; the pupil, thanks to the poem inside and outside of himself, and thanks to the guidance of his teacher, is placed within a complex web of connections, literary and historical, with himself and with others, with the dead and with the living. The recitation of a memorized poem is an essential element in Bennett's dramatization of an idealized tutorial.[50]

This moving scene from *The History Boys*, while clearly a fantasy of pedagogy, nevertheless helps us both to gauge the vital importance of the sympathetic instructor and to imagine more fully the possible texture of the exchanges in Bert Linn's classroom all those years ago. And might not such fostered moments—the alliance of the memorized poem and the exercise of thought—have happened in other schools too? Thousands of miles from Walworth, another good teacher tried hard to get his pupils to understand, and visualize, the poem they would soon begin to memorize. Writing about his days in an "old country school" in Indiana in the 1920s, Larken L. Beeman remembered that his teacher "wanted us to actually see in our minds eye, the 'lowing herd winds slowly o'er the lea,' and would ask what 'lowing' meant, and what the 'lea' was" (quoted in Fuller, 152). These specific forms of pedagogical guidance and practice did not necessarily have to take place in the classroom, of course. Consider this tract from 1921, written in the form of an open letter from the Seafarers' Educational Service, a charity set up under the auspices of the Workers' Educational Association to provide men of the royal and merchant navies with books free of charge.[51] The letter encouraged the would-be poetry reader to begin by committing a poem to memory, to "say it over to yourself while you are at work," and thus "get to understand it and like it more and more." "You will enlarge your mind and increase your power of thinking for yourself," it promised. And which poem should the sailor learn to find this tranquil place? Where should he go to get away from the noise of the engines and the press of the bunkroom?

> Take the first two verses of Gray's Elegy [the letter says]. Well, the ideas are very simple. The bells ring at 8 o'clock; the cows and the ploughman go home, leaving the poet in the dark, where it is so quiet that he can only hear a beetle flying by and sheep bells in the distance. But if you learn those verses, you will probably find that they give you the feeling that you would have in a country churchyard on a summer's evening. (284)

And once you had reached the place of solitude, what might happen next? What would you do when you got there?

Some sixty years after the hypothetical sailor settled down to learn Gray's Elegy by heart, Richard Rodriguez's first work of autobiography, *The Hunger of Memory*, was published in the United States. According to Colombo, Cullen and Lisle, the editors of *Rereading America: Cultural Contexts for Critical Thinking and Writing*, the book "set off a storm of controversy in the Chicano community. Some hailed it as an uncompromising portrayal of the difficulties of growing up between two cultures; others condemned it because it seemed to blame Mexican Americans for the difficulties they encountered assimilating into mainstream American society" (143). Born in 1944 into an immigrant family living in California, the young Rodriguez excelled at elementary and high school in Sacramento, successively winning places at Berkeley, Stanford, and Columbia, and, in due course, a Fulbright fellowship to study English literature in London and a grant from the National Endowment for the Humanities. Despite this record of academic success, however, Rodriguez came to abandon his dissertation on the question of genre in the Renaissance, and returned home to live with his parents, eventually establishing a career as a writer, editor, and journalist. According to his autobiography, the fog of loneliness and depression that engulfed the diligent Ph.D. student sitting with his growing stacks of file cards in the British Museum Reading Room cleared only when he stopped checking out books of literary criticism and turned to works by "educational experts" (71). Desperate to understand how it was that he had moved, as he says, so "far . . . from my past," desperate "to determine how fast I would be able to recover something of it once again," Rodriguez finally found what he was looking for "in a chapter in a book by Richard Hoggart" (72).

Thanks to the American dominance of the English language Internet, if you enter "scholarship boy" into Google's search engine today, the majority of hits will take you to excerpts from *The Hunger of Memory*; parts of this text are regularly assigned in college and university courses across the United States, and on occasion also make it into the high school classroom. For Rodriguez, and perhaps now significant numbers of other American readers too, Hoggart's definition of a psychological syndrome gives explanatory form to deeply felt sensations and experiences. The dissimilarities between a British individual who won a scholarship to a grammar school in the first half of the twentieth century and an American individual educated in very different educational systems in later times prove to be less important than the similarities. Although in Rodriguez's case the perceived gap between home and school is constituted by language and ethnicity as well as class, *The Uses of Literacy* provides him with an immediately recognizable image of his own split self.

"In the sixth grade," Rodriguez tells us, "I simply concluded that what gave a book its value was some major idea or theme it contained. If that core essence could be mined and memorized, I would become learned like my teachers" (62). At the point when he decided to turn his back on the academy, Rodriguez felt that he was for the most part working the same seam, trying to accumulate knowledge "to fill the hollow within me and make me feel educated" (64). But, in the days and months that followed, as he sat at home and endeavored to figure out, with the help of Hoggart, exactly how he was now placed, he discovered it was this very "ability to consider experience so abstractly" that was the real benefit of all those

hours in the classroom and with his books (72). "If, because of my school-
ing," Rodriguez writes, "I had grown culturally separated from my par-
ents, my education finally had given me ways of speaking and caring
about that fact" (72). Now able to look back on his past with an analyti-
cal eye, he could see that the best of his Sacramentan classrooms had not
encouraged sheer acquisition of knowledge, but had "emphasize[d] the
value of a reflectiveness that opens a space between thinking and immedi-
ate action"; even more importantly, Rodriguez perceived that a signifi-
cant proportion of his university days had in fact focused on a nexus of
issues that carried strong connections to those that ultimately engrossed
his attention on the home front (72). In certain ways, the two different
modes of Rodriguez's twentieth-century existence—life as a member of
his family, life as an academic—could be mapped onto topics he had al-
ready studied in the English poetry of earlier ages. Only after he had
reached his own understanding of what he had gained from a relation-
ship with two ways of being did Rodriguez realize that he had been
taught a variant of this lesson long before:

> My best teachers in college and graduate school tried to prepare me
> for this conclusion, I think, when they discussed texts of aristocratic
> pastoral literature. Faithfully, I wrote down all that they said. I memo-
> rized it: "The praise of the unlettered by the highly educated is one of
> the primary themes of 'elitist' literature." But "the importance of the
> praise given the unsolitary, richly passionate and spontaneous life is
> that it simultaneously reflects the value of a reflective life." (72)

Given his Renaissance bent, Rodriguez is not, I think, gesturing explic-
itly towards the "Elegy Written in a Country Churchyard" at this point;
nevertheless, as one of the most celebrated heirs of this tradition, Gray's
work can easily claim its place in the discussion. However we may jib at
the potential sentimentalities and misrepresentations that tend to afflict
depictions of the "unsolitary, richly passionate and spontaneous life" of
the poor and uneducated—within pastoral literature generally; within
the Elegy; within *The Hunger of Memory* itself—elements of Rodriguez's
conclusion are useful inasmuch as they help to focus our attention on
Gray's speaker and his work within the churchyard. What is the poem,
after all, but a sending forth of his thoughts on a range of connected top-
ics? Any given reader may choose to agree or disagree with the conclu-
sions the speaker reaches, but no one can argue with the fact that he
models contemplation. It is this aspect of the Elegy, I think, that consti-
tutes the most important role that this poem could play in the times and
places under scrutiny. And further, thanks to the inherent properties of a
particular pedagogical practice, it had the opportunity to keep on per-
forming this function for many years after the gates of elementary school

had closed. In the best of classrooms, children might have learned to think from, and through, this poem in an encouraging atmosphere in which the pleasures of investigation and debate were shared. They might have discovered that different viewpoints on the same lines could coexist; that they could develop their ideas by listening to the questions and answers of teachers and schoolmates; that they could find new ways of responding to the poem each time they heard its words, in their own tones or the tones of others. Under ideal circumstances, perhaps the scholarship-child-in-training did not suffer the loneliness of the long distance runner, but found others to talk to along the way.

This may well be my own pedagogical fantasy. In placing it here, I run up against not only many of this project's arguments about the problems inflicted upon, and by, poetry within a certain disciplinary structure, but also many of our commonsensical assumptions about the essentially solitary nature of extended thought. To pick up this latter theme is to depart from the major concerns of this chapter—after all, I have mainly concentrated here upon education's potential to separate the one from the many when that education is understood primarily as a mechanism of social differentiation. But does intellectual development actually require, and result in, an individual's isolation—for some portion of the time at least? "We perished, each alone," recites Mr Ramsay in *To the Lighthouse* (225); would he (not to mention Cowper) also insist that we read and we think alone? Ex-scholarship boys and girls may well have felt cut off from both working-class and middle-class communities in later life, yet perhaps at the same time they found pleasure and enlightenment in another kind of solitude, in that schoolroom-acquired ability to immerse themselves in the remembered words of a poet. Or is it a mistake to think that they were really alone at such moments? They were, after all, in conversation with the ideas of another.[52]

Did memorized poems change the way people thought? The next case study will attempt to address this question through the lens of another poem and in contexts different from those that have occupied us here. Yet before we leave Gray's Elegy, it is perhaps worth making one last point. While it is impossible to establish every role that this poem may have played in the minds of individuals over the years, I can nevertheless say this: since 1751, whenever anyone has written about the broad issues of class, education, and unrealized talent in British life, letters, and history, then more often than not, the words and ideas of Gray's poem have had a tangible effect upon their compositions. Historians, essayists, biographers, novelists, poets, politicians—a wide range of authors have used, and will continue to use, the Elegy as an explicit or implicit reference text for their own explorations of these topics. Thanks to the breadth of their dissemination and the firmness of their installation in the minds of countless individuals, Gray's expressions have set the terms in which certain charged clusters of ideas are habitually invoked; in the face of this fact, any given author's estimation of the meaning of the Elegy, in its parts or as a whole, and any given author's decision to agree or disagree with that estimated meaning, become subsidiary affairs. The poem has played an undeniably important role for writers who hail from distinctly nonelite social grades: such authors may burst the bounds that Gray originally set around the life of the poor, but the existence of those bounds has proven to be intensely energizing. At the beginning of the nineteenth century, for example, Gray's work was securely fixed in the minds of Britain's two best-known "peasant poets," Robert Burns and John Clare,[53] the former using the Elegy's "short and simple annals" stanza as the epigraph for "The Cotter's Saturday Night"; later in the century, a builder's son from Dorset found not only the titles of two, and the themes of many more, of his novels in Gray's poem, but also the conditions for existence for the vast majority of his poems as well.[54] We cannot know just how many Miltons were rendered mute and inglorious in the years both before and after Gray composed his Elegy, but for some individuals from cottages, back-to-back houses, or tenements, his words have taken the form of a gauntlet thrown in their paths.

In the second half of the twentieth century Gray exercised a profound imaginative and structural influence upon Tony Harrison, that bitterest scholarship boy of them all. "On Not Being Milton," the sonnet that furnishes the ironic quotation in this chapter's title, hardly disguises its allusions; other Harrison poems are similarly explicit about their point of departure. Most important here is the controversial *V*, a 448-line re-configuration of the Elegy, which retains the original poem's stanza form but moves the speaker from a tranquil country churchyard in the mid-eighteenth century to a desecrated urban cemetery in the 1980s, and transforms that speaker's alter ego from Gray's prematurely deceased "youth of humble birth" into an aerosol-toting, foul-mouthed skinhead. Frequently called to account for his unfashionable and unwavering commitment to the meter and rhyme schemes of traditional poetic forms, Harrison tends to provide explanations that encompass and interlock the personal and the political, the immediate and the historical. In his compositional process, says Harrison the poetic craftsman, the challenge of a formal requirement operates as a thrillingly creative catalytic agent. Harrison the highly educated son of the poor, however, asserts that it his right and his duty to take up residence in the structures that have generally been off-limits to his class ("So right, yer buggers, then! We'll occupy / your lousy leasehold Poetry").[55] When Harrison claims Gray's place in the graveyard, he is simultaneously inspired and infuriated by what the past, no less than the present, offers up to him; the Elegy, like the vandalizing skinhead, both rouses him to write and provides the grounds for his despair.

But is that quite right? Throughout my investigation, I have acted as if Thomas Gray is an unproblematic representative of the elite, a cardboard figure of effete ruling-class privilege who stands languidly by while others do the hard work of hewing wood, plowing fields and even waging war. Harrison, at least, knows better than this. In the late 1990s, in the midst of the speculation about who would succeed Ted Hughes (yet another Yorkshire scholarship boy) as poet laureate, the *Guardian* published a new Harrison poem entitled "Laureate's Block." Once again, the poet employs the Elegy's stanzaic form, but this time Gray himself makes an extended appearance within the poem. "Appalled" by newspaper reports that he is "'widely tipped' for a job [he'd] never seek," the fiercely republican Harrison retires under the duvet with "four vols of Gray," and is delighted to read, in a letter dated December 19, 1757, of the Elegist's disgusted repudiation of the laureateship ("rat-catcher to his Majesty"), a post Gray refused that same year. Co-opting a lengthy excerpt from the letter into his poem, Harrison revels in his kinship with the earlier writer: "That's Gray 2 centuries and more ago / with sentiments I find quite close to mine." Seemingly unlikely bedfellows, Gray and Harrison are found to be united not only by their shared skill with an iambic line and the turn of a quatrain, but also by a joint scorn for what the former called "the bland emollient saponaceous qualities of sack and silver," the prize offered up to poets by the Establishment. There, we might think, the similarities end. Yet if we look still closer, can we discover any more marks of resemblance?

As it turns out, Thomas Gray was a scholarship boy himself. Gray had a scrivener for a father, just like Milton, but whereas Milton's father was proud to finance his clever son's education, Philip Gray was perpetually unwilling to put his hand in his pocket. It was left to Gray's mother, who ran a small millinery shop with her sister, to sort things out. Two of her brothers, Robert and William Antrobus, were assistant masters at Eton College; thanks to their good offices, the eight-year-old Gray was awarded a small scholarship and admitted to the school in 1725. At Eton, Gray was part of a close-knit circle of friends that included Horace Walpole, the youngest son of Sir Robert Walpole, the prime minister. In due course, after they had been at Cambridge together for around five years, Walpole invited Gray to travel to Europe as his companion on the grand tour. What happened next has been the subject of considerable speculation: certainly a quarrel ensued, and the two went their separate ways. On his return to England in 1741, Gray soon found himself obliged to bury his father. Thereafter, because that parent had recently managed to lose what little fortune he possessed, Thomas felt himself too poor to continue to train for the bar, and lived most of his life as an academic in Cambridge on extremely straitened funds, only accepting a sinecure professorship in 1771 when he was fifty-two years old. The breach with Walpole, however, had long since been healed. In 1773, two years after Gray's death, his friend, the eventual Earl of Orford, described to a mutual acquaintance what he felt had happened around a third of a century earlier:

> I am conscious that in the beginning of the differences between Gray and me the fault was mine. I was too young, too fond of my own diversions, nay, I do not doubt, too much intoxicated by indulgence, vanity, and the insolence of my situation, as Prime Minister's son, not to have been inattentive and insensible to the feelings of one I thought below me; of one, I blush to say it, that I knew was obliged to me; of one whom presumption and folly, perhaps, made me deem not my superior then in parts, though I have since felt my infinite inferiority to him. I treated him insolently; he loved me, and I did not think he did. I reproached him with the difference between us, when he acted from convictions of knowing he was my superior. (Quoted in Gosse, 43)

Samuel Johnson was not convinced by these (admittedly somewhat edged) protestations of guilt.[56] "[U]nequal friendships," he remarks in that account of Gray in his *Lives of the English Poets*, "are easily dissolved":

> Mr Walpole is now content to have it told that it was by his fault. If we look however with prejudice on the world, we shall find that men, whose consciousness of their own merit sets them above the compliances of servility, are apt enough in their association with superiors to watch their own dignity with troublesome and punctilious jealousy and in the fervour of independance to exact that attention which they refuse to pay. Part they did, whatever was the quarrel, and the rest of their travels was doubtless more unpleasant to them both. (4:176)

What are we to believe? Did Gray really chafe under a sense of his simultaneous mental superiority and social inferiority to his urbane and monied friend? Was the former scholarship boy aware of the strength of his intellectual gifts, yet continually discomfited by the gap between his place in life and that of those who were born into privilege? Johnson certainly thinks so, and soon follows his analysis of the failed European tour with further evidence to support these impressions. The biographer quotes from a letter on Gray's character by the Rev. Mr. Temple:

> Though [Gray] seemed to value others chiefly according to the progress they had made in knowledge, yet he could not bear to be consid-

ered himself merely as a man of letters; and though without birth, or fortune, or station, his desire was to be looked upon as a private independent gentleman, who read for his amusement. (4:179)

Approached from this angle, our supersensitive poet seems to bear a keen resemblance to that youth of "humble birth," that youth unknown to Fortune, who lies buried at the Elegy's close. Writing in 1923 on the perpetually engaging topic of the identity of the poem's melancholy scholar, critic Odell Shepard raises the idea that the end of the Elegy might be "considered as Gray's description of himself," but then dismisses it: the "tone" of the conclusion, he decides, "is that of the sentimental and lachrymose self-pity which most boys put behind them in the earlier stages of adolescence" (347). It is a fair guess that most readers would wish to avoid the curtailment of interpretative potential that results if these lines are taken as covert autobiography only, but has Shepard chosen quite the best argument to convince us that the hypothesis is entirely untenable? Within the confines of this chapter's investigation of Gray's verses and their connection to the history of thousands and thousands of humble scholars, I prefer to leave alive a final, haunting, possibility. The Elegy did not simply become a poem for the scholarship boy: it had been the scholarship boy's poem from the very first.

Charles Wolfe, "The Burial of Sir John Moore after Corunna"

Not a drum was heard, not a funeral note,
    As his corse to the rampart we hurried;
Not a soldier discharged his farewell shot
    O'er the grave where our hero we buried.

We buried him darkly at dead of night,
    The sods with our bayonets turning,
By the struggling moonbeam's misty light
    And the lanthorn dimly burning.

No useless coffin enclosed his breast,
    Not in sheet or in shroud we wound him;
But he lay like a warrior taking his rest
    With his martial cloak around him.

Few and short were the prayers we said,
    And we spoke not a word of sorrow;
But we steadfastly gazed on the face that was dead,
    And we bitterly thought of the morrow.

We thought, as we hollow'd his narrow bed
    And smooth'd down his lonely pillow,
That the foe and the stranger would tread o'er his head,
    And we far away on the billow!

Lightly they'll talk of the spirit that's gone,
    And o'er his cold ashes upbraid him—
But little he'll reck, if they let him sleep on
    In the grave where a Briton has laid him.

But half of our heavy task was done
    When the clock struck the hour for retiring;
And we heard the distant and random gun
    That the foe was sullenly firing.

Slowly and sadly we laid him down,
    From the field of his fame fresh and gory;
We carved not a line, and we raised not a stone,
    But we left him alone with his glory.[1]

Carving a Line and Raising a Stone: Memorization and Memorialization

SIR THE BURIAL SIR OF SIR JOHN MOORE
SIR AT CORUNNA SIR

(a titter from 2B they are wet and I will tuough them up after)

Notadrumwasheardnotafuneralnote
shut up peason larffing
As his corse
As his corse
what is a corse sir? gosh is it
to the rampart we carried
(whisper you did not kno your voice was so lovely)
Not a soldier discharged his farewell shot.
PING!
Shut up peason I know sir he's blowing peas at me
Oer the grave where our hero we buried.

Geoffrey Willans and Ronald Searle, *How To Be Topp*, 1954 (59)

Not so long ago, I discovered that my first acquaintance with the poem that forms the focus of this chapter had been forged at an early age.[2] As a nine-year-old, I was wholly addicted to a now-neglected classic of schoolboy humor, a book that featured the caustic observations and idiosyncratic spelling of Nigel Molesworth, a dyspeptic pupil at St. Custard's, the minor preparatory school of a minor public school. The dog-eared Puffin reprint that I had stolen from my older brother, and that I returned to again and again over the next few years, was entitled *How To Be Topp*;[3] both a literary and an artistic delight, the book was written by a former prep schoolmaster, Geoffrey Willans, and is regularly punctuated with scratchy pen-and-ink drawings by Ronald Searle, a survivor of the Japanese prison camps and the Burma railway.

Although I attended a state school, both my private reading and popular culture had already made me conversant with the distinctive fictional world of the British boarding school, a microcosm compounded of unfamiliar objects like tuck boxes and Latin prep, and peopled by the equally perplexing figures of blubbing maters, undermatrons, cads and rotters, and masters (not teachers) with canes. Fascinating in itself as a picture of an alien culture, a culture that spoke a language something like mine, this enclosed and self-sufficient realm was infinitely more amusing when refracted through the preternaturally cynical spectacles of Nigel Molesworth.[4] But while many of the narrator's stylistic tics lodged themselves firmly inside my head, to resurface from time to time for private amusement or to establish communion with a fellow adherent, Molesworth's rendition of "SIR THE BURIAL SIR OF SIR JOHN MOORE SIR AT CORUNNA SIR" failed to stick.

The reason why is not hard to fathom. Although many of the targets of *How To Be Topp*'s satire were unknown to me, it was often possible to work out what was going on, and why it was funny, from the context. The English lesson in which Molesworth's performance occurs, however, bore no relation whatsoever to the kind of teaching I experienced in West Yorkshire in the 1970s. Poetry at primary school was something we wrote ourselves, in free form, and with our own illustrations, after we had been encouraged to look out of the window at the driving rain or the falling leaves. When I made it to secondary school in 1973 as a member of the first year's intake in the new comprehensive system, English—now the subject of separately time-tabled lessons and with its own dedicated teacher—was still connected, by and large, to what was out of the window. Our reading matter—*Kes, A Kind of Loving, The Loneliness of the Long-Distance Runner*—was as gritty, as northern, as contemporary, and as depressed, as the landscape of defunct collieries and disused factory chimneys that we could see from our recently renamed Secondary Mod. The poetry we studied came from *Voices*, an attractive new series of illustrated anthologies from Penguin, but even here, although the range of subjects, authors, and historical periods seemed wider, we did not travel far from the desolation of our designated terrain: "Close the coal-house door, man, / There's blood inside" intoned the folk songs, while Blake told us about those dark satanic mills.[5]

Steeped in gloomy working-class experience, then, our English lessons had no place for Wolfe's poem, despite its doleful theme. We didn't often lament the death of titled gents. (Not that I would have known at the time that one of the "SIRs" in Molesworth's title belonged to "John Moore," rather than to a member of the group of ominously black-gowned figures in Searle's illustrations. The joke was lost on me.) And "Corunna" rang no bells either: History was as resolutely proletarian as English, and while we learned a great deal about the Industrial Revolution (the subject for us of a kind of latter-day regional studies, with many a field trip up the Colne Valley and plenty of actual physical contact with bobbins and spinning jennies), the Napoleonic Wars were out. We knew about Peterloo, not Waterloo; Captain Ludd, but not General Moore. War did figure, both in the history and the English classrooms, but it was always World War I, with Wilfred Owen as our chief guide to the horrors of the trenches. His "Miners," indeed, with "those who worked dark pits of war," made this land of nightmare comprehensibly continuous with our habitual literary universe. Within such a world it was axiomatic that a wartime elegy that lamented the lack of funeral rites was not for an officer, but for a common soldier, or, more likely, for soldiers in the mass: "What passing-bells for these who die as cattle?" ("Anthem for Doomed Youth"). Workingmen were the heroes, and not their commanders; a high-ranking officer was an out-of-touch and incompetent blimp, a donkey who sent those men, those lions, to their death. Siegfried Sassoon told us all we needed to know about the general, and from the right perspective: "'He's a cheery old card,' grunted Harry to Jack / As they slogged up to Arras with rifle and pack. / . . . But he did for them both by his plan of attack" ("The General").

So, for all these reasons, *How To Be Topp*'s mocking riff on Wolfe's solemn ode as an archetypal text for schoolroom recitation failed to make itself fully intelligible to me. I now see the brilliance of Willans's attack—the deft skewering of the poem's dual delivery of obscure diction and morbid subject-matter in a single thrust ("What is a corse sir? gosh is it"); the accurate discharge from Peason's peashooter of the missing farewell shot (PING!). But because the real "Burial of Sir John Moore," or in fact anything remotely resembling it, had never made itself felt in childhood or adolescence, I never cherished this part of Molesworth's beloved text, and it did not imprint itself upon my memory. And if I had read Wolfe's poem, either then or for a long time afterwards, I probably would have rejected it outright. The form would have seemed repellant: it is hard to get past the preponderance of feminine rhymes, and still harder, perhaps, is the insistent thrum of the anapest. Yet it is through that very rhythm that I can now begin to feel my way towards an appreciation of the coherence of Wolfe's governing plan. The poet's point of entry to his topic is clearly the contrast between the greatness of the man, his consummate heroism, and the circumstantial lowness and incompleteness of his funeral. In the gap that is thereby created, Wolfe offers his poem as a gesture of restitution after the fact. Words of negation—"not," "no," and "nor"—are repeatedly countered with "but," the conjunction of substitution: the poem repeatedly insists that apparent lack is actually remedied ("he didn't get this, but he did get that"), and ultimately transcended. Within this structure and the military setting of the scene, the poem's dominant anapestic rhythm makes perfect sense. As a reader 150 years ago would have been quicker to recognize, Wolfe borrows the rhythm of a drumbeat to make reparation for the respectful tattoo that was missing from Moore's inadequate burial service—"Not a drum was heard," until now, and now forever more (or as long as the poem is recited).[6]

But even if I had been able to overcome my resistance to the poem's form by recognizing the unified economy of Wolfe's method, the content would still have presented severe difficulties. In the wake of the terrible toll of wartime deaths in the twentieth century, and most especially in the cataclysm of World War I, the situation that Wolfe describes does not appear that awful in the overall scale of things. Moore's brother officers were, after all, able to give him a burial, even if it did not contain the full military honors a general would normally have received. Still more problematic would have been the fact that the poem seems to invoke all the concepts, the so-called "big" or "old" words of "hero," "warrior," "fame," and "glory," plus the euphemistic treatment of death as a "sleep" in a "narrow bed," which I had been taught were one of the contributory causes that led so many young men to offer themselves up as lambs to the slaughter in the trenches of northern France.[7] It may be that I did run across the text at some point of my postsecondary academic career, and, as with Molesworth's rendition, it simply made no impact. This poem would have had nothing to say to me.

Consequently I can date the firing of my interest in "The Burial of Sir John Moore" to a much later stage in my studies. In the summer of 1996 I was working on "Drummer Hodge," Thomas Hardy's poem about the burial of a young British soldier in South Africa during the Second Anglo-Boer War. (Given the content and ideological slant of my formative educational experiences, the fact that I was concentrating on this particular author is entirely predictable. As Peter Widdowson's analysis *Hardy in History* makes clear, Hardy's doom-filled and class-sensitive later novels were the paradigmatic, and thus the most taught, texts within English curricula in the early phase of the comprehensive system for secondary schools in Britain.) It runs as follows:

> They throw in Drummer Hodge, to rest
>   Uncoffined—just as found:
> His landmark is a kopje-crest
>   That breaks the veldt around;
> And foreign constellations west
>   Each night above his mound.
>
> Young Hodge the Drummer never knew—
>   Fresh from his Wessex home—
> The meaning of the broad Karoo,
>   The Bush, the dusty loam,
> And why uprose to nightly view
>   Strange stars amid the gloam.
>
> Yet portion of that unknown plain
>   Will Hodge for ever be;
> His homely Northern breast and brain
>   Grow to some Southern tree,
> And strange-eyed constellations reign
>   His stars eternally.

First published as "The Dead Drummer" in a journal in 1899, Hardy's poem at that time carried the following explanatory headnote: "One of the Drummers killed was a native of a village near Casterbridge." As research for a paper on the different ways in which the graves of boys and girls are represented in Victorian literature, I was trying to track down this particular soldier, to locate the source of the poet's inspiration in some record of the death of a drummer from a Dorsetshire regiment in the first few months of the war ("Girls Underground . . ."). Hardy may of course have simply heard the story from a friend or neighbor, but I thought that the loss might have been reported in the local newspaper. He subscribed to the *Dorset County Chronicle*; there were a number of others he could have read. Combing through the columns at Colindale, the British Library's newspaper archive, I did not find a drummer (though there was a trumpeter, and a bugler), but I began to notice, incidentally, that the frequent brief obituaries and accounts of hasty battlefield burials often carried the same title. The item about General Symons that appeared in the *Dorset and Somerset Standard* on November 2, 1899, was typical. Above the description of the interment in Umsinga in Natal five days earlier, in which the general's body "was simply enshrouded in the Union Jack," ran the heading "No Useless Coffin." On occasion the phrase also cropped up in the text of these accounts—enough times to make me realize that it was a quotation, a phrase that was obviously so well known to the writers and the readers of these newspapers that it did not require identification.

Wolfe's poem became a recitation standard just like the other works in my case studies, but the role it played in the years after the classroom was significantly different from that performed by many other poems in the juvenile canon. "Casabianca" stands as a fit representative of this larger group. The subject of Hemans's work is so singular, so entirely removed from normal human experience, that memories of the poem in the nineteenth and twentieth centuries tended to take the individual back not to its content, *per se*, but to the experience of its first memorization: "The Boy Stood on the Burning Deck," either in its pristine or its parodic form, was remembered most often as an example of a poem learned at school or in the playground. When its words are summoned up in reference to another kind of experience, then it is usually used analogically: for example, although not actually standing on board a ship about to suffer a devastating explosion, the Oklahoma bomber Timothy McVeigh, in his determination to stand alone in his trial for the attack on the Alfred P. Murrah Federal Building, was for Gore Vidal *like* the boy on the burning deck (352). Because the incident described in Hemans's poem was extremely unlikely to occur again, references to "Casabianca" redound primarily upon the poem as an entity in itself, or to distinct situations that remain separate from its particular, peculiar, drama.

In contrast, the event described in Wolfe's poem was endlessly repeated during the nineteenth century in times of war or in other circumstances that did not permit the performance of a decent burial. In their attempts to come to terms with such a distressing situation, individuals who had committed this poem to memory in childhood found that its words came back to them to provide a genuine source of solace. Straddling the gap between what should have been, and what has to be, the speakers in Wolfe's poem ultimately assert that honor is nevertheless satisfied, and that the glory of the fallen soldier shines through. Such a positioning not only proves extraordinarily comforting to those in similar situations, but is also open enough to allow individuals to substitute the details of their own predicament for those Wolfe mentions, and thus render the poem even more intimate and consoling. Offering itself up at a time of crisis and providing a shared framework for personal expression, "The Burial of Sir John Moore" validates a hope expressed by the 1868 Schools Inquiry Commission in Britain. If literature could be taught so as "to kindle a living interest in the learner's mind," the report ventured, "it would certainly have one merit that could hardly be overestimated, namely, that the man would probably return to it when the days of boyhood were over" (*British Parliamentary Papers*, 2:267). Although there are inevitably times when Wolfe's poem is summoned up chiefly for its schoolroom associations, the recourse the commission envisaged frequently occurred for profound and deeply melancholy reasons.

This case study both focuses on the experiences of individuals facing the burials of soldiers and comrades on the field of battle and attempts to connect this topic to a discussion that has exercised cultural historians of Britain for some time: how do we account for the massive change in memorial practices that occurs roughly between the time of Sir John Moore and 1915, between the Napoleonic Wars and World War I?[8] After the Battle of Corunna, the 800 common soldiers who died alongside their general were dealt with as common soldiers had been dealt with for millennia: they were piled in a heap and so buried. After all the major battles of this long war, Waterloo included, there were no individual, marked graves for rank-and-file soldiers, and very few mentions of names on any memorials back in Britain. From March 1915 onwards, however, a separate military unit logged the sites of burial of every soldier, whenever and wherever possible, an operation that culminated in the massive endeavor of the Imperial War Graves Commission. This organization ultimately managed to provide over 800,000 individual graves for soldiers' bodies, around 600,000 of which also carried the soldier's name. For most of the unidentified remainder, plus another third of a million cases where the body was never found, the name of the soldier was carved at a commemorative site as close as possible to the last place that the individual had been known to be alive.

In the year after the war had ended, Rudyard Kipling set out the policy of the commission he chaired in an official publication entitled "The Graves of the Fallen":

> In a war where the full strength of nations was used without respect of persons, no difference could be made between the graves of officers or men. Yet some sort of central idea was needed that should symbolize our common sacrifice wherever our dead might be laid; and it was realised, above all, that each cemetery and individual grave should be made as permanent as man's art could devise. (5)

Recent work by historian Michèle Barrett has given the lie to this: some casualties in the Indian Army, it turns out, received mass, not individual, burial, but the commission's public voice, at least, stated that each dead soldier would receive his own marked grave or memorial in perpetuity, and that all headstones would be of a uniform type. Given the scale of grief suffusing the empire, it is not surprising that Kipling makes no mention of precedents here, and what was proposed and achieved was indeed truly innovative. Nevertheless, the personalized commemoration of the rank-and-file soldier does have a traceable history from the French Revolution onwards, a history that gathers momentum in the second half of the nineteenth century.[9] In particular, the practices that originated in the American Civil War have led historians to credit this conflict as a kind of way station en route to the mass memorialization of World War I. It is in the context of this war that I make my case about the functional presence of Wolfe's poem in the minds of ordinary individuals, and its role in creating the social expectations that led to the establishment of the American National Cemeteries. Once "The Burial of Sir John Moore" becomes the common possession of the common soldier, I argue, it contributes to a major shift in the commemorative practices of the English-speaking world.

◆ ◆ ◆

Corunna was the Dunkirk of its day. Remembered and recorded as a stirring example of British pluck, the battle at La Coruna was actually part of the British army's retreat from Spain: it was a victory inasmuch as it allowed the safe evacuation of 27,000 men. At the head of 20,000 soldiers, General Sir John Moore had marched into the country from Portugal in October 1808 to assist the attempt to thwart Napoleon's intention of placing his brother Joseph on the Spanish throne. With the knowledge that his troops would be augmented by a force of 10,000 men under the leadership of General Sir David Baird, Moore approached Madrid, only to discover that Spanish resistance had collapsed in the face of the 300,000-strong

French army. Pursued by corps led by Marshals Soult and Ney, Moore's forces then began a disastrous three-weak retreat across rugged terrain in appalling winter weather, shedding morale and discipline along the route; further, it was estimated that 5,000 men were also lost in one way or another during the journey (many were said to be drunk from looted stores). Because of an error in communication, the necessary transport ships for the evacuation of the now-combined troops of Generals Moore and Baird were not waiting for them on their arrival at La Coruna. Faced with the choice of giving battle or making terms with Marshal Soult "to allow us to embark quietly," as he stated in his last despatch on January 13 to the prime minister, Lord Castlereagh, Moore decided on the former course of action, despite the fact that his "position in front of this place [was] a very bad one," and that he was outnumbered in men (at this stage "the French force exceeded 20,000," while "the British did not amount to 15,000") and artillery (Moore, 135).

The battle was fought on January 16, 1809. According to Pococke, an ordinary "soldier of the 71st" whose military memoirs were published in 1819, "Sir John was at the head of every charge. Everything was done under his own eye" (92). All the chronicles of the battle that began appearing from 1810 onwards told the same story of the commander's bravery, recording his cry of "Remember Egypt!" as he joined the 42nd regiment, the Highlanders, in their attack. Dispatching an officer to fetch a battalion of guards to support the left flank of the Highlanders, Moore then saw that his move had been misunderstood: because the 42nd were practically out of ammunition, their commanding officer assumed that the summoned guards were intended to replace them, and he ordered his men to fall back. "My brave 42nd, join your comrades; ammunition is coming, and you have your bayonets," shouted Moore, and they moved forward with him once again (92). It was at this moment that he received his death wound. In *The Spanish Campaign of 1808*, published in 1831, Adam Neale provides a full account:

> A cannon-shot here struck Sir John Moore, and carried away his left shoulder and a portion of the collarbone, leaving the arm hanging merely by the flesh. He dropt from his saddle on the ground, stretched on his back; but his fine manly countenance changed not, neither did he exhibit the least sensation of pain. Captain Hardinge dismounted, and grasping his hand, observed him anxiously watching the 42d, which was warmly engaged, and told him they were advancing, whereon his countenance brightened. His friend Colonel Graham, (Lord Lynedoch), who now came up to assist him, observing the composure of his features, began to hope that he was only slightly wounded, till he observed the dreadful laceration. From the extent of the wound, it was vain to

attempt to check the bleeding, and Sir John consented to be removed in a blanket to the rear. In raising him up, his sword, hanging on the wounded side, touched his arm and became entangled, which induced Captain Hardinge to unbuckle it; but the General said, in his usual tone and manner, "It is as well as it is: I had rather it should go out of the field with me." Six soldiers of the 42d and guards now bore him away. Hardinge, observing his composure, began to hope that the wound might not prove mortal, and expressed his wish that he might still be spared to the army. Moore turned his head, and looking steadfastly at the wound for a few seconds, replied, "No, Hardinge, I feel that to be impossible." (203)

Moore lived long enough to hear that his forces had won the battle, and that they would be able to make an honorable departure from Spain; at the end of that day, the French had lost 2,000 men, and the British 800.

The account of the burial of Sir John Moore that inspired a young Irishman to compose a poem came from the *Edinburgh Annual Register*'s 1810 "History of Europe" by Robert Southey, the same writer whose mention of the "brave boy" at the Battle of the Nile in his *Life of Horatio Lord Nelson* (1813) was to capture Felicia Hemans's interest to similar effect. Here is the paragraph that Charles Wolfe, then a student at Trinity College, Dublin, heard read aloud by a fellow student at some point in 1816:

He had often said that if he was killed in battle, he wished to be buried where he fell. The body was removed at midnight to the citadel of Corunna. A grave was dug for him on the rampart there, by a party of the ninth regiment, the aides-de-camp attending by turns. No coffins could be procured, and the officers of his staff wrapped the body, dressed as it was, in a military cloak and blankets. The interment was hastened; for, about eight in the morning, some firing was heard, and the officers feared that, if a serious attack was made, they should be ordered away and not suffered to pay him their last duty. The officers of his family bore him to the grave; the funeral service was read by the chaplain; and the corpse was covered in earth. (458–59)

There is only one important factual difference between this narrative and Wolfe's reimagining of the scene. While Southey, and every other chronicler, states that the burial took place in the early morning of January 17, the poem seizes upon the evocative detail that "the body was removed at midnight to the citadel" and repositions the funeral service to the "dead of night." (As in the case of Casabianca, the poetic version of events was to win the battle of representations, at least in the mind of the artist Thomas Ballard, whose painting of a moonlit interment hangs in the Sir

John Moore Memorial Library at the army camp in Shorncliffe. Chronicles that appear after the popularization of the poem also follow the same path as accounts of the Battle of the Nile; just as later historians draft Mrs. Hemans's boy into their texts, a writer like Neale, for instance, feels "that no apology is necessary for introducing" Wolfe's verses into his narrative, given that they "are so faithfully descriptive of the last obsequies of the hero whom they commemorate" [206].)

Apart from the time shift, then, Wolfe sticks closely to Southey for the circumstantial details of his poem.[10] For his form, he seems to have turned to the recently published *Irish Melodies* of his countryman, Thomas Moore, a debt apparently unnoticed until 1882, when it was first suggested by a reviewer in the *Athenaeum*. In "The Field of His Fame: A Ramble in the Curious History of Charles Wolfe's Poem 'The Burial of Sir John Moore,'" Harold A. Small cites the support for this claim in his admirably comprehensive survey, and also notes some marked similarities in content. Most interestingly, however, Small tracks the courses of the numerous controversies about the true authorship of the poem that arose throughout the nineteenth century. Although the facts of the matter turn out to be well-nigh indisputable—there are really no grounds to challenge the notion that Wolfe did indeed write this poem—the evident discrepancy between the obscurity of the author and the eventual ubiquity of the poem seems to have fostered the growth of a remarkable number of stories, some in earnest and most in jest, about alternative contenders.

One of the elements that promoted this development, Small notes, was the fact that the poet was not the person who submitted the work for publication. As Wolfe's friend, the Rev. John A. Russell, was to explain in 1825, "the poem found its way to the press without the concurrence or knowledge of the author. It was recited by a friend [Samuel O'Sullivan] in presence of a gentleman [the Rev. Mark Perrin] travelling towards the north of Ireland, who was so much struck with it, that he requested and obtained a copy; and immediately after, it appeared in the *Newry Telegraph* [April 19, 1817], with the initials of the author's name. From that it was copied into most of the London prints, and thence into the Dublin papers; and subsequently it appeared, with some considerable errors, in the *Edinburgh Annual Register*, which contained the narrative that first kindled the poet's feelings on the subject, and supplied the materials to his mind" (5). Russell's publication history appeared as part of the introduction to a slim collection of poems and sermons entitled *Remains of the Late Rev. Charles Wolfe*; his friend had now been in his grave for two years, having succumbed to tuberculosis at the age of thirty-two.

If Wolfe, a curate in a quiet rural parish, had been buried with little notice in a country churchyard, the frequent reprintings of the poem ultimately ensured that "The Burial of Sir John Moore" would enjoy a glorious afterlife. Although it seems to have brought no fame to him in Ireland, an important development had already occurred in June 1817, when *Blackwood's Edinburgh Magazine* reprinted the poem.[11] From this point onwards, the poem began the gradual rise towards its anthological omnipresence. By 1851, D. M. Moir could comment in his *Sketches of the Poetical Literature of the Past Half-Century* that "'The Ode on the Burial of Sir John Moore' went directly to the heart of the nation, and it is likely to remain for ever enshrined there" (292). Just over a hundred years later, and not foreseeing the dramatic falling-off that would occur in the second half of the twentieth century, Small, an American critic, echoes Moir's opinion and summarizes the poem's subsequent history:

> The poem is known correctly enough throughout the English speaking world; it has been read, memorized, recited, ever since our great-grandfather's day. Because it celebrates martial glory, and memorializes a British soldier who, whatever his shortcomings, beat, or at least beat off, the French, it is not likely to be discarded for a while yet. Britain never forgets her heroes. And the poem is easy for any reader, British or not, to remember. It is one of those poems which, once read, it is almost impossible not to remember; as Lowell remarked, long ago "We have heard many ingenious persons try to explain the cling of such a poem as The Burial of Sir John Moore and the results of all seemed to be, that there were certain verses that were good, not because of their goodness, but because one could not forget them." (9–10)

Although we may object a little to Small's perception of British culture (even for 1953, this seems a little dated), he nevertheless encapsulates some of the received opinions about this poem, and provides a useful link to a brief survey of its pedagogical history.

The canonization of "The Burial of Sir John Moore" as a schoolroom recitation piece began in the United States. The poem cropped up in numerous "speakers" and reading books in the 1840s and 1850s, but it was its arrival in the series published by the redoubtable McGuffey brothers that ensured its broad distribution; Wolfe's poem first appeared in their *Fifth Eclectic Reader* in 1844.[12] In time, it would gravitate to the *Sixth*, gaining, in 1857, a short biographical introduction about the author, and then, much later in the century, a note on Sir John Moore and definitions of the more difficult words ("martial," "upbraid," "reck," and "random"), but for a long period, the poem, like all the others in the McGuffey books, stood without editorial apparatus. Across the Atlantic, the poem found itself reproduced in numerous general anthologies in the first half of the nineteenth century, but it took a little longer to establish a commanding presence in classroom readers. Although it featured in Sheridan Knowles's

Elocutionist in 1825, "The Burial of Sir John Moore" only really came into its own in British schools after the institutionalization of recitation as an all-elementary-school practice in 1882. From now onwards, the poem's ability to illustrate British history and promote patriotism ensured its repeated use. Placing it in a reading book for Standard IV (which is to say, for ten-year-olds), the Chambers series of 1883 (*Select Poetry for Recitation*) is entirely representative: as in all the rival publications, the editors provide an explanatory historical note ("By a masterly retreat to the seaport of Corunna . . . but died in the moment of victory") and a selection of glosses for words and phrases. Its inclusion in W. E. Henley's long-lived and widely assigned *Lyra Heroica* of 1892 was inevitable: the drumbeat of Wolfe's anapests would now be heard for many years to come.

The prominence gained by "The Burial of Sir John Moore," then, was out of all proportion with the modest standing of its author, and indeed, the minimal size of his otherwise uncelebrated oeuvre. One-hit wonders may be a familiar phenomenon in popular music today, but in other fields they usually have had a tendency to provoke suspicion. "In the lottery of literature," commented Moir, "Charles Wolfe has been one of the few who have drawn the prize of probable immortality from a casual gleam of inspiration thrown over a single poem, consisting only of a few stanzas" (292),[13] but from the time of the poem's first general popularity onwards, others had been expressing the opinion that the trophy had been awarded to the wrong man. "When single-speech Hamilton made in the Irish Commons that one memorable hit, and persevered ever after in obdurate taciturnity, folks began very justly to suspect that all was not right; in fact, that the solitary egg on which he thus sat, plumed in all the glory of incubation, had been laid by another": with these words, and under the heading of "The Original of 'Not a Drum Was Heard,'" the first number of *Bentley's Miscellany* in 1837 launched itself forth upon a jeu d'esprit that was to prove remarkably congenial to this particular poem (96). In brief, the article purported to have discovered that Wolfe's version was a mere "translation," and proceeded to supply not only the historical circumstances of the poem's first flowering ("Colonel de Beaumanoir . . . killed in defending, against the forces of Coote in Pondicherry, the last stronghold of the French"), but also the full "original" ("Ni le son du tambour . . .") (96). The playfulness of the piece ensures that few would have been fooled, and the jest was repeated again, this time in German, with another fake scene of origin. Many other translations were to follow—usually, it is true, without claims of any existence anterior to Wolfe—but they played their part in blurring the issue of authorial origin.

A much more serious challenge to the question of Wolfe's ownership of the poem had been inadvertently initiated by Lord Byron back in 1822. In his *Journal of the Conversations of Lord Byron* (1824), Captain Medwin told the story of an after-dinner conversation on "the lyrical poetry of the day":

> [A] question arose as to which was the most perfect ode that had been produced ... "I will show you [said Byron] an ode you have never seen, that I consider little inferior to the best which the present prolific age has brought forth." With this he left the table, almost before the cloth was removed, and returned with a magazine, from which he read [the lines on Sir John Moore's burial]. The feeling with which he recited these admirable stanzas, I shall never forget. After he had come to the end, he repeated the third, and said it was perfect, particularly the lines
>
> > But he lay like a warrior taking his rest,
> >   With his martial cloak around him.
>
> "I should have taken," said Shelley, "the whole for a rough sketch of Campbell's."
> "No," replied Lord Byron: "Campbell would have claimed it if it had been his." (113–14)

Medwin then expresses his view that "the ode was Lord Byron's; that he was piqued at none of his own being mentioned; and, after he had praised the verses so highly, could not own them. No other reason can be assigned for his not acknowledging himself the author, particularly as he was a great admirer of General Moore" (114). Adding in a footnote to this passage, "I am corroborated in this opinion lately by a lady, whose brother received them many years ago from Lord Byron, in his Lordship's own handwriting," Medwin thus set in circulation a remarkably long-lived myth. (Medwin himself, however, soon recanted: in the second edition of his *Conversations*, he quietly confessed that his "supposition was erroneous"). Indeed, traces of some form of connection between the poem and the most celebrated poet of its age persisted in the most public of places: the annotated McGuffey's *Fifth* of 1879 concluded its headnote with the words, "Byron said of this ballad that he would rather be the author of it than of any one ever written" (301).

But if Byron was bruited to be the author, then so, at different times, were lesser-known figures such as Christopher North, Barry Cornwall, William Frederick Deacon, and numerous others. The most inventive, and laboriously developed, hoax occurred in a book entitled *The Memoirs of Sergeant Paul Swanston* and published in 1840. The author, ostensibly a servant to an official in the commissariat, meets a young man called Wolfe, a British soldier in the Peninsula expeditionary force. Thrown together once again in a transport ship returning home after the battle at Corunna, the two men begin a lengthy conversation that ultimately results in the composition of a poem. Wolfe, now "made a corporal ... by Sir John Moore himself, at least, by his order," tells Swanston that he "was one of those ... that helped to make his grave, and bury him," and that he has it in mind "to make some verses" (chapter 6). Unable, in the bowels of the rocking ship, to lay his hands upon a pen and paper, Wolfe tries out his lines on the obliging Swanston and between the two of them they work towards a perfected version of something that is at first called "the 'Death of Sir John Moore'" but swiftly metamorphoses into a more familiar form. It is a fascinating scene, and spins itself out for page after page: Small, who reproduces at least 2,500 words of it in over six pages of his text, remarks that Swanston's ingenious fiction "seems to have been the only attempt to prop an 'original' in English" (28). He finds it "at best a lame performance," commenting that "aside from its occasional success in provoking a smile, it may hardly offer an excuse for its resurrection," but the exercise, I think, shows "Swanston" to have been a fairly astute literary critic (28–29). Certainly the concocted discussions about the evolution of each stanza allow our fiction writer to address the issue of the poem's less successful moments. Here is an extract from a couple of pages into the conversation, with "Wolfe" speaking first:

"The next verse I think would do better were it the last one of the whole, because it would make a goodish ending; but I'll let you hear it—it's the only second one I have at present:—

"Slowly and sadly we laid him down,
From the field of his fame fresh and gory;
We carved not a line, we raised not a stone,
But we left him—alone with his glory!

"*Gory* and *glory* are not altogether admissible words for a rhyme; but I've tried all the other words that I can think of to rhyme with *glory*, and I cannot find another that answers the sense."

"The poetry of that stanza is too good," said I, "to allow of criticism on a word; but, perhaps, if I might dare to name a word to you, I would say *sorrow*; don't you think you could alter a line, so as *sorrow* could come in, if you are not pleased with *glory*?"

"I have *sorrow* in use already," he said. (Chap. 6)

Swanston was not to be the only reader who would have a problem with this line (Tennyson, otherwise a great fan of the poem, "wished the last line but two could be changed" [Hallam Tennyson, 844]), but it is probably more relevant to my purpose here to pay attention simply to the fact that "fraud," as Small says, "may beget error" (29). More than half a century later, a certain R. C. Newick picked up the ball that Swanston had lobbed, and ran with it, as we can see from the opening paragraph of his small book, *The Writer of "The Burial of Sir John Moore" Discovered* (1908):

> There is no poem in the English language more often quoted in speech or printed in books, no poem about whose authorship there has been more controversy, none of which grips more firmly both the mind of a child and the intellect of a cultivated scholar, than the immortal threnody "The Burial of Sir John Moore." The purpose of this pamphlet is to prove that the ode was not written by the Rev. Charles Wolfe, but by a soldier of the 9th Regiment, named Joseph Wolfe, who was one of the party that actually dug Moore's grave. This necessarily involves the charge that the Rev. Charles Wolfe was an impostor. (7)

Newick appears to have drawn no followers, but his earnest text adds another strand to the fabric of confusion that became wrapped around the body of the verses. Of a different twist altogether were the many parodies that played with the poem's form. Small notes that Walter Hamilton's collection of 1884–89, *Parodies of the Works of English and American Authors*, "gives, wholly, or in part, no fewer than thirty-one parodies of the 'Burial,' and mentions a dozen more"; the first stanza of the most well known of these, by the Rev. Richard Harris Barham of *Ingoldsby Legends* fame, must stand for all the rest:

> Not a sou had he got,—not a guinea or note,
>   And he looked confoundedly flurried,
> As he bolted away without paying his shot,
>   And the landlady after him hurried.

The experiences of all the poems at the center of this study reveal that parody generation is an inevitable side-effect when verses with a distinctive rhythmical pattern are the common possession of a substantial population. "None of the parodies is spitefully aimed at the poem itself," comments Small in a summary of the good-natured quality of these burlesques (29). "One, which is a thrust at body-snatching, is in questionable taste . . . but none is disrespectful of Wolfe's hero in his grave. And none is satirical or contemptuous of Wolfe for having written his ode; to borrow a phrase from D' Israeli's essay on parody, 'some ingenuity in the application' is all that Wolfe's parodists have intended" (29). The fact that "The Burial of Sir John Moore" gave rise to so many spoofs from the 1830s onwards disproves any thesis that would try to assert that the poem was once held in high reverence, and then became ridiculous to its community at some later date; perhaps it is also worth making the rather obvious point that anapestic rhythms clearly have always carried the potential for comedy that today seems to be the sole justification for their employment. Some allusion to original content, then, may or may not be present in the parody, but faithful reproduction of the poem's original meter is key, and intention is all: parodists may be more or less successful in their attempt to amuse, but they generally borrow the form for comic effect, and we usually know that it is meant to be funny.

When verses with a distinctive theme are the common possession of a substantial population, however, the potential exists for other kinds of borrowing that serve very different intentions and needs. As noted in Part I, promoters of recitation in both Britain and the United States were keen to talk about the exercise's lifelong benefits, and often employed the language of the bank vault to make their points. For instance, in 1883 the American compiler of a school poetry book, Lambert's *Memory Gems*, selected the following words from British essayist Sir Arthur Helps for its title page: "We should lay up in our minds a store of goodly thoughts in well-wrought words, which should be a living treasure of knowledge, always with us, and from which, at various times, and amidst all the shifting of circumstances, we might be sure of drawing some comfort, guidance and sympathy" (1:232). To John Henry Newman, however, in *The Grammar of Assent* (1870), the return to lines memorized as a child takes an altogether more poignant form. As befits his own classical education, Newman is here writing more particularly about "the words of some classic author, such as Homer or Horace," lines that are "the birth of some chance morning or evening at an Ionian festival, or among the Sabine hills," but it is the contrast between "how differently young and old are affected" that is his principal concern:

> Passages, which to a boy are but rhetorical commonplaces, neither better nor worse than a hundred others which any clever writer might supply, which he gets by heart and thinks very fine . . . at length come home to him, when long years have passed, and he has had experience of life, and pierce him, as if he had never know them before, with their sad earnestness and vivid exactness. (75)

Newman here describes a piercing, a sudden entering into the self of the meaning of words that had been there all along.[14] But could the "sad earnestness and vivid exactness" of those lines also work to heal, or at least, comfort, if they sprang forth from the heart at a time when that heart was in terrible pain? And if those lines had been memorized not just by a few people here and there, but by entire generations together, how might that change the ways in which individuals used such words? And how might those words, so employed, change their worlds?

Here is Patrick Henry Taylor (or Henry, as he was known), a former schoolteacher from Belle Prairie, Minnesota, and now a sergeant in the First Minnesota regiment, writing in his journal after the Battle of Gettysburg in 1863: "I helped our Colonel off the field but fail to find my brother who, I suppose, is killed. I rejoin the regiment and lie down in the moonlight, rather sorrowful. Where is Isaac?" (quoted in Carley, 5). The next morning, another soldier tells Taylor that he has found his brother's body and takes him to the spot. "I find my dear brother dead!" continues the entry. "A shell struck him on the top of his head and passed through his back, cutting his belt in two." Taylor records that he retrieved Isaac's pocket watch as a keepsake, wrapped his brother up in the half-tent that soldiers carried to sleep in, and then, with the help of some comrades, buried him. He put up a board, marked it "I L Taylor, 1st Minn Vols," and then added the following lines:

> No useless coffin enclosed his breast,
>   Nor in sheet nor shroud we bound him,
> But he lay like a warrior taking his rest,
>   With his shelter tent around him.

He closes the account in his journal with these words: "As we laid him down, I remarked, Well Isaac, all I can give you is a soldier's grave" (5).

What we witness here, I would suggest, is an intersection of two distinct worlds. When Henry writes that stanza of poetry on the board at Isaac's grave, it is a public act, for he chooses to honor and commemorate his brother with words that are intelligible to his society. Yet at the same time it is also an intensely private act. In his adaptation of Wolfe's words to the precise circumstances of Isaac's burial (that "shelter tent" in place of the "martial cloak"), Henry shows that the poem that he has memorized is his, his to change in the ways he needs it to change, at a moment when he is experiencing intense grief. At this distance, it is difficult for us to know exactly how to understand the broader dimensions of Henry's behavior, and how it might relate to past practices in the English-speaking world. We may like to think that individual soldiers in conflicts before the American Civil War usually attempted to pay respect to their dead relatives, friends, and comrades by giving them whatever kind of burial the immediate situation permitted, but no historical records have been found to confirm such a supposition. It seems reasonable to assume, though, that Henry's feelings about the final rites owed to his brother were probably influenced by his knowledge of the kind of funeral Isaac would have received if he had died back home in Minnesota, and it is certainly easier to discover evidence about changing forms of civilian burial, in different regions, and at different socioeconomic levels, in this period (Laderman). But whatever comparative frames we bring to bear on this moment in Gettysburg, one thing is clear. There is an explicit belief, evident in Wolfe's poem and in the instance of a soldier like Taylor calling upon it as a resource, that the hasty burial stands in for one that should have been furnished. For Wolfe, as we have seen, the omission of full military honors creates the occasion for the poem, which is thus forged in the space between what a general should have received and what he does receive. For the common rank-and-file soldier, however, there was in this historical period no secure tradition of any such ceremony or permanent marking of his death, either where he died or on a memorial elsewhere ("all I can give you is a soldier's grave"). Yet once the poem, stored within the memory of an ordinary soldier, is summoned up in response to the ad hoc burial of his brother and comrade, then it points towards the absence of a proper commemoration.

The broad distribution of the *Fifth Eclectic Reader* across North America and the presence of "The Burial of Sir John Moore" in other popular schoolbooks ensured that the poem would be quoted on both sides of the division, by Confederates and Unionists who shared a common cultural heritage. Here is another extract from a wartime journal, this time kept by Kate Cumming, who was working as a nurse for the Confederate forces in Corinth, Tennessee. The entry for May 6, 1862, runs as follows:

> Mr. Jones died today; he was 18 years of age. He died the death of a Christian; he was a brave soldier; true to his God and his country. Miss H. sat up all night with him. She is endeavoring to procure a coffin for him. We have none now in which to bury the dead, as the Federals have destroyed the factory in which they were made. At one time, I thought it was dreadful to have the dead buried without them, but there is so much suffering among the living that I pay little attention to such things now. It matters little what becomes of the clay after the spirit has left it. Men who died as ours do, need no useless coffin to enshrine them. (24)

Reading between the lines, we can see that Kate needs to assert that she has worked through a crisis. Miss H., who has sat for hours at the bedside of a dying young man, is, in the face of the obvious impossibility of her quest, desperately searching for a coffin for him. "At one time," Kate implies, she too was in Miss H.'s position, but she is trying hard here to tell herself that she has overcome her sense of the "dreadful[ness]" of committing a shattered body to the earth without the cultural dignity of the containing form of a coffin. "I pay little attention"; "it matters little": with these repetitions, Kate protests that in the face of "so much suffering among the living," the manner in which the dead are buried does not matter, especially when they (and here she reaches towards a further argument) met their ends as nobly as these. "Men who died as ours do, need no useless coffin to enshrine them," she insists, borrowing words from a poem, not from Scripture, to attempt to reconcile herself to this seeming betrayal of last respect. The grief, shock, and horror that concentrate themselves with the greatest intensity at this one defined point—the direct meeting of body and soil, of "clay" with clay—are wrapped round and consoled by Wolfe's quiet insistence that heroes need no coffins.

Sometimes allusions to "The Burial of Sir John Moore" in Civil War writings were less poignant. Writing from his base with the Ninth Illinois regiment in Kentucky, war correspondent Loren Webb filed a report on February 11, 1862, that co-opted other, less charged, lines from Wolfe's poem into an impromptu verse celebration of the triumphant routing of an Alabama regiment from a half-built fortification:

> Not a drum was heard, not a rally note,
>   On the field where the chivalry was fleeing,
> Not a rebel fired his farewell shot,
>   From the works which the chivalry were building.[15]

A sense of glee, rather than sorrow, here infuses Webb's parody, and it is surely rhythm (albeit rhythm badly handled), rather than any true appropriateness of content, that drives his decision to wax "poetical," as he says to his editor, in his description of how the "Southern chivalry . . . did skedaddle." After the passage of time, too, the poem's appearance in chronicles and memoirs of the conflict seems formulaic rather than deeply felt. S. F. Horrall's *History of the Forty-Second Indiana Volunteer Infantry* (1892) provides a representative example: describing the battlefield burial of the gallant Captain Chas. G. Olmstead, whose words "This is as good a place to die as any other" had "scarcely died on his lips when he fell," Horrall states that "the lines of Wolfe are appropriate," quotes the "No useless coffin" and the final stanzas correctly and in full, and moves on (78).

In the midst of the war's horrible carnage, however, "The Burial of Sir John Moore" seemed to play a more important role for its quoters. Even in the generally less personal genre of a newspaper report, the "no useless coffin" phrase (used here not as a heading, as in the preponderance of cases of Anglo-Boer War journalism, but in the body of the text), appears to speak to the individual needs of one particular writer as he attempts to come to terms with the intensely distressing sights around him. In a dispatch that appeared in the *London Times* on February 4, 1863, a Canadian correspondent writing from Fredericksburg describes the "unusual care" that is being taken by the Federals "to make arrangements for the wounded." The number of casualties is "overwhelming":

> The air in the hut hospitals became intolerable, the ground literally soaked with blood. Close by were the pits into which was [*sic*] placed the bodies of those who had died. All possible respect was paid to the dead with an exception—the chaplain could never be had to read the

burial service. The writer saw about a dozen in one place being buried together. The pits were about 4 ft. deep. No useless coffin was seen; but there they lay, each with his camp-blanket around the inanimate form which alone separated the features so dear to faraway friends, from the cold, damp earth. Silently the soldiers did the work of the gravedigger, and one form after another disappeared from view and reposed from strife beneath the red Virginian soil. At the head of each was a rough board, upon which was written the name and regiment of the person. This was done as far as was possible, but there were many who died before they could tell who they were, or to what company they belonged. Upon the headboard of these was written simply "Unknown." Upon one I read "Unknown lieutenant." One could not but associate with these "unknowns" the heart-throbs of waiting friends, of anxious mothers, and distracted wives, who waited and waited till time alone said he must be gone. ("The Soldier's Grave," 1)

Here the quotation draws little enough attention to itself, but its significance is clear: the writer fights to assuage his horror of that coming together of the "cold, damp earth" and the beloved features of someone's husband, of someone's son, but he is mounting a rear-guard battle. While Kate Cumming is able to reach towards consolatory justifications (we should try to help the living, and not worry about the dead; heroes have no need of elaborate funerals), the journalist struggles: only a camp blanket and Wolfe's insistence that the coffin is "useless" keep the "red Virginian soil" at bay.

One last extract, this time from the private correspondence of a young "Georgian sharpshooter," William Rhadamanthus Montgomery, shows once again the exact site at which one cultural form, Wolfe's poem, offers itself up as the substitution for another cultural form, the coffin, and allows the suffering individual to carry on in otherwise unbearable circumstances. At the front line near Knoxville, Tennessee, on November 27, 1863, William has had to break off from writing to his "dear Aunt Frank" to attend to another task. He returns to the letter with these words:

A few hours later—Since writing the above Aunt Frank I have just finished the painful task of burying one of our men (was killed). "No useless coffin encloses his breast, but he lays like a brave warrior taking his rest with only his blanket around him." It is awful to think of, to be called upon so suddenly to bury an intimate friend & associate. But such is the fate of War, cruel War. Oh! How heartily I would we all hail a happy peace. Do write soon Aunt Frank & tell me all the news about old Marietta. I will write you again soon & will try & have more time to do it in. Our Boys keep up a prettie heavy fire all the time.

If you could hear us you would think a battle going on. My love to all the family, & write soon to Your Loving Nephew. (99)

What is so impressive about the writings of these individuals immersed in the trauma of violent and untimely death is the resourcefulness of their response: with few comforts to hand in desperate wartime straits, they call upon something deep within to help them survive the emotional devastation of the moment—something "inwoven with the very fabric of [their] mind[s]" since schooldays, as the American compiler of *Memory Gems for School and Home* put it in 1907 (W. H. Williams, 5). It is plain enough, I think, that on the material level, some wrapping of the body, whether it be in cloak, blanket, or even shelter tent, is at this time and for these people an absolute cultural necessity. More surprising, perhaps, is the way in which the bare adequacy of this gesture is repeatedly transformed and ennobled by the internalized memory of another such burial, of a poem that told them that respect and glory are not dependent upon planks of wood and a proper funeral.

"No useless coffin," then, is not the beginning and the end of this story. Although this strand of text serves to suture the purest point of pain, it is important to recognize that these three words function as synecdoche, and can only do their work if the entire poem is implicitly present within the hearts of its onetime reciters, and of those who will read and recognize their allusions. Worthy of comment, too, is the fact that Wolfe's poem manages to take on such significance for individuals who to us might seem distanced from its specific referents. That the poem is written by an Irishman about a Scotsman appears to have carried precious little punch—standing, as it did, in the *Fifth Eclectic Reader* without annotation, "The Burial of Sir John Moore" did not declare these affiliations to its first waves of memorizers, and only the word "Briton" signals national difference within the original text. For the purposes of my argument, though, the question of rank, or rather the absence of its markers, is far more resonant than the question of nationality. It is significant, I think, that the word "General" crops up nowhere in the text, and that Moore's honorific title features only in the poem's own title (and, as we noted with "Casabianca," titles have a curious habit of drifting away from otherwise successfully memorized texts, so this would make the effect of its presence there even more negligible). For Wolfe and the poem's early adult British readers, this was specifically an ode to a high-ranking leader, a commander whose social and military standing would almost have guaranteed him the status of "hero" even if his conduct had not been particularly valorous (in Moore's case, of course, the appellation was more than honestly earned). But for individuals who had learned "The Burial of Sir John Moore" at school in a different country and within a different social system, the poem they carried with them in a time of war threw up no internal hindrances to their applying it to any combatant, whatever his rank; their sense of it not as an alien cultural entity but as their own common property is more than amply illustrated by the fact that they were quick to adapt it to their personal needs. It is in this way, I am suggesting, that both a consolatory thought and an expectation that today seem entirely natural and understandable were supported and advanced by a work of literature: lamenting, and redeeming, an inadequate burial through the structure of Wolfe's poem, those who were left behind to mourn the common soldier thought of him as a hero who deserved more than an unmarked mass grave. The functional significance of "The Burial of Sir John Moore," then, extends beyond its structural presence within the immediate recollection, or imagination, of the scene of interment by individuals, to a contributory role in the development of new social practices for the memorialization of the rank-and-file solder.

There was no official policy about the marking of soldiers' graves at the outset of the Civil War: as Laqueur notes, "troops of neither side were issued the regular means of identification that would have made this possible" (158), and thus later efforts to provide accurate commemoration for individual burial sites were fraught with difficulty.[16] Throughout the war, too, a marked division persisted between the treatment allotted to the bodies of officers and enlisted men in Unionist and Confederate forces alike: the former could be sent home for burial if their families wished to invoke this privilege. Nevertheless, this turbulent era witnessed signal shifts in communal attitudes towards the soldier's corpse. Tracking the official proclamations that led to the establishment of a national burial system, however, has the inevitable effect of making the process seem more streamlined than it actually was; in the midst of the conflict, combatants had to respond quickly to rapidly changing circumstances, and orders were often more honored in the breach than in the observance. The first significant attempt to ensure the preservation of "accurate and permanent records of deceased soldiers and their place of burial" came in General Order 75, which was issued after the disastrous First Battle of Bull Run (Manassas) in July 1861 (Mollan).[17] This debacle made it clear to the War Department that the conflict would certainly be of a longer duration than initially envisaged, and that there would be a flood of inquiries about the whereabouts of missing loved ones. In April of the next year, another order came through, this time requiring commanding officers to mark off plots of ground "in some suitable spot in every battlefield, so soon as it may be in their powers, and to cause the remains of those killed to be interred, with headboards to the graves bearing numbers and, when practicable the names of the persons buried in them" (quoted in Mollan, 58). Few commanders found themselves able to comply with these orders, given the crush of their other responsibilities, and so it fell to the Office of the Quartermaster to take control; this was, indeed, a logical extension of its traditional duties, which since 1775 had included the administration of burial grounds within army posts.[18] Another important measure was pushed through a few months later: in July 1862, Lincoln signed an omnibus act that in section 18 ensured that "the President of the United States shall have power, whenever in his opinion it is expedient, to purchase cemetery grounds and cause them to be securely enclosed, to be used as a national cemetery for the soldiers who shall die in the service of their country" (quoted in Mollan, 59). This was the origin of the National Cemetery System; Gettysburg, begun in 1863, was the first, and arguably the most symbolically significant, site.

From this stage onwards, and after the end of the Civil War, there were various moves to develop new practices of memorialization, and, eventually, to ensure the permanence of these measures. By 1866, forty-one National Cemeteries containing the bodies of over 100,000 Union soldiers had come into existence; the following year, Congress passed an act dedicated to the further establishment and protection of such sites. The quartermaster general, Montgomery C. Meigs, repeatedly called for reports on the burials recorded during the course of the conflict, announcing his department's intention to mark the graves of all Union soldiers and prisoners of war "so far as can be ascertained" and to "publish a record of the names and places of interment" (quoted in Mollan, 59). As can be imagined, attempts to locate, identify, and re-inter remains were beset with problems: by 1870, the bodies of 300,000 men had been moved to seventy-three National Cemeteries, but over 40 percent of these had to be marked "Unknown," while the compiled reports of burial locations were shot through with errors. The cost of replacing short-lived wooden boards soon became apparent, and debates about appropriate permanent substitutes began: in March 1873, a million dollars were appropriated to furnish the graves with markers of "durable stone." At this time, too, the right of burial in a national cemetery was extended to all honorably discharged Union veterans; six years later, the secretary of war was further authorized to erect official headstones "over the graves of Union soldiers who have been interred in private, village, or city cemeteries" (quoted in Mollan, 61). Only in 1906 did Congress authorize the provision of comparable headstones to mark resting places of Confederate soldiers within both National Cemeteries and Confederate burial plots.[19]

Gradually, then, the United States moved towards a system that would make the single, named site for each and every fallen soldier its ideal. Yet we should be wary of any back projection that would make the Civil War battle graves exact precedents for the vast cemeteries of World War I, with their serried rows of identical markers for officers and enlisted men alike. Laqueur makes the following monitory statements to this effect:

> Gettysburg, with its individual graves, was itself a major innovation ... [but] something of an exception. ... Similar cemeteries were not built on other and even bloodier battle sites; there are no rows of individual graves at Antietam, for example. Finally, those who planned Gettysburg were still only groping toward the creation of national burial grounds or cemeteries that primarily marked individuals. Between 1864 and 1895 the landscape, as one historian noted, became "a vast outdoor gallery of state and regimental monuments," not singular or national ones. (158)

The validity of these points is supported, in an interesting fashion, by a speech delivered by William James on the event of the unveiling in Boston in 1897 of the celebrated Saint Gaudens monument to Colonel Robert Gould Shaw and the 54th Massachusetts Regiment, the Union's first troop of black soldiers.[20] So nervous was James about his responsibility that he made the uncharacteristic decision to memorize his entire oration, a speech that included a couple of lines from a poem that he had learned by heart years before. As he moved towards the end of his long and moving address, James described how the newly formed regiment, on only its third day of fighting with the Confederates, participated in the desperate attack on Fort Wagner, losing two-thirds of its officers and nearly half of its men, some three hundred in all, in the process. In James's account of the burial of the dead the following day, the enemy's indiscriminate interment of officers and men, white and black, together, is converted from a calculated insult into an apt and noble symbol of their common cause and bravery:

> As for the colonel, not a drum was heard nor a funeral note, not a soldier discharged his farewell shot, when the Confederates buried him, the morning after the engagement. His body, half stripped of its clothing, and the corpses of his dauntless negroes were flung into one common trench together, and the sand was shovelled over them, without a stake or stone to signalize the spot. In death as in life, then, the Fifty-fourth bore witness to the brotherhood of man. The lover of heroic history could wish for no more fitting sepulchre for Shaw's magnanimous young heart. There let his body rest, united with the forms of his brave nameless comrades. There let the breezes of the Atlantic sigh, and its gales roar their requiem, while this bronze effigy and these inscriptions keep their fame alive long after you and I and all who meet here are forgotten. (*Exercises at the Dedication*, 49)

James delivers a liberal and uplifting speech here, and so it may seem churlish to take issue with his rhetoric, but, whether he knew it or not, this poetic invocation of those "nameless" comrades is quite inaccurate: a tally of 106 names of "the Enlisted Men of the 54th Regiment Mass. Vols Missing After the Assault on Ft. Wagner July 18th 1863" was compiled immediately thereafter and still survives in army records. (The "inscriptions" James mentions, which can be found on the back of the monument, listed only the names of the officers, all white, who died in the attack; it took eighty-four more years before sixty-two of the names of black soldiers were also carved into the stone.) More germane to our purposes here, though, is the indication we receive from James's words that the concepts of both the unmarked and the mass grave are not so culturally repellant that they cannot be redeemed and transfigured. Admittedly, these are highly specialized circumstances, and James was quite definitely building on what were by this point long-standing discussions about the national symbolism of this particular grave. (Shaw's father, choosing not to have his son's body disinterred for a private funeral, had stated that he held "that a soldier's most appropriate burial place is on the field where he has fallen"; whether he, or, as was widely believed, a Confederate commander, had also said that Shaw was "buried with his niggers" was the source of some confusion, but the remark was widely believed to have attracted large numbers of black recruits to the Union Army [quoted in McPherson, 687].) But if the disturbing notion of the mingling of corpses in the mass grave can be transformed through the abstract image of "the brotherhood of man," anxieties about the ignominious burial of the colonel's body and the lack of a "stake or stone to signalize the spot" receive much more direct succor. Via the cultural shorthand of a brief reference to Wolfe's poem, James links South Carolina to Corunna, and thus can leave Shaw's mortal remains alone with their glory.[21]

That Wolfe's poem also came to inhabit the British consciousness is clear from the responses of those caught up in the two Anglo-Boer wars (Van Wyk Smith), but the situation changes dramatically thereafter. Because of the horrific circumstances of long entrenched warfare in northern France and Belgium, the poem, predictably enough, receives little direct quotation in the public and private literature of World War I; as I have already noted, Sir John's "maimed rites" seem lavish and elaborate when considered in relation to a world in which any kind of burial was regularly impossible. In a sense, though, the work of "The Burial of Sir John Moore" was already done, and not just in its role of promoting the creation of the American precedent. In contributing to the consolidation of the long-standing archetype of the noble soldier in the minds of millions of people, Wolfe's poem helped to ensure that men who died in

World War I received not only some form of individual commemoration abroad, but also commemoration as heroes back home. Until fairly recently, it was a commonplace both in the cultural history and the literary criticism that addressed this period to assert that the nineteenth-century ethos and those "old" words we find in poems like "The Burial of Sir John Moore" rendered them repugnant to a substantial majority of the British population after the war. There are complex, but understandable, reasons why such a belief should have prevailed for so long, but massive physical evidence has always existed to contradict it. Most notably, war memorials, in every village, in every town, and in every city across Great Britain stand in silent but impressive rebuke to the concept of such a dismissal. The spirit of the martial and patriotic poems of the past infuses these stony commemorations of World War I—memorials that do not reject "the old words" but carry their carving again and again and again above the names of the listed individuals, the Glorious and Immortal Dead. "The Burial of Sir John Moore" ends by asserting that the general is left overseas with his glory. The mass memorization of this poem played a part in ensuring that in the wake of World War I, glory was general all over Britain.

To venture into the fray of the cultural history of war and commemoration bearing nothing more substantial than a thirty-two-line poem may seem foolhardy, or quixotic at least. I should make it clear that my poetic standard functions in this argument both as the thing itself—the lines of the poem genuinely affected the way in which some individuals in distress represented their situation to themselves and to others—and as the emblem of a number of broad social changes that had the result of making people feel very differently about the positions in which they and their loved ones were placed in wartime. It would be uncontroversial to suggest that the state begins to maintain graves and mark the names of all its soldiers, regardless of rank, because of the increasing democratization and spread of individualism within its society; these were processes that made it possible for a large proportion of the population to achieve a high level of literacy and thus a new relationship to identity. Yet such an abstract statement does not take us very close to how and why specific, felt, needs arose. Standing as both representative symbol and result of major social shifts, the memorized poem affords a significantly different point of access to this instance of historical change; a focus on words that were carried far and wide within countless individuals helps to bring us nearer to the changing of hearts and the changing of minds. I suggest that it is through our examination of moments like Henry Taylor's description of his brother's burial or Kate Cumming's account of her struggle to accept the unacceptable that we can best begin to understand those mass cemeteries, the permanent memorials of northern France and Belgium, those hundreds of thousands of individually named and preserved graves, soldiers of all ranks together. I have argued here that Wolfe's poem is about reparation, that it functions as a belated attempt to provide what should have been given at the time: "We carved not a line, and we raised not a stone." The mass memorization of "The Burial of Sir John Moore after Corunna," I believe, played its part in the modern phenomenon of mass memorialization, and thus in the carving of a million lines, and the raising of a million stones.

Afterword

W. E. HENLEY: "INVICTUS"

Out of the night that covers me
    Black as the Pit from pole to pole
I thank whatever gods may be
    For my unconquerable soul.

In the fell clutch of circumstance,
    I have not winced nor cried aloud.
Under the bludgeonings of chance,
    My head is bloody, but unbowed.

Beyond this place of wrath and tears,
    Looms but the Horror of the shade.
And yet the menace of the years
    Finds, and shall find, me unafraid.

It matters not how strait the gate
    How charged with punishments the scroll
I am the master of my fate:
    I am the captain of my soul.

RUDYARD KIPLING: "IF –"

If you can keep your head when all about you
    Are losing theirs and blaming it on you;
If you can trust yourself when all men doubt you,
    But make allowance for their doubting too;
If you can wait and not be tired by waiting,
    Or being lied about, don't deal in lies,
Or being hated, don't give way to hating,
    And yet don't look too good, nor talk too wise:

If you can dream—and not make dreams your master;
    If you can think—and not make thoughts your aim,
If you can meet with Triumph and Disaster
    And treat those two impostors just the same;
If you can bear to hear the truth you've spoken
    Twisted by knaves to make a trap for fools,

Or watch the things you gave your life to, broken,
    And stoop and build 'em up with worn-out tools:

If you can make one heap of all your winnings
    And risk it on one turn of pitch-and-toss,
And lose, and start again at your beginnings
    And never breathe a word about your loss;
If you can force your heart and nerve and sinew
    To serve your turn long after they are gone,
And so hold on when there is nothing in you
    Except the Will which says to them: "Hold on!"

If you can talk with crowds and keep your virtue,
    Or walk with Kings—nor lose the common touch,
If neither foes nor loving friends can hurt you,
    If all men count with you, but none too much;
If you can fill the unforgiving minute
    With sixty seconds' worth of distance run,
Yours is the Earth and everything that's in it,
    And—which is more—you'll be a Man, my son!

Recitation's Legacy: The Nation's Favo(u)rite Poems

In December 2009 a film called *Invictus* opened in American cinemas; its London premiere occurred a month later. The movie tells the story of how Nelson Mandela, in his first term as the South African president, strove to unite his apartheid-torn country by enlisting the help of the national rugby team; the team's victory in the final of the 1995 Rugby World Cup provides the film with its uplifting conclusion. Although Mandela's autobiography actually makes no mention of his reciting W. E. Henley's poem in prison, and although the text he handed to Springbok captain Francois Pienaar for inspiration was apparently not "Invictus" but Theodore Roosevelt's "Man in the arena" speech, director Clint Eastwood decides to have it otherwise.[1] In consequence it is a fair guess that for some time to come, both the word "Invictus" and Henley's lines will be connected in the popular mind with Mandela and the indomitability of spirit he demonstrated during his twenty-seven years of captivity as a political prisoner.

Sitting watching the movie in a northern Californian cineplex in January 2010, I was not best pleased—and not just because I found it for the most part a leaden and predictable piece of work. I was annoyed because a long-planned scheme to write about Henley's poem for this book's coda had been effectively derailed. I had been intending to explore the poem's

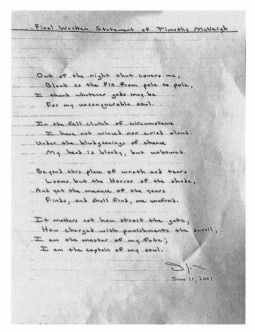

3. Timothy McVeigh's final statement, June 2001

relation to Timothy McVeigh, the man who bombed the Alfred P. Murrah Federal Building in Oklahoma City on April 19, 1995. On the night before his execution in June 2001 McVeigh wrote out Henley's poem from memory, signed it, and left it in place of a final statement (figure 3).

I had imagined that my coda would speculate about how McVeigh had come to know the poem. He might have learned it while in high school in Lockport, New York, but it is more likely, I think, that he was first exposed to its lines while watching another American film that used the words of "Invictus" to set forth its central message. *Kings Row* was the smash hit of 1942 and has been regularly screened on American television over the years; adapted from a best-selling 1940 novel of that title by Henry Bellaman, the movie unreels, in the words of its best-known star Ronald Reagan, "a slightly sordid but moving yarn" about a group of friends growing up in a small midwestern town at the turn of the nineteenth century (4). Their little world beset by social pressures, sexual jealousies, dark secrets, and a series of overwrought challenges and tragedies, the characters are the denizens of the Peyton Place or the Wisteria Lane of their day. In the film's climactic scene Reagan's character, who is recovering from the amputation of both his legs, is told that the surgery was medically unnecessary, an act of revenge by a sadistic doctor. The deliv-

erer of this shocking piece of information then recites the first two stan-
zas of "Invictus" to inspire his bed-bound friend to receive the news with
all possible fortitude. After a moment or two, a laughing Reagan proves
equal to the challenge. The film then comes to a triumphal close, the
soundtrack featuring a choir singing the final stanza of "Invictus" in rous-
ing chorus.

Yet much as I wished to draw an indisputable line of descent from
Kings Row to McVeigh, I had yet to uncover hard evidence; furthermore,
I was also finding it difficult to make a definitive case for a causal rela-
tionship between the condemned man's citational act and some subse-
quent deployments of Henley's poem. Nevertheless, my hypothetical coda
would have noted that the image that is reproduced as figure 4 appeared
a couple of years after McVeigh's death. Part of an advertising campaign
for a company called SureFire that makes gun-mounted flashlights, the
poster superimposes the text of "Invictus" on a photograph taken during
the second Gulf War (McVeigh's service, we might note, had been hon-
ored by the U.S. Armed Force's Bronze Star in the first). I would also have
referred to the fact that another of America's "home-grown terrorists"
quoted the poem from the confines of his prison cell a few years later; the
nine-paged "manifesto" issued by Atlanta Olympic Games bomber, Eric
Rudolph, concluded with the words, "I say to you people that by the . . .
grace of God I am still here—a little bloodied, but emphatically unbowed."
I had material, then, to connect "Invictus" to a certain constituency of
ultra-right American extremists (or to products that they might find at-
tractive), and I had planned to talk about how and why this might have
come about.

Those who toil within reception studies are hostages to fortune; we
take aim at a moving target (with or without a flashlight), or, like some
especially hapless rugby player, try to kick our ball through a set of con-
tinually shifting goalposts. I should perhaps make it clear that I had not
been intending to argue that Henley's poem had been prized solely by
militant separatists until Eastwood's film came along to change my mind.
Every decade since the poem's first publication in 1888 furnishes evidence
testifying to its extraordinarily broad appeal, and further supportive ma-
terial appears all the time. January 2008, for example, witnessed U.S.
presidential candidate John McCain's remark, "We are the captains of
our fate" after he had won the South Carolina primary,[2] an event that
prompted a *New York Times* editorial by William Kristol proclaiming
that this candidate's relation to "Invictus" demonstrated an estimable
neo-Victorianism that America would be wise to respect. I was also well
acquainted with the poem's importance not just to the famous and the
infamous, but to large numbers of the general public as well. My file of
examples grew steadily. To mention only two: I learned from the chair of

4. A poster produced by SureFire to promote its
range of gun-mounted flashlights, circa 2003

my department that she had read the lines at a Berkeley memorial service for a friend who had died of cancer and who had always cherished the poem that she had memorized at school fifty years earlier. Another colleague mentioned that when she last taught the poem, one of her students broke down in tears: her brother, who had died of AIDS, had kept a copy of it pinned up by his bedside.

En route to whatever its argument might have turned out to be, then, that coda would obviously have had to acknowledge that any cultural object in wide circulation cannot be fixed; cannot be made to have a single meaning; and cannot be owned categorically by any one person or community. While these remain necessary and important admissions here, this afterword takes a different direction from that originally planned. Instead of examining "Invictus" primarily in relation to McVeigh and American extremism, I consider why these lines have become so extraordinarily important to so many, and such a variety of, individuals; I also place the poem next to Rudyard Kipling's "If –," another short work that has claimed huge numbers of adherents. "Invictus" and "If –" figure here as prime examples of poems that have been widely memorized and have gained the status of national favorites. It would seem reasonable to assume that there is an easy causal relationship between these two characteristics and that the reception histories of the two works will therefore follow neatly parallel paths. Yet this is not the case. The trajectories described tell two divergent stories, stories that bring us closer to an understanding of the nationally distinct aftereffects of the cultures of mass poetry recitation that were formally consolidated within public education in both Britain and the United States. "Invictus" and "If –" ultimately serve as optics for an examination of recitation's different legacies in these two countries.

One of this book's aims has been to show, in a variety of ways, how a poem learned by heart has the potential to create a pronounced and particular form of the affective relation that can pertain between individuals and works of art. Why has "Invictus" encouraged such highly charged instances of this bond? My answers to this question consider features that are both intrinsic and extrinsic to Henley's poem. While it is perhaps self-evident that its contents are exceptionally nonreferential, this quality was enhanced by certain events in the work's early publication history. Thereafter, once "Invictus" came to enjoy mass dissemination, the poem's inherent and acquired traits of openness and detachability gave it the power to perform as a concrete instantiation of the ideological belief in mass individualism that underwrites liberal democratic society—the belief that "We are all individuals," as Monty Python pithily expressed it in *Life of Brian*. Although "Invictus" undoubtedly has had, and has, a relationship with English-speakers in many different countries, its importance to the American psyche has been especially profound. Within the nation that subscribes more wholeheartedly to a faith in individualism than any other, the recitation of Henley's lines packs a tremendously effective emotional punch.

One of the notable features of the poem's history was the speed of its rise to preeminence. "It was published ten years ago in Mr. Henley's first book of verse," said Sir William Archer in 1898, "and already it is a classic"; American writers in this year and the next also referred to the lines as "now famous" and "justly famous" (Archer, 151; Chapman, 276; Page, 451). The rapidity of this embrace was no doubt assisted by the open question of the poem's stance on theological matters, an ambiguity best illustrated by line 3, "I thank whatever gods may be." (Arthur Symons indicated delicately in an early review that Henley had most likely filched the construction from Swinburne's "Garden of Proserpine" [191].) Some applauded the poem's expression of classical, heathen, or humanist beliefs: "stoicism has waited all these centuries for its superbest utterance," said Archer (151); Alice Brown in 1895 pronounced it "the greatest pagan cry of modern years" (44); atheist G. W. Foote reprinted it in *The Freethinker* three years later. Yet the following year the poem could appear as the entry for May 19 in *Prayers from the Poets: A Calendar of Devotion*; a broad swathe of church magazines and diocesan newsletters in both Britain and America also featured it within their pages in the last decade of the nineteenth century. Wide open to interpretation, Henley's poem was more than acceptable to Christians and non-Christians alike, and found admission everywhere.

Yet none of these appearances saw those sixteen lines reprinted under the heading "Invictus." The poem's curious titular history is both symbol and component of a process that saw the work move progressively further away from its connection to Henley, or, more precisely, from the biographical circumstances of its genesis. As Edward H. Cohen argued nearly forty years ago, there is no reason to doubt that the poem was indeed written in 1875, the date printed below it when it first appeared in 1888 under the enigmatic inscription "To R. T. H. B" (the letters indicated Hamilton Bruce, one of the three founders of the *Scots Observer*, the paper that had given Henley much-needed employment as editor that same year). The 1875 composition date makes the poem one of those that Henley drafted in his midtwenties, long before he knew Bruce, during the twenty months he spent in the Edinburgh Royal Infirmary under the care of Joseph Lister, pioneer of antiseptic surgery. Henley suffered from tuberculosis of the bone, and had had his left leg amputated in his teens; thanks to Lister, his right was saved. Henley gave poetic form to his infirmary experiences in the twenty-eight poems of "In Hospital," the sequence that constituted the opening and longest section of that first *Book of Verses*, and which also attracted most comment in initial reviews. In the early years of its existence in print, critical mentions of the poem we now know as "Invictus" habitually linked it to this sequence and thus inevitably to the known facts of Henley's courage in the face of terrible disease.

At the same time, however, the poem's titular inadequacy had already begun to disturb; both anthologists and subeditors started to append their own inventions. *The Esoteric* magazine dubbed it "Unconquered" in 1890; six years later it was "Urbs Fortitudinis" for *A Treasury of Helpful Verse*; Foote called it "Undaunted" for *The Freethinker*. Henley himself muddied the water when he reprinted the poem in his 1899 volume *Echoes of Life and Death* under an expanded, and now memorial, heading, "I. M. R. T. Hamilton Bruce (1846–1899)." The two authorized dedications may have played their part in helping to detach the verses from a connection to Henley's own biography, but they were rarely used in reprintings. *Le mot juste* was supplied instead by Arthur Quiller-Couch when he included the poem in the first edition of the *Oxford Book of English Verse* in 1900 under a now-famous one-word title. "Invictus" was not accepted immediately or in all quarters, but Quiller-Couch's formulation has largely won the day.

Yet although "Invictus" and the poem under discussion became bound together, the tie between these two and Henley's lifelong battle with disease has been less secure. So insecure, in fact, that the 1917 *Cambridge History of English Literature* could blithely refer to the poem as "the portrait of [Robert Louis] Stevenson," despite the fact that it also discusses Henley's medical condition and the "Hospital Verses" at some length (Ward, 238). As the years went by and the poem continued to enjoy multiple reprintings in a range of publication venues, it was less and less likely to take with it a link to the circumstances of its composition. To a degree, this was related to the textual conventions of the types of places in which it tended to appear. "Invictus" was often dropped into a newspaper or magazine page otherwise devoid of poetry or featured in a popular anthology of verse; in neither venue has it been common to include biographical details about an author. But to focus only on Henley's poem in mainstream print media leaves untouched a further important site of dissemination, that of the school. What happened to "Invictus" in the classroom?

Henley's poem has had markedly different experiences within British and American education. Arnold Smith, an English pedagogue already mentioned in this study, may have praised the poem's closing lines in his 1915 *Aims and Methods in the Teaching of English* for their "ethical value and bracing effect" and suggested that they could "bring solace . . . in some despondent mood" (101), but the powers of "Invictus" were not broadly distributed in Great Britain; a key text for many grammar and private schoolboys, it never took root in the elementary school. Thanks to that longer and wider reach of recitational culture across the Atlantic, it was a different story in the United States; the poem came into its own as a text for memorization in the upper grades of the high school in the mid-1930s, when it also began to be a frequently named item on college entrance requirements for English literature (Applebee, 278). From then on until the beginning of the 1960s and the general decline of mandatory recitation in the United States, "Invictus" was a staple. Thereafter, if the practice happened to survive in any given institution, there was a good chance that Henley's poem would survive with it. Some years ago one of my graduate students told me that her high school in Connecticut had, and still has, a scheduled "Invictus" day each year: on the appointed date, any teacher can point at any person and ask for an immediate recitation of the poem (performed, *Dead Poets* fashion, upon a chair or table).[3]

But for the most part, these experiences with Henley's poem also floated free of knowledge of Henley's life, whatever the degree of information dispensed by teacher or textbook may have been. Indeed, these sixteen lines have frequently enjoyed an existence independent not just of biographical details but of any connection to their author whatsoever. To be sure, the majority of reprintings bear the poet's name, but the ascription "W. E. Henley" has been unlikely to trigger any broader recollections. Like Charles Wolfe, Henley is a one-hit wonder whose only poetic claim to fame is this piece; in the height of the McVeigh or McCain or Mandela moments, pieces of American journalism that mentioned "Invictus" habitually assumed that readers needed to be given the basic facts (the words "nineteenth-century cripple" have on occasion sufficed, but "Long John Silver"—the *Treasure Island* character Stevenson reputedly based upon his one-legged friend—often gets mentioned as well).[4]

I have here been pulling upon a number of threads within the poem's production and reception histories to illustrate how their lines worked loose from a connection to the man who wrote them. Yet this has teased out a process that in truth always operated in concert with at least two other factors. The first of these connects to that status of "Invictus" as a memorized poem; as these pages have repeatedly demonstrated, those who learn a work by heart and recite it frequently come to feel that it belongs to them, not the author of its being, or, even further, that it actually speaks for them. When the work is in the first person, then this sensation can be still more intense: where does one "I" end and the other begin? The second factor is constituted not just by the word "I" but by all the other words inside the poem as well.

What is it about those five sentences that created their massive appeal? This question is best approached by way of that frequently ignored site of composition and their coincident verses. I do not suggest such a move simply to shrink "this place of wrath and tears" to the size of Edinburgh Royal Infirmary or to demystify the "clutch of circumstance" by noting it bears a relation to the "clutch of chloral" that appears in "Interior," Poem III in the longer work. Rather, because entering "Invictus" from "In Hospital" reveals that the structure of the experiences and the spaces represented within the individuated poem is coextensive with those in the sequence. "Invictus" delivers all three major tenses—present, past, and future—but we are hard put to locate its "I" in anything like orderly or organized temporality. We are no less bereft of a sense of place. The poem demonstrates a marked prepositional insistence—"Out," "In," "Under," and "Beyond" are all important, capitalized, line-beginning words—but where on earth (or out of it) are we? Yet when we come "Out of the Night" through the hospital verses, we are able to smell the "thick, sweet mystery of chloroform" that pervades the air in "Before," Poem IV of "In Hospital"; we can sense how that "clutch of chloral" dissolves the outlines of the knowable world and renders reemergence into consciousness a dissociated jumble of returning sensation. "[B]rokenly / Time and the place glimpse onto me again," says the speaker in Poem VI, "After," but it could just as well be the speaker of "Invictus."

To recognize that "I" as a postanesthetic self is not a terminus but a beginning, for it helps us to start defining the peculiar nature of the poem's most prominent patterns. By repeatedly conjoining the tangible with the intangible, "Invictus" delivers above all an experience of intensity without specificity. In their fusion of overt physicality with absolute abstraction, the phrases "the fell clutch of circumstance" and "the bludgeonings of chance" illustrate this most compactly, but the entire poem is created out of meshings of the literal and the metaphorical. It is this quality, I would argue, that has made this hospital poem endlessly hospitable to others; at every turn "Invictus" offers reciters an open opportunity to understand its expressions not as the contingent utterances of somebody else in a particular historical moment or geographical site, but rather as entirely personal to themselves in their own time of trial. If you happen to be the leader of a rugby team, a member of the official armed services, or a soldier in your own private militia, then you will pronounce the word "captain" with a certain assurance that this poem is speaking literally, uncannily, for you. But if you are none of these things, there is still no bar to identification given that the poem's pivots always provide a choice of figurative or factual embrace. "Invictus" can produce such strong effects within all comers not because the narratives it offers are hazy, but because its stories of what has happened, what is happening, and what will happen to the speaker are equally characterized by unlocatable definition.

All comers? Or do you have to be going through a time of trial, as I stated a few sentences back? One might counter that everybody finds life to be a bit of a trial at some point or another, but this is a little too glib. Better to acknowledge that to date "Invictus" has been most passionately claimed by individuals in two types of circumstance—those whose bodily mobility has been checked either by illness or accident, or by imprisonment (just or unjust, state-sanctioned or otherwise). *Kings Row* and Eastwood's *Invictus* nicely illustrate this bipartite division (did Casey Robinson, the screenwriter who inserted Henley's lines into the former film, know that the lines he uses to cheer up the legless Ronald Reagan had been written by an amputee? I have been unable to find out). There are of course exceptions—a recent autobiography by the emphatically two-legged Andre Agassi testifies to the poem's importance to an unincarcerated tennis player—but on the whole, the rule stands firm. "Invictus" has become associated with states of being in which freedom and self-determination can be achieved only within an imagined internal realm. Whether or not we choose to see this as an allegory for the state of man within modern society depends upon which way we lean, politically.

"Invictus" appears within *Americans' Favorite Poems*, an anthology published in 2000 in the wake of the highly successful "Favorite Poem Project" mentioned in the introduction. In common with the other 199 poems in the book, the lines are printed without any explanatory notes or details about their author and are prefaced instead by remarks from some of the individuals who chose the work as their favorite. Here are the three quotations that precede Henley's poem:

> It came to my mind during the attack on Pearl Harbor and nearby Hickam Field. I was a private stationed at Hickam. For two-and-a-half to three hours, a buddy and I dodged strafing, bombing and the usual horrors of the wounded and the dead. Fearful of dying and in despair, I raised a clenched fist to the skies and "master of my fate" took hold in my mind, and "captain of my soul" fortified my resolve. We hadn't lost; we had a God-given direction to turn to. Later I learned that I had recalled part of "Invictus." (Arthur Scevola, 80, Retired Optometrist, Debany, Fl.)

> I am submitting this powerful poem to the Favorite Poem Project. I am a forty-nine year old woman and I have been incarcerated for the past twenty-three years, serving a life sentence. I have never done violence to anyone, yet I have paid dearly for my mistakes in my youth. I have handled the nightmare of prison with dignity, courage and maturity. There had been times of despair when I thought I couldn't go on, yet somehow I have. This beautiful poem has been an inspiration and a source of strength and comfort to me whenever I close my eyes and recite it to myself. (Diane Metzger, 49, State Prisoner, Newcastle, Del.)

> I am an aged exile from New England, confined at home after a stroke some eighteen years ago. I hold Henley's poem to be a true masterpiece of inspiration. On the night of the stroke, as my inert body was being wheeled by paramedics down the corridors of Mass. General Hospital, my mind staved off panic by silently repeating this poem. (Joe Sabia, 74, Corpus Christi, Tx.) (114)

I will pass over the second two citations, noting only that they serve as further illustrations of my point about the poem's appeal to those enduring physical confinement, in hospital or in prison.[5] It is the first quotation that gives me pause here, for it corrects my former assertion that Henley's poem has been of primary importance to two types of individuals. I should have said three: "Invictus" is not just the invalid's poem and the prisoner's poem, but also the soldier's poem.[6] This is an identity that is always readily available through that word "captain"; that is implicit in its importance to McVeigh and McCain; and that can also make us think again about the nature of the bond that forms when the "I" of the poem becomes the "I" of the reciter. Relatively speaking, there are not all that many poems in the first person in the canons of recitational verse; within those that do exist, the "I" is usually springing "to the stirrup" as the narrator of a dramatic tale; or wandering "lonely as a cloud" in some kind of pleasant and enriching relationship with the natural world; or, indeed, ventriloquizing that natural world itself ("I come from haunts of coot and hern").[7] But just as the soldier who puts his life at risk for other people or who dies for the nation exists at the sharpest point of intersection between the self and others, between the self and an abstract idea outside the self, so do the memorized lines of Henley's poem balance themselves at the spot on the Möbius strip where individual and communal ideals become one, where the internal and the external converge.

No other widely known poem, I believe, has encouraged quite so much emotional blurring of the "I's" as "Invictus." But if we tried to think of another work that makes strong men cry; if we wanted to invite a second person to join the first; if we wished to find a "you" to meet the "I," where might we turn? "If –." Bringing Kipling's poem into relation with Henley's enables me to advance a few final ideas about those very different attitudes towards memorizing poetry in present-day Britain and the United States that I noted at the beginning of this study. Yet this is a quasi-allegorical deployment that requires that I downplay the similarities between the two works and treat a number of other issues somewhat cavalierly. So let me confess upfront: much of what I have said about Henley's poem could also be said about Kipling's. It is not hard to argue that the two pieces, emerging in more or less the same moment and climate, address a similar subject and share numerous poetic strategies; it is not difficult to make the case that they have done very similar cultural work in their active afterlives. Further, in my moves to have "Invictus" stand representative of certain American tendencies, and "If –" of certain British ones, I am not suggesting that "Invictus" is unknown or uncherished or unquoted in Great Britain, for this is clearly not the case. Nor would I be so foolish as to argue that "If –" is without status in the United States. It may not feature in Pinsky's anthology but it is there, for instance, in *The Best Loved Poems of the American People*, that hugely popular book from the

1930s that has been endlessly reprinted. I will not conduct an extended close analysis of this poem's exceptionally peculiar form—a form that is literally breathtaking for the reciter, indeed breathtakingly difficult, that single run-on, conditional sentence with its twenty "you's" and seemingly interminable list of hypothetical propositions—but I will make a few remarks about its production and reception history.

It seems likely that "If –" was composed some time before it was published; Kipling claims in his melancholy autobiography of 1937, *Something of Myself*, that he had drawn his inspiration for the verses from the character of his friend Dr Leander Starr Jameson, the Scots-born colonial adventurer and politician whose failed raid against the Boers in the Transvaal at the end of 1895 ultimately led to his imprisonment the following year by the British Government. But the poem first appeared in print only in 1910, inside a collection of short stories entitled *Rewards and Fairies* that formed a companion volume to *Puck of Pook's Hill* of 1906. In both books, a series of generically-diverse tales are told to two Sussex children, Dan and Una, by individuals magically plucked out of history by the elf Puck, or by Puck himself. Poems are liberally sprinkled throughout, generally appearing at the beginning and end of each story. "If –" comes at the close of "Brother Square-Toes," in which an old salt called Pharaoh Lee spins a yarn of his adventures in 1793 and 1794, when he fell in with French revolutionaries at sea, crossed the Atlantic, fetched up with Moravians and Seneca Indians in the hinterlands of Philadelphia, and then ultimately overheard, in a woodland clearing, George Washington making the case for a treaty of peace—what would become the Jay Treaty of 1795—between the United States and Great Britain.

Almost immediately upon first publication, "If –" was singled out for special attention;[8] it would take many pages to do full justice to the poem's wild and wonderful reception history thereafter. Suffice to say that it was reprinted here, there, and everywhere—often in places that did not meet with its author's approval. As Andrew Lycett describes in his biography of Kipling, sometimes the writer bestirred himself to call "Hold on!"—he won an injunction preventing the manufacturers of the tonic wine Sanatogen from advertising their product with the last four lines of the third stanza, and birth-control advocate Marie Stopes was told politely, but firmly, that she was not allowed to feminize the language at the end to make it an appropriately aspirational text for her clinics (503, 550). At other times, though, Kipling acceded to demands—happy, for example, to inscribe the poem into a miniature volume for the Lutyens-designed doll's house for the royal family in 1924 (510). Kaiser Wilhelm was said to keep a copy of the poem on his desk in exile in Holland; the king of Siam translated it into Thai; Antonio Gramsci into Italian (576).

Kipling himself commented astutely in his autobiography upon the scale and types of reception his poem had experienced:

> Among the verses in *Rewards* was one set called "If," which escaped from the book, and for a while ran about the world. They were drawn from Jameson's character, and contained councils of perfection most easy to give. Once started, the mechanisation of the age made them snowball in a way that startled me. Schools and places where they teach, took them for the suffering Young—which did me no good with the Young when I met them later. ("Why did you write that stuff? I've had to write it out twice as an impot.") They were printed as cards to hang up in offices and bedrooms; illuminated text-wise and anthologised to weariness. Twenty-seven of the Nations of the Earth translated them into their seven-and-twenty tongues, and printed them on every sort of fabric. (205)

It is Kipling's reference to schools that most attracts my attention, for it gives us some useful information about the poem's place in Britain's educational history. The "Young" upon whom "If –" was imposed was not a general, but a specific, young; it was composed of the kind of schoolchildren (or rather, schoolboys) who might plausibly refer to the lines they had to write out as punishments as "an impot." or imposition. Which is to say, the pedagogical take-up of "If –" in Britain mirrors that of Henley's poem, inasmuch as it has occurred primarily within grammar schools, private schools, and public schools—a point not lost on the film director Lindsay Anderson, who turned to Kipling's title when he needed a name for his 1968 attack on the latter institution. Insofar as "If –" has been a school text it has been within the education of, if not always the elite, then the aspirational, of those who were lifted—or who were in the process of lifting themselves—above the mass. As with "Invictus," Kipling's most famous verses never became part of the canon of recitational standards that reigned within the elementary school.

These days, when television programs or radio stations or newspapers in Britain conduct polls about "best-loved" poems, "If –" has a remarkable record of coming top. In 2009 it got the number one spot when the British radio station Classic FM asked listeners to vote for their "all-time favourite poem"; in 1995, *The Bookworm*, a BBC TV book program, declared it "a clear and unassailable winner" after it received twice as many votes as the next-placed work ("The Lady of Shalott"). Containing, in rank order, the one hundred most popular poems, an anthology entitled *The Nation's Favourite Poems* was published after the competition and has since been reprinted forty-five times. The book's title is of course a fudge; this volume does not tell us which verses that abstraction "the nation" likes best, only which poems are favored by the people who responded to calls for their opinion. Yet notwithstanding the problematical statistical and methodological features of this and other similar surveys, it is interesting to me that a poem that carries within its history no link to recitation in the elementary school should occupy such a commanding position. There is a correlation, I think, between this fact and the general attitude in Britain towards the phenomenon of the memorized poem that I noted at the beginning of the introduction.

Part I of this book demonstrated that the routes by which mandatory poetry recitation came to take its central place in the emergent mass public education of Britain and the United States were not the same; it also showed that once the exercise had been enshrined within their highly dissimilar school systems, it was subject to certain procedural variations. Yet these differences, interesting though they may be, appear minor in comparison to the pronounced contrast between the ways in which onetime cultures of widespread verse recitation are now remembered in these two countries. In short: the idea of the memorized poem typically evokes mixed feelings in Britain and overwhelmingly positive emotions in the United States. Despite the fact that rote learning was the default mode of installation in both countries, it is only in Britain that discussions of the topic regularly make reference to this fact and intimate that this invalidated the enterprise of schoolroom recitation as a whole.

The British response, I believe, is informed by a broader but incompletely understood distaste; the derogatory remarks about a certain pedagogical technique that are called up by mentions of poetry recitation stand in for a more general, underexplored, anxiety about "Our Victorian Education," as the title of Dinah Birch's book neatly puts it. Attitudes to the memorized poem in Britain, it seems to me, are still conditioned by the facts that its initial engine of dissemination was the Revised Code of 1861–62 and that the site of that dissemination was the elementary school; disavowal of the Victorians' massive feat of educational expansion is the norm, even though (or because?) many of its elements continue to exert structural and imaginative power over everyday British life. Today it is a part of the country's national mythology, its Whiggish history, that the 1944 Education Act created wholly new forms of class mobility (which is not true) and that it destroyed institutional formations such as the elementary school and its associated pedagogical forms that were wholly bad (which is debatable). One of this book's aims has been to correct and bring focus to such false and fuzzy beliefs.

In the reading I have staged in this afterword, "If –" stands forth as a work that offers the potentially deep emotional sustenance of a memorized poem but which does not invoke memories of Britain's discredited primal scene—its elementary scene—of pedagogical recitation. While some of those who vote for it in those national surveys may have learned it within one privileged form of educational institution or another, others will have discovered it for themselves at some later stage of life, and committed it to heart, or kept it close to hand, because those thirty-two lines said something to them that they felt better for hearing, that they wanted to make their own, to make part of themselves. For those who cherish "If –," we might ask, who is the poem's "you"? The obvious way to answer this question is to point to its final words and say, "the son"; the speaker of the poem obviously stands in the position of the father, an appropriately modest yet preternaturally wise individual (a better Polonius) who never utters the first-person pronoun but who (we might imagine) draws on his lifetime's stock of accumulated experience and observation to deliver invaluable words of guidance to his child. But is that how the poem works for its adherents? Don't they—we—you—don't you treasure it because it is giving you words to live your life by, words to help you "Hold on" when there is nothing in you except the words themselves? When an individual runs through "If –" silently or out loud, he may be dispensing advice to an external "you" but he is also hearing the lines address him, and so the "you" of the poem is also the "I" that is speaking it. But whichever way you look at it, "If –" is a poem predicated upon a hierarchical relationship, a relationship in which there is always a difference in power between the two positions; "If –" recognizes that some advise and some receive advice, that some teach while others are taught. Ironically enough, then, it is a deeply pedagogical poem.

In contrast, there is no congruency between the contents of "Invictus" and its existence as a beloved memorized poem in the United States; no scene of instruction within the text; no trace of the process by which the words of another become the most precious personal expressions of an individual—or rather, of this individual, of that individual, again, and again, and again. The top-down directive that drives "If –"—indeed, that drove the mandatory memorization of poetry in British elementary schools—the enforcement from above, or from outside, is instead wholly naturalized and internalized here, just as it was throughout verse recitation's American reign, where the decentralization of educational decision-making meant that the mass adoption of the practice was affirmed by the separate, yet identical, acts of innumerable individuals across the country and over the years. Britain and the United States both experienced the phenomenon of widespread juvenile recitation but in nationally distinct fashions. Today, thoughts and feelings about this cultural formation on two sides of the Atlantic are shaped by profoundly different attitudes to the educational past, to the operation of class, and to the ideology of individualism. It is therefore impossible for the peoples of these two nations to remember the memorized poem in exactly the same way.

Appendix 1

Table 1.
The Contents of *Poetic Gems* (1907) and the *Manual of the Elementary Course of Study for the Common Schools of Wisconsin* (1910)

Poetic Gems	*Wisconsin Course*	Works that appear in both
	Anon	
*Joseph Addison	†Alfred Austin	
William E. Aytoun (2)	William Blake	
Robert Browning	**Robert Browning** (2)	
M. Bruce or J. Logan		
William C. Bryant (2)	**William C. Bryant** (3)	
Robert Burns (2)	**Robert Burns**	
Lord Byron	**Lord Byron**	"There was a sound of revelry . . ." (from *Childe Harold*)
Thomas Campbell (2)	*Emily Dickinson*	
†Will Carleton		
William Cowper (3)		
Lady Dufferin		
G. R. Emerson	Ralph Waldo Emerson	
Oliver Goldsmith	Francis Miles Finch	
Thomas Gray		
Felicia Hemans *(2)*	**Felicia Hemans**	"The Voice of Spring"
	†*Ella Higginson*	
James Hogg	**James Hogg** (2)	"The Skylark"
Josiah Gilbert Holland		
Oliver Wendell Holmes	**Oliver Wendell Holmes** (2)	"The Chambered Nautilus"
Mary Howitt	Thomas Hood	
	William Howitt	

Table 1. (*Continued*)

Poetic Gems	Wisconsin Course	Works that appear in both
John Keats (2)	Sir William Jones	
	Charles Kingsley	
†Rudyard Kipling	†**Rudyard Kipling**	"Recessional"
	James Henry Leigh Hunt	
	Abraham Lincoln	
Henry W. Longfellow (4)	**Henry W. Longfellow** (3)	Selections from *Evangeline* and *Hiawatha*
James Russell Lowell	**James Russell Lowell**	
Lord Macaulay (2)	*Harriet McEwen Kimball*	
†Henry Newbolt		
Adelaide Ann Procter		
†Charles G. D. Roberts		
Sir Walter Scott (4)	**Sir Walter Scott**	
*William Shakespeare (6)	*William Shakespeare (6)	(1) "The Quality of Mercy" (*The Merchant of Venice*)
		(2) "A Lesson from the Bees" ("Therefore doth heaven divide . . .," *Henry V*)
Percy Bysshe Shelley (2)	**Percy Bysshe Shelley**	"To a Skylark"
Algernon C. Swinburne	Samuel Francis Smith	
Alfred, Lord Tennyson (5)	**Alfred, Lord Tennyson** (5)	"The Charge of the Light Brigade"
*James Thomson	*Celia Thaxter*	
John G. Whittier (2)	**John G. Whittier** (3)	
	Samuel Woodworth	
William Wordsworth (5)	**William Wordsworth** (3)	

Note: **Bold** indicates author with work in both volumes; underline indicates North American author; *italic* indicates female author; * indicates born over 200 years before 1910; † indicates still living in 1910.

Appendix 2

"Pieces Suitable for Recitation (English)" appeared in *The Teachers' Aid*, January 23, 1886. I have added the bracketted information in italics giving the line lengths required per standard at this date; the poet's name; and the length of each poem.

As we have been frequently asked for a list of pieces suitable for recitation, we append a number, from which a selection can be made:

Standard 1: (20 lines)
"The First Grief" (*Hemans: 28 lines*)
"The Better Land" (*Hemans: 28 lines*)
"The Blind Boy" (*Cibber: 20 lines*)
"The Soldier to his Mother" (*MacKellar: 40 lines*)

Standard 2: (40 lines)
"The Beggar Man" (*Aikin: 40 lines*)
"A Night With a Wolf" (*Bayard Taylor: 40 lines*)
"We are Seven" (*Wordsworth: 64 lines*)
"Casabianca" (*Hemans: 40 lines*)

Standard 3: (60 lines)
"After Blenheim" (*Southey: 66 lines*)
"Lucy Gray" (*Wordsworth: 64 lines*)
"The Wreck of the Hesperus" (*Longfellow: 88 lines*)
"Bruce and the Spider" (*Barton: 50 lines*)

Standard 4: (80 lines)
"Death of Marmion" (*Scott: variable*)
"Lord Ullin's Daughter" (*Campbell: 56 lines*)
Selections from "The Ancient Mariner" (*Coleridge: variable*)
"Llewelyn and his Dog" (*W. R. Spencer: 92 lines*)

Standard 5: (100 lines)
Gray's "Elegy" (*128 lines*)
"King Robert of Sicily" (*Longfellow; 216 lines*)
Selections from *The Deserted Village* (*Goldsmith: variable*)
Selections from *The Traveller* (*Goldsmith: variable*)

Standards 6 and 7: (150 lines from Shakespeare or Milton)
Death of Julius Caesar
The Fall of Wolsey (*Henry VIII*)
Arthur and Hubert (*King John*)
Ghost Scene (*Hamlet*)
Selections from *The Merchant of Venice*
Master of the Fallen Angels (*Paradise Lost*)
Selections from *Samson Agonistes*

An Overworked Elocutionist
By Carolyn Wells

ONCE there was a little boy, whose name was Robert Reece;
And every Friday afternoon he had to speak a piece.
So many poems thus he learned, that soon he had a store
Of recitations in his head, and still kept learning more.

And now this is what happened: He was called upon, one week,
And totally forgot the piece he was about to speak!
His brain he cudgeled. Not a word remained within his head!
And so he spoke at random, and this is what he said:

"My Beautiful, my Beautiful, who standest proudly by,
It was the schooner *Hesperus*,—the breaking waves
    dashed high!
Why is the Forum crowded? What means this stir
    in Rome?
Under a spreading chestnut tree there is no place like home!

When Freedom from her mountain height cried, Twinkle, little star,
Shoot if you must this old gray head, King Henry of Navarre!
Roll on, thou deep and dark blue castled crag of Drachenfels,
My name is Norval, on the Grampian Hills, ring out, wild bells!

If you 're waking, call me early, to be or not to be,
The curfew must not ring to-night! Oh, woodman,
    spare that tree!
Charge, Chester, charge! On, Stanley, on! And let
    who will be clever!
The boy stood on the burning deck, but I go on
    forever!"

His elocution was superb, his voice and gestures fine;
His schoolmates all applauded as he finished the last line.
"I see it does n't matter," Robert thought, "what words I say,
So long as I declaim with oratorical display!"

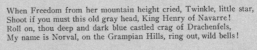

5. Carolyn Wells, "An Overworked Elocutionist," *St. Nicholas Magazine* (1908)

Key to citations:

"My beautiful, my beautiful! That standest meekly by"
Caroline Sheridan Norton, "The Arab's Farewell to His Steed"

"It was the schooner Hesperus"
Henry Wadsworth Longfellow, "The Wreck of the Hesperus"

"The breaking waves dashed high"
Felicia Hemans, "The Landing of the Pilgrim Fathers"

"Why is the Forum crowded? What means this stir in Rome?"
Epes Sargent, "The Fate of Virginia" (Thomas Babington Macaulay)[1]

"Under the spreading chestnut tree"
Henry Wadsworth Longfellow, "The Village Blacksmith"

"There's no place like home"
John Howard Payne, "Home, Sweet Home"

"When Freedom from her mountain height"
Joseph Rodman Drake, "The American Flag"

"Twinkle, twinkle, little star"
Jane Taylor, "The Star"

"Shoot, if you must, this old gray head"
John Greenleaf Whittier, "Barbara Frietchie"

"King Henry of Navarre"
Thomas Babington Macaulay, "Ivry"

"Roll on, thou deep and dark blue Ocean"
Lord Byron, *Childe Harold's Pilgrimage*

"Castled crag of Drachenfels"
Lord Byron, *Childe Harold's Pilgrimage*

"My name is Norval; on the Grampian Hills"
John Home, *Douglas*

"Ring out, wild bells"
Alfred, Lord Tennyson, *In Memoriam A. H. H.*

"You must wake and call me early"
Alfred, Lord Tennyson, "The May Queen"

"To be, or not to be"
William Shakespeare, *Hamlet*

"The curfew must not ring tonight"
> Rose Alnora Hartwick Thorpe, "Curfew Must Not Ring Tonight"

"Woodman, spare that tree"
> George Pope Morris, "Woodman, Spare That Tree!"

"Charge, Chester, charge! On, Stanley, on!"
> Sir Walter Scott, *Marmion*

"And let who will be clever"
> Charles Kingsley, "A Farewell"

"The boy stood on the burning deck"
> Felicia Hemans, "Casabianca"

"But I go on forever"
> Alfred, Lord Tennyson, "The Brook"

NOTES

Introduction

1. The recitation of poetry in English has a rich history throughout the British Empire and all countries where English was spoken and taught. Nevertheless, for the most part I purposely limit the geographical scope of this project to just two nations. Even after I have drawn these parameters, I am aware that my uses of the words "British" and "American" throughout the pages of this book are convenient rather than accurate. In the first instance, it is important to state here that even though many of the comments I make about educational history do pertain at times to all parts of the British Isles, others of them should more strictly be related to conditions within England and Wales only, and that there are significantly different stories to be told about recitation in Scotland; as will become apparent in Part I, Ireland also constitutes its own fascinating case here. In the second instance, I slight the larger geography of the Americas the way nearly everyone else does, and use "American" in its popular contemporary sense, i.e., as an adjectival form that refers to the United States of America only.

2. For a representative sampling of pieces written between 1997 and 2009, see, for instance, Beran; Collins; Ediger; Freedman; Hipple; Holt; and "Letters," *City Journal*.

3. See http://www.favoritepoem.org/.

4. For a rare exception, listen to Geoff Nunberg's National Public Radio piece from June 21, 2005 at http://www.npr.org/templates/story/story.php?storyId =4712745.

5. The issue of memorization is central to studies of both purely oral forms of transmission and forms that depend on the existence of written texts. George Steiner comments, "In other epochs, societies, or traditions, the commitment to memory, the availability to total recall and reiteration, of massive bodies of texts—epic, ritual, liturgical, historical, taxonomic—was, or still is, routine" (444).

6. Information on these programs is best gleaned from their respective websites, http://poetryoutloud.org/; http://www.nationalpoetryday.co.uk/; and http://www.bbc.co.uk/schools/teachers/offbyheart/.

7. For the most part, supportive material and citations for the claims made in the next several paragraphs therefore appear in the body of, and notes to, Part I.

8. I am especially fond of the claims made in this extract from the preface of Epes Sargent's *Standard Speaker*: "The pupil will be astonished to find how much his voice will gain in power by daily exercise. 'Reading aloud and recitation,' says Andrew Combe, 'are more useful and invigorating muscular exercises than is generally imagined; at least, when managed with due regard to the natural powers of the individual, so as to avoid effort and fatigue. Both require the varied activity of most of the muscles of the trunk to a degree of which few are conscious until

their attention is turned to it. In forming and undulating the voice, not only the chest, but also the diaphragm and abdominal muscles, are in constant action, and communicate to the stomach and bowels a healthy and agreeable stimulus'" (36).

9. Cf. J. Dover Wilson: "the teacher is . . . the host whose business it is to introduce these two natural friends to each other" (18); L. Logie: "A poet is in some ways very much a child" (68).

10. Which is not to say that it would be impossible to conduct such surveys, given that a proportion of these people are still alive at the time of writing.

11. Jonathan Rose makes the point that a "valid objection to using memoirs as a source for educational history is that they overrepresent the winners" (148).

12. Frequently working in concert, these fields have helped to produce increasingly nuanced and historicized understandings of the many complex relationships that can inhere between literature and life. The first two areas have only attained the status of recognized fields during this period; the third carries a longer history, but has in these years undergone radical reconfiguration, thanks in large part to the influence of the reception theory of Hans Robert Jauss.

13. Peter Widdowson's study *Hardy in History* is a good example; this book stands as an important achievement within a narrow field.

14. These new kinds of works take as their central organizing principle a feature that on occasion played a part in earlier studies, but only as a minor theme in larger designs. Here I think, for instance, of Paul Fussell's recognition in *The Great War and Modern Memory* of the pervasive presence of Bunyan's *Pilgrim's Progress* throughout the disparate forms of literature (notebook jottings, letters home, poems) produced in the trenches of northern France, and of Carolyn Steedman's awareness in *Strange Dislocations* of the ways in which Goethe's Mignon haunts all manner of nineteenth-century writings on the troubled child. For examples of afterlife studies published since 2000, see Clayton; Joyce; Kaplan; and Kucich and Sadoff.

15. I return to this question as a theoretical issue at the end of the introduction.

16. This historical happenstance also justifies, I hope, the project's interchangeable uses of the words "recitation" and "memorization." In other times and places memorizing and reciting, and the relation between these two activities, can of course function differently; in such contexts it would not be possible to substitute one term for the other quite as glibly as I do throughout these pages.

17. See, for instance, studies by Picker; Kreilkamp; and Stewart.

18. For instance, Celeste Langan's "Understanding Media in 1805: Audiovisual Hallucination in 'The Lay of the Last Minstrel'" bases itself upon Friedrich Kittler's influential argument that mass literacy taught a silent and private way of reading. See his "Gramophone, Film, Typewriter" and *Discourse Networks 1800/ 1900*.

19. Work on the phenomenon of mass recitation is to date not extensive, but see, on the American side of things, the studies by Sorby and Rubin already mentioned, and an essay by Leslier Fiedler entitled "The Children's Hour, or The Return of the Vanishing Longfellow: Some Reflections on the Future of Poetry." On the British side, Richard D. Altick's landmark *The English Common Reader: A Social History of the Mass Reading Public, 1800–1900* makes some brief but important nods to the practice; Jonathan Rose's book, cited earlier, also contains

valuable references in the course of its more general survey of working-class reading; there is also an interesting essay on verse choirs by Mark Morrisson.

20. I return to these volumes in the afterword.

21. Serving as an assistant commissioner on the 1858 Newcastle Commission, which first suggested that memorization of poetry be added to the program of studies for pupil teachers, the exceptionally industrious Arnold was employed from 1852 to 1886 as one of her Majesty's Inspector of Schools and thus knew perhaps as much as anyone in the country about the actual practice of classroom recitation; the frequent references to the exercise within his annual reports provide the most comprehensive consideration we have of both its ideal effects and quotidian shortcomings. Dedication to pedagogical causes shaped the life's work of this son of Thomas Arnold, the famous reforming headmaster of Rugby School; the contributions of Arnold fils to the improvement and extension of Great Britain's educational institutions constitute a huge and genuinely admirable achievement. Even as he performed these Herculean bureaucratic labors, however, Arnold was active in other areas. Up until the late 1850s, he was a regularly publishing poet; in the second half of the nineteenth century he was the most powerful English-speaking cultural critic of the day. Arnold's essays on English literature had a dominant effect upon the canon of works and the line of literary history that would be taught for many years within university courses. The fact of Arnold's active involvement with what evolved into opposed notions and forms of literary study is instructive; it helps us to see that in the high noon of the Victorian period at least, the distance between the halting recitation of a thirteen-year-old trainee elementary-school teacher and the most elevated of poetic critiques was not so great that it could not be encompassed on a daily basis in the vision of a single individual.

22. See, as casebook examples, T. S. Eliot's well-known comments about Tennyson and Browning in "The Metaphysical Poets" (247).

23. See Fussell, *The Great War and Modern Memory*.

24. The poem closes with an address to "My friend," asserting that had this individual witnessed the gas attack viscerally rendered in its first twenty-four lines, then "you would not tell with such high zest / To children ardent for some desperate glory, / The old Lie: Dulce et decorum est / Pro Patria Mori." The addressee has been identified as Jessie Pope, a writer of jingoistic poetry in simple verse forms, to whom "Dulce et Decorum Est" was originally to have been dedicated. Arguably, the poem begins an attack upon juvenile recitational culture even before the turn to the "friend." The "blood" that comes "gargling from the froth-corrupted lungs" of the man who failed to put on his gas mask in time is described as "Obscene as cancer, bitter as the cud / Of vile, incurable sores on innocent tongues." This simile always appeared puzzlingly unlocated to me until I realized that Owen may here be imagining the poems of versifiers like Pope as "sores" upon the "tongues" of reciting children.

25. Susan Warner's *The Wide, Wide World* (1850) and Mary Elizabeth Braddon's *Lady Audley's Secret* (1862) represent exemplary cases here.

26. For the locus classicus, see Cleanth Brooks, *The Well Wrought Urn*.

27. I explore the *Alice* books' relation to recitation in an essay entitled "Reciting Alice: What is the Use of a Book without Poems?"

28. Cf. Dames's discussion of the lengthy quotation in "On Not Close Reading."

29. The text of the poem reprinted here is taken from *English Poetry*, Harvard Classics edition, vol. 2.

Part One

1. For an indication of how frequently this work by Richard Monckton Milnes (later Lord Houghton) seems to have been assigned in Britain, see this comment from *The Teachers' Aid* periodical in 1887: "Having decided the time to be spent over the subject, the next point to consider is the piece. *Do not select hackneyed ones.* An Inspector told me he was heartily sick of 'A fair little girl sat under a tree,' for nine out of ten schools had selected that for Standard I" ("Recitation").

2. This part of my historical fiction grounds itself upon two facts. The volume of *Poetic Gems* in my possession carries a stamp that says, "With the Compliments of W. & R. Chambers, Ltd." and the inscription "G. Greenwood, Battyeford Nat. School" written in an adult, copperplate hand.

3. Appendix 1 sets out some of the points of convergence and divergence between this set of poems and the collection of works named in the Wisconsin course of study.

4. See note 1.

5. The "Casabianca" case study explores in greater detail the ways in which regular verse's most pronounced stylistic features possess intrinsic aide-mémoire characteristics.

6. David Vincent argues that the schooling systems developed for the poor were notable for the way in which they engineered "a deliberate narrowing of the range of pedagogic options." Such narrowness, he contends, must be seen in contradistinction to the broad range of styles and modes of literacy tuition that prevailed before the nineteenth century and in venues other than the public classroom. My study of just one strand in this variegated plait, then, should rightly acknowledge that any single activity, such as recitation, was intertwined with "an essential plurality of methods embodied in a multiplicity of formats" by teachers amateur and professional, inside and outside the home. It would have been the rare individual who reached literacy by following only one line; an analysis of the history and importance of a particular technique must needs be aware of the simultaneous and contributory roles of numerous other learning behaviors (189, 188). See also Kittler, *Discourse Networks*.

7. It is hard to discover if Watts's ideal program was matched by widespread practice in the years in which his book held sway, but there is evidence that some children were encouraged to follow his regimen. From the *Papers and Diaries of a York Family*, for instance, we learn the following about one Margaret Gray, whose education started in the first decade of the nineteenth century: "As soon as she was able to speak, she was taught to commit to memory Dr. Watts' *Divine Songs for Children*; at the age of four she could read the Bible and repeat the Church Catechism; and from that period for some years she regularly committed to memory the Gospel for the day" (cited in Cruse, *Englishman and His Books*,

75). Such memorization and performance of poetry before introduction to the printed page may well have been a common experience.

8. In his inspector's report of 1861, Matthew Arnold argues that poetry memorization should be added to the curriculum of pupil teachers because "their taste will be formed by it, as the learning of thousands of lines of Homer and Virgil has insensibly created a good literary taste in so many persons, who would never have got this by studying the rules of taste" (*Reports*, 88).

9. The three named works appear in all editions of both volumes. For discussion of *The Speaker*'s contents, see Michael, 185–86.

10. For general histories of the expansion of education in Great Britain in the nineteenth century and further information on Bell and Lancaster, see Goldstrom; Adamson; Wardle; Hurt; Silver and Silver; Digby and Searby; and Ball.

11. Lancaster and other hardline BFSS adherents had hoped that edifying biblical extracts would constitute their pupils' sole source of reading material, but by 1820 a bespoke classroom reader entitled *Scripture Lessons* had been published in book and sheet form; this contains no poems (Goldstrom, 40).

12. Most general histories of British education make some reference to the pupil-teacher system, but it is to date an inadequately studied phenomenon. Robinson's *Pupil Teachers and Their Professional Training in Pupil-Teacher Centres in England and Wales, 1870–1914* is currently the only extensive exploration of one aspect of the topic.

13. Although "[u]niversity courses in English had been taught at Edinburgh, and other universities in the eighteenth century" (Court, 796), and the "first professor of English in England" had been "appointed to his position at University College, London" in 1828 (Dharwadker), the topic was accepted as part of London University's bachelor of arts course only in the 1850s, a period that also saw the introduction of an English literature examination paper into the Indian Civil Service. It took considerably longer before Oxford and Cambridge fully embraced English language and literature as an admissible subject; for example, it was not possible to take a degree in English alone at the latter university until 1926 (Palmer, quoted in Burnett; Baldick).

14. For general and specific histories of the growth of public education in the United States, see McClennan; Bartlett; Klose; Gordon and Gordon; Finkelstein; Beauchamp; Pulliam; Button and Provenzo; Spring; Parkerson and Parkerson. Elson's *Guardians of Tradition: American Schoolbooks of the Nineteenth Century* is also an useful source of information.

15. "In fact, during the seventeenth and eighteenth centuries, the names of the subjects and the names of the textbooks were often one and the same" (Kliebard, *Changing Course*, 9).

16. Monitorial systems appeared in the United States in the years between 1800 and 1830, although only in its larger cities; population patterns explain why this trend did not travel far.

17. Such teaching methods were very similar in form to those that prevailed when children were taught at home in both Britain and America; before, during, and after the historical period under scrutiny, parents, or other literate members of the household, would test the child in this way to make sure she had "learnt her lesson." This of course is a scene that appears in any number of nineteenth-

century novels, both British and American, with *David Copperfield* providing perhaps the most celebrated example (see the "Casabianca" case study, p. 104).

18. As Wayne E. Fuller explains, the average schoolteacher thus "put a heavy burden on the memory" of her charges: "she drilled her students and taught them to memorize because that was the way she had been taught, and because, in her commonsense way, she believed that unless a student remembered what he had learned and could say it, he had not learned it.... This was so uncomplicated that the poorest teacher could understand it. So the country teacher reviewed her students and drilled them over and over, and when they failed to learn their lessons, which usually meant memorizing them, she was prone to insist they do so" (202).

19. The *Spelling Book* had become the best-selling American introductory text by 1790, and then occupied this position for almost fifty years.

20. This phenomenally successful series, which grew to a seven-book sequence by 1863, sold around 120 million copies between 1836 and 1920, with its strongest sales (60 million units) occurring between 1870 and 1890. See Spring, 141; Venezky, 251; Bartlett, 390–92. There is a considerable literature on the meaning and reach of the "McGuffeys" as a social phenomenon; see, for instance, Minnich; Mosier; Westerhoff.

21. For example, consider the representative McGuffey series. Nine of the 85 lessons in the *Second Reader* of 1836 are poems, compared to 19 of the 67 lessons in the *Third Reader* of 1838; 51 of the 130 in the *Fourth* of 1838; 120 of the 235 in the *Fifth* of 1844; and 89 of the 179 in the *Sixth* of 1857. As a glance at the 1901 ratios reveals, these proportions remained relatively constant over the years: 18 of 72 readings in the *Second* are poems; 25 of 68 in the *Third*; 27 of 60 in the *Fourth*; and 48 of 97 in the *Fifth*.

22. This development can be linked to the spread of new pedagogical theories, especially those emanating from German-Pestalozzian schools, which encouraged the division of children, according to age and attainment, into a grade system. Given the piecemeal development of American education in this period, however, the graded school did not arrive in many parts of the United States until the late 1800s, and in others, not until the twentieth century. For huge numbers of students over a relatively long period, the operative divisions within the classroom were instead provided by the schoolbook series. As many memoirs attest, "you were placed by the book you were reading" (Woody, 43).

23. As Parkerson and Parkerson comment, the graded McGuffey readers, for instance, "provided both students and teachers with questions that encouraged thinking and comprehension" (105–6).

24. See also Clifton Johnson, 112–13.

25. Citations from the Code up to 1899 are taken from the *Minutes and Reports of the Committee of Council on Education 1839-99*; thereafter, from the Board of Education's *Codes, Reports, Circulars* and *Handbooks of Suggestions*.

26. Three quarters of all pupil-teachers moved upwards to teaching-training colleges. The syllabi here underwent a degree of fluctuation in the four decades after 1862, but their poetic requirements generally followed the pattern laid down in the Revised Code's initial incarnation. For male students, this was 300

lines of poetry in their first year, followed by an additional 300 lines of poetry, or 200 of prose, in the second year; female students, however, had only to proffer 200 lines of poetry in their second year.

27. Royal Commission on Popular Education in Britain, 1861, *British Parliamentary Papers*, 1:108. The remark herein that the pupil-teachers' course contained "no literary subject whatever" is puzzling. Either this is a simple error, or it reveals that the kinds of things that the apprentice-instructors had been doing with poetry and prose during the first fourteen years of their training system were viewed under substantively different heads. The 1860 edition of *The Pupil-Teacher's Hand-Book to the Annual Government Examination* gives a good picture of the nature of these activities in its "Questions adapted to each year of apprenticeship." Trainees at the end of their second and third years are, for instance, required to perform parsing exercises with short poetic extracts to satisfy the examiners that the subject "English grammar" had been adequately learned. For the fourth and fifth years, however, the tasks are more diverse, and would seem to lie somewhere within the province of "literary studies": candidates are asked to "[g]ive examples of the figures of speech most commonly used in English poetry"; to "[e]xplain the metre" of some lines of verse, or "what is necessary to make a perfect rhyme"; to provide "a short sketch of the Elizabethan period of English Literature"; and, above all, to write paraphrases of selected passages of esteemed poetry and prose.

28. Although "recitation" was detached from "English" in 1890, its successful performance continued to be tied to a school's income-earning potential until 1900. The 1890 Code stated, "No school shall receive the higher of the two Principal Grants unless the Inspector reports that the scholars throughout the school are satisfactorily taught Recitation" (*Minutes and Reports of the Committee of Council on Education 1889–90*, 132). In 1895 it explained that although "the Recitation of poetry no longer forms part of English as a Class Subject. . . . [t]he usefulness of this exercise as a means of enlarging the range of the scholar's thoughts, cultivating the imagination and improving the taste, has been so generally recognised that it has been deemed expedient to retain Recitation as one of the conditions indispensable to the award of the higher principal grant" (*Minutes and Reports of the Committee of Council on Education 1894–95*, 175).

29. Cf. *A Manual of Method* prepared by Abraham Park in 1875, when recitation could be offered as a "Specific Subject" by the upper standards. Park suggests works by Scott, Longfellow, Goldsmith, Dryden, Thomson, Wordsworth, and Burns for the "First Stage," and for the "Second and Third," selections from "Milton, Shakespeare, Cowper, Wordsworth, Southey, Keats, Rogers, Kirke White, Hannah More, Felicia Dorothea Hemans, &c."

30. See appendix 2 for "a list of pieces suitable for recitation," as provided by the workaday British periodical *The Teachers' Aid* in 1886.

31. See, for instance, Janet A. Miller's comments in "Urban Education and the New City: Cincinnati's Elementary Schools, 1870 to 1914": "The board allowed little or no deviation from the adopted course, asserting that 'grading, course of study, and textbooks prescribed, shall be strictly adhered to, and no other studies or textbooks prescribed, shall be introduced, nor shall any pupil be required to

provide or be permitted to use other books than those herein specified.' Trustees on the board not only controlled the course and the books used, but specified amounts of material to be covered by a certain date in the school" (156).

32. This comment about "even for the girls" repeats the gender discrimination already noted in the discrepancy between syllabi in the men and women's teacher-training colleges in Britain.

33. See, for a generically diverse range of treatments of the affective experience of the Friday afternoon recitation, Stephen Crane's short story, "The Making of an Orator" and the Clinkscales' memoir, both of which are discussed in the "Casabianca" case study, and Hamlin Garland's autobiography: "it was in the Friday exercises that I earliest distinguished myself . . . it was the custom at the close of every week's work to bring a section of the pupils upon the platform as essayists or orators, and these exercises formed the most interesting and the most passionately dreaded feature of the entire school. No pupil who took part in it ever forgot his first appearance. It was at once a pillory and a burning. It called for self-possession, memory, grace of gesture, and a voice!" (197). Other "Friday afternoon" references abound. For instance, in 1905 Paul Lawrence Dunbar challenged the idea that "the love for poetry is declining" in the following manner: "Go into any school on a Friday afternoon, in our Middle West, and I think after you have gotten through listening to the 'Friday afternoon exercises,' you will agree with me" (quoted in Rubin, *Songs of Ourselves*, 50). For a citation embedded in a poem, see the first lines of Carolyn Wells's 1908 comic verse "The Overworked Elocutionist," which is provided in full in appendix 3.

34. Stoutemyer provides this course of study's recitation requirements in full in his essay, "Memory Work in the Grades" (32–33). In common with many others, the architect of this curriculum felt that there were appropriate links between boys and girls at different stages of the course and certain poetic forms, authors, and works.

35. See Kliebard, *Forging the American Curriculum*: the last decades of the nineteenth century "marked the beginning of a massive influx of new students, the secondary school population rising from a mere 6 to 7% of 14–17 year olds in 1890 to more than 50% by 1930" (12).

36. Chubb was a leading figure in the Ethical Culture movement: he emigrated from Britain to the United States in 1889, and was principal first of a Brooklyn high school and then the Ethical Society's New York high school department.

37. My formulation is indebted both to Elson's general view of the dominant trends in American textbook contents over the nineteenth and twentieth centuries, and the description of curriculum change given in Arthur N. Applebee's *Tradition and Reform in the Teaching of English*.

38. The recent resurgence of interest in poetry recitation is frequently accompanied by the revival of a species of the "memory training" argument. In discussions of recitation as a desirable practice for juveniles, this is usually linked to right-leaning pundits' longing for "training" (understood as rigorous disciplinary activities) in public education more generally, but in other contexts it works differently. For instance, contemporary journalists and commentators are often quick to link the potential value of restoring poetry memorization to research

that suggests that the mental powers of older adults are retained only if continually exercised (the "use or lose it" doctrine). See, for instance, Bader.

39. The marked emphasis upon "race" here and in the Hall and Huey citations connects to the increasingly imperialistic and nationalistic ends served in this period both by recitation in particular, and by dominant pedagogical approaches to English or American literature more generally. I investigate this theme below.

40. With various emphases, commentators had been insisting that literature for children "should treat of such subjects as are within the range of their experience [and] pleasing to their imaginations" since at least the 1830s (see Cobb, *Juvenile Reader, no. 1*, i). As we shall see, references to the necessary "relevance" of poetic selections to children's lives increased exponentially towards the end of recitation's heyday.

41. Daughters, it must be said, do not get much of a look in.

42. The American side of this topic is covered by Sorby and Rubin; the British story has to date been less explored, but offers a strong parallel narrative.

43. Betts comments that "for decades the topic most frequently advocated in the British teachers' press, usually for timetabling in the period around Empire Day, was 'the Flag,' and readily permeated into geography, history, drama, needlework and religious instruction" (277).

44. The event was officially adopted in Britain in 1916 and experienced its greatest popularity in the interwar years (Springhall; Ben Shepard).

45. His lectures were later published in two books, *On the Art of Writing* and *On the Art of Reading*. This quotation appears on page 45 of the earlier volume.

46. In Great Britain the practice of whole classes reciting in unison was clearly widespread. This is evident not only from numerous memoirs, but from the number of times that official government documents and associated writings inveigh against it. Here, for example, are a couple of passages from that 1906 *Companion to the N. U. T. Code*, already quoted in part at the beginning of this chapter: "The pieces selected should always be read to the teacher before being committed to memory, but should be learnt individually, and never by the class in unison. Such a device is the merest mechanical drill, and destroys any value recitation may have. . . . Simultaneous recitation and simultaneous reading aloud are as objectionable on musical as on educational grounds, because the use of such methods is sure to produce reading and recitation which is either frankly unintelligent or marked by a fictitious or imitated intelligence. Such reading or recitations is, therefore, both monotonous and mechanical, and will blunt a child's sensibility to musical influences" (33).

47. As noted in the discussion of Charles William Bond's experiences at the beginning of the chapter, the Board of Education's *Handbook of Suggestions* took a similar line. In one of its later revisions (1927), it further asserted that "the main story or leading idea of a poem should be within [a child's] grasp," but "it is even less necessary in poetry than in prose that every phrase or word should be understood" (82).

48. A 1967 report from the Department of Education and Science (*Children and their Primary Schools* [London: Her Majesty's Stationery Office]) commonly known as the Plowden Report), provides an interesting overview of the coun-

try's history of poetry teaching. It comments that at the time of writing, "[f]ew children learn poems because, once the nursery rhyme stage is past, few teachers speak poems to them," and then concludes that "[c]hildren may lose much when they are not set an example of getting poetry by heart" (216–17).

49. See, for a good example of this approach, May R. Pringle's 1925 article, "Comparison in Method," for the in-house journal of the American National Council of Teachers of English, which sets out the difference between the "old" and a "new" style of teaching poetry in conveniently schematic form. Pringle discusses an experiment conducted with two sets of fourteen-year-olds in Detroit: the "control group" experienced a series of lessons in which the memorization, and then recitation, of Longfellow's poem "The Builders" was the central focus, whereas the "experimental group" made a "thorough study" of the same work, first "discussing the life-problems solved . . . by this poem," and then using the findings to construct individual projects for investigation (307).

50. Michael observes that the idea that "religious and moral training can be reinforced through poetry is expressed" throughout the nineteenth century (222). See also Elson and Goldstrom.

51. To make the point in a somewhat gross fashion: while "Speaker" volumes frequently feature speeches from *Othello*, midcentury classroom readers do not.

52. Lorna Sage's memoir *Bad Blood* provides this witty summation of the prevailing inclinations of the classroom canon as it existed at the acme of Britain's culture of juvenile recitation: "I owned a book that could stand for all the rest . . . *Poetry for the Young*, a fat School Prize anthology published in 1881, and much reprinted, a treasury of heroical and sentimental verses culled mostly from the Romantics and their Victorian followers, particularly Mrs. Hemans and Longfellow. *Poetry for the Young* had murky engravings of castles by moonlight, shipwrecks and birds —the only form of wildlife ethereal enough to carry its message, for although it was packed with rhymes about nature's busy doings (storms, torrents, tides) it was absolutely silent on animal appetites, and contrived to confuse love with waving goodbye to one's native land. Its real subject was death: death in infancy, death in the far corners of the empire, death at sea on the way there —and just plain old death. Death was *Poetry for the Young*'s great prize. Dying, anyone was elevated to the condition of poetry: Blake's chimney sweep, Byron's gladiator 'Butcher'd to make a Roman holiday,' the boy on the burning deck, the minstrel boy, Somebody's Darling, Ozymandias, Poe's Lenore, Lord Ullin's daughter who rhymed with water, the Forsaken Merman, the Solitary Reaper, Simon Lee the old huntsman, Gray's mute inglorious Milton, and Lucy like a violet by a mossy stone even while she lived, which wasn't long" (177–78).

53. Michael argues that "[i]t is not until Palgrave that literary values are explicitly given priority over (but not in opposition to) moral values. Palgrave's attitude is best seen in *The Children's Treasury* [1875], to which nothing is admitted 'which does not reach a high rank in poetical merit'" (222).

Felicia Hemans, "Casabianca"

1. This is the version of Hemans's poem that most frequently appeared in nineteenth-century textbooks in England. At one important moment, this differs

from the version that first appeared in 1826 and is now generally reproduced in scholarly editions. In the original text, the word "And" at the beginning of line 19 is included in the quotation marks designating the child's speech, which is thus dramatically interrupted at this point. In every Victorian textbook version I have seen, the child's outburst ends after "gone" in the previous line; thus all the words of line 19 are given to the narrator, which results in the nonsensical utterance "And but the booming shots replied." As will become apparent in my developing argument, the textbooks' elimination of the original version's metrical irregularity at this juncture is not without significance.

2. "Casabianca" also has an important place in the United States and other countries that conducted elementary education in English in the nineteenth and twentieth centuries, but in this case study I focus primarily upon the question of its recitation in Great Britain.

3. Cf. Wolfson, xiv, and others.

4. The commonly used English phrase "by heart" reaches back at least to the fourteenth century (the OED cites *Troilus and Criseyde*'s "She told ek al [th]e prophesies by herte"), and find its exact reflection in the long-standing French phrase *par coeur*. Alas for any wider theory about the heart as the western European seat of memory, the Germans invoke agility (*auswendig*) or the cranial (*aus dem Kopfe*) rather than the cardiological; the Spanish and the Italians opt for the cerebral (*de memoria* and *a memoria*).

5. The best-known American parody is considerably more benign: "Who does not know, 'The boy stood on the burning deck, eating peanuts by the peck?'"(Rubin, "They Flash," 259). It also, interestingly enough, alters the rhyme scheme.

6. See Clarke, 44; and Hemans, ed. Kelly, 79, for references to parodies, and the appearance of "Casabianca's" first line in Judge Dread's risqué pop song "Big 6" in 1972.

7. Both the Wolfson and Kelly editions provide useful bibliographies of the growing number of late twentieth and early twenty-first century books and articles on Felicia Hemans. Curran, Ross and Clarke are generally recognized to have heralded the recovery. In addition to these, and works already cited above, the following writings have been of particular importance to me: Armstrong; Lootens, "Hemans and Home" and "Hemans and her American Heirs"; Sweet; Feldman; and Armstrong and Blain.

8. Once again, I am indebted to Guillory.

9. The work that challenges this perception that has been important to me falls primarily within new historicism; I am thinking especially of studies by Catherine Gallagher and Thomas W. Laqueur. See their coedited volume, *The Making of the Modern Body*, Laqueur's *Making Sex*, and Gallagher's work on the cultural construction of hunger in *Practicing New Historicism*.

10. See McGann, 70; and Wolfson, 428. This "wrong side" issue is less puzzling once we know that "Casabianca" gained its reputation as a preeminent work for juvenile recitation over the middle years of the nineteenth century. Thereafter, the avowedly nationalistic justifications for the memorization exercise that gained strength from the 1870s onwards did not have sufficient power to displace well-established standards like Hemans's poem from the pedagogical canon. See Part I.

11. For maternal presence, see McGann: "The upshot is a poem of violent death brooded over by a beautiful but ineffectual angel of maternal love" (71).

12. For comparison to Christ's abandonment, see Hemans's poem "Prisoners Evening Hymn" (Kelly, 379–80):

> by the anguish of thy Son
> When his last hour came darkly on—
> By his dread cry, the air which rent
> In terror of abandonment.

13. P. G. Wodehouse (born 1881 and educated at Dulwich College) unintentionally makes the point in *The Luck of the Bodkins* (first published 1935) that "Casabianca" transcended class boundaries. Part of the plot hinges on the fact that Ikey Llewellyn, a Hollywood movie magnate, has been erroneously informed that the Ambrose Tennyson he has hired as a screenwriter is the celebrated author of "The Boy Stood on the Burning Deck." When he discovers he has employed "the wrong Tennyson," Mr. Llewellyn is understandably annoyed, but Monty Bodkin points out that this hardly matters, because "Shakespeare wrote 'The Boy Stood on the Burning Deck'" (165). American starlet Lottie Blossom takes up the issue with her steward, the working-class polymath Albert Peasemarch:

> "Say, listen, buddy," said Miss Blossom, "didn't you tell me Tennyson wrote 'The Boy Stood on the Burning Deck'"?
> "Quite right, miss."
> "Mr. Bodkin says he didn't."
> Albert Peasemarch smiled a pitying smile.
> "Mr. Bodkin, miss, so I understand from the ties in his drawer, was educated at Eton. That's where he's handicapped in these matters. Eton, as you may have heard, is one of our English public schools, and the English public-school system," said Albert, warming to a subject to which he had given a good deal of thought, "isn't at all what an educational system should be. It lacks practicality and inspiration. If you ask me, they don't learn the perishers nothing. The whole essence of the English public school system with its hidebound insistence on . . ." (166).

14. This claim is based on my own examination of a wide range of school textbooks in the British Library rather than on thoroughgoing statistical analysis. Michael reveals the popularity of Hemans in its tabulation of the number of times works by a select number of authors appear in a broad swathe of schoolroom readers, but it does not correlate these occurrences with patterns of assignment or textbook sales figures. Goldstrom provides very useful information about the typical content and structure of the most frequently assigned working-class school readers in England and Ireland between 1808 and 1870, but there is no comparable historical study of the teaching of English literature in middle- and upper-echelon schools in the nineteenth century. To be sure, the Clarendon Commission (1864) and the Taunton Commission (1868), which inquired into the state of education in the public and grammar schools respectively, were both dismayed by the general neglect of the subject, but there is evidence that the practice of recitation found a much stronger foothold in well-to-do institutions in the last quarter of the nineteenth century (Gordon and Lawton; Shayer).

15. Consider, in particular, the findings of Thomas W. Laqueur, who in his exploration of one particular pioneering branch of mass education, the burgeoning Sunday school movement in the first half of the nineteenth century, blasts our assumptions about the Evangelical desire to rout juvenile wickedness, noting that "there was great reluctance . . . to exercise severe discipline and that stress was always more on rewards than on punishments" (*Religion and Respectability*, 225). But Laqueur is also careful to stress that practices in the Sunday Schools were necessarily related to their special status: "corporal punishment was condemned as inappropriate for the sabbath" (225), and in any case, class size tended to be far smaller than in weekday schools, allowing a less-regulated atmosphere. E. S. Lawrence's *Origins and Growth of Modern Education* also provides useful information about institutions that did not use the cane (Manchester Grammar School, for example, had done away with corporal punishment by 1800, and, according to De Quincey, the "self-discipline of the older boys and the efficacy of their examples were enough to keep order" [qtd. in Lawrence, 214]).

16. Foucault's detailed analysis of the regimen in Christian Brothers Schools, does, however, make reference to "punishments borrowed directly from the judicial model (fines, flogging, solitary confinement)," but is most interested in the punishment that is "isomorphic" with the required, but inadequately performed, task, "so much so that the corrective effect expected of it involves only incidentally expiation and repentance; it is obtained directly though the mechanics of a training. To punish is to exercise" (179).

17. Corporal punishment (generally in the form of "paddling") is currently still permitted in the public schools in twenty-two of the United States of America, and in private schools in all states.

18. See especially Ian Gibson, *The English Vice*.

19. Dr. Spencer began as a pupil-teacher, rising to Chief Inspector for the London County Council and H. M. Divisional Inspector of Schools.

20. I thank Karol Berger for his suggestion that I examine *Buddenbrooks*. For a consideration of the theme of forgetting in this novel, see Harald Weinrich's *Lethe: The Art and Critique of Forgetting*.

21. "Ich bin allein auf weiter Flur": asserting the solitariness of the depicted figure, Ludwig Uhland's "Schäfers Sonntagslied" offers another version of "Casabianca's" mirrored relationship between the poem's subject and its reciter.

22. "[U]nd schlug die Verse auf, die für heute auswendig zu lernen waren. . . . Er verstand kaum ihren Sinn, geschweige denn hätte er eine einzige davon aus dem Kopfe hersagen können," *Buddenbrooks*, 544. See note 4.

23. Cf. John George Clinkscales's account from a memoir of school life in South Carolina in the mid-1860s, a rare example of a noncelebratory personal narrative about classroom recitation:

> That was not the last severe trial I had during that year at school. After a week, Miss Pendle announced that on the following Friday afternoon all of us would have to "say a speech." Every one of us must "speak a piece." The next week there was a great stir among the boys and girls selecting and committing to memory their "pieces."
>
> My piece was thoroughly committed, but all week I was very nervous. The very thought of the approaching ordeal made me weak in the knees.

Friday afternoon came, and I was the first boy the teacher called on for a speech. I didn't know whether my legs would carry me out on the floor to the spot she designated or not, but, with a desperate effort, I made the attempt. I entered the ring marked on the floor by the teacher, made my bow, which was a short, sharp jerk of the head, and, instead of delivering my own speech, started off on one learned by one of the other boys. I had heard him repeat it so often out of school I knew it about as well as I knew my own.

That blunder ruined me. The boys laughed, the teacher frowned, I bit my lip, cleared my throat, stammered, finally started on my own, forgot it after repeating one line, burst into tears and ran to my seat.

That was a terrible ordeal. My humiliation and suffering were something fierce. The fact is, no man can ever know the suffering that failure caused me. And I am quite sure that grown people do not, can not, fully sympathize with children in their heartaches.

Every Friday afternoon during that school year I suffered. I wanted to declaim, was anxious to, but just couldn't. I would cry in spite of everything I could do. The other boys spoke their pieces and enjoyed it. I was humiliated beyond measure because I couldn't do what the others did. I suffered. Let no man say that it was an inexcusable weakness. Weakness it was, to be sure, but one I could not possibly help. I am now quite sure that my nerves were responsible for the whole trouble. And I had no way of getting rid of the nervous affection but by growing out of it. I was seventeen years old before I could face an audience with anything like reasonable composure. (249–50)

24. A full consideration of this issue would require a careful examination of the opinions of contemporary novelists about the status of poetry and their own genre.

25. For illustrations of the phenomenon of lifelong retention in the twentieth century, see Rubin's "They Flash."

26. See note 7 for the important recent critical writings on "Casabianca" alluded to here. McGann and Sweet are especially interested in the trope of fragmentation.

27. See, for instance, chapter 2 of Jameson's *The Political Unconscious*.

28. A particularly interesting nineteenth-century discussion of the ballad tradition appears in William Allingham's introduction to *The Ballad Book*.

29. See, however, Wolfson's attention to metrical stanza and line in her study of Hemans and Byron, and other considerations of questions of poetic form and genre in the Sweet and Melnyk collection of essays.

30. For a consideration of suspicions of rhyme in an earlier historical period, see chapter 3 of Ramie Targoff's *Common Prayer*.

31. As Fussell states in *Poetic Meter*, "most of the actual poems that ordinary people remember (and recite) are written in quatrains, as are most common mnemonic verses, nursery rhymes, rhymed saws and proverbs and admonitions, hymns and popular songs. The unsophisticated person's experience of poetry is almost equivalent to his experience of quatrains, which tends to suggest that there is something in four-line stanzaic organisation (or in the principle of alternate

rhyming) that projects a deep and permanent appeal to human nature. The presence of the quatrain at the heart of the sonnet bespeaks its appeal to the sophisticated as well" (141).

32. The account that follows is substantially indebted to Lavery.

33. "Many lives of Nelson have been written," states Southey on the frontispiece, "one is yet wanting, clear and concise enough to become a manual for the young sailor, which he may carry about with him, till he has treasured up the example in his memory and in his heart."

34. See, though, McGann: "Hemans' central myth represents a home where the father is (for various reasons) absent" (71).

Thomas Gray, "Elegy Written in a Country Churchyard"

1. As far as I can ascertain, this phrase was coined by William Makepeace Thayer as a title for his popular 1881 biography of James A. Garfield; it later came to be used for a biography of Lincoln as well.

2. Some critics maintain that the "lines" that "relate" the "artless tale" of "th' unhonour'd Dead" must be those inscribed upon the grave markers; for them, the "thee" thus refers to the man who chiselled them (this is the so-called "Stonecutter theory"). A more persuasive majority, however, argues that Gray here has his speaker address a hypothetical version of his own self, the same individual who has been telling the story of the churchyard's lowly inhabitants in the "lines" of his poem. This latter reading inevitably places the poem into a logically untenable temporal loop, but it nevertheless offers (to my mind at least) a more psychologically compelling account than the former reading. See the essays by Herbert W. Starr, Frank H. Ellis, and John H. Sutherland collected in *Twentieth Century Interpretations of Gray's Elegy*, ed. Starr.

3. It is interesting to note that Hoggart's investigation of a phenomenon that only becomes properly apparent in the twentieth century is peppered with numerous *nineteenth*-century descriptions of early emanations of the type: sentences from Anton Chekhov, Turgenev, George Eliot, William Hazlitt, Herbert Spencer, and Matthew Arnold appear in chapter 10, "Unbent Springs: A Note on the Uprooted and the Anxious."

4. In theory, by abolishing grammar school fees, the 1944 Education Act should have brought the "production" of scholarship children to a close (see note 21 for details of the act's provisions). Yet such an ending did not occur. It is revealing, I think, that in working-class communities the 11+ examination that determined which child was sent to which institution was still referred to as "the scholarship" for many years, despite the fact that there were no more scholarships to win; more broadly, the persistent relevance of the category of "the scholarship boy" to Britain's post-1944 social landscape has resulted in the continued use of the tag to describe the individual who rises from the working to the middle class via education. See, for instance, Eagleton, 52.

5. Talbot Baines Reed's hugely popular *Fifth Form at Saint Dominic's* (published in 1880, but in wide circulation up to the 1930s) cannot be said to provide documentary evidence of what actually happened in a minor public school of the period, but its basic illustration of classroom techniques probably bears some

relation to the true state of affairs. Chapter 17 presents an extended episode in which the headmaster enters the English master's room, and takes over the lesson:

> "What have the boys been reading?" inquired Dr. Senior of Mr. Rastle.
> "Grey's [*sic*] Elegy, sir. We have just got through it."
> "Oh! Grey's Elegy," said the Doctor; and then, as if forgetting where he was, he began repeating to himself
> "The curfew tolls the knell of parting day,
> The lowing herds wind slowly o'er the lea."
> "The first boy,—what can you tell me about the curfew?"
> The first boy was well up in the curfew, and rattled off a "full, true, and particular account" of that fine old English institution, much to everybody's satisfaction. (167)

As the scene progresses, and the Doctor continues to recite the verses of the Elegy (from memory, naturally), he regularly interrupts himself to ask the boys to supply historical glosses and semantic paraphrases. This deadeningly dull pedagogical mode notwithstanding, we are clearly meant to respect both the worthy old master and his noble absorption within the similarly worthy and noble old poem. The reward for such good behavior on our part is the vicarious thrill of the pupils' bad behavior, the opportunity to enjoy the boys' boisterously ingenious cheek, however implausible it may be. To what do the words "The rude Forefathers of the hamlet sleep" refer? "Four rude old men who used to sleep in church!" shouts an unfeeling ignoramus. The lesson continues:

> The Doctor passed the question on no further; but gravely explained the meaning of the line, and then proceeded with his repetition in rather a sadder voice. Now and again he stopped short and demanded an explanation of some obscure phrase, the answers to which were now correct, now hazy, now brilliantly original. On the whole it was not satisfactory; and when for a change the Doctor gave up reciting, and made the boys read, the effect was still worse. One boy, quite a master of elocution, spoilt the whole beauty of the lines
>
> —"Nor Grandeur hear with a disdainful smile
> The short and simple annals of the Poor . . ."
>
> by reading "animals" instead of "annals"; while another, of an equally zoological turn of mind, announced that—
>
> "On some fond beast the parting soul relies,—"
> instead of "breast." (168)

6. Cf. the use to which the Elegy is put in these exemplary questions provided in John Smith's *Key to Reading*:

> Q. What is the meaning of *parting day*?
> A. That the daylight is departing.
> Q. Then you do not conceive that the word *parting* is an adjective to the word *day*, as *meeting-day, wedding-day*, &c.?

A. No: I think it is the participle of a verb implying the parting away, or departure, of the daylight.

Q. Why do you say *daylight*? The word is *day*.

7. Cf. Guillory, 87: "It may no longer be possible now to distinguish this effect from the effect of the poem's recitation and memorization in the classroom."

8. It is true that the government's Hadow Report of 1928, *Books in Public Elementary Schools*, lamented that "many of the old favourites of English tradition, such as Byron's stanzas on The Eve of Waterloo, Cowper's John Gilpin, Campbell's Hohenlinden and Gray's Elegy, have been neglected of late," but of these works, the last named seems to have clung on with the greatest persistence (2, para. 29).

9. Presenting combinations of shorter works was directly endorsed within the Code itself, but inspectors periodically complained about the dangers of abstracting sections from longer pieces. The practice later received the following censure in a discussion of pupil-teacher training in the *Day School Code* of 1900: "The recitation is often unsatisfactory, owing . . . partly to the mischievous practice of placing in the hands of the learner the passage which has to be committed to memory as an isolated fragment, without context or introduction" (137).

10. Hambrook School's archive can be found online at http://www.frenchay museumarchives.co.uk/Archives/Schools/Hambrook_SchLog_1870-10.rtf.

11. A similar pattern is apparent in the United States: Gray's Elegy tends to crop up in the pages of the last textbook of the elementary reader series, whatever the highest number of that series happens to be. Thus in 1858, the poem features in Osgood's *Progressive Fifth Reader*, "designed for . . . the highest classes in public and private schools"; in 1879 it is to be found in McGuffey's *Sixth Eclectic Reader*, the final volume in that sequence.

12. Gosse substantiates the story's veracity as follows: "This beautiful anecdote of Wolfe rests on the authority of Professor Robison, the mathematician, who was a recruit in the engineers during the attack upon Quebec, and happened to be present in the boat when the General recited Gray's poem" (145). Other versions of the story, as I mentioned in the introduction, attribute slightly different utterances to Wolfe.

13. Lingering there in Gray's churchyard, listening to the poem that captured for him the spirit of his own village in Dorset ("Stinsford *is* Stoke Poges," he said on another occasion), Hardy experienced the sensation of déjà vu: "With startling suddenness, while duly commending her performance, he seemed to have lived through the experience before" (326). Hardy explains what had happened: "in love of recitation, attitude, and poise, tone of voice, and readiness of memory, the fair lady had been the duplicate of the handsome dairymaid who had insisted on his listening to her rehearsal of the long and tedious gospels, when he taught in the Sunday school as a youth of fifteen" (327). So much for the "thin veneer . . . of rank and education over the natural woman" (327), he remarked (to himself, we hope).

14. For this reason, much of the poem's reputation as a declamatory standard rests upon its being performed in parts, rather than as a whole. Contemporary

poet and critic John Hollander suggests just such a strategical abbreviation in *Committed to Memory: 100 Best Poems to Memorize*, an exhortation in favor of learning verse by heart: "An otherwise wonderful set-piece like Gray's 'Elegy Written in a Country Churchyard,' at 128 lines, would be too long (although celebrated individual quatrains from it might be taken as short pieces in themselves—one thinks, for example, of 'The boast of heraldry, the pomp of pow'r, / And all that beauty, all that wealth e'er gave, / Awaits alike th' inevitable hour, / The paths of glory lead but to the grave' (preface)." In past years too, many fans of the Elegy followed this course, which is in essence the guiding principle of the "memory gem" practice mentioned in Part I. The stanza that Hollander recommends was, as it happens, Thomas Edison's favorite piece of poetry: the man who first captured the reciting voices of the great poets of the nineteenth century on his wax cylinders was apparently very fond of repeating these lines within the earshot of his many associates. Such instances of partial declamation might encourage us to wonder more generally exactly how many words have to be repeated, and in what demeanor and circumstances, for a performance to count as a recitation proper rather than an act of quotation. Certainly in the history of the Elegy as a text spoken without book, the line between these two associated, though substantially different, arts is frequently blurred.

15. Harland's autobiography is to be found online at http://bosonbooks.com/boson/freebies/harland/harland.pdf.

16. Robert would not, however, have learned Gray's Elegy with this teacher. Earlier in the book the man who was later to become a noted educational reformer and the founder of Summerhill school writes as follows: "Long poems are an abomination to children; to ask them to commit to memory a long poem like Gray's *Elegy* is unkind." He also "hate[s] the poems that crowd the average school-book.... 'Little Jim,' 'We are Seven,' 'Lucy Gray,' 'The Wreck of the Hesperus,' 'The Boy stood on the Burning Deck,' and all the rest of them" (36–37).

17. Interestingly enough, the Selfridge's piece preempts the main thrust of Empson's analysis, opening, as it does, with pretty much the same point about the same lines: "Gray's lines about undiscovered merit are so beautifully written that they throw a cloud over our judgment.... When we repeat them we come to believe that it is almost as it should be that the mute inglorious Milton should rest unknown in the country churchyard, that the flower should be born to blush unseen and waste its fragrance on the desert air" (12).

18. To provide just a few illustrations: the Elegy was apparently "translated by revolutionists and monarchists alike in the French Revolution"; it is reported that "in the mid nineteenth-century agricultural labourers [in Britain] were seen to have the lines 'Some village-Hampden, that with dauntless breast / The little tyrant of his fields withstood' embroidered on their union banners" (Goodridge, 15). A quite literally cryptic instance of the poem's place in the history of class warfare occurred in the late 1920s, when members of the British Communist Party were attempting to stir up insurrection among students in India. As revealed in a report in *The Times* on a trial in Meerut in 1929, communications between agent Philip Spratt and Comintern, the Third International, were conducted

through the medium of invisible ink and a certain 128-line work of literature: the cipher employed figures such as 26/7 to represent the seventh word of the 26th line, and so forth (15).

19. It was also apparently one of these chance encounters that brought William Whewell, born in 1794 and the son of a carpenter, to the attention of the Master of Lancaster Grammar School. Offered a free place, Whewell in time made it to Cambridge, where he ultimately became the Master of Trinity in 1842. See Sanderson, xiii.

20. While I recognize that it is both intellectually and politically objectionable to reify an absolute line of division between the middle and the working classes in any time or place, I take my lead here from nineteenth- and twentieth-century Britain's apparently general belief in the actual and important existence of such a divide.

21. Under the stewardship of Rab Butler, the president of the Board of Education in the wartime coalition government, this famous piece of legislation was designed to inaugurate a decisively new era in educational and social policy—the complement to, and extension of, Forster's pioneering Elementary Education Act of 1870. Raising the school-leaving age to fifteen, Butler's Act aimed to replace the elementary school with a sequence of primary, and then some form of secondary, education for all. Through the sorting device of a nationwide test in the last years of primary school (a reconfiguration of the by-this-point long-standing "11 +" into an obligatory qualifying exam), it would be determined whether a child should attend a grammar (the appropriate destination for those capable of thinking in "abstract" terms); a secondary modern (for the "concrete" thinkers); or a junior technical school (intended for the "mechanically" minded, but in actuality something of an abstract concept itself, given that only a very few were established). All three forms of secondary school were to be free. I acknowledge that these moves had some very important consequences, not least for the institutions under my specific scrutiny here, the grammar schools: (1) the fact that access was now limited to those who could pass the 11+ meant that the affluent could no longer buy places for their less bright children; (2) the abolition of fees removed a charged marker of difference between pupils with disparate social backgrounds. Nevertheless, my point is this: as far as academically inclined working-class children were concerned, the new provisions simply altered some of the characteristics of the structures the government had instituted since 1902. Certainly a good number of the sociological studies, both quantitative and qualitative, early and late, which sought to investigate the class constitution of the grammar school in its post–World War II incarnation, concluded that little seemed to have changed. As an examination of institutions in Middlesborough and South West Hertfordshire reported in 1953, "the likelihood that a working class boy will reach a grammar school is not notably greater today, despite all the changes, than it was before 1945" (Floud et al., 33); another scrutiny estimated that both before and after Butler's Act, the children of the professional classes were three times more likely to receive a grammar school education than the children of the working classes. The demographics of attendance did not undergo profound alteration; although proportions varied from school to school, district to district, working-

class children still constituted a minority presence at grammar schools, and class differences continued to be evident to all in the classroom.

22. The practice of racial segregation in public schooling was eventually declared illegal in the landmark *Brown v. Board of Education* case of 1954; whether widespread racial equity has been achieved with American schools is a different issue. The inequitable treatment of children from different socioeconomic backgrounds has been investigated in numerous studies: here is one example, on the question of access to secondary education that dominates this chapter, from 1922. In his *Selective Character of American Secondary Education*, George Counts found clear disparities in the rates at which different urban classes ascended to high school: the lower your social class, the less likely were you to continue in education after elementary school. For important later studies, with various different political slants, see Coleman; Conant; Harrington.

23. Some measures were taken to establish Higher Elementary Schools and forms of vocational secondary education for the less academic child. See Sanderson, 24–25.

24. "By the time we were half way up the school," writes Kathleen Betterton, "the likely scholarship winners had been marked down, and from then on they received a quite special degree of attention" (quoted in Burnett, 211). Cf. Beer, 77: "So for three years we were trained not for life but for the Scholarship."

25. See note 4.

26. Hughes, however, was not able to take up the scholarship; after the outbreak of war, she was sent to live with her grandmother in Essex. Hughes's autobiography, to be found only online at http://www.mdx.ac.uk/www/study/arcjknow.htm, contains the fullest description I have found of the scholarship application process, at least as it functioned in this particular time and place. For instance, she recalls the large amount of work that her teacher set for scholarship hopefuls, even over the summer holidays: "the teacher always insisted on lots of repetition. She was terrified that her best pupils might 'slip back.' Each week, we had to send the batch of questions back to the school by post." Once Hughes had won the Junior County Scholarship, she still had to take a further entrance exam at the school which her parents had selected, and to pass a London County Council medical exam at County Hall. "'Do try hard to please the doctor,' said my teacher."

27. There are no prizes for identifying the text from which Burnett takes the title of this work, or that of its companion volume, *Useful Toil*.

28. For a directly opposing view, however, see Rowse, *A Cornish Childhood*, 180.

29. Three of Britain's prime ministers in the second half of the twentieth century were scholarship winners in its first half; of these, one (Harold Wilson) was the leader of the Labour party, and two (Edward Heath and Margaret Thatcher, nee Roberts), of the Conservative party. Few, however, would allot thoroughgoing working-class status to their original homes: the Wilsons are generally thought of as upper working class, and the Heath and Roberts families as lower middle class.

30. Given that the assigned narratives usually described the exploits of the ruling classes only, then middle-class children would have also experienced this disjunction, but, I think, to a significantly lesser degree: is it fair to assume that

because the prototypical middle-class son imagines that the course of his life will take an upwards trajectory, he is more likely to identify easily, not to mention pleasurably, with elite heroes? And—just to make a very quick point that connects to a large topic that has been hugely discussed in recent years—if white, Christian, working-class boys felt a sense of disjunction, how would it be for those who were not white, not Christian, and not male? Yet—as I hope will be apparent in due course in my discussion of the possible ways of responding to "He fell among thieves"—it is of course overly simplistic to assume that any given reader necessarily judges a poem according to its representation (or nonrepresentation) of individuals from groups with which he or she might identify.

31. "He fell among thieves," published in Newbolt's *Admirals All* of 1897, was based, with some poetic license, on the extraordinary life story of explorer George Whitaker, recipient of the 1869 Royal Geographic Society's medal, who was beheaded in Kashmir in 1870.

32. The lines are from Gray's pindaric ode "The Bard."

33. One of the important topics in such a study would be the recited poem's role within speech training. In the United States, poetry recitation in public institutions often occurred in a session of the school day that was called, or otherwise linked to, "Elocution." In Great Britain, however, thanks to the nation's obsessive concern with the relationship between speech and class, the issue has historically been much more fraught. Some early advocates of juvenile recitation spoke explicitly and enthusiastically about the exercise's ability to bestow refined pronunciation on lower-class pupils; teacher-training colleges in the Victorian era also stressed the importance of "correct speech" and required their students to apply themselves to both the "improvement" of their own accents, and eventually, those of their charges. In the twentieth century official educational documents, at least, appear to become more wary of approaching this complex topic; how such statements relate to the behavior of teachers in actual classrooms is of course another question. Generally speaking, in twentieth-century Britain only those institutions and individuals who deliberately blazoned their ability to facilitate class rise presented verse recitation as a valuable means towards this end; in practice, this meant that private schools, and perhaps even more importantly, after-school elocution lessons (often paid for by socially aspirant parents who could not afford full-time private education for their children), were the sites of the most enthusiastic promotion of poetry memorization. Indeed, these venues kept juvenile recitation alive in Britain long after the state's educational system had discarded it.

34. Burrell, for instance, is adamant that pronunciation training is an essential element of the recitation exercise. Stating that he "know[s] how difficult this is" (note that he dedicates his volume to "all teachers in elementary schools . . . with sympathy and with respect"), Burrell nevertheless maintains that "[d]istinct and correct pronunciation must be insisted on in the lower classes . . . it ought not to be impossible now that children of a very tender age are at school for several hours in the day" (6).

35. *The Big H* is the title of a play, screened on BBC 2 on Boxing Day, 1984, in which Harrison explored this issue further. Performed by twenty-four pupils from Yorkshire and three actors from the National Theatre, the work, in the form of a

school nativity play, takes the story of the Massacre of the Innocents as its theme. Herod first appears in triplicate in the figures of three schoolteachers who impose "H" sounds on their unaspirating charges.

36. For a different perspective, see *A Cornish Childhood*. Rowse speaks both prose and verse in his grammar school's production of *Twelfth Night*, but the fact that he plays Malvolio, an example par excellence of a man with ideas above his station, perhaps tells its own story.

37. Appending "Shuttleworth" to his name after his marriage in 1842, Kay had trained as a doctor, and, after he moved to Manchester, was instrumental in setting up that city's statistical society. Author of *The Moral and Physical Condition of the Working Class Employed in the Cotton Manufacture in Manchester* (1832), he worked as a poor law commissioner from 1835, and then, four years later, became the secretary of the newly constituted Committee of Council on Education. Ill health caused him to resign in 1849 (the same year in which he was given a baronetcy), but he later recovered and resumed various educational, medical, and governmental labors.

38. For one thing, as discussed earlier, a good number of the works assigned for memorization, particularly in the earlier years of the exercise, could hardly be described as the "treasures" of English literature. Even after later versions of the Revised Code sought to ensure that the elementary canon featured the "classics" of English literature, such revisions affected primarily the selections for the upper standards, leaving classes lower down the school with poetic material that few would wish to claim for the national canon. See Part I.

39. As illustrated in an earlier portion of this chapter, the Elegy's relation to this tradition was not created by the poem's author, but its reciter, General Wolfe.

40. See Hoggart, *Tyranny of Relativism*, 85; Williams, *The Country and the City*, 72–75. Williams mentions the Elegy in a discussion of changes in structures of feeling. Writing first about the anger he experienced when his father had to memorize Herrick's "A Thanksgiving" (1647), with its whining about a "little house" and its "humble roof," for an evening class, Williams is less harsh about Gray's poem than Empson, finding it less blameworthy than Herrick's work or Shenstone's "The School Mistress' (1748), but he is still critical: "It cannot really be had both ways: the luck of the 'cool sequester'd vale' and the acknowledged repression of 'Chill Penury.'" For a considerably more extreme example of working-class rage with bourgeois literature, see *Solo Trumpet*, the fascinating autobiography of T. A. Jackson (b. 1879), who left his board school at thirteen to work as a "printer's devil" and ultimately became a leading figure in the British Communist Party. Jackson, seduced in his early independent reading by "the sheer magic" of Macaulay's words and the "sensuous form" of poetry and drama, came to distrust the way in which literature could distract the working classes from "the world of every-day actuality," and was particularly suspicious of the quietistic bent of the literary canons pressed upon the proletariat by schools and such devices as Sir John Lubbock's list of the "One Hundred Best Books." "[I]t was a salutary precaution," he writes, "to take care that the books within reach of the newly-taught generation were such as would lead their minds to 'higher things' and away from such 'barbarities' and 'sordidness' as strikes, struggles, agitations, barricade battles and Socialism" (32).

41. Rowse constitutes a complicated case, in that he takes up various different political stances over the course of his career, but I am here fixing him in the position he expresses in his autobiography of 1942. Here is a representative sampling of his opinions in that text: "There may be people silly enough to think it snobbery to prefer civilized standards and a world of culture and tradition to the great heart of the people. I have no use for the great heart of the people. Or rather that is about all of theirs I have any use for: their emotional life, its depth and sincerity and vitality and directness, is their greatest strength, not their intelligence, their wit, their brilliance, subtlety, variety of conversation or understanding. After all, the magnificent achievements of English literature, of the English political tradition, of English history science, are the work of the upper and middle classes, not of the people. I have never much liked Piers Plowman as against Chaucer, the nasty Puritans as against Sir Thomas More and Marlowe and Shakespeare, the fantastic Levellers as against the Cavaliers or Hobbes or Milton, Ebenezer Elliott and the Corn Law Rhymers compared with Tennyson and Arnold, the Socialist tradition in English thought compared with the magnificent line of Bacon-Hobbes-Locke-Hume-Bentham-Mill. In history I have always been bored by Popular Movements and Revolts: such fools, led by such nit-wits—Jack Cade, Robert Aske, John Ket, and the rest of them. What a dreary quagmire is the history of the Labour Movement—Robert Owen, the Chartists, Bronterre O'Brien, Feargus O'Connor, the Trade Unions, the Junta, Ramsay Macdonald—compared with the splendour and magnificent achievement of Elizabeth and the Cecils, the resplendent services to the nation of the Churchills, the Pitts, Nelson or Drake. I find an entry in a note-book, jotted down casually, saying that I could never hear the name of Nelson without tears coming into my eyes—such genius, such courage, so transcendent a fate. When William Pitt died, worn out with his labours, at the age of forty-six, the spirit of European resistance to Napoleon, at the mention of that name in the Commons, taking their leave of him, a hush passed over the whole House. Is it any wonder that I prefer such men to the drab Levellers and all the Chartists and Socialist Leaguers that ever were?" (105).

42. As Rose notes in his chapter on "The Whole Contention concerning the Workers' Educational Association," far-left figures such as Rowland Kenney, the Independent Labour Party journalist, accused Mansbridge of seducing workers into "the development of the Servile State": "he nets in hundreds of striving workers [writes Kenney] and inoculates them with the virus of university 'culture,' and preaches a non-party, unsectarian doctrine which makes a fool of him every time he is lumped up against one of the brutal facts of our modern social system" (Rose, 266–67). This is unfair to Mansbridge, as a reading of *The Trodden Road* reveals; nevertheless, as we shall see in due course when we turn to consider this work's appendix, he appears to be in favor of an "unpolitical" reading of Gray's Elegy.

43. The cultural object of the poem, when disseminated by the school as an entity to be memorized, thus manages to perform as a wry encapsulation of the three forms of cultural capital, as defined in the sociological theory of Pierre Bourdieu. For Bourdieu, cultural capital exists not only in "the objectified state" as "cultural goods" (such as poems), but also in "the institutionalized state" (a prime example of which are "educational qualifications"), and in "the embodied state," "in the form of long-lasting dispositions of the mind and body" (241).

44. Cf. Dewey, *Democracy and Education*: that which is learned only for purposes of moving up the educational ladder quickly degenerates "into a miser's accumulation, and a man prides himself on what he has, and not on the meaning he finds in the affairs of life" (288).

45. See, for instance, the example of Dorothy Burnham (b. 1915), quoted in Rose, 24:

"Although I spoke—in my back street urchin accents—of La Belly Dame Sans Murky, yet in Keats's chill little poem I seemed to sense some essence of the eternal ritual of romantic love. And Tennyson's 'Morte D'Arthur' bowled me over. I read it again and again until I fairly lived in a world of 'armies that clash by night' and stately weeping Queens. So the poets helped me escape the demands of communal living which now, at thirteen, were beginning to be intolerable to me." Cf. this finding in Rubin's "They Flash upon That Inward Eye": "I grew up during the depression, the child of immigrant parents. At that time, I perceived everything about my life as ugly—the drab tenement furniture, the worn clothes we wore. Lowell's 'The Vision of Sir Launfal' made me think 'I, too, could experience beauty . . .'" (266).

46. The issue of the difficulty of finding a (warm enough) space in which to think and work quietly frequently comes up in the autobiographies of ex-working-class children, most often in relation to homework. See Marsden and Jackson, 117: "Some children went into the front room, others retired to a bedroom, but many did their homework in the living-room/kitchen at the very centre of family activity. This immediately produced difficulties. Should the wireless be on or off? Could the younger children play noisily? Could the father stretch his legs and tell the day's tales? . . . 'Sometimes he used to go up into the bedroom and do it. Aye, he'd have the eiderdown wrapped all round him to keep him warm, wouldn't he?'" Cf. Harrison on "the foldaway card table, the green baize . . . the frosted attic skylight" (*Selected Poems*, 89), and Quiller-Couch's *On the Art of Reading*: "I have been talking to-day about children; and find that most of the while I have been thinking, if but subconsciously, of poor children. Now, at the end, you may ask 'Why, lecturing here at Cambridge, is he preoccupied with poor children who leave school at fourteen and under, and thereafter read no poetry?'. . . Oh, yes! I know all about these children and the hopeless, wicked waste; these with a common living-room to read in, a father tired after his day's work, and (for parental encouragement) just the two words 'Get out!'" (57).

47. Following up this statement with an attack upon false memories of the idyllic classroom, Leacock chooses to work the same ground as Talbot Baines Reed:

Let's see. This is the class in English poetry and the children are to study Gray's "Elegy." Now sit tight in your seat and listen for the questions. First of all the teacher will read out a verse—

"The boast of heraldry, the pomp of power,
And all that beauty, all that wealth e'er gave,
Awaits alike the inevitable hour.
The paths of glory lead but to the grave."

Now come the questions:—

"Boast—first boy, how do you distinguish boast from boost?"

"Would it be an improvement, second boy, to say, 'The boost of heraldry'? Distinguish this again, third boy, from 'the booze of heraldry.'"

"Heraldry—fourth boy, what is Greek for this?"

"Now in the next line, fifth boy, 'all that beauty.' All WHAT beauty? and in the line below, sixth boy, 'lead but to'; explain the difference between but to and but in."

"Now for the whole class—take your exercise books and write a life of the poet Gray, being particular to remember that his grandfather was born in Fareham, Hants, or perhaps in Epsom, Salts." (184)

48. I cite Bennett's work not only because it has much to say about poems and memorization, but because it is preeminently a play in the Hoggartian line: its title could, in fact, easily have been "The Scholarship Boys." With regard to these issues, it is interesting to note that the relationship of *The History Boys* to the period in which it is primarily set is decidedly unhistorical. This is a fact that Bennett freely admits in the play text's introduction, an essay that is sprinkled with quotations from many of the same works that I cite in this chapter, from *The Uses of Literacy* to *Education and the Working Class*. Some of the play's historical unlikeliness resides in the following areas: an (implausibly large) group of sixth formers is working (ultimately—and again implausibly—all successfully) to win scholarships in history to take them to Cambridge and Oxford from their 1980s Sheffield grammar school (itself a somewhat anomalous institution in a time and place dominated by comprehensives). Bennett himself (born in Leeds in 1932, and another important example of one of those figurative, if not literal, "scholarship boys" produced after the 1944 Education Act) had won such awards, successively, to both universities. After he was "well on with the play," the playwright learned from a friend who had sat the exams with him all those years ago that he "was hopelessly out of date . . . that scholarship examinations such as we'd both experienced were a thing of the past, and even that scholarships themselves were not what they were" (xix). All this is quite correct—but just as the "scholarship boy" tag persisted even after scholarships to grammar school disappeared, so the general disappearance of scholarships to university did not erase the demarcation line that hovered—and hovers—around the student with a working-class background. The historical "errors" of Bennett's play, then, provide further evidence that Hoggart's concept easily floats free of actual "scholarship" systems, such is its continuing relevance to Britain's class-stratified society.

49. See the "Burial of Sir John Moore" case study, and an extended discussion of the historical contexts of this Hardy poem in my "Girls Underground, Boys Overseas."

50. "[I]t is as if a hand has come out and taken yours," says Hector of the moment when literature yields up this personal connection. A stage direction follows: "*He puts out his hand, and it seems for a moment as if Posner will take it, or even that Hector may put it on Posner's knee. But the moment passes*" (56). Much of Bennett's play is taken up with the fact that Hector is simultaneously an

example of one kind of ideal instructor and a man who is fond of surreptitious caresses of the genitals of some of his students (Posner, it is worth pointing out, is not one of the boys who receives such attentions). The connections between pedagogy and erotics are out of my remit here.

51. The open letter is provided as an appendix in Mansbridge's autobiography, *The Trodden Road*. Founded in 1919, the Seafarers' Education Service established the College of the Sea in 1938 "to provide the means whereby those who made their living at sea could continue their education and benefit from similar educational facilities as was enjoyed by their counterparts ashore." In 1976, the college became an operation of the still-extant Marine Society, a charity founded by Jonas Hanway in 1756. I have been unable to discover how widely, and for how long, the quoted tract was distributed.

52. Cf. Georges Poulet: "I am someone who happens to have as objects of his own thought, thoughts which are part of a book I am reading, and which are therefore the cogitations of another. They are the thoughts of another, and yet it is I who am their subject . . . I am thinking the thoughts of another" (54–55). In what ways does memorization of the thoughts of another heighten or otherwise alter this experience? The next case study and the afterword both return, in different ways, to this question.

53. Clare's prose writings include the line "Grays Letters great favourites of mine . . . they are the best letters I have seen," but some responses the poet is said to have made during his later years in the lunatic asylum are especially poignant. Visitors to the asylum in 1860 attempted to stir Clare to converse about poetry:

> Ingenious Della Cruscan rhymes and florid poetry made no impression on Clare . . . But Mr. Godfrey, the secretary, knew more truly how to touch his heart.
> "John," he said, "do you know those lines—
> 'The curfew tolls the knell of parting day'?"
> "Oh, yes, " said Clare, "I know them, they are Gray's."
> And then, with that appropriativeness which we have already remarked,
> "I know Gray, I know him well."

I cite this from J. W and Anne Tibble's biography *John Clare: A Life* (397)— Anne Tibble, by the way, being the same individual that we encountered as a Yorkshire scholarship girl earlier in this chapter. I am not convinced, however, by their argument that Clare's last comment necessarily displays "appropriativeness."

54. For an extended consideration of Hardy's relationship to Gray's work, see Dennis Taylor and my "Where Heaves the Turf."

55. Harrison, "Them & [uz]: II," *Selected Poems*.

56. Johnson's relation to the scholarship boy construct bears examination too; consider, for example, his spurning of the shoes that were left outside his college door at Oxford to replace his worn-out pair. See Boswell, 1:52.

Charles Wolfe, "The Burial of Sir John Moore after Corunna"

1. The text of the poem reprinted here is taken from Quiller-Couch's *Oxford Book of English Verse*.

2. I thank Ceri Sullivan for bringing this to my attention.

3. Only now do I learn that it was the third volume in a Molesworth tetralogy, running from *Down With Skool!* and *Back In The Jug Agane* to *A Whizz With Atomes!*

4. Fans of "the curse of st custard's" are likely to wish that Harry Potter's elongated epic had inherited even a modicum of Molesworth's ironic perspective on institutional life. Certainly J. K. Rowling filches enough else from Willans— "Hogwarts," for instance, is both the title of an imaginary Latin play by "Marcus Plautus Molesworthus," and the name of the headmaster of St Custard's "grate rival, porridge court."

5. Geoffrey Summerfield's five volumes (*Voices: An Anthology of Poems and Pictures*) were published from 1969 onwards.

6. For Oliver Elton, in his *Survey of English Literature: 1780–1830*, the rhythm is even more resonant and admirable: "The plummet-like fall of the heavy syllables of grief, as into an unknown depth, and the elastic rise, proper to an anapaestic measure, of the lighter ones, as though for heroic consolation, is worthy of the masters" (47).

7. For a concise summary of this prevailing "myth of the war," see Samuel Hynes, *A War Imagined: The First World War and English Culture*. As Hynes and others have argued, Paul Fussell's *The Great War and Modern Memory* has played an important role in perpetuating and disseminating the "myth." Nevertheless, Fussell's book continues to be indispensable reading matter for anyone interested in this topic.

8. See, in particular, Winter; Bourke; and Laqueur's "Memory and Naming in the Great War." I rely especially upon Laqueur's essay in the pages ahead.

9. As Laqueur notes, Reinhart Koselleck claims that the earliest monument to dead soldiers who were not also aristocrats or commanders was erected in Lucerne to the memory of the Swiss Guards killed in the attack on the Tuileries in 1792 (159).

10. Over the years, there have been debates as to whether "the precise correspondence of the details with the prose narrative" increased or diminished the poem's merit, but few have agreed with Edmund Gosse, who rejected the "fable" of the poem's connection to Southey's report, asserting that "the newspaper account is quite bald and commonplace, and the poet has supplied all the salient points out of his own imagination" (*The English Poets*, 4:322).

11. Missing the point, it seems, about Wolfe's insistence that coffins are unnecessary, *Blackwood's* explained its decision to copy the verses out of the newspapers by asserting they were "too beautiful not to deserve preservation in a safer depository" (277).

12. It also appears in Cobb's *Fifth Reading Book* in 1844, John Frost's *American Speaker* in 1845, and Epes Sargent's *Standard Speaker* in 1852.

13. Cf. a later, more acerbic, comment on the "one-hit wonder" issue. In "Slender Reputations," Alexander Brent-Smith writes the following: "When we study history, the ridiculous ease with which some men have picked up immortal crowns, compared with the hopeless struggles of others who have had to be content with picking up crusts from the gutter, is immediately apparent. A cursory glance at any anthology of verse will be sufficient for our purpose. We shall find

the great names duly represented by poems which we more or less know and respect, but real familiarity, even though it be accompanied by contempt, will be reserved for Mr. Charles Wolfe. I do not suppose that one person in a thousand knows who he was. Well, he was an Irish clergyman who wrote 'The Burial of Sir John Moore,' a poem with little value either as history or as poetry. Written more than a hundred years ago, it has been printed in every English Reader from that day until this and will probably continue to be printed until the decline and fall of the British Empire" (499).

14. For Andrew H. Miller, the emphasis on belated recognition that appears in the quoted passage constitutes Newman's primary theme, preeminently in relation to the necessity of apprehending as if for the first time the sufferings of Christ (158–60).

15. See http://www.webbdeiss.org/webb/lorenwarcorres.html.

16. Union General Horace Porter noted on the night before the first day of the Battle of Coldharbour on June 3, 1864, that he had seen men in his forces writing their names and addresses on slips of paper, and fixing them to the back of their jackets, so that their families might be informed of their deaths if necessary (Bowman and Commager, 163).

17. See also Drew Gilpin Faust's *This Republic of Suffering*, which appeared after I wrote this case study.

18. The dispatch from Fredericksburg in 1863, quoted earlier, provides a vivid picture of this work in practice.

19. Many Confederate graves had of course long been marked and maintained without national support. The first monument erected in honor of unknown Confederate soldiers was dedicated on October 21, 1869, in Union City, Tennessee.

20. There is a considerable literature on the 54th Massachusetts Regiment, the Saint Gaudens monument, and the occasion of its dedication. See, in particular, Tatum; Nudelman.

21. The battlefield, and burial site, has now been washed into the ocean.

Afterword

1. The autobiography of another Robben Island inmate, Eddie Daniels, does however mention Mandela reciting "Invictus" in his cell (244).

2. McCain's misquotation of line 15 of "Invictus" is a common error.

3. I thank Kerry Hanlon for this information.

4. Gore Vidal relates in his *Vanity Fair* article on Timothy McVeigh that he emailed one offending journalist's network to insist that Henley be called "extremities challenged" instead (352).

5. It is however interesting that the incarcerated individual is in this instance female. My use of the phrase "all comers" should really have been qualified: on the whole, "Invictus" appeals to men more than to women. One might argue that the poem deftly sidelines worries that words are womanly and only deeds manly, or indeed fears that verses are for girls; by removing the speaker's potential for action and presenting measured language as an achievement of superior strength, the poem forecloses concerns about the effeminacy of poetic utterance.

6. I thank Tricia Lootens for helping me see this point more clearly.

7. These familiar lines come from Browning's "How They Brought the Good News from Ghent to Aix"; Wordsworth's "Daffodils"; and Tennyson's "The Brook" respectively.

8. For instance, in a quite literal detachment of the poem, Kipling's American publisher Doubleday published a little book containing "If –" and nothing but "If –" just months after *Rewards and Fairies*. This is not to say that the original context counts for nothing; a lingering and understandable inference in some quarters that the lines were a gloss on George Washington's character did "If –" no harm in its American afterlife.

Appendix 3

1. "Virginia," one of the *Lays of Ancient Rome*, appeared in Sargent's *Standard Speaker* as "The Fate of Virginia" and with the following note: "In order to render the commencement less abrupt, six lines of introduction have been added to this extract from the fine ballad by Macaulay."

WORKS CITED

British Official Reports

British Parliamentary Papers. Ed. P. Ford and G. Ford. Shannon: Irish University Press, 1968–70.

    Minutes and Reports of the Committee of Council on Education, 1839–99

    Report of the Commissioners appointed to inquire into the State of Popular Education in England (Newcastle Commission), 1861. Vol. 21.

    Report of the Commissioners appointed to inquire into the revenues and management of certain schools and the studies pursued and instruction given therein (Clarendon Commission), 1863. Vols. 20, 21.

    Report of the Schools Inquiry Commission (Taunton Commission), (1869), 1873, vol. 28.

    Board of Education:

        Code of Regulations for Day Schools, 1902

        Handbook of Suggestions for Teachers, 1905, 1923, 1927, 1937

        The Teaching of English in England (The Newbolt Report), 1921

        Report of the Consultative Committee on the Primary School (Hadow Report), 1926, 1931

        Report of the Consultative Committee on Books in Public Elementary Schools, 1928

    Department of Education and Science:

        Report of the Central Advisory Council for Education (England): Children and Their Primary Schools (Plowden Report), 1967

Other

Ablow, Rachel, ed. *The Feeling of Reading: Affective Experience and Victorian Literature*. Ann Arbor: University of Michigan Press, 2010.

Adamson, John William. *English Education, 1789–1902*. Cambridge: Cambridge University Press, 1930.

Agassi, Andre. *Open: An Autobiography*. New York: Knopf, 2009.

Allingham, William, ed. *The Ballad Book: A Selection of the Choicest British Ballads*. London: Macmillan, 1864.

Altick, Richard D. *The English Common Reader: A Social History of the Mass Reading Public, 1800–1900*. Chicago: University of Chicago Press, 1957.

Anderson, Amanda. "Victorian Studies and the Two Modernities." *Victorian Studies* 47.2 (2005): 195–203.

Applebee, Arthur N. *Tradition and Reform in the Teaching of English: A History*. Urbana, Ill.: National Council of Teachers of English, 1974.

Archer, Sir William. "Some Living Poets." Lecture reported in *The Academy*, February 5, 1898, 151–52.

Armstrong, Isobel. *Victorian Poetry: Poetry, Poetics and Politics*. London: Routledge, 1993.

Armstrong, Isobel, and Virginia Blain, eds. *Women's Poetry: Late Romantic to Late Victorian*. London: Macmillan, 1999.

Arnold, Matthew. *Reports on Elementary Schools, 1852–1882*. London: Macmillan, 1889.

———. *Schools and Universities on the Continent*. Ed. R. H. Super. Ann Arbor: University of Michigan Press, 1964.

Austen, Jane. *Mansfield Park*. London: Penguin, 2003 [1814].

Bader, Jenny Lyn. "Britney? That's All She Rote." *New York Times*, September 16, 2007.

Baldick, Chris. *The Social Mission of English Criticism 1848–1932*. London: Oxford University Press, 1983.

Ball, Nancy. *Educating the People: A Documentary History of Elementary Schooling in England,1840–1870*. London: Maurice Temple Smith, 1983.

Barrett, Michèle. "Subalterns at War: Colonial Forces and the Politics of the Imperial War Graves Commission." *Interventions* 9.3 (2007): 451–74.

Bartlett, Richard A. *The New Country: A Social History of the American Frontier, 1776–1890*. New York: Oxford University Press, 1974.

Beauchamp, George A. *The Curriculum of the Elementary School*. Boston: Allyn and Bacon, 1964.

Beer, Patricia. *Mrs. Beer's House*. London: Macmillan, 1968.

Bennett, Alan. *The History Boys*. London: Faber and Faber, 2004.

Beran, Michael Knox. "In Defense of Memorization." *City Journal* 14.3 (2004): 71–80.

Betts, R. S. "A Campaign for Patriotism in the Elementary School Curriculum: Lord Meath, 1892–1916." *History of Education Society Bulletin* 46 (1990): 40–44.

Birch, Dinah. *Our Victorian Education*. Oxford: Blackwell, 2008.

Bishop, Elizabeth. *North and South*. Boston: Houghton Mifflin, 1946.

Boswell, James. *The Life of Samuel Johnson, LL.D.: Including a Journal of a Tour to the Hebrides*. Ed. John Wilson Croker. 10 vols. London: John Murray, 1831.

Bourdieu, Pierre. "The Forms of Capital." Trans. R. Nice. In *The Handbook of Theory and Research for the Sociology of Education*. Ed. John G. Richardson. Westwood, Conn: Greenwood Press, 1986.

Bourke, Joanna. *Dismembering the Male: Mens' Bodies, Britain, and the Great War*. Chicago: University of Chicago Press, 1996.

Bowman, John Stewart, and Henry Steele Commager. *The Civil War Day by Day*. New York: Dorset Press, 1989.

Brent-Smith, Alexander. "Slender Reputations." *Musical Times* 65.976 (1924): 499–500.

Brodhead, Richard H. "Sparing the Rod: Discipline and Fiction in Antebellum America." *Representations* 21 (1988): 67–96.

Brontë, Charlotte. *Jane Eyre*. Harmondsworth: Penguin, 1996 [1847].

Brooks, Cleanth. *The Well Wrought Urn: Studies in the Structure of Poetry*. New York: Harcourt, Brace, 1947.

Brown, Alice. *Robert Louis Stevenson: A Study*. Boston: Copeland and Day, 1895.

"The Burial of Sir John Moore after Corunna." *Blackwood's Edinburgh Magazine* 1.3 (1817): 277–78.

Burrell, Arthur. *Recitation: A Handbook for Teachers in Public Elementary Schools*. London: Griffin, Farran, Okeden and Welsh, 1891.

Burnett, John. *Destiny Obscure: Autobiographies of Childhood, Education and Family from the 1820s to the 1920s*. London: Allen Lane, 1982.

———. *Useful Toil: Autobiographies of Working People from the 1820s to the 1920s*. Harmondsworth: Penguin, 1984.

Burnett, John, David Vincent, and David Mayall, eds. *The Autobiography of the Working Class: An Annotated, Critical Bibliography*. 3 vols. New York: New York University Press, 1984–89.

Butler, Samuel. *The Way of All Flesh*. Harmondsworth: Penguin, 1986 [1903].

Butler and Noble. *A Practical Grammar of the English Language*. Louisville: John P. Morton, 1846.

Button, H. Warren, and Eugene F. Provenzo, Jr. *History of Education and Culture in America*. Englewood Cliffs, N.J.: Prentice-Hall, 1983.

Campkin, J. *The Struggles of a Village Lad*. London: Tweedie, 1858.

Carley, Kenneth. *Minnesota in the Civil War: An Illustrated History*. St. Paul: Minnesota Historical Society Press, 2000.

Cary, C. P. *Manual of the Elementary Course of Study for the Common Schools of Wisconsin*. 14th ed. Madison: Democrat Printing Company, 1910.

Chapman, Edward Mortimer. "The Religious Significance of Recent English Verse." *Biblioteca Sacra* 1898 (55): 259–80.

Chesterton, G. K. "On Mr. Thomas Gray." In *All I Survey: A Book of Essays*. London: Methuen, 1933.

Chubb, Percival. *The Teaching of English in the Elementary and the Secondary School*. New York: Macmillan, 1902.

Chorley, Henry F. *Memorials of Mrs. Hemans with Illustrations of Her Literary Character from Her Private Correspondence*. 2nd ed. 2 vols. London: Saunders and Otley, 1837.

Clarke, Norma. *Ambitious Heights: Writing, Friendship, Love—The Jewsbury Sisters, Felicia Hemans and Jane Welsh Carlyle*. London: Routledge, 1990.

Clayton, Jay. *Charles Dickens in Cyberspace: The Afterlife of the Nineteenth Century in Postmodern Culture*. New York: Oxford University Press, 2003.

Clinkscales, John George. *On the Old Plantation: Reminiscences of His Childhood*. Spartanburg: Band and White, 1916.

Cobb, Lyman. *New North American Reader, or Fifth Reading Book*. New York: Caleb Bartlett, 1844.

———. *Cobb's Juvenile Reader, no. 2*. Baltimore: Joseph Jewett, 1831.

———. *Cobb's Juvenile Reader, no. 1*. Dansville, N.Y.: Stevens & Flagler, 1835.

Cohen, Edward H. "Two Anticipations of Henley's 'Invictus.'" *Huntington Library Quarterly* 37 (1974): 191–96.

Collins, Billy. "The Companionship of a Poem." *Chronicle of Higher Education* 48.13 (2001): 5.

Cook, F. C. *Poetry for Schools*. London: Longman, Green, Brown and Longmans, 1849.

Coleman, James S., et al. *Equality of Educational Opportunity*. Washington, D.C.: U.S. Government Printing Office, 1966.

Colombo, Gary, Robert Cullen, and Bonnie Lisle, eds. *Rereading America: Cul-*

tural Contexts for Critical Thinking and Writing. New York: St. Martin's Press, 1989.

Conant, James B. *Slums and Suburbs: A Commentary of Schools in Metropolitan Areas. New York:* McGraw-Hill, 1961.

Cornish, Frances Warre. *The Public School Speaker: A Selection of Pieces for Recitation*. London: John Murray, 1900.

A Correspondent. "Gray on a White Night: Reconstructing the Elegy through the Small Hours." *London Times*, April 22 1960.

Court, Franklin E. "The Social and Historical Significance of the First English Professorship in England." *PMLA* 103.5 (1988): 796–807.

Crane, Stephen. *The Complete Short Stories and Sketches of Stephen Crane*. Ed. Thomas A. Gullason. Garden City, N.Y: Doubleday, 1963.

Cruse, Amy. *The Englishman and His Books in the Early XIXth Century*. London: G. G. Harrap, 1930.

———. *Victorians and their Books*. London: Allen and Unwin, 1935.

Cumming, Kate. *A Journal of Hospital Life in the Confederate Army of Tennessee from the Battle of Shiloh to the End of the War*. Louisville, Ky.: W. Evelyn, 1866.

Cunningham, J. V. "The Problem of Form." In *The Collected Essays of J. V. Cunningham*. Athens: Ohio University Press, 1976.

Curran, Stuart. "Romantic Poetry: The 'I' Altered." In *Romanticism and Feminism*. Ed. Anne K. Mellor. Bloomington: Indiana University Press, 1988.

Dames, Nicholas. "On Not Close Reading: The Prolonged Excerpt as Victorian Critical Protocol." In Ablow, ed.

Daniels, Eddie. *There and Back: Robben Island, 1964–79*. Bellville, South Africa: Mayibuye Books, 1998.

Dead Poets Society. Directed by Peter Weir. Touchstone Pictures, 1989.

De la Gravière, Captain E. Jurien. *Sketches of the Last Naval War*. Trans. The Hon. Captain Plunkett. London: Longman, 1848.

Dewey, John. *Democracy and Education*. New York: Free Press, 1916.

Dharwadker, Vinay. "Orientalism and the Study of Indian Literatures." In *Orientalism and the Postcolonial Perspectives: Perspectives on South Asia*. Ed. Carol A. Breckenridge and Peter van der Veer. Philadelphia: University of Pennsylvania Press, 1993.

Dickens, Charles. *David Copperfield*. Harmondsworth: Penguin, 1966 [1849–50].

Digby, Anne, and Peter Searby, *Children, School and Society in Nineteenth-Century England*. London: Macmillan, 1981.

Downing, Lucia B. "Teaching in the Keeler 'Deestrict' School." *Vermont Quarterly*, n.s., 19.4 (1951): 233–40.

Dukes, Carol Muske. "A Lost Eloquence." *New York Times*, December 29, 2002.

"The Duty of Discovering Merit." *The Times*, July 15, 1927.

Eagleton, Terry. *The Gatekeeper: A Memoir*. London: Penguin, 2003.

Ediger, Marlow. "Memorization of Poetry: Good or Bad?" *Journal of Instructional Psychology* 24 (1997): 273–77.

Eliot, T. S. "The Metaphysical Poets." In *Selected Essays*. London: Harcourt, Brace, 1932.

Elliott, Sir George. *Memoirs*. London: Privately printed, 1863.

Ellis, Alec. "Books in Victorian Elementary Schools." London: Library Association pamphlet, 1971.

———. *Educating Our Masters: Influences on the Growth of Literacy in Victorian Working-Class Children*. London: Gower, 1985.

Elson, Ruth Miller Elson. *Guardians of Tradition: American Schoolbooks of the Nineteenth Century*. Lincoln: University of Nebraska Press, 1964.

Elton, Oliver. *Survey of English Literature: 1780–1830*. London: Macmillan, 1912.

Empson, William. *Some Versions of Pastoral*. New York: New Directions, 1950 [1935].

English Poetry. Harvard Classics ed. Vol. 2. New York: P. F. Collier & Son, 1910.

The English Poets: Selections with Critical Introductions by Various Writers. London: Macmillan, 1880.

Enright, D. J. *Injury Time: A Memoir*. London: Pimlico Press, 2003.

Exercises at the Dedication of the Monument to Colonel Robert Gould Shaw and the Fifty-fourth Regiment of Massachusetts Infantry, May 31, 1897. Boston: Municipal Printing Office, 1897.

Faust, Drew Gilpin. *This Republic of Suffering: Death and the American Civil War*. New York: Alfred A. Knopf, 2008.

Feldman, Paula. "The Poet and the Profits: Felicia Hemans and the Literary Marketplace." *Keats-Shelley Journal* 46 (1997): 148–76.

Felleman, Hazel, comp. *Best Loved Poems of the American People*. Garden City, N.Y.: Doubleday, 1936.

Fiedler, Leslie. "The Children's Hour, or The Return of the Vanishing Longfellow: Some Reflections on the Future of Poetry." In *Liberations: New Essays on the Humanities in Revolution*. Ed. Ihab Hassan. Middletown, Conn.: Wesleyan University Press, 1971.

Finkelstein, Barbara J. "The Moral Dimensions of Pedagogy: Teaching Behavior in Popular Primary Schools in Nineteenth-Century America." *American Studies* 25.2 (1974): 82.

Floud, Jean E., A. H. Halsey, and F. M. Martin. *Social Class and Educational Opportunity* London: Heinemann, 1958.

Foucault, Michel. *Discipline and Punish: The Birth of the Prison*. Trans. Alan Sheridan. New York: Vintage, 1979.

Freedman, Morris. "Poetry, Dead or Alive?" *Education Week* 19.33 (2000): 43–46.

Freud, Sigmund. "A Child is Being Beaten." In *The Standard Edition of the Complete Psychological Works of Sigmund Freud*, vol. 17, *An Infantile Neurosis and Other Works*. Ed. James Strachey. London: Hogarth Press and the Institute of Psycho-Analysis, 1953–74.

Frost, John. *The American Speaker*. Philadelphia: Thomas, Cowperthwaite, 1845.

Fuller, Wayne E. *The Old Country School: The Story of Rural Education in the Middle West*. Chicago: University of Chicago Press, 1982.

Fussell, Paul. *The Great War and Modern Memory*. New York: Oxford University Press, 1975.

———. *Poetic Meter and Poetic Form*. New York: Random House, 1965.

Gallagher, Catherine, and Stephen Greenblatt. *Practicing New Historicism*. Chicago: University of Chicago Press, 2000.

Gallagher, Catherine, and Thomas W. Laqueur, eds. *The Making of the Modern Body: Sexuality and Society in the Nineteenth Century.* Berkeley: University of California Press, 1987.

Garland, Hamlin. *A Son of the Middle Border.* New York: Macmillan, 1917.

Gibson, Ian. *The English Vice: Beating, Sex and Shame in Victorian England and After.* London: Duckworth, 1978.

Gill, Brian, and Steven Schlossman. "'A Sin against Childhood': Progressive Education and the Crusade to Abolish Homework, 1897–1941." *American Journal of Education* 105.1 (1996): 27–66.

Goldstrom, J. M. *Education: Elementary Education 1780–1900.* Newton Abbott: David and Charles, 1972.

Goodridge, John. "'Three Cheers for Mute Ingloriousness!': Gray's Elegy in the Poetry of John Clare." *Critical Survey* 11.3 (2000): 11–20.

Goldman, Ronald, ed. *Breakthrough: Autobiographical Accounts of the Education of Some Socially Disadvantaged Children.* London: Routledge and Kegan Paul, 1968.

Gomm, Amy Frances. "Water Under the Bridge." Brunel University Library archive of unpublished working-class autobiographies, 39–40.

Gordon, Edward E., and Elaine H. Gordon. *Literacy in America: Historic Journey and Contemporary Solutions.* Westport, Conn.: Praeger, 2003.

Gordon, Peter, and Denis Lawton. *Curriculum Change in the Nineteenth and Twentieth Centuries.* London: Hodder and Stoughton, 1978.

Gosse, Edmund. *Gray.* English Men of Letters Series. New York: Harper, 1882.

———, ed. *The English Poets: Selections with Critical Introductions by Various Writers.* London: Macmillan, 1880.

Guillory, John. *Cultural Capital: The Problem of Literary Canon Formation.* Chicago: University of Chicago Press, 1993.

Haddow, Alexander. *On the Teaching of Poetry.* Glasgow: Blackie and Son, 1925.

Hall, G. Stanley. *Adolescence: Its Psychology and Its Relations to Physiology, Anthropology, Sociology, Sex, Crime, Religion and Education.* New York: D. Appleton, 1904.

Hall, Stuart. "A Sense of Classlessness." *Universities and Left Review* 5 (Autumn 1958): 26–31.

Hamilton, Walter, ed. *Parodies of the Works of English and American Authors.* London: Reeves and Turner, 1884–89.

Hardy, Florence E. *The Early Life of Thomas Hardy, 1840–1891.* London: Macmillan, 1928.

Hardy, Thomas. *The Complete Poetical Works.* Ed. Samuel Hynes. 5 vols. Oxford: Clarendon Press, 1982.

———. *Tess of the d'Urbervilles.* Ed. Scott Elledge. New York: Norton 1991.

Harrington, Michael. *The Other America: Poverty in the United States.* Baltimore: Penguin, 1966 [1963].

Harrison, Tony. "Laureate's Block." In *Laureate's Block and Other Poems.* Harmondsworth: Penguin, 2000.

———. "Them & [uz]." In *Selected Poems.* Harmondsworth: Penguin, 1984.

———. *V.* Newcastle upon Tyne: Bloodaxe Books, 1985.

Helps, Arthur. *Friends in Council.* 3 vols. New York: Thomas R. Knox, [1849].

Hemans, Felicia. *Selected Poems, Letters, Reception Materials.* Ed. Susan J. Wolfson. Princeton, N.J.: Princeton University Press, 2000.

———. *Selected Poems, Prose and Letters.* Ed. Gary Kelly. Toronto: Broadview Press, 2002.

Henley, W. E. *A Book of Verses.* London: D. Nutt, 1888.

———. *Echoes of Life and Death.* Portland, Maine: T. B. Mosher, 1908 [1898].

———, ed. *Lyra Heroica: A Book of Verse for Boys.* London: Methuen, 1892.

Herndon, William H., and Jesse W. Weik. *Abraham Lincoln: The True Story of a Great Life.* New York: D. Appleton, 1893, reprinted 1917.

Hipple, Ted. "Let's Hear it for Memorization." *English Journal* 93:4 (2004): 20–21.

Hitchman, Janet. *The King of the Barbareens.* Harmondsworth: Penguin, 1972.

Hoggart, Richard. *A Local Habitation.* London: Chatto and Windus, 1988.

———. *Speaking to Each Other.* London: Chatto and Windus, 1970.

———. *Tyranny of Relativism: Culture and Politics in Contemporary English Society.* New Brunswick, N.J.: Transaction, 1997.

———. *The Uses of Literacy.* London: Chatto and Windus, 1957.

Hollander, John. *Committed to Memory: 100 Best Poems to Memorize.* New York: Academy of American Poets, 1996.

Holt, Jim. "Got Poetry?" *New York Times Book Review*, April 5, 2009, 23.

Horrall, Spillard F. *History of the Forty-second Indiana Volunteer Infantry.* Chicago: Donohue & Henneberry, 1892.

Huey, Edmund Burke. *The History and Pedagogy of Reading: With a Review of the History of Reading and Writing Methods, Texts and Hygiene in Reading.* New York: Macmillan, 1908.

Hughes, Ted. *By Heart: 101 Poems to Remember.* London: Faber and Faber, 1997.

Hughes, Thomas. *Tom Brown's School-Days.* London: Macmillan, 1868 [1857].

Hurt, John. *Education in Evolution: Church, State, Society and Popular Education 1800–1870.* London: Paladin, 1972.

Hynes, Samuel. *A War Imagined: The First World War and English Culture.* London: Bodley Head, 1990.

If.... Directed by Lindsay Anderson. Memorial Enterprises, 1968.

Imperial War Graves Commission. *The Graves of the Fallen.* London: His Majesty's Stationery Office, 1919.

Invictus. Directed by Clint Eastwood. Warner Brothers, 2009.

Iremonger, Frederic. *Dr. Bell's system of instruction, broken into short questions and answers for the use of masters and teachers in the national schools.* London: F. C. and J. Rivington, 1817.

Jack, Ian. *English Literature, 1815–1832.* Oxford: Clarendon Press, 1963.

Jackson, Brian, and Dennis Marsden. *Education and the Working Class.* London: Routledge and Kegan Paul, 1962.

Jackson, T. A. *Solo Trumpet.* London: Lawrence and Wishart, 1953.

Jackson, Virginia W. *Before Modernism: Nineteenth-Century American Poetry in Public.* Princeton, N.J.: Princeton University Press, 2012.

———. "Who Reads Poetry?" *PMLA* 123.2 (2008): 181–87.

Jameson, Frederick. *The Political Unconscious: Narrative as a Socially Symbolic Act*. Ithaca, N.Y.: Cornell University Press, 1981.

Jauss, Hans Robert. *Towards an Aesthetic of Reception*. Trans. Timothy Bahti. Minneapolis: University of Minnesota Press, 1982.

Johnson, Clifton. *The Country School*. New York: Thomas Y. Crowell, 1907.

Johnson, Samuel. *The Lives of the Poets*. Ed. Roger Lonsdale. 4 vols. Oxford: Clarendon Press, 2006.

Jones, Griff Rhys, ed. *The Nation's Favourite Poems*. London: BBC Books, 1996.

Joyce, Simon. *The Victorians in the Rearview Mirror*. Athens: Ohio University Press, 2007.

Kallgren, Daniel. "Race, Place, and Poverty in the Pattern of Southern School Attendance, 1850–1950." *Historical Geography* 27 (1999): 167–92.

Kaplan, Cora. *Victoriana: Histories, Fictions, Criticism*. New York: Columbia University Press, 2007.

Kendall, Cavin Noyes, and George Alonzo Mirick. *How to Teach the Fundamental Subjects*. Boston: Houghton Mifflin, 1915.

Kincaid, James R. "Girl-Watching, Child-Beating and Other Exercises for Readers of *Jude the Obscure*." In *The Sense of Sex: Feminist Perspectives on Hardy*. Ed. Margaret R. Higonnet. Urbana: University of Illinois Press, 1993.

Kingsmill Moore, H. *An Unwritten Chapter in the History of Education: Being the History of the Society for the Education of the Poor of Ireland, generally known as the Kildare Place Society, 1811–1831*. London: Macmillan, 1904.

Kings Row. Directed by Sam Wood. Warner Brothers, 1942.

Kipling, Rudyard. *If –*. Garden City, N.Y.: Doubleday, 1910.

———. *Puck of Pook's Hill*. London: Macmillan, 1906.

———. *Rewards and Fairies*. London: Macmillan, 1910.

———. *Something of Myself*. London: Macmillan, 1937.

Kittler, Friedrich. *Discourse Networks 1800/1900*. Stanford, Calif.: Stanford University Press, 1990.

———. "Gramophone, Film, Typewriter" in *Literature/Media/Information Systems*. Ed. John Johnston. Amsterdam: G&B Arts, 1997.

Klapper, Paul. *Teaching Children to Read*. New York: D. Appleton, 1914.

Kliebard, Herbert M. *Changing Course: American Curriculum Reform in the 20th Century*. New York: Teachers College Press, 2002.

———. *Forging the American Curriculum: Essays in Curriculum History and Theory*. London: Routledge, 1992.

Klose, Nelson. *A Concise Study Guide to the American Frontier*. Lincoln: University of Nebraska Press, 1964.

Knowles, James Sheridan. *The Elocutionist: A Collection of Pieces in Prose and Verse*. Belfast: Simms and McIntyre, 1825.

Koselleck, Reinhart. "Kriegerdenkmale als Identitatsstiftungen der Überlebenen." In *Identität*. Ed. Otto Marquand and Karlheinz Stierle. Munich: Wilhelm Fink, 1979.

Kreilkamp, Ivan. *Voice and the Victorian Storyteller*. Cambridge: Cambridge University Press, 2005.

Kristol, William. "Thoroughly Unmodern McCain." *New York Times*, January 21, 2008.

Kucich, John, and Dianne Sadoff, eds. *Victorian Afterlife: Postmodern Culture*

Rewrites the Nineteenth Century. Minneapolis: University of Minnesota Press, 2000.

Laderman, Gary. *The Sacred Remains: American Attitudes towards Death, 1799–1883*. New Haven: Yale University Press, 1996.

Lambert, W. H. *Memory Gems: Graded Selections in Prose and Verse for the Use of Schools*. Boston: Ginn, Heath, 1883.

Laqueur, Thomas W. *Religion and Respectability: Sunday Schools and Working Class Culture 1780–1850*. New Haven: Yale University Press, 1976.

———. *Making Sex: The Body and Gender from the Greeks to Freud*. Cambridge: Harvard University Press, 1990.

———. "Memory and Naming in the Great War." In *Commemorations: The Politics of National Identity*. Ed. John R. Gillis. Princeton, N.J.: Princeton University Press, 1994.

Langan, Celeste. "Understanding Media in 1805: Audiovisual Hallucination in 'The Lay of the Last Minstrel'" *Studies in Romanticism* 40.1 (2001): 49–70.

Lavery, Brian. *Nelson and the Nile: The Naval War against Bonaparte, 1798*. London: Chatham, 1998.

Lawrence, E. S. *Origins and Growth of Modern Education*. London: Penguin, 1970.

Lawrence, D. H. *Phoenix II: Uncollected, Unpublished, and Other Prose Works*. Ed. Harry Thornton Moore. New York: Viking Press, 1968.

Lawrence, Paul. "The Slump in Poetry." *Critic*, April 1905, 267–68.

Leacock, Stephen. *Short Circuits*. New York: Dodd, Mead, 1928.

"Letters." *City Journal* 14.4 (2004): 120.

Life of Brian. Directed by Terry Jones. Handmade Films, 1979.

Lincoln, Abraham. *The Autobiography of Abraham Lincoln*. New York: Francis D. Tany, 1905.

———. *The Collected Works of Abraham Lincoln*. Ed. Roy Basler. 9 vols. New Brunswick, N.J.: Rutgers University Press, 1953.

Loeffelholz, Mary. *From School to Salon: Reading Nineteenth-Century American Women's Poetry*. Princeton, N. J.: Princeton University Press, 2004.

Logie, L. *Self Expression in a Junior School*. London: H. Milford, 1928.

Lootens, Tricia. "Hemans and her American Heirs: Nineteenth-Century Women's Poetry and National Identity." In *Women's Poetry, Late Romantic to Late Victorian: Gender and Genre, 1830–1900*. Eds. Isobel Armstrong and Virginia Blain. London: Macmillan, 1999.

———. "Hemans and Home: Victorianism, Feminine 'Internal Enemies,' and the Domestication of National Identity." *PMLA* 104 (1994): 238–53.

Lowndes, G. A. N. *The Silent Social Revolution: An Account of the Expansion of Public Education in England and Wales, 1895–1935*. Oxford: Oxford University Press, 1937.

Lycett, Andrew. *Rudyard Kipling*. London: Weidenfeld and Nicholson, 1999.

Lynch, Thomas. "Iambs for the Day of Burial." *Still Life in Milford: Poems*. New York: Norton, 1998.

Magnus, Laurie, and Cecil Headlam, eds. *Prayers from the Poets: A Calendar of Devotion*. London: Edinburgh: Blackwood and Sons, 1899.

Mann, Thomas. *Buddenbrooks: Verfall einer Familie*. Frankfurt am Main: Fischer, 1967.

Mansbridge, Albert. *The Trodden Road: Experience, Inspiration, and Belief.* London: J. M. Dent and Sons, 1940.

Mayer, David. "Parlour and Platform Melodrama." In *Melodrama: The Cultural Emergence of a Genre.* Eds. Michael Hays and Anastasia Nikolopoulos. London: Macmillan, 1996.

McClennan, B. Edward. *Moral Education in America: Schools and the Shaping of Character from Colonial Times to the Present.* NY: Teachers College Press, 1999.

McGann, Jerome. *The Poetics of Sensibility: A Revolution in Literary Style.* Oxford: Clarendon Press, 1996.

McGavin, Harvey. "Learning by Rote Kills Verse for Life." *Times Educational Supplement,* July 5, 1996.

McGeorge, Colin. "Death and Violence in Some Victorian Reading Books." *Children's Literature in Education* 29 (1998): 109–17.

McGill, Meredith L. *American Literature and the Culture of Reprinting, 1834–1853.* Philadelphia: University of Pennsylvania Press, 2003.

———, ed. *The Traffic in Poems: Nineteenth-Century Poetry and Transatlantic Exchange.* New Brunswick, N.J.: Rutgers University Press, 2008.

McPherson, James. *Battle Cry of Freedom: The Civil War Era.* New York: Oxford University Press, 1988.

Medwin, Thomas. *Journal of the Conversations of Lord Byron: Noted during a Residence with His Lordship at Pisa in the Years 1821 and 1822.* London: Henry Colburn, 1824.

Michael, Ian. *The Teaching of English: From the Sixteenth Century to 1870.* Cambridge: Cambridge University Press, 1987.

Miller, Andrew H. *The Burdens of Perfection: On Ethics and Reading in Nineteenth-Century British Literature.* Ithaca and London: Cornell University Press, 2008.

Miller, D. A. *The Novel and the Police.* Berkeley: University of California Press, 1988.

Miller, Janet A. "Urban Education and the new City: Cincinnati's Elementary Schools, 1870 to 1914." *Ohio History,* 88. 2 (1979): 152–72.

Minnich, Harvey C. *William Holmes McGuffey and His Readers.* New York: American Book Company, 1936.

Moir, D. M. *Sketches of the Poetical Literature of the Past Half-Century.* Edinburgh: W. Blackwood and Sons, 1851; third edition, 1856.

Mollan, Mark C. "Honoring Our War Dead: The Evolution of the Government Policy on Headstones for Fallen Soldiers and Sailors." *Prologue* 35 (Spring 2003): 56–65.

Montgomery, George, Jr. ed. *Georgia Sharpshooter: The Civil War Diary and Letters of William Rhadamanthus Montgomery, 1839–1906.* Macon, Ga.: Mercer University Press, 1997.

Moore, James Carrick. *A Narrative of the Campaign of the British Army in Spain: Commanded by His Excellency Sir John Moore, Authenticated by Official Papers and Original Letters.* London: J. Johnson, 1809.

Morrison, Arthur. *Child of the Jago.* London: Methuen, 1987 [1896].

Morrisson, Mark. "Performing the Pure Voice: Elocution, Verse Recitation, and

Modernist Poetry in Prewar London." *Modernism/Modernity* 3.3 [1996]: 25–50.

Mosier, Richard D. *Making the American Mind: Social and Moral Ideas in the McGuffey Readers.* New York: King's Crown Press, 1947.

Muske-Dukes, Carol. "A Lost Eloquence." *New York Times*, December 29, 2002.

National Educational Association. *Report on the Committee of Twelve on Rural Schools, 1895.* Chicago: University of Chicago Press, 1897.

Neale, Adam, John Hope Hopetoun, John Malcolm and Albert Jean Michel Rocca. *Memorials of the Late War.* Edinburgh: Constable, 1831.

Neilan, Sarah. "Hook, Line and Sister Helena: Secrets of Memorizing Poetry." *Times Educational Supplement.* 8 March 1991, no. 3897: 27.

———. "Survival Tactics." *Times Educational Supplement.* 30 November 1990, no. 3883: 25.

Neill, A. S. *A Dominie's Log.* New York: McBride, 1916.

Newbolt, Henry. *Admirals All.* London: E. Mathews, 1897.

The New England Primer: a reprint of the earliest known edition, with many facsimiles and reproductions, and an historical introduction. Ed. Paul Leicester Ford. Dodd, Mead and Company, 1899.

Newick, R. C. *The Writer of "The Burial of Sir John Moore" Discovered.* Bristol: T. Thatcher, 1908.

Newman, John Henry. *An Essay in Aid of a Grammar of Assent.* London: Burns, Oates, 1955.

Nudelman, Franny. *John Brown's Body: Slavery, Violence, and the Culture of War.* Chapel Hill: UNC Press, 2004.

Okley, Judith. "Privileged, Schooled and Finished: Boarding Education for Girls." In *Defining Females: The Nature of Women in Society.* Ed. Shirley Ardener. London: Croom Helm, 1978.

"The Original of 'Not a Drum Was Heard.'" *Bentley's Miscellany*, January 1837, 96–97.

Osgood, Lucius. *Osgood's Progressive Fifth Reader.* Pittsburgh: A. H. English, 1872.

Owen, Wilfred. *The Collected Poems.* Ed. C. D. Lewis and Edmund Blunden. London: New Directions, 1965.

Page, Curtis Hidden. "The Plays and Poems of Richard Hovey." *Bookman* 8 (1899): 449–53.

Palgrave, F. T., ed. *The Golden Treasury.* London: Macmillan, 1861.

Palmer, D. J. *The Rise of English Studies: An Account of the Study of English Language and Literature from its Origins to the Making of the Oxford English School.* London: Oxford University Press, 1965.

Park, Abraham. *A Manual of Method.* London: Blackie and Son, 1882.

Parkerson, Donald H., and Jo Ann Parkerson. *Transitions in American Education: A Social History of Teaching.* New York: Routledge Falmer, 2001.

Picker, John. *Victorian Soundscapes.* Oxford: Oxford University Press, 2003.

"Pieces Suitable for Recitation (English)." *Teachers' Aid*, January 23, 1886, 397.

Pinsky, Robert, and Maggie Dietz, eds. *Americans' Favorite Poems: The Favorite Poem Project Anthology.* New York: Norton, 2000.

Pococke, Thomas. *Journal of a Soldier of the 71st, or Glasgow Regiment, High-*

land Light Infantry, from 1806 to 1815. Edinburgh: William and Charles Tait, 1819.

Poetic Gems: A Selection of Good Poetry for Young Readers. London: W. & R. Chambers, 1907.

Poulet, Georges. "Phenomenonology of Reading." *New Literary History* 1.1 (1969): 53–68.

Pringle, May R. "Comparison in Method." *English Journal of the American National Council of Teachers of English* 14.4 (1925): 305–24.

Pulliam, John D. *History of Education in America.* Columbus: Charles E. Merrill, 1968.

A Practical Teacher. *The Pupil-Teacher's Hand-Book to the Annual Government Examination.* London: Collins, 1877.

Quiller-Couch, Arthur. *On the Art of Reading.* Cambridge: Cambridge University Press, 1920.

———. *On the Art of Writing.* Cambridge: Cambridge University Press, 1916.

———, ed. *The Oxford Book of English Verse, 1250–1900.* Oxford: Clarendon Press, 1900.

Reagan, Ronald, with Richard G. Hubler. *Where's the Rest of Me?* New York: Duell, Sloan and Pearce, 1965.

"Recitation: Why It Should be Taught, and How." *Teachers' Aid,* January 29, 1887, 419–20.

Reed, Henry. *Introduction to English Literature from Chaucer to Tennyson.* London: Shaw, 1865.

Reed, Talbot Baines. *Fifth Form at Saint Dominic's.* London: Religious Tract Society, 1894 [1880].

Robinson, Wendy. *Pupil Teachers and Their Professional Training in Pupil-Teacher Centres in England and Wales, 1870–1914.* Lewiston, Maine: Edwin Mellen Press, 2003.

Robson, Catherine. "Girls Underground, Boys Overseas: Representations of Dead Children in Nineteenth-Century British Literature." In *Dickens and the Children of Empire.* Ed. Wendy Jacobson. London: Macmillan, 2000.

———. "Reciting Alice: What is the Use of a Book without Poems?" In Ablow, ed.

———. "Standing on the Burning Deck: Poetry, Performance, History." *PMLA* 120 (2005): 148–62.

———. "'Where Heaves the Turf': Thomas Hardy and the Boundaries of the Earth." *Victorian Literature and Culture* 32 (2004): 495–503.

Rodriguez, Richard. *The Hunger of Memory.* New York: Bantam Books, 1983.

Rose, Jonathan. *The Intellectual Life of the British Working Classes.* New Haven: Yale University Press, 2001.

Ross, Marlon. *The Contours of Masculine Desire: Romanticism and the Rise of Women's Poetry.* New York: Oxford University Press, 1989.

Rowse, A. L. *A Cornish Childhood.* London: Jonathan Cape, 1944.

———. *The Spirit of English History.* New York: Oxford University Press, 1945.

Rubin, Joan Shelley. "'Listen, My Children': Modes and Functions of Poetry Reading in American Schools, 1800–1850." In *Moral Problems in American Life: New Perspectives on Cultural History.* Ed. Karen Halttunen and Lewis Perry. Ithaca, N.Y.: Cornell University Press.

————. *Songs of Ourselves: The Uses of Poetry in America*. Cambridge: Belknap Press of Harvard University Press, 2007.

————. "'They Flash upon That Inward Eye': Poetry Recitation and American Readers." In *Reading Acts: US Readers' Interaction with Literature 1800–1950*. Ed. Barbara Ryan and Amy Thomas. Knoxville: University of Tennessee Press, 2002.

Russell, the Rev. John A., ed. *Remains of the Late Rev. Charles Wolfe*. Hartford, Conn.: Huntington, 1828.

Sacred Poetry Adapted to the Understanding of Children and Youth, Selected for the Use of the Irish National Schools. Dublin: National Education Board, 1835.

Sage, Lorna. *Bad Blood*. London: Fourth Estate, 2000.

Sanderson, Michael. *Educational Opportunity and Social Change in England*. London: Faber and Faber, 1987.

Sargent, Epes. *Standard Speaker*. Philadelphia: Thomas, Cowpenthwaite, 1852.

Sassoon, Siegfried. "The General." In *Collected Poems*. London: Faber and Faber, 1947.

Sedgwick, Eve Kosofsky. "A Poem is Being Written." *Representations* 17 (1987): 110–43.

Select Poetry for Recitation. London: Chambers, 1883.

Shayer, David. *The Teaching of English in Schools, 1900–1970*. London: Routledge and Kegan Paul, 1972.

Shepard, Ben. "'The grit of our forefathers': Invented Traditions, Propaganda and Imperialism." In *Imperialism and Popular Culture*. Ed. John MacKenzie. Manchester: Manchester University Press, 1989.

Shepard, Odell. "A Youth to Fortune and to Fame Unknown." *Modern Philology* 20.4 (1923): 347–73.

Shuttleworth, James Kay. *Four Periods of Public Education, as reviewed in 1832, 1839, 1846, 1862*. London: Longman, Green, Longman, and Roberts, 1862.

————. *The Moral and Physical Condition of the Working Class Employed in the Cotton Manufacture in Manchester*. Manchester: J. Ridgway, 1832.

Silver, Harold, and Pamela Silver. *Education of the Poor: The History of a National School 1824–1974*. London: Routledge, 1974.

Small, Harold A. "The Field of His Fame: A Ramble in the Curious History of Charles Wolfe's Poem 'The Burial of Sir John Moore.'" *English Studies* 5 (1952–53): 1–49.

Smith, Arnold. *Aims and Methods in the Teaching of English*. London: Constable, 1915.

Smith, Nila Banton. *American Reading Instruction: Its Development and Its Significance in Gaining a Perspective on Current Practices in Reading*. Newark, Del.: International Reading Association, 1965 [1934]).

"The Soldier's Grave." *The Times*, February 4, 1863.

Sorby, Angela. *Schoolroom Poets: Reading, Recitation and Childhood in America, 1865–1917*. Lebanon, N.H.: University of New England Press, 2005.

Southey, Robert. "History of Europe." In *The Edinburgh Annual Register for 1808*. Vol. 1, part 1. Edinburgh: Ballantyne, 1810.

Spencer, F. H. *An Inspector's Testament*. London: Unwin, 1938.

Spencer, Herbert. *An Autobiography.* 2 vols. London: Williams and Norgate, 1904.

Spring, Joel. *The American School 1642–1985: Varieties of Historical Interpretation of the Foundations and Development of American Education.* New York: Longman, 1986.

Springhall, J. O. "Lord Meath, Youth and Empire." *Journal of Contemporary History* 5.4 (1970): 97–111.

Steedman, Carolyn. *Strange Dislocations: Childhood and the Idea of Human Interiority, 1780–1930.* Cambridge: Harvard University Press, 1995.

Steiner, George. "Critic"/"Reader." *New Literary History* 10.3 (1979): 423–52.

Stephen, Leslie. *Hours in a Library.* London: Smith and Elder, 1909.

Stewart, Garrett. *Reading Voices: Literature and the Phonotext.* Berkeley: University of California Press, 1990.

Stoutemyer, J. Howard. "Memory Work in the Grades." *Elementary School Journal* 18.1 (1917): 32–33.

Summerfield, Geoffrey, comp. *Voices: An Anthology of Poems and Pictures.* Harmondsworth: Penguin, 1969.

Swanston, Paul [pseud.?]. *Memoirs of Serjeant Paul Swanston.* London: B. D. Cousins, 1850 [1840].

Sweet, Nanora. "History, Imperialism and the Aesthetics of the Beautiful: Hemans and the Post-Napoleonic Moment." In *At the Limits of Romanticism: Essays in Cultural, Feminist and Materialist Criticism.* Ed. Mary A. Favret and Nicola J. Watson. Bloomington: Indiana University Press, 1994.

Sweet, Nanora, and Julie Melynk, eds. *Felicia Hemans: Reimagining Poetry in the Nineteenth Century.* London: Palgrave, 2000.

Swett, John. *Common School Readings: Containing New Selections in Prose and Poetry for Declamation, Recitation, and Elocutionary Readings in Common Schools.* San Francisco: H. H. Bancroft, 1868.

Swinburne, Algernon Charles. "The Flogging Block." In *Lesbia Brandon.* Ed. Randolph Hughes. London: Falcon Press, 1952.

Sylvester, David. *Robert Lowe and Education.* Cambridge: Cambridge University Press, 1974.

Symons, Arthur. "Mr. Henley's Poetry." *Fortnightly Review,* August 1, 1892, 182–92.

Targoff, Ramie. *Common Prayer: The Language of Public Devotion in Early Modern England.* Chicago: Chicago University Press, 2001.

Tatum, James. *The Mourner's Song: War and Remembrance from the Iliad to Vietnam.* Chicago: University of Chicago Press, 2004.

Tawney, R. H. *Secondary Education for All.* London: Labour Party, 1922.

Taylor, A. J. P. *English History, 1914–1945.* London: Oxford University Press, 1965.

Taylor, Dennis. "Thomas Hardy and Thomas Gray: The Poet's Currency." *ELH* 65.2 (1998): 451–77.

Tennyson, Hallam. *Alfred Lord Tennyson: A Memoir by His Son.* London: Kessinger, 2005.

Thackeray, William. *Vanity Fair.* Harmondsworth: Penguin, 1968 [1848].

Thayer, William Makepeace. *From Log-Cabin to White House: A Biography of James A. Garfield*. Boston: James H. Earle, 1881.

Theobald, Paul. *Call School: Rural Education in the Midwest to 1918*. Carbondale Southern Illinois University Press, 1995.

The Third Book of Lessons. Dublin: National Education Board, 1836.

Thomas, Woody, "Country Schoolmaster of Long Ago." *History of Education Journal* 5 (1954): 41–53.

Thompson, Flora. *Lark Rise to Candleford: A Trilogy*. London: Penguin, 2000.

Tibble, Anne. *Greenhorn: A Twentieth-Century Childhood*. London: Routledge and Kegan Paul, 1973.

Tibble, J. W., and Anne Tibble. *John Clare: A Life*. Oxford: Oxford University Press, 1972.

Treneer, Anne. *School House in the Wind: A Trilogy*. Exeter: University of Exeter Press, 1998.

"Trial in Meerut." *The Times*, June 25, 1929, 15.

Twain, Mark. *The Adventures of Tom Sawyer*. New York: Bantam, 1966 [1876].

Urban, Wayne, and Jennifer Wagoner. *American Education: A History*. New York: McGraw Hill, 2000.

Uttley, Alison. *The Country Child*. Harmondsworth: Penguin, 1970.

Van Wyk Smith, Malvern. *Drummer Hodge: The Poetry of the Anglo-Boer War 1899–1902*. Oxford: Clarendon Press, 1978.

Venezky, Richard L. "A History of the American Reading Textbook." *Elementary School Journal* 87.3 (1987): 247–65.

Vidal, Gore. "The Meaning of Timothy McVeigh." *Vanity Fair,* September 2001, 347–53: 409–15.

Vincent, David. "Reading Made Strange: Context and Method in Becoming Literate in Eighteenth and Nineteenth-Century England." In *Silences and Images: The Social History of the Classroom*. Ed. Ian Grosvenor, Martin Lawn, and Kate Rousmaniere. New York: Peter Lang, 1999.

Ward, Sir A. W., and A. W. Waller, eds. *The Cambridge History of English Literature: The Nineteenth Century*. New York: G. P. Putnam's Sons, 1917; Cambridge: Cambridge University Press, 1917.

Wardle, David. *English Popular Education*. Cambridge: Cambridge University Press, 1970.

Warner, Oliver. *The Battle of the Nile*. London: Batsford, 1960.

Watts, Isaac. *Divine and Moral Songs*. Derby: T. Richardson, Friar-Gate; London: Hurst, Chance, 1829 [1715].

Weinrich, Harald. *Lethe: The Art and Critique of Forgetting*. Trans. Steven Rendall. Ithaca, N.J.: Cornell University Press, 2004.

Wells, Carolyn. "An Overworked Elocutionist." *St. Nicholas Magazine* 35.6 (1908): 41.

Wells, W. H. *The Graded School: A Graded Course of Instruction for Public Schools*. New York: A. S. Barnes & Burr, 1862.

Westerhoff III, John H. *McGuffey and His Readers: Piety, Morality, and Education in Nineteenth-Century America*. Nashville: Abingdon, 1978.

Widdowson, Peter. *Hardy in History*. New York: Routledge, 1989.

Willans, Geoffrey, and Ronald Searle. *How to be Topp*. Harmondsworth: Puffin, 1964 [1954].

Williams, Raymond. *The Country and the City*. New York: Oxford University Press, 1973.

Williams, W. H. *Memory Gems for School and Home*. New York: A. S. Barnes, 1907.

Wilson, J. Dover. *Poetry and the Child*. London: F. Hall, 1916.

Winter, Jay. *Sites of Memory, Sites of Mourning: The Great War in European Cultural History*. New York: Cambridge University Press, 1995.

Wodehouse, P. G. *The Luck of the Bodkins*. Harmondsworth: Penguin, 1964 [1935].

Woodward, Kathleen. *Jipping Street*. London: Longmans, 1928.

Woolf, Virginia. *To the Lighthouse*. Oxford: Oxford University Press, 1998 [1927].

Wolfe, Charles. "The Burial of Sir John Moore after Corunna." *Blackwood's Edinburgh Magazine* 1.3 (1817): 277–78.

Wolfson, Susan. "Hemans and the Romance of Byron." In Sweet and Melnyk, eds.

Wordsworth, William, and Samuel Taylor Coleridge. *Lyrical Ballads*. Ed. R. L. Brett and A. R. Jones. London: Methuen, 1963.

Yoxall, J. H., and Ernest Gray. *The Companion to the N. U. T. Code*. London: Educational Supply Association, 1906.

INDEX